D1523385

Living and Leaving

Living and Leaving

A Social History
of Regional Depopulation
in Thirteenth-Century
Mesa Verde

DONNA M. GLOWACKI

THE UNIVERSITY OF
ARIZONA PRESS

TUCSON

To my family, friends, and perseverance
You all made this possible

The University of Arizona Press
www.uapress.arizona.edu

Printed in the United States of America
20   19   18   17   16   15   6   5   4   3   2   1

ISBN-13: 978-0-8165-3133-2 (cloth)

Jacket designed by Leigh McDonald
Jacket photo by Robert Jensen

Library of Congress Cataloging-in-Publication Data
Glowacki, Donna M., author.
    Living and leaving : a social history of regional depopulation in thirteenth-century Mesa Verde / Donna M. Glowacki.
        pages cm
    Includes bibliographical references and index.
    ISBN 978-0-8165-3133-2 (cloth : alk. paper)
    1. Pueblo Indians—Colorado—Mesa Verde National Park—Migrations.   2. Pueblo Indians—Colorado—Mesa Verde National Park—History.   3. Pueblo Indians—Colorado—Mesa Verde National Park—Antiquities.   4. Indians of North America—Southwest, New—Migrations.   5. Indians of North America—Southwest, New—History.   6. Indians of North America—Southwest, New—Antiquities.   7. Mesa Verde National Park (Colo.)—Antiquities.   I. Title.
    E99.P9G55 2015
    978.8'27—dc23
                            2014039731

♾ This paper meets the requirements of ANSI/NISO Z39.48–1992 (Permanence of Paper).

CONTENTS

ILLUSTRATIONS

Figures

Tables

ACKNOWLEDGMENTS

It takes a village, in this case, a large, aggregated one. A book like this cannot be written without the help, advice, assistance, support, expertise, time, and generosity of many. I am truly grateful for all of the help and encouragement I have received along the way. This research began as a dissertation at Arizona State University. My committee—Keith Kintigh, Kate Spielmann, Michelle Hegmon, and George Cowgill—encouraged me to take on a challenging and ambitious project. Their mentoring, insightful comments, and critiques resulted in a strong foundation for a regional synthesis. I am also grateful for their continued friendship and support.

As a synthesis of one of the most densely occupied areas of the pre-Hispanic U.S. Southwest with over a century of research, this study would not have been possible without the work of the many archaeologists who came before, and collaboration with munificent researchers from many institutions. The initial compilation of the PIII regional site and NAA data involved gaining access to site and pottery data through institutions in three different states, lots of site reports, and the help of many individuals. Those assisting with gathering site data included Tim Seaman and Karyn de Dufour at ARMS, Cynthia Williams and Larry Nordby at Mesa Verde National Park, Kristin Jensen and Kevin Jones at the Utah SHPO, and Mary Sullivan at the Colorado SHPO; Jim Allison provided data from his survey work in Utah, and Jim Potter and Warren Hurley provided data from A-LP. I was also able to update site data through my work on the VEP with the support of Tim Kohler, Mark Varien, and Scott Ortman via VEP I (SES-0119981). Pottery samples were obtained with the help of Bill Lipe, R. G. Matson, Mary Collins, and Garth Portillo, who assisted with the Cedar Mesa permissions and sampling. Dale Davidson provided permission to collect clays in Utah on BLM land. C. Dean Wilson selected pottery samples from La Plata sites and clay samples. Access to these collections was also facilitated by the efforts of Eric Blinman and Wolkie Toll (New Mexico Office of Archaeological Studies) and Chris Turnbow, Tony Thibodieu, and Julia Clifton (Museum of Indian Arts and Culture). Gary Brown, Terry Nichols, and Frank Hayde helped with obtaining the Aztec Ruins National Monument samples. Larry Nordby, Carolyn Landes, Kathy Fiero, and Ted Oppelt assisted with the samples from Step House at Mesa Verde National Park. Robin Lyle, Chelsea Dunk, Jamie

Merewether, and Melita Romasco helped in obtaining the samples from the McElmo area that were then curated at Crow Canyon Archaeological Center, and Fumi Arakawa and I had great adventures collecting clay in southeastern Utah. Jim Judge and Jim Kendrick generously allowed me use of their NAA data from the Lowry community. Michael Glascock, Jeff Speakman, and their lab technicians processed and analyzed the samples at MURR providing the raw NAA data.

Initial data collection, analysis, and writing were funded by an NSF Dissertation Improvement Grant (BCS-012487), an ASU Department of Anthropology Research Grant, a MURR NSF Grant (SBR-9802366), Colorado Historical Society Grant 95-02-028, an ASU Dean's Circle Scholarship and Writing Fellowship, the Joe Ben Wheat Scholarship (University of Colorado–Boulder), and the Florence C. and Robert H. Lister Fellowship (Crow Canyon Archaeological Center). In addition to those already mentioned, conversations along the way with Cathy Cameron, Kari Chalker, Margie Connolly, Linda Cordell, Fred Harden, Tim Kohler, Steve Lekson, Bill Lipe, Linda Martin, Steve Plog, Ruth Van Dyke, Carla Van West, Mark Varien, and Richard Wilshusen (and "the Maya") were particularly helpful in advancing my thinking and research.

As I was beginning the publishing process, a bit of a monkey wrench got thrown into the mix that required several years of attention. I am grateful for the good care I received from surgeons, medical staff, physical therapists, colleagues, friends, and family who helped with my recovery; I would not have been able to write this book (or do much of anything, really) without their care and support during some tough times.

During the bionic interlude, much had happened archaeologically, and I needed to update and reanalyze the database. Winston Hurst, Gary Brown, and Paul Reed provided new data to revise my site database for the Totah and West Central Mesa Verde. I was also able to incorporate my own survey work at Mesa Verde National Park, which was supported by National Geographic, the Institute for Scholarship in the Language Arts (ISLA) at Notre Dame, and VEP II (DEB-0816400), as well as the efforts of Scott Travis, Julie Bell, Kay Barnett, the MV-CCS crew, and many others at Mesa Verde National Park. These new data improved and changed my results, making it a more interesting study. Special thanks to Aron Adams, Jim Allison, Kay Barnett, Ben Bellorado, Grant Coffey, Winston Hurst, Robert Jensen, Stephen Matt, Marit Munson, Sarah Payne, Susan Ryan, Jonathan Till, Tom Tweed, and Laurie Webster, who all provided important last-minute details, conversations, and images for the book as I made the final push.

I also appreciate the support and encouragement I have received from my colleagues and friends in the Department of Anthropology at Notre Dame. The final production of the book was supported by the Institute for Scholarship in the Language Arts (ISLA) at Notre Dame. I appreciate the sustained support, patience, and assistance from Allyson Carter, the staff at the University of Arizona Press, and the press's editorial board to make this book possible. The final product was much improved by the thorough and thoughtful comments of Patrick Lyons and an anonymous reviewer. I am also grateful for the careful reading and copyediting of Kathy Cummins and Sally Bennett Boyington. Eric Carlson drafted the graphs, and Grant Coffey produced the maps and line drawings. Robert Jensen not only provided amazing landscape images but also helped with image processing.

I am very fortunate to have been involved with both Mesa Verde National Park and Crow Canyon Archaeological Center for the past twenty years. Both institutions have profoundly affected my life and career. I am also forever grateful for the support, encouragement, and friendship of a great many people over the course of my archaeological career and life. I wish I could list you all by name. Learning and laughing with you all is a true wonder. Thank you. And finally, thank you to my family, whose love and support have made all of this possible, especially my parents, who have always, unwaveringly, done everything within their power to help me make my life the best it could possibly be.

Living and Leaving

CHAPTER ONE

Explaining Regional Depopulation

Stories such as the collapse of the Maya are enthralling. That a once vibrant and thriving society can come to a seemingly sudden end is at once fascinating and horrifying. We want and need to understand it. How is that possible? Will it happen to us? It seems so final, an epic failure, "The End"—an association that in part arises from conceiving of collapse as an event rather than a process. Yet the people who lived through these turbulent periods carried on, making cultural and behavioral changes as they adjusted to their new circumstances. *Collapse**
does not imply a permanent end; it means there was a breakdown or critical loss of the effectiveness of some aspect of society and *things can no longer be the way they were*. It is useful shorthand for referring to the complex circumstances involved during periods of rapid change, if we are precise about what it is that collapses and what carries over (Yoffee 1988:18). For when we talk of collapse, we also obscure the details, histories, and contingencies that are so important to shaping the lived experience of people during this time, which is actually what we really want to know.

Cases of large-scale societal collapse and change are particularly intriguing when they involve the complete depopulation of a region, such as happened with the Classic period Mayas or, as discussed here, the

---

*When I use the term, it is *collapse* with a lowercase *c*, and the implication is that since not all aspects of a society or culture break down, something comes after (see also Cowgill 1988; Eisenstadt 1988; McAnany and Yoffee 2010; Middleton 2012).

ancestral Pueblo people. Regional abandonments are atypical.* Our connections to place are strong because they are both practical and emotional (e.g., Basso 1996). Memory, investment, tenure, and experience all play a role in forging our links to particular landscapes and locations, and the strength of these connections is such that place becomes an inseparable part of our identity and history. When confronted with challenges that affect our livelihood, the first response is to find local solutions to our problems. On balance, people prefer to avoid moving and to instead make changes that could be reversed if conditions improve (Di Lernia 2006:52; Minnis 1996:71). Therefore, when people move, the implication is that there are problems that could not be resolved locally. If moving involves not only everyone leaving but also moving far enough away that an entire region is emptied, then the problems are so pervasive and unsettling (literally) that monumental, large-scale change is required, which has cascading effects across space and through time. Why is it that in some cases societies can solve their problems through reorganization, but in others, the solution requires leaving?

Regardless of whether people stay or go, more often than not dramatic societal change corresponds with climatic catastrophes that, on the surface, appear to have been the root cause. The end of the Maya Classic period in the tenth century and the reorganization of the Mochicas in the sixth century, for example, both coincided with periods of drought, erratic rainfall patterns, or other climatic disruptions (deMenocal 2001; Haug et al. 2003; Shimada et al. 1991). The coincidence of major climatic changes with large-scale societal change naturally places the impact of the climatic catastrophes at the forefront of our explanations, a perspective reinforced by today's renewed interest in climate change and sustainability. All too often this leads to Malthusian explanations that rely heavily on the "standard trio" (Plog 2003:184) of environmental change, population growth, and resource stress.

Climate and the natural environment undergird resource availability and affect the prevailing conditions with which people contended; we, of course, need to learn about their effects on society and our impact on them. This explains only part of the story, however, and although it is an essential part, environmentally based explanations are not completely satisfying, for as Hewitt (1983:25) reminded us, the social order of things and their historical circumstances are what "shape or frustrate these matters." Climatic and environmental conditions and their severity are

---

*I use the word *abandonment* to indicate instances when residents moved away, leaving structures and/or geographic areas largely vacant. Such a situation does not necessarily mean, however, that the "abandoned" places were no longer important to or connected with those who emigrated from the area or that they never returned or had relinquished their territorial claims.

perceived through cultural ideals influenced by economics, politics, religion, history, settlement organization, social boundaries, and traditions, among other factors (Eisenstadt 1988; Hassan 2002; Hewitt 1983; Hoffman and Oliver-Smith 1999; Ingold 2000; Van Buren 2001). They are then acted on or not at individual, group, community, and societal scales in ways that are situational and may not always make sense. As Hassan (2002:21) succinctly stated, "Climate is not destiny." Social and cultural constructions define our choices and to a large extent our perception of the natural environment (Eisenstadt 1988). Many factors, including social conflict, political mismanagement, invaders, and economic problems, can lead, and have led, to collapse and change without any connection to climatic or environmental downturns. Consequently, a thorough assessment of the cultural and historical contexts of cases of large-scale societal change is required if we are to understand the role, if any, of environmental and climatic change.

Take the Mayan regional depopulation at the end of the Classic period (which represents a useful comparative case for the thirteenth-century ancestral Pueblo people considered here): beyond the challenges of drought, deforestation, and soil erosion, there was also a Mayan "Game of Thrones" in which kings and other elites vied for power both within and among more than forty city-states. Religion played a central role in these political machinations, as elites expanded upon traditional rites and successively increased the scale of public ritual and performance, presumably to engender social cohesion and investment in the royal system (Inomata 2001, 2006; Lucero 2006). This increasingly tied royal power to the supernatural, which eventually helped weaken the Classic Maya kingship system when challenges could not be adequately surmounted despite the powerful connections with the gods claimed by the elites. As royal dynasties waxed and waned, the competitive climate disrupted their political system and fostered war and other conflicts (Demarest et al. 2004a; Webster 2002). Even though drought and anthropogenic degradation played an integral role in the demographic reorganization that marks the end of the Maya Classic period, clearly, political, religious, and social factors are just as culpable, if not more so. This point is underscored by the fact that the ancient Mayans left some of the wettest parts of the Mayan territory in the southern lowlands to settle in the generally drier north, drought notwithstanding (Webster 2002:243–44). All of these circumstances were configured in various ways and undermined the traditional royal power concentrated in the southern lowlands, disrupting a system—a way of organizing—that had been in place for centuries.

As this example highlights, what we really want and need to know is, What were people actually doing before and during periods of great change? How did their actions, decisions, and histories contribute to causing far-reaching societal changes like regional depopulations? Answering these questions is made difficult because of the complex webs of interrelated, multiscalar factors involved (Demarest 2004:240–42; Hassan 2002; Robb and Pauketat 2013b; Yoffee 1988) and the role that history plays in how these situations are perceived and acted upon (Pauketat 2001; Robb and Pauketat 2013a). Individuals often do not experience exactly the same combination of social and natural circumstances as other individuals, and if they do, they may not have the same perceptions of these circumstances even as they are happening. This is also true at the group, village, and community levels, where multiple agendas and needs beyond the individual and household further affect decisions and actions. This milieu is also deeply enmeshed in political, religious, and economic forces that further influence decisions, actions, and outcomes.

Regional Depopulation of the Northern San Juan

The ancestral Pueblo occupation of the Northern San Juan (Mesa Verde) region is famous for its regional depopulation at the end of the AD 1200s, which has captivated archaeologists and laypeople alike since North American archaeology began. This fascination has driven more than 120 years of research, producing a wealth of information on past environmental conditions and agricultural productivity (Ahlstrom et al. 1995; Berry 1982; Cordell et al. 2007; Dean et al. 1985; Huckleberry and Billman 1998; Kohler 2010; Van West and Dean 2000; Wright 2010) and regional settlement history (Fewkes 1911; Glowacki and Ortman 2012; Hayes 1964; Holmes 1878; Hurst and Till 2009; Kleidon et al. 2007; Lipe and Varien 1999a, 1999b; McKenna and Toll 1992; Nordenskiöld 1990; Reed 2011; Toll 2008; Varien 1999; Varien et al. 1996; Varien et al. 2007). Pueblo perspectives and historical accounts (Dozier 1954, 1964; Malotki 2002; Naranjo 1995, 2008; Ortiz 1969; Silko 1996; Suina 2002; Swentzell 1993) and Pueblo ethnography (Eggan 1950; Ellis 1964; Fox 1967; Parsons 1939; Titiev 1944; Whiteley 1998, 2008) are also essential, for we cannot understand the long-term impacts and outcomes of the significant changes evident in the archaeological record of the late thirteenth and early fourteenth centuries without them.

Widespread emigration from the Northern San Juan region in the late AD 1200s was, in many ways, the continuation of a long history of migration and movement across the Southwest that was, and is, integral to Pueblo culture (Naranjo 1995, 2008). Most of the time, migrations

were small scale and localized, but there were also periods of intensified population movement, such as the late AD 800s to early 900s
(Schlanger 1988; Wilshusen and Van Dyke 2006; Wilshusen, Ortman,
et al. 2012) and the early to mid-1100s (Dean et al. 1994:65; Judge
1989:245–49; Kantner and Kintigh 2006:184–86), when people moved
longer distances and depopulated certain areas. Viewed from this perspective, the Mesa Verde migrations were not the exception but the
natural course of things, the rule. Nevertheless, they were conceivably
the most remarkable and transformative of all the pre-Hispanic Pueblo
migrations.

The first and probably most compelling reason for their importance
is that the Northern San Juan region—an area of nearly 20,000 square
kilometers—was completely depopulated by ancestral Pueblo people
(figure 1). Not only did *everyone* leave the region and adjacent areas,
but Pueblo people never returned residentially. The scale of this emigration differed from that of any other period and perhaps from most
cases of migration and regional depopulation in the world.* For example,
as one might expect, the ancestral Pueblo population in the San Juan
Basin declined during the severe drought, violence, and reorganization
associated with the attenuation of the Chacoan system in the early to
mid-1100s. Yet throughout this uncertain period at least some people
continued living in Chaco Canyon (Hayes 1981:33–34, 51; Judge 1989;
Van Dyke 2007a:230) and the Northern San Juan (Brown et al. 2013;
Glowacki and Ortman 2012; Kleidon et al. 2007; Toll 2008:table 16.1;
Varien et al. 2007). Although people could have stayed in the Northern
San Juan during the late 1200s and beyond as well (Duff et al. 2010; Van
West 1994; Van West and Dean 2000; Wright 2010), they did not. The
ancestral Pueblo people had "weathered" previous periods of climatic and
environmental hardship, so what made this period so different that the
entire population was compelled to leave the entire Four Corners region
and did not return to live there again?

The distinctive character of this exodus is accentuated by the fact
that most cases of migration are accompanied by "return migration," a
countermigration stream of people who for a variety of reasons return
after having moved away (Anthony 1990; Lee 1966). Because the rate
of return is largely dependent on the perceived opportunities at both the
destination and the point of origin, when return migration decreases or

*In many cases, chronological resolution and survey coverage make it difficult to know
whether people truly left regions altogether or whether they started living in a more dispersed settlement pattern than previously (e.g., Nelson 1999). In the Mayan case, for example, archaeological evidence is now pointing to dispersed populations continuing to live in
the southern lowlands even after a political vacuum and depopulation at the end of the
Maya Classic period (Lucero 2006:191–92; Webster 2002).

FIGURE 1. Map of the Southwest with the Northern San Juan and adjacent regions shown. Illustration by Grant D. Coffey.

stops altogether, this is an indication that it has become either undesirable to return home or too difficult to make the return trip (Lee 1966). The implication of this for the Northern San Juan case is that conditions in the mid to late 1200s must have deteriorated and altered so much that people not only could not stay but also did not want to risk returning to the region.

The second distinguishing aspect of the Mesa Verde migrations is that they involved an unprecedented number of people who needed to find new homes. At the beginning of the 1200s, the region contained the highest population density in the Southwest (Duff 1998; Hill et al. 2004, 2010), yet by the end of the century the region was vacated.

Recent population estimates suggest that there may have been as many as 14,000 to 19,000 people who lived in a 1,817-square-kilometer portion of Central Mesa Verde alone (i.e., the Village Ecodynamics Project study area; Varien et al. 2007:table 4). Even if this estimate is high—a likely possibility since it is based on the density of small sites in block surveys, which is then applied to the whole study area—there is the entire region to consider. Thus, even though the timing of migration varied across the region (Glowacki 2010), many thousands of people were leaving the Northern San Juan throughout the thirteenth century, and many of these left in the latter fifty years (see also Varien 2010:15–19; chapter 4 herein). The extent of this relocation had widespread effects as people negotiated the social and cultural dynamics at their southern destinations while they tried to join existing pueblos or to establish new ones.

Finally, the Mesa Verde migrations were transformative because the cultural changes that emerged from acculturation and syncretism as people shifted across the Colorado Plateau engendered a sea change in Pueblo history—sometimes referred to as the Pueblo III–Pueblo IV transition, circa AD 1250 to 1350 (e.g., Adams 1996)—that reoriented Pueblo ideology (Adams 1994; Crown 1994, 1998; Pauketat 2011). This momentous transition is reflected in widespread changes in the form, location, technology, and artistic perspective of kiva murals, rock art, and painted pottery. For example, rock art and kiva mural aesthetics shifted from geometric abstractions and horizon markers to anthropomorphic and naturalistic figures (figure 2; Munson 2011; Newsome and Hays-Gilpin 2011; Smith 1952), and decorated pottery, which had predominantly been black-on-white, became increasingly dominated by polychrome and glaze ware types (Habicht-Mauche et al. 2006; Hays-Gilpin and Van Hartesveldt 1998; Huntley 2008; Van Keuren 2011). The marked change in aesthetics suggests that this was a deeply transformative period that affected core ideals and practice among all Pueblo groups.

The scale and scope of cultural changes in the fourteenth century are particularly striking because Pueblo culture is often described as being conservative and traditional—traits that tend to promote slower rates of change and long-term continuities. Thus, the late thirteenth and early fourteenth centuries were a particularly pivotal time in Pueblo history, of which the Mesa Verde migrations were an instrumental part. To fully understand their impact and role in this transformation requires a thorough assessment of the circumstances that prompted the Mesa Verde migrations, including historical variation in settlement and interaction across the region.

FIGURE 2. Examples of geometric and anthropomorphic murals. (a) Cliff Palace mural dating to the thirteenth century. Photograph taken by Kay E. Barnett. (b) Fourteenth-century kiva mural from Awatovi. Drawing by Marit K. Munson, after Smith 1952:fig.78b.

Intraregional Variation: Historical Landscapes and Linked Histories

Gustav Nordenskiöld, a young Swedish aristocrat with a penchant for exploration and thorough documentation, is credited with the first scientific archaeological investigation of the Mesa Verde cliff dwellings. Early in the summer of 1891, Nordenskiöld arrived in the beautiful Mancos Valley by horse and buggy as a tourist planning to stay for a week at the Wetherill ranch with Richard Wetherill as his guide. Instead, he became so enthralled with the ancient Pueblo dwellings that he explored the canyons and alcoves of the Mesa Verde uplift for the next four months. During this time, he investigated at least twenty-seven different alcove sites, assigning each a unique number that was inscribed in the sandstone exposed at each dwelling.* Nordenskiöld also excavated in at least six cliff dwellings—Painted Kiva (No. 9), Long House, Kodak House, Mug House, Step House, and Spruce Tree House (in this order)—with the aid of the Wetherill brothers and a crew of laborers.

These early archaeological explorers were among the first of European descent to have wondered, Why did they leave? The translation of Nordenskiöld's (1990:170) 1893 response to this inexorable question is "from causes difficult of elucidation, a period of decay set in," and he further posited that the cliff dwellings were the last refuge of the Mesa Verde Pueblo people before they left entirely, a belief that has withstood the test of time. Nordenskiöld's difficulty in elucidating why the ancestral Pueblo society in Mesa Verde declined was attributable to how little was known about these ancient people and how sudden and dramatic their departure seemed. Today we know much more about the ancestral Pueblo occupation of not only the cliff dwellings but also the entire region. Even after more than 120 years of research, however, Nordenskiöld's words still ring true, for elucidation is made difficult by the complex interrelationships among social histories, climate, environment, contingency, and the everyday decisions and actions of individuals and their families.

The large-scale, long-term processes we are trying to understand are complex, embedded, and dynamic, with multiple intersecting historical strands. Within broadly shared cultural patterns and geographic

---

*These numbers are commonly referred to as Nordenskiöld's numbers and are attributed to his study of the cliff dwellings. Although he makes specific references to the numbers in his book, he does not explicitly mention implementing the numbering system, nor does he reference carving the numbers. Given the length of his expedition and his intention to document his findings, we can most likely assume that he initiated the numbering system. However, Nordenskiöld may have used an existing numbering system that originated with the Wetherills, for it is curious that Spruce Tree House was labeled "House No. 1" even though it was the last of the dwellings he excavated.

landscapes, particular landforms, specific places, variation in resource availability and technology, and distinctive social networks and cultural configurations created varying historical landscapes (Robb and Pauketat 2013a). These "complex webs of association" (*sensu* Pfaffenberger 1988:249) shaped the experiences and choices of the people whose lives were enmeshed with them, and they need to be understood on their own terms so that we can better define the connections involved in large-scale changes. The linkages within and among these historical landscapes—what Demarest and his colleagues (2004b) termed linked regional culture-histories—will allow us to better understand what transpired.

Delineating historical landscapes is particularly crucial for understanding large-scale change and regional depopulation, because recognizing these entwined elements elucidates the critical factors and influences involved during periods of upheaval and change. Although events can stimulate population movements, regional depopulations and migrations are processes (Cameron 1993; Nelson 1999). Processes take time, so there is variation in how depopulation unfolds. For example, there are differences between groups of peoples in the circumstances leading to the decision to move away, the timing of these moves, and the social scales involved at various stages (Anthony 1990; Duff 1998; Tainter 1988). By unpacking the variation in social, political, religious, climatic, and environmental contexts, and thereby also identifying continuities, we can better realize the relationships among these variables and better discern how social and cultural boundaries are reconfigured prior to and during large-scale change and regional depopulation (Eisenstadt 1988). A focus on the variation in historical and social contexts avoids generalizing about social and cultural change via universal or normative behaviors, which masks how the process actually unfolded.

The importance of understanding these nuances is exemplified by current trends in Mayan research whereby archaeologists are revealing the complex mosaic of the varied local histories of major and minor centers that eventually collided and occasioned the end of Mayan royalty and the Maya Classic period (Demarest 2004; Demarest et al. 2004a; Lucero 2006:186–91; Webster 2002:260–94). To illustrate, in the western part of the Maya region (the Petexbatun portion of the Usumacinta drainage), warfare and deep-seated political rivalries led to the dramatic collapse of the major centers of Los Pilas and Aguateca. North of this area, the decline and collapse of Tikal and Calakmul was a more protracted process—one that appears to be linked to overpopulation that, in part, was due to immigrants escaping from the warfare and disruptions that occurred in the west (i.e., Petexbatun/Usumacinta). However, in the east, Lamanai was relatively resistant to the turbulence happening elsewhere in Maya lands, and although political systems shifted, this city-state persisted well beyond the Post-Classic period. These different cases show that the cascading impact of the decline of royal power differentially affected the dissolution of each center depending on its local circumstances, connections, and history.

To understand how complexity such as this contributed to the dynamics of large-scale social change requires examining social processes and interactions at multiple scales and the interrelationships among them. The foundation of these studies is the considered and comprehensive analysis of regional patterns and processes. The historically situated cultural contexts and social processes evident at regional scales shape the social landscape within which daily interactions and sociopolitical and economic networks operated. Examining the material and spatial contingencies affecting cultural practice and social interactions at the regional scale allows us to determine how trajectories of change emerged and to assess their cascading impact across space and through time. My goal with this book is to present one such study that focuses on the regional and subregional scales of the Northern San Juan to allow us to better understand how people living across such a large and diverse geographic area decided to leave it.

Regional studies are not new, of course (e.g., Adams 1981; Fish and Kowalewski 1990; Sanders et al. 1979; Willey 1953), and have been integral to archaeological research in the U.S. Southwest from its beginning. Regional archaeology, circa the early 1900s, was descriptive and focused on defining the distribution of settlement patterns and associated material culture at its most inclusive scale (e.g., culture areas and culture histories; see Kroeber 1939). Defined culture areas were assumed to reflect the spatial extent of shared normative behaviors and were typically viewed as culturally homogenous. Nels C. Nelson's (1919) description of the distribution of Puebloan cultural traits is one of the earliest culture area studies in the U.S. Southwest (see also Gladwin and Gladwin 1934; Kidder 1924; Kroeber 1939:32–37). This static view changed as descriptive knowledge accumulated and it became increasingly evident to archaeologists that uniformity was not the norm (Cordell and Plog 1979). Research subsequently shifted to understanding the connections maintained through economic, political, and ritual organization and the movement of goods and ideas within these systems and across large geographic areas (regional systems or interaction spheres).

In the U.S. Southwest, this paradigm shift elucidated the extent and influence of the Chaco and Hohokam regional systems, which were defined by the distribution of key attributes such as great houses and ballcourts, respectively (Crown and Judge 1991; Judge and Schelberg 1984; Wilcox 1979). Subsequent regional studies have focused on regional-scale interaction (Ericson and Baugh 1993; Hegmon 2000), the role of hinterlands in regional dynamics (Sullivan and Bayman 2007), and macroregional perspectives that address connections between the Southwest and Mesoamerica (Mathien and McGuire 1986; McGuire et al. 1994; Wilcox 1999).

To fully grasp the implications of these "big picture" studies, we must also understand how these regional-scale patterns developed by unpacking the variability within these broad areas (Hegmon and Plog 1996; Kowalewski 2003; Neitzel 2000), which has been the focus of more-recent regional-scale research (Duwe 2011; Glowacki 2006a; Peeples 2011; Schachner 2007).

Most regional-scale studies in the Northern San Juan (e.g., Lipe 1995; Rohn 1989; Varien 1999; Wright 2010) have focused on Central Mesa Verde. Although previous studies have considered the influence of the Totah and western areas such as the Comb Ridge locality and Cedar Mesa (e.g., Lipe 1995:145–48; Lipe and Varien 1999b:322, 324), none have methodically analyzed settlement history across the entire region from northwestern New Mexico to the extreme western margins in southern Utah. In part, this has been because the expansive area contains numerous tribal, federal, and private entities with differing goals and mandates for archaeological research and cultural preservation. The National Park Service (NPS) and Bureau of Land Management (BLM), for example, are responsible for key areas of the ancestral Pueblo occupation of the region. NPS manages three national parks (Mesa Verde, Canyonlands, and Arches) and three national monuments (Aztec Ruins, Yucca House, and Hovenweep), and BLM manages large parcels of land in southeastern Utah and also Canyons of the Ancients National Monument, which contains 170,000 acres of mesas and canyons in the heartland of Central Mesa Verde. Although we have learned much about these important areas and provided for their sustained preservation, research has also been compartmentalized, inherently promoting provincial views of intraregional dynamics. In recent years, new collaborations and the increased capacity for building and analyzing large data sets have enabled the synthesis of site data across the region, which is transforming our understanding of cultural dynamics in the Northern San Juan (Brown et al. 2013; Glowacki 2006a, 2010; Varien et al. 2007).

The compartmentalized nature of research in the Northern San Juan affects how we approach problems such as the Mesa Verde migrations (see also Lekson 1999a:103, 2008:158–63). Our narratives have been particularly biased toward the southwestern Colorado portion of Central Mesa Verde because of the prominence of the Mesa Verde uplift, the incredible preservation of the cliff dwellings, the concentrated occupation of this area by ancestral Pueblo people (chapter 3), and the sustained research program directed by Crow Canyon Archaeological Center archaeologists. This bias is manifest in *Leaving Mesa Verde* (Kohler et al. 2010), a synthesis of current research on the depopulation of the region. Although this volume takes a broad approach to the problem by including analyses that address the Rio Grande (see chapters by Boyer et al., Lipe, and Ortman) and the western Virgin Branch and Kayenta ancestral Pueblo people (see chapters by Allison and Dean), it only tangentially addresses the role of Aztec, a major religious and political center in northwestern New Mexico (see chapter by Glowacki), and portions of southeastern Utah traditionally associated with Central Mesa Verde are also underrepresented (but see chapters by Wright and Glowacki).

To achieve an inclusive understanding of regional dynamics across the Northern San Juan, I analyzed intraregional settlement patterns and gauged interconnectedness through pottery circulation. The available data for sites with occupation between AD 1150 and 1300 were compiled and used to assess variation in population distribution, occupational histories, settlement organization, and the distribution of civic-ceremonial architecture across the region (chapter 3). My research builds on the work of many archaeologists who have recorded data over multiple generations and was facilitated by my longtime professional associations with Mesa Verde National Park, Crow Canyon Archaeological Center, and the Village Ecodynamics Project (VEP), a multi-institutional interdisciplinary NSF-funded team of researchers who seek to understand the relationship between ancestral Pueblo people and their environment from AD 600 to AD 1290.

When the key variables that are fundamental to understanding societal change are isolated, the historical processes and social networks underlying the Mesa Verde migrations, including the population relocation and reorganization that preceded the widespread migrations of the late 1200s, become more apparent. Assessing the degree to which people were connected establishes the extent to which developments in one part of the region would have impacted those in other parts of the region. It also addresses how well people were able to mitigate uncertainty, for one way people coped with stress and risk was through their social networks (Braun and Plog 1982; Minnis 1996; Rautman 1993, 1996). I summarize trends in intraregional exchange, drawing heavily on a regional-scale compositional study that uses neutron activation analysis to evaluate pottery circulation of Mesa Verde jars and bowls as a proxy for interconnectedness (chapter 4).

These data on settlement and interaction networks enable the delineation of historical landscapes across the Northern San Juan to enhance our understandings of the complexities of the circumstances during the thirteenth century and how they differed across the region. For example, a crucial part of understanding the sociopolitical landscape during the thirteenth century is clarifying the role of Aztec as a religious and political center in the Northern San Juan. There are various views on the subject. One model views Aztec as the presumed successor of Chaco Canyon and the principal religious and political center of the late twelfth and thirteenth centuries. From this perspective, Aztec became a hegemonic force that continued to dictate social, ceremonial, and political interactions across the Northern San Juan much as Chaco had for the northern Southwest, except with a more restricted sphere of influence (Cameron and Duff 2008; Lekson 1999a, 2008). Another model sees Aztec as one of many prominent large centers that structured intraregional sociopolitical and ceremonial networks (Lipe 2002, 2006; Lipe and Varien 1999b:322–25), with several centers, such as Aztec and Yellow Jacket Pueblo, being significantly larger and potentially more influential than others. A third view emphasizes that Aztec and its associated cultural landscape were independent of Chaco or Mesa Verde (Brown et al. 2008; McKenna and Toll 1992; Reed 2008a, 2011; Toll 1993, 2008). All of these scenarios recognize that Aztec was a direct outgrowth of the great houses at Chaco Canyon and that it became an important force in the region to at least some degree. In actuality, the role of Aztec in the region is more complex and nuanced than current models allow and likely involved elements of all these perspectives, because as discussed later (chapters 5 and 6), the role of Aztec and its regional influence changed over time.

There's Still Juice in the Orange

To some, the regional depopulation of the Northern San Juan may seem a well-trodden topic, a veritable "sucked orange," to use the well-known metaphor (Kidder 1958:322). Archaeologists and ethnologists have long been trying to answer questions about how and why it happened and where people went (Davis 1964; Gladwin 1957; Jett 1964; Kelley 1952; Kidder 1924; Lipe 1995; Nordenskiöld 1990:170), and we have a general sense of the factors involved. For some, this may be enough. Edgar Lee Hewett certainly gave this impression, for it was he who used the "sucked orange" metaphor to dissuade A. V. Kidder from working in the Southwest (Kidder 1958:322). However, I believe, as did Kidder, that there is still much to learn.

The long history of research on this topic was well summarized by Varien (2010), who focused on theories commonly used to explain why the ancestral Pueblo people left Mesa Verde. His grouping of these theories into four main categories—human impacts on the environment, climatic change, warfare, and disease—also highlights a history of research that has focused predominantly on some key factors affecting ancestral

Pueblo people, but not the social and cultural circumstances involved. Varien (2010) acknowledged this understudied area when he concluded by noting that new research on the topic was emphasizing the social, political, and religious contexts of the Mesa Verde migrations (e.g., Glowacki 2010, 2011; Lipe 2010; Ortman 2012).

Social and cultural change was integral to Southwestern research early on (e.g., Steward 1937), and it has been recognized as an important influence prompting the late thirteenth-century migrations (Cordell et al. 2007; Davis 1964; Lipe 1995; Van West and Dean 2000:38–39; Varien 1999:216; Varien et al. 1996:103–5; Varien et al. 2000). The "standard trio" has garnered much more attention from scholars, however, with much of the focus on the role of environmental change, the impact of the drought, and the prevalence of raiding and conflict. Social and cultural change was not divorced from these commonly cited factors, nor are climate and violence necessarily the primary stimuli for change. Shifting social networks, changing attitudes or beliefs, and individual agendas that are unrelated to environmental or climatic change can also cause significant social and cultural change in society. These changes, in turn, can have widespread and varied effects on a society, especially if they develop into viable social, political, or religious movements (Glowacki 2011; Harkins 2004; Pauketat 2011; Peeples 2011; Vokes 2007; Wallace 1956). The consequences of movements and social change—both intended and unintended—are particularly acute when times are uncertain or when social and political organization may not be flexible enough to accommodate them (Hegmon et al. 2008). More specifically, addressing the role of social change in the Northern San Juan during the 1200s is an important next step for understanding the regional depopulation, and for Pueblo society, social change has everything to do with religion.

The Role of Religion

Religion is inextricably enmeshed in all aspects of Pueblo society, including politics and government, thus, Pueblo culture is theocratic. Studying changes in Pueblo society, ancient or recent, is impossible without considering the role of religion (see, e.g., chapters in Glowacki and Van Keuren 2011; Ware 2014; Ware and Blinman 2000). For Pueblo people, religion and ceremonialism maintain balance and underlie everything, including where and how to live, when and how to plant or harvest, whom one can marry, and how problems are resolved (Bernardini 2008; Dozier 1970; Eggan 1950; Glowacka 1998; Ortiz 1969; Parsons 1939; Titiev 1944; Whiteley 2008:24–31). As Pauketat (2011:238) succinctly stated,

"Indigenous Pueblo history is religion, so to speak." Through Pueblo oral histories and ethnographic records, we know that religious differences were often at the root of conflict, and various mechanisms, including the development of new rituals, reviving past practices, and adopting rituals from either Pueblo or non-Pueblo groups, were used to solve problems or effect change in Pueblo society (Bernardini 2011; Levy 1992; Malotki 2002; Parsons 1939; Ware and Blinman 2000; Whiteley 2008).

Not only are religion and ceremonialism the essence of Pueblo culture, but also they can become increasingly important for any culture during times of strife and uncertainty. Religious change is one of the many social actions taken to mitigate problems, climatic or otherwise (Harkins 2004; Vokes 2007). Thus, religion and the politics of religion are clearly integral to understanding the period leading up to the Mesa Verde migrations. Yet discussions of religion have been largely absent from our explanations of the thirteenth-century depopulation of the Northern San Juan (but see Glowacki 2011; Ortman 2012). This omission is understandable given the nature of the archaeological record and difficulties of inferring religion from material culture; however, we cannot ignore it, because religion shaped how climatic, environmental, and social changes were perceived and acted upon and was at least as important as climatic and demographic changes in structuring the circumstances of the 1200s, if not more so.

Pueblo religious practices are not uniformly shared; they vary across space, differing from group to group and village to village, and are often expressed in settlement organization and architecture. The regional-scale approach taken here allows for an examination of this variation to permit a better understanding of the role religious change may have had in the Mesa Verde migrations. I previously suggested that religious movements intended to revitalize communities may have had the unintended consequence of destabilizing Mesa Verde society (Glowacki 2011). I develop these ideas here by incorporating a consideration of historical processes, which differentially affected developments within and between the eastern and western portions of the region (chapter 5). Eastern and western regional differences were deeply rooted and developed from differing social histories as various cultural groups moved into and out of these areas. These differences are particularly evident during the Pueblo I period, AD 750 to 900 (Allison et al. 2012; Chuipka 2009; Potter et al. 2012; Wilshusen and Ortman 1999; Wilshusen, Ortman, et al. 2012) but are less well understood for later time periods, even though they remained important until the Northern San Juan region was depopulated (Glowacki 2010). It is especially important to understand these historical differences, since strong differences between Eastern and Western Pueblos persist today.

Detaching from Place

In the following pages, I lay out the details of the thirteenth-century Pueblo occupation in the Northern San Juan to establish the social contexts and historical landscapes that influenced how and why Mesa Verde Pueblo people left this place. Places become a part of who we are and how we understand the world. Leaving a place is therefore a significant act and a big moment in a person's life. When people decide to leave and do not know when or if they might return, individuals undergo a separation process as they come to terms with their reasons for leaving and the uncertainty that comes with it. For some the bond with a place is stronger than for others, particularly if they are well situated with good access to land and other resources or have prominent standing and influence in the community. In these cases, people may be hesitant to leave, especially if leaving means giving up perceived security. In other cases, individuals and families have more-tenuous bonds, either because their lifestyles already involve mobility or, in more sedentary situations, they have somehow become marginalized or disillusioned with leaders or ideological beliefs and would therefore welcome relocation as a means to improve their situation. In either case, although the actual leaving may be perceived as immediate and swift, the process of detaching from place can be protracted, continuing through migration and resettlement. A traumatic event or dire circumstances that force people to leave regardless of their druthers, however, truncate the detachment process, making it wrenching and abrupt.

Layered into the decision-making process are the influential factors that compel leaving. Dorigo and Tobler (1983) conceived of these factors as the "Push Pull Migration Laws." Their framework has been productively used by Mesa Verde archaeologists to better understand the influences of local pressures, such as climate change and population aggregation, and the attractive benefits at possible destination areas, such as the northern Rio Grande (e.g., Lipe 1995; Varien et al. 1996). The push-pull paradigm places emphasis on the agency of external forces, yet it is the agency of individuals and households that constitutes leaving (Cameron 1993). To reorient this emphasis, McAnany and Lamoureux St-Hilaire (2013) recently offered the notion of stressors and enablers, instead of push and pull, to allow for the fact that the act of leaving a place is socially, politically, and culturally negotiated by individuals, households, villages, and communities. The stressors and enablers are what attenuate relationships with place enough that people become willing to relocate.

As discussed by McAnany and Lamoureux St-Hilaire (2013), stressors, like push factors, are those circumstances that heighten insecurity, either perceived or actual, and erode social dynamics by making a living situation inhospitable and unbearable. Stressors come from a variety of sources, including environmental and climatic downturns, changes in politics or religion, economic challenges, and warfare. Enablers, though similar to pull factors, differ in that they include not only gains found at potential destinations but also advantages held by the potential migrants that allowed them to more readily relocate. Conceived of in this way, enablers include having adequate resources to facilitate moving, maintaining established connections with people in different areas, and possessing knowledge and/or skills that could benefit a new community. For example, economic and social networks connected individuals and villages with other places. These links were relied on to buffer resources during difficult times (e.g., Braun and Plog 1982; Rautman 1993) and when necessary could also aid migration by providing information or even a possible destination.

Stressors and enablers are both always at work to some degree, but their configurations and intensity vary for each person, household, and village, resulting in numerous narratives of leaving. During periods of stability, it is the enablers that tip the scale toward emigration. Those individuals and families with the means and connections would be more likely to move under stable conditions (Anthony 1990) and would also be among the earliest to emigrate as the intensity of stressors began to increase. Enablers also tend to have more influence when en route and settling at destinations, whereas the intensity, duration, and diversity of stressors have the greatest effect on the scale of depopulation.

There are periods when the number and intensity of stressors steadily increase rather than subside, particularly if new factors, such as the onset of a severe drought, come into play. As specific stressors intensify, they can also compound, causing an increasing proportion of the population to experience shared and prolonged stress. Consequently, emigration—a common method of coping with deteriorating social and environmental conditions (e.g., Minnis 1996; Tainter 1988:199)—becomes more prevalent. Population loss begins to take a toll on the remaining residents as keeping essential services and village-level institutions functioning becomes more difficult, which contributes to the disintegration of social order (Hill et al. 2004; Tainter 1988). If these circumstances persist and emigration continues, the strain becomes too great and the bonds that held the village or community together completely unravel. The reduced population is no longer able to sustain village life, particularly if key ritual specialists have already left, which forces the remaining residents to leave as well. These same dynamics found within villages also affect interactions and social coherence at larger scales, eroding the ties that once allowed the society to exist in that specific way and at that place. The dissolution of one village, particularly if it was an important hub, would have cascading impacts on nearby centers and villages, altering social and ceremonial networks. As increasing numbers of people migrate, perceptions of place for those who stay also changes as they readjust to new social configurations in a shifting social landscape that is being steadily depopulated (McAnany and Lamoureux St-Hilaire 2013; Tainter 1988). In extreme cases, the stressors become so acute and sense of place so altered that it becomes perceived as being uninhabitable, and the abandonment of the region becomes complete. Conceived of this way, the emigration process itself is historicized and the varied reasons for which people began emigrating from a diverse region are not the same as the more broadly shared reasons that caused the depopulation to be complete (Cameron 1993; Glowacki 2010).

Although the end of the 1200s saw a uniform outcome across the Northern San Juan, the circumstances of depopulation differed across the region and involved a mixture of strategies, processes, and responses. By understanding the interplay of stressors and enablers, the nature of these factors, the extent to which they become widely shared among the entire society, and the degree of change over time, we can better characterize the processes of emigration and abandonment at different scales and for different geographic areas. The lower population density, drier environment, and occupation history of the western portion of the region with affinities toward Kayenta and the east presented different circumstances than the dramatic population and settlement growth in the politically charged social landscape of the eastern half of the Northern San Juan. These circumstances and their implications are detailed in the following pages.

CHAPTER TWO

Laying the Groundwork

Since 1861 when T. Stangl carved his name in the alcove wall at Bone Awl House, the impressive architecture, excellent preservation, and picturesque settings of the cliff dwellings have made them a prime destination for early explorers, archaeologists, and tourists. Over the years, the attraction of these iconic and well-preserved sites inherently promoted a Mesa Verde–centric view of the ancient Pueblo occupation of the Four Corners region (Lekson 1999a; Toll 1993; Varien 2000:5–6), a circumstance evidenced by the use of the term *Mesa Verde* to describe a culture, a region, two pottery types, and a national park. Regional archaeologists have also come to refer to specific areas as Central Mesa Verde for the core area (Lipe 1995:143, 2006; Varien 2000:6–7; Varien et al. 1996); Eastern Mesa Verde for the territory associated with the La Plata, Animas, and Piedra drainages (Bellorado 2013; Lipe 1995:145; Wilshusen 2009), an area also known as the Middle San Juan (Reed 2008a) and the Totah (Lipe 1995:145, 2006; McKenna and Toll 1992:133; Stein and Fowler 1996:123; Toll 2008:311); and Western Mesa Verde for the portion of the region in what today is known as Utah (Lipe 1995:145). Yet using the term *Mesa Verde* emphasizes the landform and cliff dwellings, unduly influencing the way researchers think about the region as a whole (Lekson 1999a:102–3; McKenna and Toll 1992:133; Reed 2008a:20; Varien 2000:5–6). To counter the Mesa Verde–centric perspective, regional archaeologists began using the term *Northern San Juan region* to refer to the northernmost extent of the ancestral Pueblo world and U.S. Southwest (e.g., Lipe 1995; Rohn 1989). Although I prefer the "Mesa Verde" region framework and its ready recognition in popular venues, when referring to the region as a whole I use *Northern San Juan,* as this term is both more geographically specific and more inclusive than *Mesa Verde.*

Defining the Northern San Juan Region

Regions are spatial units that are "roughly equivalent to the space that *might* be occupied by a social unit" and are composed of "space in which *at a given time*, a high degree of cultural homogeneity may be expected but not counted on" (Willey and Phillips 1958:19, 20; emphasis added). Therefore, regional boundaries do not necessarily correspond with cultural entities. If they do, the designated boundaries merely indicate an area within which there are strongly associated material cultural patterns; they do not convey the complexity of the social networks at numerous scales intersecting at a variety of nodes that actually produce the large-scale patterning we see. The spatial extent of social and cultural networks within geographically defined regions—and the corresponding distribution of the people who produced them—is not fixed; it is socially negotiated, crosscutting, multiscalar, conditional, and constantly changing (Kowalewski 2003; Kowalewski et al. 1983; Lightfoot and Martinez 1995; Van Dyke 2007a). It is important to specify not only what you are describing, culturally and geographically, and how and why the area is defined, but also when the entity occurred. For example, when Rohn (1989:149) first described the Northern San Juan region, he was careful to specify how occupation within this area fluctuated over time and space, noting that the ancestral Pueblo occupation expanded westward beyond Comb Ridge during some periods but not in others. Similarly, McKenna and Toll (1992:133) account for spatial and temporal correlations when they note that it was not until after AD 1080 that major settlements developed and came to define the Totah.

Defined as the land associated with the northern tributaries of the San Juan River from its headwaters to its confluence with the Colorado River, the Northern San Juan region is a geographically related system (figure 3; Lipe 1995:143–44; Rohn 1989:149; Varien 2000:6). The prominent river, for which the region is named, may have also been an important social or political boundary in the past (Adams and Adams 1959). For example, today, the San Juan River is one of the four sacred rivers of the Navajo people and the northern boundary of the Navajo Nation (McPherson 1995:15). To understand the extent to which this type of association was true in the past as well requires further research to assess settlement patterns on both sides of the San Juan River, and much of this land is tribally owned. The San Juan, Abajo, and Carrizo Mountains further delimit the region, and Ute Mountain (figure 3) is a prominent feature near its center (Rohn 1989:149; Varien 2000:6).

I take an inductive approach to better understand the role of regional dynamics in the depopulation of the Northern San Juan; this approach starts from an inclusive perspective and then unpacks intraregional

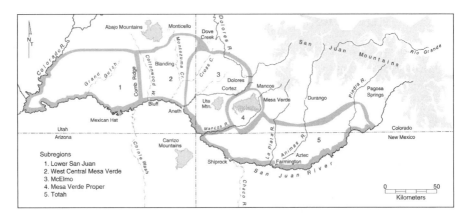

FIGURE 3. Map of the Northern San Juan region showing major physiographic features and subregions. Illustration by Grant D. Coffey.

variation. From AD 1150 to the end of the 1200s, the distribution of sites with Mesa Verde pottery types and shared architectural traits nearly covers the maximum extent of the geographically defined Northern San Juan region, which includes portions of northwestern New Mexico, southwestern Colorado, and southeastern Utah (figure 4; Lekson 1999a:100; Lipe 2006:261–62; Varien 2010:fig. 1.2). During this period, Mesa Verde society was at its peak in spatial extent and population levels. I use the Northern San Juan region as the first-order level of organization and consider areas within this geographic region, such as the Totah, as subregions—an analytical heuristic that allows consideration of not only the local developments within them but also interrelationships across this geographically related area in an equivalent way. My analysis differs from the conventional approach, which prioritizes one area over others, such as Central Mesa Verde or the Totah (Middle San Juan), which inherently promotes oppositional paradigms. Using comparable spatial units within the broader geographic area to think about the variation within it frees us from our preconceived notions, allowing an integrative analysis of developments and interactions across the Northern San Juan.

Figure 4 shows a relatively continuous site distribution paralleling the San Juan River from AD 1150 to 1300, a pattern that would be reinforced if site data from Navajo Nation and Ute Mountain Ute lands were included. One of the lines of evidence that has been used to argue for distinct regions is a potential "settlement gap" between those sites concentrated along the La Plata, Animas, and San Juan drainages in northwestern New Mexico and those on the Mesa Verde cuesta (uplift) in southwestern Colorado (Lipe 2006:309; Lipe and Varien 1999b:322). However, the perceived gap is to some extent an artifact of low population

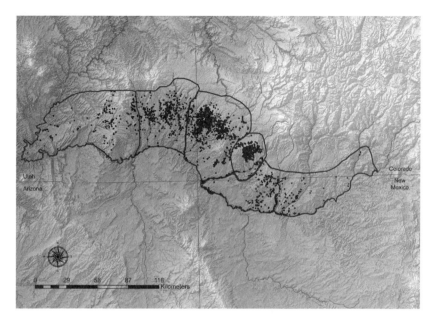

FIGURE 4. The regional distribution of sites with a Pueblo III period component (AD 1150–1300). Illustration by Grant D. Coffey.

density in the Piedra district by AD 1200 (Varien et al. 1996), state and tribal boundaries, and insufficient survey. Although site density in this area is low, the distribution is similar to that found in the western portion of the region, particularly in the vicinity of Comb Ridge (see chapter 3). Further research and survey are required to better evaluate site distribution before a convincing argument that the low site density represents a distinct social, cultural, or political boundary can be made.

Intraregional Variation

Regions are not homogenous. The shared geographical and cultural traits associated with the Northern San Juan region do not preclude differences in history, cultural identity, language, and organization across it, particularly since these attributes are multiscalar, malleable, and subject to local social and geographic variability. The varied influence of location, climate, and environmental conditions across the Northern San Juan invariably led to different opportunities, interaction networks, experiences, contingencies, and responses to the circumstances of the 1200s. People living in the western and eastern peripheries of the region not only experienced markedly different environmental and climatic conditions

but also were closer to those living in other regions. For example, in
the far western portion of the Northern San Juan there were stronger
connections with those living in the Kayenta region (see figure 1). The
ancestral Pueblo people of the Kayenta area differed markedly from those
living in the Northern San Juan in just about every way. Their settlements were smaller and were not organized around kiva-focused household units, their structures were built with both masonry and jacal, their
habitation rooms contained an entrybox feature not found among Mesa
Verde groups, and their pottery was produced using different technological and stylistic attributes that included polychrome types (Colton
1955, 1956; Dean 1996; Jennings 1966; Kidder and Guernsey 1919;
Lipe 1970; Sharrock et al. 1961). Unlike most of the Colorado Plateau,
there were no evident material or architectural connections to Chaco
Canyon (Dean 1996:40–41, 2010:337). Interactions and exchange with
ancestral Pueblo people in the Kayenta region contributed to variation in
settlement patterns and social networks on the western periphery of the
Northern San Juan in ways that are not apparent in the eastern portion
of the region (see chapters 3 and 5).

Understanding this variation requires us to focus on subsets of the
areas we typically study to avoid conflating important intraregional differences that may help explain large-scale social processes like migration
and depopulation. For example, using *Central Mesa Verde* to refer to the
densely settled core of the Northern San Juan region (Lipe 1995:143;
Varien 2000:6–7, 2010) is useful because settlement patterns within this
area are more similar to each other than to those in the far eastern and
western portions of the region. Nonetheless, using this defined area also
homogenizes settlement and cultural variation; yet the lived experiences
of ancestral Pueblo people across Central Mesa Verde differed. Consider,
for example, the ancestral Pueblo people living in the cliff dwellings and
other villages on the Mesa Verde cuesta. This area is included in Central
Mesa Verde because of similar settlement patterns, demographic trends,
and material culture (Lipe 1995, 2006; Varien 2000; Varien et al. 1996);
however, there are also pertinent differences. The Mesa Verde cuesta is
in the southeastern part of Central Mesa Verde, which is closer to areas
in New Mexico, such as the La Plata River and Aztec, and farther from
southeastern Utah. Thus, even though San Juan Red Ware from southeastern Utah has been recovered from many sites on the Mesa Verde
cuesta, exchange and communication networks were strongly influenced
by connections with the east and south. For example, Chaco, Puerco,
and Gallup Black-on-white pottery and White Mountain Red Ware types
such as Puerco, Wingate, and St. John's Black-on-red, and Wingate and
St. John's Polychrome, have been found in low frequencies at thirteenth-
century Mesa Verde Proper sites such as Spring House (Nordenskiöld

FIGURE 5. View of Mesa Verde Escarpment looking south. Photograph by Robert D. Jensen.

1990:plate XXXVIII), 5MV34 (O'Bryan 1950), and Far View (Rohn 1977:242).

The Mesa Verde cuesta has a noticeably different physiographic setting, with a higher elevation than the rest of Central Mesa Verde, a difference of about 460 meters, and a southern aspect that increases sun exposure (figure 5). These differences produce both more precipitation and a longer growing season. Despite its elevation, the Mesa Verde cuesta has ample frost-free days for growing corn (153 days), which is not the case for other parts of the region (Adams and Petersen 1999:26). These environmental conditions differ greatly from those of the western portion of Central Mesa Verde, which can be 600 meters or more lower and receives 15–25 centimeters less moisture than the eastern portion (Wright 2010:table 4.1). These physiographic advantages likely made farming on the Mesa Verde cuesta more successful than in other parts of Central Mesa Verde (Adams and Petersen 1999; Benson 2011), particularly during the challenging climatic conditions of the thirteenth century. The differences in interaction networks and agricultural potential for ancestral Pueblo people residing on the Mesa Verde cuesta established conditions that were not experienced by those living in other parts of Central Mesa Verde.

Intraregional variation is also conflated when using the term *Western Mesa Verde* to refer to the area from the Utah state line west to the Colorado River (Lipe 1995:145). In fact, this area encompasses the greatest range of variation possible within the region. There are major geological changes from the Dakota Formation of the Cretaceous period and the Morrison Formation of the Jurassic period east of Comb Ridge to the more ancient Wingate, Chinle, and Moenkopi Formations deposited during the Triassic period and the Cutler Formation of the Permian period on the west side of Comb Ridge (figure 6; table 1). The nature of the canyons

FIGURE 6. View of Butler Wash and Comb Ridge looking south. Photograph by Jonathan D. Till.

also changes with this geologic shift, becoming narrower and steeper in the Triassic and Permian formations with great cliff-face expanses that are difficult to traverse (e.g., the Wingate Formation). Settlement patterns, specifically site size, also differ. For example, one of the largest villages east of Comb Ridge is the Nancy Patterson Village (42SA2110) in the Montezuma drainage, which has 7 room blocks, 21 kivas, a plaza, and more than 300 rooms (Hurst and Till 2009:fig. 4.5; Rohn 1989:161; Thompson et al. 1988); whereas Moon House (42SA5005), one of the largest sites west of Comb Ridge, has 3 room blocks, 2 kivas, a plaza, and 42 rooms (Bloomer 1989). We need to understand how intraregional variation in lived experience created different histories and contingencies across the region so that we can reconstruct how these varied histories coalesced into the circumstances prompting the thirteenth-century migrations and regional depopulation.

To unpack intraregional variation in settlement and interaction networks, I use subregions—an intermediate spatial scale between the region and localities or communities—as an analytical unit. The term *subregion*, however, should not be understood as implying some sort of hierarchy or inferior quality (i.e., one area/subregion is not better or worse than another). Recognizing that social entities are complex and transcend boundaries at different scales, I am not using subregions to define social or political entities within the region. Instead, I use them as

TABLE 1. Generalized geological column for the Northern San Juan

Million years ago	Period	Geology			Description
	QUATERNARY	Stream and glacial deposits			Gravels
	TERTIARY	Nacimiento, San Jose, and Telluride Formations			Andesites, rhyolites, ash-flow tuffs, and conglomerate
78	CRETACEOUS	Animas Formation			Conglomeratic, greenish-gray and tan sandstone, siltstone, and shale
		Kirtland Shale			Gray shale interbedded with sandstone
		Fruitland Formation			Gray-white and brown sandstone, gray and olive-brown shale, and coal
		Pictured Cliffs Sandstone			Cliff-forming white sandstone interbedded with shale; marine
		Mesa Verde Group	Cliff House Sandstone		Sandstone; transgressive marine
			Menefee Shale		Dark shale, bentonite, coal, and plant remains; continental stream and swamp
			Point Lookout Sandstone		Sandstone; near-shore marine
		Mancos Shale			Dark shale, thin sandstone, limestone, bentonite, and fossiliferous; transgressive offshore marine
		Dakota Sandstone			Sandstone, dark shales, and coals; transgressive, near-shore marine
		Burro Canyon Formation			Conglomerate; continental rapid stream

(continued)

TABLE 1. Generalized geological column for the Northern San Juan (*continued*)

Million years ago	Period	Geology		Description
138	JURASSIC	Morrison Formation	Brushy Basin Member	Shale, sandstone, limestone, and dinosaur fossils; continental swamps and broad streams
			Salt Wash Member	
		Junction Creek Sandstone		Pink, reddish-orange, and brown sandstone; eolian dune and interdune origins
		Summerville Formation		Sandy shales; continental inland lake
		Entrada Sandstone		Reddish-orange and pinkish to white fine sandstone; continental sand dunes
205	TRIASSIC	Dolores Formation		Sandstone, conglomerate; continental stream, lake, floodplain
		Wingate Formation		Massive, cliff-forming sandstone, light orange-red to brick red
		Chinle Formation		Variegated shale and clay; brownish-gray and reddish sandstone
		Moenkopi Formation		Chocolate-brown and reddish-brown sandstone and siltstone
240	PERMIAN	Cutler Formation		Red-brown sandstone; continental floodplain

spatial units to facilitate intraregional comparison of settlement, demography, and architecture. Subregions divide the region into components that capture robust variation obscured by the regional scale but that do not get overwhelmed by the detailed nuances of smaller scales, which can sometimes make it difficult to see important patterning. At a subregional scale, discernable intraregional variation provides relevant cultural and environmental contexts for the more specific social and political interactions, allowing us to see how local-scale social organizations and networks created regional-scale processes.

Defining the Subregions

The Northern San Juan has great topographic diversity, ranging from the southern margins of the Rocky Mountains (approximately 4,200 meters above sea level) to lower elevations at the confluence of the Colorado and San Juan Rivers and in the deep canyon bottoms of southeastern Utah (approximately 1,300 meters above sea level). These differences in elevation underlie variability in temperature, rainfall, and vegetation (see Adams and Petersen 1999:29). The diverse regional geology (see table 1) affects vegetation, agricultural productivity, water tables, and raw material distributions (e.g., the availability of suitable clays for pottery production [see chapter 4]).* Agricultural productivity in each subregion is further affected by variation in annual precipitation, and the resulting differences in agricultural yields influenced subsistence strategies, social dynamics, and settlement location across the region. The effect of varying precipitation was a particularly important concern in the western half of the region because people living there were more susceptible to drought and near-drought conditions attributable to its typically drier climate and related agricultural challenges.

With these issues in mind, I defined subregions based on differences in geology, elevation, and physiographic boundaries that characterize the regional landscape. This seemed a good place to start, since natural settings influenced the opportunities, challenges, and conditions that affected people's daily lives. Plus, it is easier to see physical divisions than to detect cultural ones in the archaeological record. First, I identified key transitions in physiographic relief and geography, such as the shift from the Mesa Verde cuesta to the Great Sage Plain and the differences

---

*For general descriptions of Colorado Plateau geology that include the Northern San Juan, see Baars 1983 and Barnes 1978. For more-specific intraregional descriptions, largely written because of mining interests, see Anderson et al. 1997; Ekren and Houser 1965; Force and Howell 1997; Griffitts 1990; Larsen and Cross 1956; Maxfield 1979; Sears 1956; and Wanek 1959.

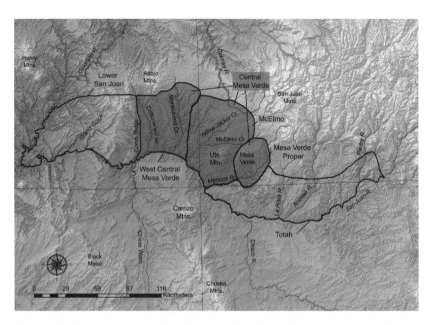

FIGURE 7. Subregion map of the Northern San Juan showing physiographic features. This is the base map used to show site and architectural feature distribution maps in chapters 3 and 4. Illustration by Grant D. Coffey.

between the areas east and west of Comb Ridge—both of which correspond with changes in geology. I then used watershed systems to further refine the physiographic and geologic boundaries. Second, I considered cultural differences in settlement patterns among these areas, such as the aforementioned differences east and west of Comb Ridge and the riverine-focused pattern in northwestern New Mexico.

Informed by these environmental and settlement attributes, I identified five main subregions within the Northern San Juan region—Totah, Mesa Verde Proper, McElmo, West Central Mesa Verde, and Lower San Juan—to facilitate intraregional comparisons (figure 7). I describe each subregion below, emphasizing the topography, geology, and agricultural conditions to provide additional details about the variables used to define them. These subregions and the following comparative analysis provide context for future studies focused on small social and spatial scales such as particular drainages, localities, communities, villages, and households.

The Totah Subregion

Because the history of Aztec and its surrounding area is so connected to both Chaco Canyon and Central Mesa Verde, researchers have had to work against the idea that Aztec and other sites in this part of northwestern New Mexico were a "backwater," a term used by Toll (1993), of Chaco and Mesa Verde by stressing its distinct history and identity (Brown et al. 2008; Lekson 1999a, 2008; McKenna and Toll 1992; Reed 2008a; Toll 1993, 2008). For this reason, McKenna and Toll (1992:133) began using the term *Totah*—Navajo for "rivers coming together"—as a regional name for this area. More recently, Reed (2008a) and his colleagues introduced the term *Middle San Juan region* because they had defined a larger geographic area than encompassed by the Totah that included the southern portion of the northern drainages feeding into the San Juan River, an area trending northeast-southwest from Chimney Rock to just west of the modern-day Four Corners that extends south of the San Juan River (Reed 2008a:fig. 1.1). Another goal was to introduce an ostensibly neutral term because of the political connotations of using a Navajo term to reference an area of ancestral Pueblo occupation, which can be viewed as disenfranchising Pueblo people from their historical homelands.*

A third way of referring to this portion of northwestern New Mexico is *Eastern Mesa Verde*, a term most recently used by Bellorado (2013) and colleagues. As defined, this area encompasses a much larger geographic area, extending slightly farther east and south of the San Juan River to include much of Largo Canyon (Bellorado 2013:fig. 1). As such, it subsumes the Upper and Middle San Juan areas.

Each of these designations has different advantages and biases, and none is ideal for every circumstance or time period (for a discerning discussion of how our understandings of these regional terms also vary based on where archaeologists work in the northern Southwest, see Bellorado 2013:342–45). Here, I continue to use *Totah* because the area defined by McKenna and Toll (1992) more closely corresponds with the geographic area I consider to examine Pueblo III (PIII) period dynamics, the term identifies this area as something distinct from the Mesa Verde core, and *Totah* is widely known since it is the earliest label for this region, one that likely predates Europeans (Toll 2008:333n1).

The Totah subregion in northwestern New Mexico (figures 7 and 8) encompasses the area associated with the confluence of the Animas,

---

*While I am sensitive to the concerns expressed by Reed (2008a), to me, the term *Totah* does not connote cultural affiliation, much as the Spanish names *San Juan* ("Saint John") and *Mesa Verde* ("Green Table") and the regional names *Kayenta* and *Chaco*, which are also Navajo terms, do not (see also Toll 2008:333n1). If we truly want to acknowledge Pueblo historical connections through our naming conventions, then we need to use Pueblo terms for regions and the physiographic features within them, but if we do this, which Pueblo terms would we use, given the many Pueblo cultural groups with distinct language groups, dialects, and connections to this area?

FIGURE 8. Historic aerial photograph of Aztec Ruins
National Monument and the Animas floodplain looking east.
Photograph taken by George J. Chambers, July 30, 1962.
Courtesy of Aztec Ruins National Monument.

La Plata, and San Juan Rivers (McKenna and Toll 1992:133) or, more
generally, the part of northwestern New Mexico that is north of the San
Juan River (Stein and Fowler 1996:123). It is where Salmon Ruins and
Heritage Park and Aztec Ruins National Monument are located. I slightly
expand this definition by including the Chimney Rock/Pagosa Springs
area because settlement and connections in this part of southwestern
Colorado are most similar to those in northwestern New Mexico (see also
Reed 2008a:fig. 1.1; Wilshusen 2009). I do not include areas south of
the San Juan River, nor do I include the upper La Plata and Piedra drainages, which were sparsely populated in the mid–AD 1100s and by AD
1200 were largely depopulated (Eddy 1977; Hannaford 1993; Varien et
al. 1996:97–98).

The Totah is roughly 6,860 square kilometers and is characterized geographically by floodplains and associated uplands formed in the Fruitland,
Kirtland, Animas, and Nacimiento Formations (see table 1).* Altitude
ranges from approximately 1,500 to 2,000 meters above sea level. Despite
an average annual precipitation of twenty-five centimeters, agricultural
conditions are good because the La Plata, Animas, and San Juan floodplains contain some of the best farmland in the region (Toll 1993). Away
from the floodplains, however, dryland farming is difficult at best (Adams
and Petersen 1999:31–33).

*For each of the subregions, the area of the polygons was measured using ArcGIS. These
measurements were rounded to the nearest ten.

The Subregions of Central Mesa Verde

The term *Central Mesa Verde* was initially used by Lipe (1995:143) to describe "the area from Mesa Verde National Park to the Colorado-Utah border." Varien (2000:7) later expanded the associated area to include the territory that arcs from the Mancos River south of Mesa Verde National Park to Cottonwood Wash in southeastern Utah. I extend the area slightly farther on the western boundary to Comb Ridge, a natural boundary with marked environmental and geologic differences to the east and west of it (see figures 6 and 7). An imposing, hundred-mile-long sandstone monocline, Comb Ridge was not a physical barrier, for people regularly traversed it, as attested to by the numerous roads, *herraduras*, and other sites along the ridge (see figure 6; Hurst and Till 2009; Till 2001).* When referring to the central portion of the Northern San Juan region, I continue to use *Central Mesa Verde*. However, based on variation in geography, geology, and settlement, Central Mesa Verde comprises three subregions: Mesa Verde Proper, McElmo, and West Central Mesa Verde (see figure 7; Glowacki 2010). When referring specifically to both the McElmo subregion and the Mesa Verde Proper subregion, I use *Mesa Verde core*, following Arakawa (2012a).

THE MESA VERDE PROPER SUBREGION.   The Mesa Verde Proper subregion includes the entire cuesta, which comprises Mesa Verde National Park and Ute Mountain Ute Tribal Park (see figure 7). Covering an area of roughly 1,030 square kilometers, this geologic uplift (cuesta) consists of a series of mesas cut by north–south-trending canyons that feed into the Mancos River (figure 9). Geologically, these canyons and mesas contain the Mesa Verde Group formations of Point Lookout sandstone, Menefee shale, and Cliff House sandstone (see table 1). Elevation ranges from approximately 2,000 to 2,600 meters above sea level. As discussed, Mesa Verde Proper has the most favorable environmental and climatic conditions in the region for successful dryland maize agriculture, including the highest yearly average precipitation of the five subregions (48 centimeters) and a longer growing season than other areas because of the southern tilt of the cuesta (Adams and Petersen 1999:32).

THE MCELMO SUBREGION.   The McElmo subregion includes the canyons and mesas associated with the McElmo and Monument drainages,

---

*For future analyses, given the site density and distribution during the AD 1150–1300 period (see figure 4; chapter 3), I would consider further modifying the boundaries of Central Mesa Verde to include the area immediately west of Comb Ridge–Comb Wash and the drainages that feed into it.

FIGURE 9. View of Park Mesa and Soda Canyon looking north. Courtesy of
Mesa Verde National Park. Photograph taken by Robert D. Jensen.

as well as the land around Ute Mountain (figure 10; see also Lipe and
Varien 1999b:fig. 9-1). Initially, I labeled this subregion "McElmo-Mon-
ument," which is geographically a more accurate name given the drainages involved (Glowacki 2006a); however, I found this label cumbersome
and have since shortened the name to McElmo (Glowacki 2010). The
McElmo subregion covers an area of roughly 3,600 square kilometers.
Most, but not all, of this subregion is in southwestern Colorado, as the
Utah portion of the Monument drainage is also included (its western
edge is roughly at the Hedley site, west of Dove Creek). The Canyons of
the Ancients National Monument, the Sand Canyon locality (figure 10),
and Yellow Jacket Pueblo are in the McElmo subregion.

The geologic setting of the mesas and canyons in this subregion
includes the Mancos, Dakota, Morrison, Summerville, and Entrada
Formations (see table 1). Altitude ranges from approximately 1,400 to
2,900 meters above sea level. The annual precipitation is 33 to 45 centimeters. Although dryland farming was, and is, possible and agricultural
productivity was relatively high compared to other areas (Adams and
Petersen 1999:33), there was also considerable local variability (Adams
and Petersen 1999; Van West 1996; Wright 2010). Consequently, farming was not as ideal as in Mesa Verde Proper. Nevertheless, the McElmo
subregion has a higher annual precipitation than does West Central Mesa

FIGURE 10. View of Sand Canyon looking north. Photograph taken by Robert D. Jensen.

Verde, making it a better location, agriculturally speaking, than the western part of Central Mesa Verde.

THE WEST CENTRAL MESA VERDE SUBREGION.   The West Central Mesa Verde subregion is in southeastern Utah and includes the areas associated with the Montezuma and Cottonwood drainages (see figure 6). Previously, I called this subregion "West Mesa Verde" (Glowacki 2006a, 2010), but this label is too similar to Lipe's (1995:145) established usage of *Western Mesa Verde*, so here I have changed it to avoid confusion and to more specifically relate this area to the western part of Central Mesa Verde. West Central Mesa Verde is roughly 2,200 square kilometers. The dominant geological formations are the Dakota, Morrison, Summerville, Entrada, and Dolores (see table 1). Elevation ranges from approximately

1,500 to 3,400 meters above sea level, and there is an annual precipitation of 18 to 33 centimeters. This subregion receives less annual precipitation than the other two, making West Central Mesa Verde a more
challenging location for ancestral Pueblo farmers, especially given local
variability.

The Lower San Juan Subregion

The term *Lower San Juan*, first used by William Adams and Nettie Adams
(1959:1), describes the 140-mile stretch of the San Juan River from
Bluff to the Colorado River and its immediately associated floodplain.
I expand their defined area to include the northern drainages feeding
into this part of the San Juan River (see figure 7). Till (2001:3) also
used *Lower San Juan* in his study of Chacoan roads in the Comb Ridge
locality, which he defined as the area west of the Montezuma drainage to
the confluence of the San Juan and Colorado Rivers. His boundaries for
the Lower San Juan include the western portion of West Central Mesa
Verde, described above.

   This subregion, the westernmost subregion of the Northern San Juan,
is markedly different from the rest of the region (Matson et al. 1988:245).
Spanning the area from west of Comb Ridge to the confluence of the San
Juan and Colorado Rivers, the Lower San Juan covers an area of roughly
5,280 square kilometers. It includes Natural Bridges National Monument, Cedar Mesa, Grand Gulch, and the Red Rock Plateau (figure 11).

FIGURE 11. View of Moon House in McLoyd's Canyon,
Cedar Mesa, Utah. Photograph taken by Sarah E. Payne.

The geological setting of the Lower San Juan is distinct from the rest of the region and contains the Wingate, Chinle, Moenkopi, and Cutler (Cedar Mesa) Formations (see table 1). Elevation ranges from approximately 1,300 to 1,700 meters above sea level. With an annual precipitation of 13 to 25 centimeters, the Lower San Juan is the most agriculturally marginal area in the region (Lipe 1970:91). It also contains the steepest canyons, sparsest vegetation, and patchiest distribution of viable agricultural lands, which makes dryland farming in this area nearly impossible (Lipe 1970:91–92).

Climate and the 1200s

As the northernmost and highest location where dryland farming was practiced in the Southwest (Adams and Petersen 1999:49; Wright 2010:81), the Northern San Juan region is a marginal environment for growing corn. Its location and the associated cold-air drainage patterns cause shorter growing seasons than experienced elsewhere in the Southwest. This situation was made more challenging for ancestral Pueblo farmers because three different precipitation patterns converge in the Four Corners area (unimodal in New Mexico; bimodal in Arizona; and low-level, yearlong in southern Utah), making rainfall extremely variable across the region (Wright 2010:77–78). The combination of these conditions makes an agriculture-based subsistence a risky endeavor that was, and is, extremely susceptible to environmental and climatic perturbations. Accordingly, climatic fluctuations—particularly drought—and their impact on agricultural productivity have played a central role in explaining the depopulation of the Northern San Juan (Berry 1982; Cordell et al. 2007; Douglass 1929; Kohler 2010; Kohler and Van West 1996; Kohler et al. 2008; Varien et al. 1996:104–5; Varien et al. 2000). Climatic changes and drought were, of course, not the only factors prompting widespread emigration (Duff et al. 2010; Glowacki 2010, 2011; Kohler et al. 2014; Kuckelman 2010; Ortman 2012), and the social and historical factors are the main focus of much of this book. Nonetheless, the effect of variation in regional climate and environmental processes on ancestral Pueblo groups in the Northern San Juan was not inconsequential.

There was much to contend with climate-wise, not the least of which was that the AD 1150 to 1300 period began and ended with major droughts. The interval from AD 1130 to 1180 was a particularly grueling time in the western United States, being one of the driest epochs during the Medieval Warming Period (AD 800 to 1300; Cook et al. 2004:1017). These conditions were locally exacerbated by low water tables, stream entrenchment, and degraded floodplains (Van West and Dean 2000:37), making the typically precarious business of farming even more uncertain than normal. The severity of these conditions required accommodation and most certainly affected decisions and behaviors daily. Among the reactions to this severe period were increased aggregation (Glowacki 2010; Glowacki and Ortman 2012; Varien et al. 2007) and settlement relocation to areas near prominent water sources and in canyon settings (Glowacki and Ortman 2012; Kleidon et al. 2007; Kolm and Smith 2012). These and other changes in the wake of drought severity created contingencies that affected thirteenth-century social networks.

From AD 1180 to 1250, there was a period of favorable convergences, such as rising water tables and aggrading floodplains, which were more conducive to productive farming (Van West and Dean 2000:35–37). However, there were also prolonged periods of cooler than normal temperatures that probably shortened what was already a minimal growing season, reducing agricultural productivity across the region (Kohler et al. 2007; Petersen 1988; Salzer 2000; Wright 2010, 2012). These cooler temperatures lasted for nearly eighty years over four different episodes throughout the 1200s and may have been just as challenging as the late 1200s drought. Recent paleoproductivity reconstructions by Kohler and his colleagues suggest that this may have been the case, since the modeled average potential maize yield during much of the 1200s is well below the mean, particularly in the first half of the century (Kohler et al. 2007:fig. 6).

Cultural behaviors may have ameliorated the impact of cooler temperatures on productivity. As noted by Van West and Dean (2000:32), the tree-ring record suggests that there was widespread wood procurement, particularly between the 1230s and 1260s (see Lipe 1995:fig. 1; Varien et al. 2007:fig. 5F), and regional population levels increased during the first half of the 1200s (see chapter 3; Glowacki 2010; Varien et al. 2007; Wilshusen 2002). Thus, even if cooler temperatures created farming challenges, these difficulties did not prevent intensification and growth in the eastern half of the region, at least for a time. The incongruity between the modeled below-average productivity and the evident increase in population levels and construction could be explained by processes of consolidation as increasing numbers of people moved into the most agriculturally productive lands in the region (Wright 2012:56), or productivity levels may have actually been higher than predicted by the models because Pueblo farmers relied on methods to enhance productivity, such as soil amendment, landscape modification, rotation, and relocation. In the case of the latter, check dams and terracing was a widely used strategy throughout the region. In the canyons of Mesa Verde Proper, for example, hundreds of check dams are associated with the habitations along the cliff edges and on the talus slopes (Hayes 1964; Kleidon et al. 2007; Kleidon et al. 2003; Rohn 1963, 1977). The enhanced water and soil retention and increase in farmable land provided by check dams and terraces would have been substantial and likely mitigated at least some of the negative impact of cooler temperatures and shortened growing seasons.

In the mid-1200s, another climatic monkey wrench was thrown into the mix when the dominant regional precipitation pattern shifted from a bimodal pattern to a unimodal one (Cordell 2000; Cordell et al. 2007; Dean 1996; Van West and Dean 2000; Wright 2010:95, 97). These changing conditions disrupted regional precipitation patterns for the next two hundred years and would have necessitated changes in agricultural practices. And then, of course, the end of the 1200s was marked by a prolonged drought from AD 1276 to 1299, also known as the "Great Drought" (Berry 1982:106, 110; Douglass 1929). Much like the one during the mid-1100s, this drought was accompanied by lower water tables, entrenched streams, and decreased spatial variability (Van West and Dean 2000:37) that further reduced agricultural productivity (Kohler et al. 2007). Although these drought conditions were not as severe as those of the mid-1100s, despite the "Great Drought" moniker, by the end of the period the Northern San Juan region was completely depopulated by ancestral Pueblo people. This outcome was not predestined: The impact of droughts is based not solely on climatic and environmental conditions but also on the ability of social, religious, and political institutions to cope with the added strain on the society (Drèze and Sen 1989:46–47; Hassan 2002; Oliver-Smith 1996:303–5). There is also great variability in the way droughts are experienced by those living through them. Thus, the drought and coincident environmental downturns were not, in and of themselves, the cause of regional depopulation (Ahlstrom et al. 1995:131). The different outcomes of the two drought periods imply that social and cultural differences existed, which in one case allowed people to continue living in the region and in the other prompted widespread emigration. To understand the role the 1270s drought played in the depopulation, we need to better understand the social conditions leading up to the onset of the drought.

CHAPTER THREE

Mapping Spatial Experience

Buildings and their configurations express the vernacular of a time, region, or group—the loosely shared cultural sensibilities for how space and place are construed. As Glassie (2000:17) beautifully elucidated in *Vernacular Architecture*, "Buildings, like poems and rituals, realize culture." Where buildings are located, how they are arranged, and their internal organization are all founded on intentional decisions that reflect experience, purpose, identity, belief, and style. The nature of architecture and settlement are also contingent. Buildings get modified and expanded, dismantled and rebuilt. They have histories that transcend the people who initially built them. As such, architecture and settlement patterns become an essential medium for examining the social and cultural milieu in which people, in this case ancestral Pueblo people, were immersed. Buildings inform on the underlying circumstances that shaped everyday lives and the historical processes behind them. Changes in architecture and settlement can also presage great cultural and societal upheavals, since relocation and renovation are often reactions to local events or circumstances from which large-scale societal transformation emerged.

To better understand the spatiality of experience across the Northern San Juan during the Pueblo III (PIII) period (AD 1150–1300), I compare and contrast subregional variation in settlement patterns, occupation histories, and the distribution of civic-ceremonial (public) architecture. Doing so not only elucidates the different cultural and historical landscapes underlying the social dynamics of the late 1100s and 1200s but also informs on how regional terminology can be clarified to better reflect this variation.

The Northern San Juan PIII Habitation
Site Database

The information presented here uses site data that I compiled from published reports and electronic site file data from the New Mexico Archaeological Records Management Section (ARMS), Mesa Verde National Park
(MVNP), the Colorado Office of Archaeology and Historic Preservation
(OAHP), and the Utah State Historic Preservation Office (SHPO), plus
data collected for the Village Ecodynamics Project (VEP) by researchers
at Crow Canyon Archaeological Center and Washington State University
(including myself). I have also included sites recorded on Navajo and Ute
Mountain Ute lands when available in published reports (e.g., Germick
1985). Numerous archaeologists and many years were involved in collecting these data, and this synthesis reflects our continued efforts to
document and preserve these important places.

I initially compiled these data in 2004 and 2005 (Glowacki 2006a,
2010). Since that time there have been several efforts to synthesize site
data in different sections of Central Mesa Verde (Glowacki 2012; Hurst
and Robinson 2014; Varien et al. 2007) and the Middle San Juan (Brown
et al. 2013; Reed 2011). Consequently, it was necessary to update the PIII
database in 2012 by adding newly documented sites and substantiating
site-specific details and to then reanalyze these data. This database contains information on 3,808 habitation sites and isolated civic-ceremonial
architecture, such as great kivas, with a PIII component (see figure 4).

Field houses, artifact scatters, and isolated features such as terraces,
check dams, reservoirs, and rooms were included in the database only
if they were associated with other residential features (e.g., a kiva or
room blocks). Many archaeologists who worked on numerous projects
for various institutions with different research goals, criteria for feature
identification, and constraints on their projects documented the key
architectural features at each site such as towers, plazas, great kivas, and
enclosing walls. Thus, there are differences in how and whether features
were recorded. For example, regional archaeologists did not consistently
discriminate between retaining and enclosing walls, which have different social and functional uses (i.e., walls that shore up sediments versus
those that define space). There are therefore issues of data consistency
that affect the architectural distributions presented here. The community center surveys have helped improve comparability among some of
the largest sites in Central Mesa Verde (Glowacki 2012; Glowacki and
Ortman 2012), as have recent large-scale survey projects (e.g., the Comb
Ridge survey [Hurst and Robinson 2014]) and research focused on specific architectural features such as towers and enclosing walls (e.g.,

Bredthauer 2010; Kenzle 1997). Issues of comparability, however, remain an important concern when interpreting large-scale, regional patterning.

Similarly, although full-coverage survey is the ideal for analyzing settlement patterns (e.g., Fish and Kowalewski 1990), it is not a feasible expectation when the study area is as large as the Northern San Juan region, nearly 20,000 square kilometers, and it contains a patchwork of private, federal, and tribal lands. Consequently, gaps in survey coverage are unavoidable, particularly with regard to tribal lands, and additional survey could alter the patterns described here. To avoid making mountains out of molehills, I focus on robust patterning that is less likely to change in significant ways with new fieldwork. A small consolation in this regard is that when my results were compared with those based on full-coverage, block surveys from key areas within the region (e.g., Varien et al. 2007), the overall trends in corresponding areas were similar.

Site Distribution and Density: Where Was Everybody?

As discussed, regional settlement was distributed along a band fifty to sixty kilometers wide that paralleled the path of the San Juan River (see figure 4; see also Varien et al. 1996). I use site density—the number of sites per square kilometer—as a proxy to compare the relative difference in population among the subregions. Since the total area surveyed was not available for all subregions, densities were calculated using the total area of each subregion. This method generalizes the site density for each subregion, since it does not account for the differing amounts of survey among the subregions or the effects of physical geography on settlement distribution. However, it does provide a reasonable measure to enable a broad comparison of site density across the Northern San Juan region. Site density data appear in table 2.

As anticipated, site density was highest in the central portion of the region and lower in the extreme eastern and western margins of the Northern San Juan (the Totah and Lower San Juan subregions; see figure 4). In the Lower San Juan, where far fewer people were living than anywhere else in the region (see also Lipe 1970, 2002; McVickar 2001:227, 231), sites were more common in the eastern part of the subregion (Grand Gulch and Cedar Mesa) and much less so west of the drainages that feed into Comb Wash (see figure 4). In the Totah, sites were concentrated along the river drainages (McKenna and Toll 1992:134; Stein and McKenna 1988), making the effective site density higher than calculated in table 2.

The Mesa Verde Proper and McElmo subregions have the highest site density in the region with a combined site density of 0.50 sites per

TABLE 2. Density of habitation sites with a Pueblo III period
component (AD 1150–1300)

Subregions and region	Number of habitation sites	Percentage of regional site sample	Area (km²)	Subregional site density
Totah	626	16	6,860	0.09
Mesa Verde Proper	653	17	1,030	0.63
McElmo	1,671	44	3,600	0.46
West Central Mesa Verde	653	17	2,200	0.30
Lower San Juan	205	5	5,280	0.04
Eastern subregions	2,950	77	11,490	0.26
Western subregions	858	23	7,480	0.11
Central Mesa Verde	2,977	78	6,830	0.44
Northern San Juan	3,808	100	18,970	0.20

square kilometer (n = 2,324, or 61 percent of the regional site sample).
To the extent that site density and the inferred population concentration
equates with central importance in regional dynamics, as the most populated, these subregions were likely the regional core. Of the two, Mesa
Verde Proper, a relatively circumscribed geographic area, had the highest
density. This was not surprising, since Mesa Verde Proper has long been
considered one of the most populated areas of the Northern San Juan
(Lipe 1995:153; Varien et al. 1996:fig. 7.5; Wilshusen 2002:114). Yet
there are two factors that bias this inference. One is that Mesa Verde
Proper has the highest percentage of surveyed land in the region because
MVNP is located there. For example, approximately 15–20 percent of the
McElmo subregion has been surveyed (e.g., Varien et al. 2007:274) versus nearly 50 percent of Mesa Verde Proper (bearing in mind that MVNP
is only half of this subregion).

The second and more influential factor is that early recording practices
in MVNP (circa 1950) used a "splitter's philosophy," and each spatially
distinct rubble mound or feature was assigned a unique site number.
Thus, villages and hamlets with multiple room blocks were recorded with
multiple site numbers. For example, Upper Battleship Rock Pueblo, which
is located on the east side of a ridge that terminates at Battleship Rock,
has 42 room blocks, 57 pit structures, a plaza, a possible great house, and
at least 33 check dams (Glowacki 2012). It is probably the largest ancestral Pueblo village in MVNP, and it was recorded as forty-three separate
sites. Therefore, the number of sites in MVNP is inflated in comparison

to the rest of the region, where multiple room block settlements were most often recorded under one site number. Although the calculated site density for the MVNP portion of Mesa Verde Proper (see table 2) is likely overestimated, this bias may have been somewhat ameliorated since site data from the western half of the subregion were largely unavailable and the area of the entire landform was used to calculate the site densities.

Central Mesa Verde has been conventionally thought of as the core of the Mesa Verde occupation in the Northern San Juan (Lipe 1995; Varien 2000). The three subregions encompassed by this area—Mesa Verde Proper, McElmo, and West Central Mesa Verde—contain 78 percent of the total site sample for the region. Thus, at first glance, Central Mesa Verde seems central to the region not only geographically but also demographically. However, site density in West Central Mesa Verde is markedly lower than that in the rest of Central Mesa Verde (see table 2). Provided that variation in survey coverage does not overly influence these data, the differences in site density suggest that West Central Mesa Verde may not have been as central as the Mesa Verde Proper and McElmo subregions.

Community Centers

The term *community center* was coined by Varien (1999:4) to refer to the large, aggregated villages that played a central role in structuring the social life of ancestral Pueblo people across the Northern San Juan. Community centers are defined as containing fifty or more structures, including rooms, pit structures, and towers, and they often had civic-ceremonial architecture, such as great kivas and plazas, for large-scale gatherings (Adler and Varien 1994; Lipe and Varien 1999b:345; Varien 1999; Varien et al. 1996). They were also frequently associated with smaller, nearby, residential sites. Many, but not all, were places with a history of continuous occupation that spanned multiple generations and were thus occupied much longer than many other villages in the region. Understanding the societal role of community centers—including when and where large villages formed, how their organization changed, and when they were abandoned—is critical if we are to reconstruct the social contexts and processes involved in leaving Mesa Verde.

Community centers in the Northern San Juan PIII habitation site database were identified as any village that met one or more of the following criteria: (1) fifty or more structures; (2) nine or more households as indicated by the number of pit structures; and (3) civic-ceremonial architecture (Glowacki and Ortman 2012). A threshold of nine pit structures was added to the criteria initially used to identify community centers (e.g., Varien 1999) because room (structure) count data were not always available at a regional scale. Previous studies show a clear difference in the number of sites with nine or more pit structures (e.g., Glowacki and Ortman 2012:fig. 14.1), which suggests that this is a useful benchmark for identifying the villages that were most likely to have played central roles in social and political dynamics. A village with six to eight pit structures, however, may also qualify as a community center based on the total number of structures if an average room-to-kiva ratio of 7:1 (Lipe 1989:table 1) is used to estimate the number of associated rooms (Lipe and Varien 1999b:345). Given the regional scope of this study, rather than muddy the waters with a possible community center category, I opted for the conservative route and used a nine-pit-structure threshold with the hope that this would elucidate robust patterns that could be explored in future analyses.

There are 253 confirmed community centers in the PIII regional database that meet the established criteria and are used to examine variation in where, when, and how people lived in the Northern San Juan (figure 12; table 3; appendix). Of course, these data account for only those people living in the largest villages, while hundreds of people lived in small and medium-sized pueblos across the region (e.g., Mahoney et al. 2000;

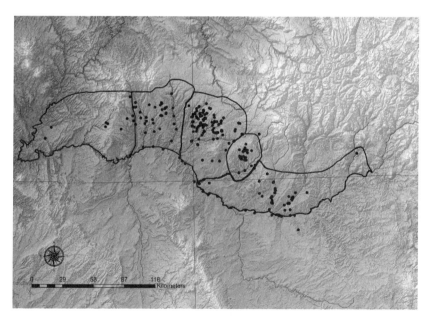

FIGURE 12. Distribution of community centers in the Northern San Juan region with a Pueblo III period component (AD 1150–1300). Illustration by Grant D. Coffey.

TABLE 3. Ratio of community centers to residential noncenters
by subregion

Subregions and region	Number of residential noncenters[a]	Number of community centers[a]	Ratio of community centers to noncenters (residential)[a]
Totah	567	59	1:10
Mesa Verde Proper[b]	617	36	1:17
McElmo	1,546 (1,565)	105 (124)	1:15 (1:13)
West Central Mesa Verde	607	46	1:13
Lower San Juan	198	7	1:28
Eastern subregions	2,730 (2,749)	200 (219)	1:14 (1:13)
Western subregions	805	53	1:15
Central Mesa Verde	2,770 (2,789)	188 (207)	1:15 (1:13)
Northern San Juan	3,535 (3,554)	253 (272)	1:14 (1:13)

[a]The number in parentheses includes 19 sites in the McElmo subregion with possible plazas that otherwise do not meet the criteria for a community center with the current available data. Further research is required to confirm whether these sites are community centers. Subsequent analyses do not include these sites.

[b]The number of residential sites for Mesa Verde Proper is somewhat inflated because of the site recording practices used when the initial site inventory was established at Mesa Verde National Park in the 1950s.

Varien et al. 2007). Thus, settlement dynamics were obviously more complex than what can be presented here.

I rely heavily on the community center data for several reasons. First, from a practical standpoint, the largest sites in the region have been a focus of research since the late 1800s, when several of them were first described by W. H. Holmes and photographed by W. H. Jackson during the Hayden Expedition (e.g., Holmes 1878). Since that time there have been numerous projects that have researched large pueblos and accumulated significant amounts of data, which in recent decades have been compiled by regional specialists (Brown et al. 2013; Glowacki 2006a; Glowacki and Ortman 2012; Hurst and Till 2009; Ortman et al. 2012; Reed 2011; Varien 1999; Varien et al. 1996, 2007). Given the visibility of community centers and the intensity of research associated with them, it is reasonable to assume that a majority of the large sites have been recorded. Community center data therefore provide a relatively consistent regional site sample, and the analyses of these data are less likely to be biased by variation in survey coverage.

Second, historically, community centers were among the last pueblos to be abandoned when ancestral Pueblo people left the Northern San Juan. Archaeological evidence shows that despite being located on productive farmland, many of the smaller settlements were abandoned as population consolidated into fewer but larger pueblos in the mid to late 1200s or moved away altogether (Glowacki and Ortman 2012; Varien et al. 1996, 2007; Wilshusen 2002). Recent analyses of the proportion of ancestral Pueblo people living in large, aggregated villages versus small or medium-sized pueblos in the VEP I study area (McElmo) suggest that more than half of the population may have lived in community centers by AD 1260 (Glowacki and Ortman 2012:231–32, fig. 14.5; Varien et al. 2007; Wilshusen 2002:118). It is therefore possible to better characterize the final decades of occupation for at least key portions of the region by focusing on the community centers.

Finally, community centers are a distinctive feature of the cultural and social landscape, constituting about 8 percent of the known PIII habitation sites in the Northern San Juan (table 3). On average, there were thirteen residential pueblos for each community center (table 3). The exception was in the Lower San Juan, where the ratio of residential pueblos to centers (28:1) was notably higher than that in the rest of the region. This marked difference shows that centers did not play a major role in the Lower San Juan and more people lived in smaller residential pueblos. In the rest of the region, the ratios were lower and similar to each other, suggesting that large, aggregated pueblos were a central feature of the social landscape. However, the ratio of residential pueblos to centers in the Totah was somewhat lower than in the Central Mesa Verde subregions (table 3). This difference in the Totah could relate to variation in either population levels or organization. The slightly higher number of residential pueblos to centers in Mesa Verde Proper may relate to the bias introduced by how sites were recorded (discussed above).

Each community center had its own history with a distinctive composition of social groups, personalities, and agendas that was shaped by historical contingencies, traditions, exigencies, and events. These influences generated complex, multiscalar relationships that uniquely positioned each center within the social, economic, ceremonial, and political networks across the region and beyond. The size of community centers and their incorporation of civic-ceremonial architecture as well as their long histories are an indication of a persistent, central presence that affected social, economic, and political interactions within and between communities. That there were materials and buildings specific to large villages reinforces this likelihood (Driver 2002; Lipe 2002; Muir and Driver 2002, 2004; Ortman and Bradley 2002). It is thus easy to envision that community centers were dynamic places and that people who lived in nearby pueblos regularly participated in ceremonial gatherings or other economic and social activities held at each of them. By delineating the roles, histories, and relational networks of these largest villages, how they varied across the region, and their relationships with other residential pueblos and centers, we will come to a better understanding of what transpired in the thirteenth century.

Subregional Occupation Histories: When Did They Live There?

An important component of reconstructing intraregional historical landscapes and understanding how they contributed to the social context of the 1200s is determining the occupation history of each subregion. Comparing similarities and differences in the timing of peak population and noticeable emigration reveals how variation in the demographic contexts and processes affected intraregional interaction and sociopolitical dynamics during this critical period. Occupation trends for each subregion were determined using room counts from community centers, which has proven to be a useful method for evaluating population trends across the Northern San Juan (e.g., Wilshusen 2002) and the U.S. Southwest in general (Hill et al. 2004, 2010). This method works particularly well for the community centers in Mesa Verde Proper and McElmo and to a slightly lesser extent for those in West Central Mesa Verde, which tend to have well-dated occupations associated with tree-ring dates and excavation data. The occupation periods of large sites in the Totah and Lower San Juan, however, are most often based on survey data and have fewer tree-ring dates, resulting in relatively broad occupation spans. Fluctuations in occupation for these two subregions are therefore not as apparent as they are for those in Central Mesa Verde.

There were room counts for 210 of the 253 community centers (83 percent). These centers include 57 percent of the McElmo centers, 78 percent of the Totah centers, 85 percent of the West Central Mesa Verde centers, 89 percent of the Mesa Verde Proper centers, and all of the Lower San Juan centers. Thus, the McElmo subregion is underrepresented in the following analysis and the occupational history was even more pronounced than as it is presented here.

Room count estimates were based on either the in-field assessment provided by the archaeologist or the number of rooms calculated by dividing architectural area by 33 square meters (the estimated average room size). Room counts could not be uniformly estimated because in many cases only an in-field estimate or architectural area was reported for each site. Note that the average room size was based on Central Mesa Verde sites, and it may have been different for the Totah and for the Lower San Juan. Since there was also no way to systematically evaluate room function for each center with the available data, all rooms were considered domestic. Because it was unlikely that all rooms were used at the same time, the raw room count for each community center was adjusted to reflect the number of rooms likely to be in use at any given time (i.e., momentary room count). For the sake of producing comparable estimates, it was assumed that the overall site population did not vary significantly during occupation, even though this was probably not the case.

The momentary room count for each site was calculated by multiplying the total room count by the average room use-life and dividing this number by the occupation period length. For example, Yucca House (5MT5006) in the McElmo subregion has an estimated 450 rooms and a 140-year occupation, from AD 1140 to 1280 (Glowacki 2001:21; Glowacki and Ortman 2012:app. B). The momentary room count for Yucca House is 129 rooms (450 multiplied by 40 divided by 140). I used an average use-life of 40 years, which is itself an average of the occupation span estimates for the small PIII sites that were tested in the Sand Canyon locality (Varien 1999:107–11). Forty years is a relatively conservative estimate for large, long-lived sites, especially for alcove sites.

The next step was to assign momentary room counts to their respective occupation period for each site. Continuing with the Yucca House example, this means that 129 rooms were assigned to the years between AD 1180 and AD 1280. This allocation method was applied to each community center in all the subregions. By assigning momentary room counts across the occupation period, these data are homogenized, and thus the trends revealed by this index of occupation history do not reflect minor fluctuations or possible hiatuses in occupation. Since the goal of this analysis is to compare the timing of peak population and notable emigration among the subregions, the insensitivity to small-scale or local variance is not overly problematic.

The momentary room counts for all centers were aggregated (table 4), and these totals were plotted by twenty-year intervals to display the trends in occupation history for each subregion (figure 13). Although this method provides a useful index to better understand how the different histories of each subregion compare, it also likely overestimates the initial occupation of each site and underestimates near-terminal peak occupations, particularly for long-lived sites. Despite these biases, the resulting occupation histories reveal important intraregional population dynamics that shaped the social landscape from AD 1140 to 1300. Technically, the resulting occupation history profiles indicate the population growth and decline associated with the community centers; however, given that ancestral Pueblo people were increasingly moving into

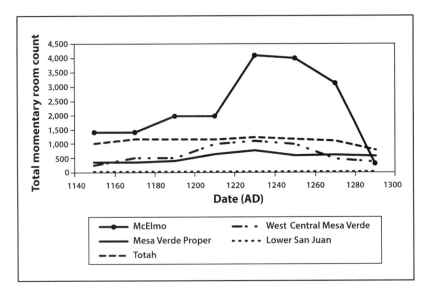

FIGURE 13. Subregional occupation histories, AD 1140 to 1300.

community centers (Glowacki and Ortman 2012; Varien et al. 2007), the profiles also reflect overall subregion population change.

The regional occupation history derived from the available momentary room counts from community centers (table 4) shows steady population increase from the mid to late 1100s and a substantial increase from 1200 to 1220, followed by two periods of marked population decline in the mid to late 1200s once widespread emigration began in earnest. This timing of growth and decline was expected and has been defined in previous population studies of the Northern San Juan (Dean et al. 1994; Euler 1988; Lipe 1995; Lipe and Varien 1999b; Varien et al. 1996, 2007; Wilshusen 2002). Looking at the occupation histories for the individual subregions, however, elucidates a more complex intraregional occupation history (figure 13). The most obvious difference is that the intensity of the occupation of McElmo greatly overshadows that of the rest of the region. With more than three to five times the population of the Totah, Mesa Verde Proper, and West Central Mesa Verde (table 4), the McElmo occupation history essentially drives the regional trend and overwhelms the variation in occupation among the other subregions (figure 13).

Differences in the nature of the occupation of each subregion are evident, however. In the McElmo subregion, the number of people living in centers increased in the late 1100s and then again from the 1220s to the 1240s, when the growth was magnitudinal. Population steadily declined

TABLE 4. Momentary room counts by subregion from AD 1140 to 1300

Period (AD)	Totah (N = 46)	% change	Mesa Verde Proper (N = 32)	% change	McElmo (N = 85)	% change	West Central Mesa Verde (N = 40)	% change	Lower San Juan (N = 7)	% change	Northern San Juan (N = 210)	% change
1140–1160	1,012		353		1,401		257		34		3,057	
1160–1180	1,166	13	353	0	1,401	0	509	50	34	0	3,464	12
1180–1200	1,166	0	405	13	1,968	29	509	0	34	0	4,083	15
1200–1220	1,151	−1	638	37	1,968	0	991	49	34	0	4,783	15
1220–1240	1,228	6	768	17	4,094	52	1,099	10	16	−53	7,204	34
1240–1260	1,177	−4	590	−23	3,991	−3	987	−10	50	68	6,796	−6
1260–1280	1,102	−6	614	4	3,122	−22	474	−52	48	−4	5,359	−21
1280–1300	795	−28	574	−7	307	−90	368	−22	34	−29	2,079	−61

after 1240, and the rate of people leaving McElmo had accelerated by the 1260s. In Mesa Verde Proper, there was steady population increase from 1180 to 1240, with the greatest increase in 1200 to 1220, following which there was a notable period of population emigration from 1240 to 1260. Unlike in other subregions, in the 1200s, there was a brief rebound in population before the ultimate exodus from the region, perhaps indicating that the cliff dwellings of Mesa Verde Proper afforded some stability during the last turbulent decades of ancestral Pueblo occupation of the Northern San Juan. In West Central Mesa Verde there were two phases of population increase (1160–1180 and 1200–1220), and population levels were in decline by 1240, with most people emigrating by the 1260s. In the Totah, population levels remained fairly constant throughout the 1200s. Although population decline began in the Totah after 1240, emigration was more gradual than in the rest of the subregions. Because of the small number of centers in the Lower San Juan, the occupation history of this subregion is more closely tied to the histories of individual centers. Thus, the population dip in the early 1200s was related to the abandonment of the Coombs site, and the increase in the mid-1200s was when the occupation of Moon House began. It is therefore difficult to make broad inferences from the occupation history of the Lower San Juan about the timing of peak population and emigration.

To better understand the subregional occupation histories, the percent change in momentary households over time was used to assess the relative magnitude and timing of the population changes that occurred in each subregion (table 4). This method provided a standardized way to evaluate the scale of population change in a way that was not overly influenced by the much larger number of centers in the McElmo subregion. These data elucidate key differences in when each of the subregions experienced significant population change (figure 14). From the 1160s to the 1180s, substantial population growth occurred in the Totah and West Central Mesa Verde. During the 1180 to 1200 period, McElmo and Mesa Verde Proper experienced marked population increase, whereas from 1200 to 1220, population growth happened in West Central Mesa Verde and continued on Mesa Verde Proper. From 1220 to 1240, population increased in all the subregions, except the Lower San Juan, but the increase was orders of magnitude higher in McElmo.

As emigration from the region became more prevalent in the late 1200s, there was variation in the rate of depopulation. For example, from 1240 to 1260, although population declined in all the subregions, the frequency of emigration was higher on Mesa Verde Proper and in West Central Mesa Verde. From 1260 to 1280, the most dramatic population loss was in West Central Mesa Verde, yet, as noted above, population

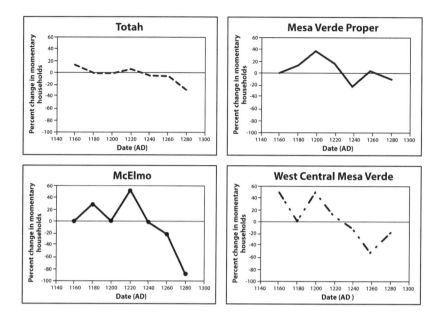

FIGURE 14. Percent change in momentary households for the Totah and Central Mesa Verde subregions.

increased on Mesa Verde Proper. In the final decades, as the remaining ancestral Pueblo people were leaving the Northern San Juan, the most dramatic population loss was in McElmo.

Summarizing the General Trends

This analysis of subregional occupation histories elucidates the variation in population growth and the rate and timing of emigration across the Northern San Juan. For example, there were different modes of population increase among the subregions, including (1) steady increase (Mesa Verde Proper); (2) periodic marked increase (West Central Mesa Verde); (3) periodic increase with an episode of dramatic increase (McElmo); and (4) nominal increase with sustained population levels (Totah). The way that population increased in each of the subregions emerged from historical processes and in turn shaped the interactions and contexts that culminated in regional abandonment. Adjusting to a rapid and dramatic increase in the number of people living in the community centers, such as was the case in the McElmo subregion, came with a different set of issues than accommodating either a steady increase of people or episodic increases of lesser magnitudes. Specifically, issues of land tenure,

alliance formation, community integration, acculturation, religious syncretism, conflict, and conflict resolution were more acute for the ancestral Pueblo people living in the McElmo subregion than for those living
in other parts of the region.

Not only did the modes of population growth differ among the subregions, so did the timing of when it occurred. In the mid-1100s, population growth was occurring in the Totah and West Central Mesa Verde, but
the regional core of McElmo and Mesa Verde Proper was experiencing
growth in the late 1100s. By the early 1200s, Mesa Verde Proper and
West Central Mesa Verde were in a growth phase, which was followed by
regionwide population growth in the subsequent decades. This temporal
and spatial variation reveals important historical differences that affected
village formation and occupation in each of the subregions.

The occupation histories also inform on potential differences in the
pace and timing of emigration from the Northern San Juan. Throughout
Pueblo history, people constantly moved for various reasons, at multiple
scales, and for varying distances (e.g., Schlanger and Wilshusen 1993).
Thus, as some researchers have suggested, the widespread emigration
from the region at the end of the 1200s had its genesis in the small-scale,
ongoing moves that occurred in the late 1100s and early 1200s (Ahlstrom
et al. 1995; Duff and Wilshusen 2000). Yet as these data and many other
studies have shown, there was also an intense phase of comparatively
rapid emigration in the late 1200s (Lipe 1995:152; Rohn 1989:166;
Varien 1999, 2010; Varien et al. 1996, 2007; Wilshusen 2002:118).

Across the Northern San Juan, people emigrated with increasing
frequency after 1240 (see table 4 and figures 13 and 14). There were,
however, subtle differences in the pace of emigration from each of the
subregions. Most of the people who emigrated from the McElmo and
Totah subregions were leaving in the final decades, whereas a higher proportion of the population in West Central Mesa Verde was leaving by the
1260s. Despite a substantial number of people leaving Mesa Verde Proper
during the 1240s and 1250s, population increased in the late 1260s and
1270s as people moved into the cliff dwellings and other large villages
before they completely left the subregion after the 1280s. Variation in the
rate of population loss differentially affected the lived experience of the
last decades of the ancestral Pueblo occupation of the Northern San Juan.

Community Centers of the Northern San Juan

Variation in the distribution and organization of community centers
emerged from the unique histories and identities of the people who
lived in them. Delineating variation among community centers provides

insights into the factors that contributed to their growth and decline and the nature of the historical landscapes in which centers were situated. The number, size, and density of community centers in each subregion affected the intensity of day-to-day interactions, the nature of social and political networks, and the size of resource catchments required to support the village. Changes in the size of centers also inform on the processes of aggregation and depopulation. Room-to-kiva ratios and the types of civic-ceremonial architecture speak to the nature of village organization.

Table 5 shows the momentary room counts from table 4, the number of centers, and their average size for each subregion. In this table, the number of centers is that used in the momentary room count calculation, not the total number for each subregion. The average size of community centers was calculated by dividing the total number of the momentary room counts for each period by the total number of sites. Since the average size is based on the momentary room counts, any increase or decrease in size relates to processes of aggregation and emigration. Community centers in the Northern San Juan were the most numerous and largest from AD 1220 to 1260, attaining their greatest frequency between AD 1220 and AD 1240 and their largest size, on average, in the late 1200s (table 5).

Varien and others have shown that the distances between community centers in Central Mesa Verde decreased throughout the 1200s (Varien 1999:158–60, fig. 7.9; Varien et al. 2000), which affected the nature of interactions among community centers. For example, in areas where the proximity (density) of centers increased, the intensity and frequency of conflict over territory or resources, and cooperative efforts, such as alliance building, were also likely to have intensified (Varien et al. 2000). Density was calculated as the number of centers per period divided by the area of the respective subregion (that is, number of centers per square kilometer). Figure 15 shows how community center density changed over time and the extent to which increasing proximity was a factor in each of the subregions.

Community center density in the Northern San Juan was the highest in Mesa Verde Proper and McElmo (figure 15; see also Varien 1999). The high density on Mesa Verde Proper is in part a result of physiographic factors, because the Mesa Verde landform inherently makes settlement in this area more concentrated than elsewhere, which also affected social processes. In all of the Central Mesa Verde subregions, community center density increased in the late 1100s and early 1200s and reached maximum density during the 1220s to 1240s (figure 15). In Mesa Verde Proper and West Central Mesa Verde, site density decreased after 1240, but in McElmo it did not decrease substantially until after 1260.

Community centers in the rest of the region were generally dispersed and in some cases were regularly spaced along drainages, a pattern particularly apparent along the San Juan River and in the Montezuma drainage

TABLE 5. Average size of community centers through time based on momentary room counts and number of sites for each subregion

Period (AD)	Totah			Mesa Verde Proper			McElmo		
	Mom. room count	Number of sites	Average size[a]	Mom. room count	Number of sites	Average size[a]	Mom. room count	Number of sites	Average size[a]
1140–1160	1,012	38	27	353	20	18	1,401	41	34
1160–1180	1,166	45	26	353	20	18	1,401	41	34
1180–1200	1,166	45	26	405	22	18	1,968	54	36
1200–1220	1,151	44	26	638	29	22	1,968	54	36
1220–1240	1,228	45	27	768	31	25	4,094	80	51
1240–1260	1,177	41	29	590	25	24	3,991	76	53
1260–1280	1,102	38	29	614	23	27	3,122	57	55
1280–1300	795	32	25	574	21	27	307	11	28
Total sites		46			32			85	

Period (AD)	West Central Mesa Verde			Lower San Juan[b]			Northern San Juan		
	Mom. room count	Number of sites	Average size[a]	Mom. room count	Number of sites	Average size[a]	Mom. room count	Number of sites	Average size[a]
1140–1160	257	21	12	34	6	6	3,057	126	24
1160–1180	509	29	18	34	6	6	3,464	141	25
1180–1200	509	29	18	34	6	6	4,083	156	26
1200–1220	991	37	27	34	6	6	4,783	170	28
1220–1240	1,099	39	28	16	5	3	7,204	200	36
1240–1260	987	31	32	50	6	8	6,796	179	38
1260–1280	474	18	26	48	5	10	5,359	141	38
1280–1300	368	15	25	34	1	34	2,079	80	26
Total sites		40			7			210	

Note: Shading indicates peak values. "Mom. room count" = momentary room count.

[a] Average size is based on the room count at each site.

[b] Because of the small sample size, there is no meaningful peak in the Lower San Juan region.

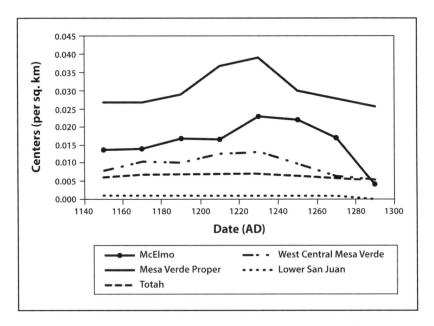

FIGURE 15. Density of community centers from AD 1140 to 1300 by subregion.

in southeastern Utah (see figure 12). Even within McElmo, where centers were most concentrated, there were areas such as the Montezuma Valley between Ute Mountain and the Mesa Verde landform where there was a line of regularly spaced centers (for example, Mud Springs, Yucca House, and Moqui Springs), a distribution suggestive of a political or social boundary (see chapter 5).

The intraregional distribution and density of centers highlight an important historical process. During the late 1100s and early 1200s, there were fewer centers regionwide than in the mid-1200s, and the distances between them were greater, which configured the social landscape and structured where and how subsequent villages could be built. Relationships with these established large villages would have required negotiation when the number of centers and people increased markedly in the mid to late 1200s, particularly in the McElmo subregion (see also Varien 1999).

Community Center Number, Size, and Density

Community centers dominated the social landscape of the McElmo subregion, where not only were there at least twice as many centers as anywhere else in the region but also centers were the largest (see tables 3

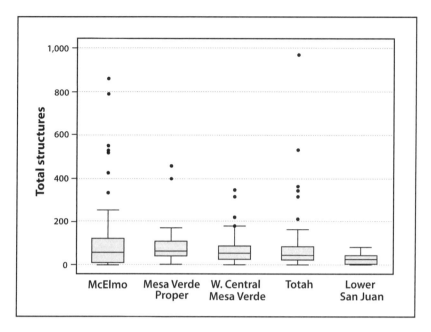

F<small>IGURE</small> 16. Boxplots showing size distributions of community centers in each subregion.

and 5). The number and size of centers in McElmo remained the highest in the region through the end of the occupation. On average, community centers in McElmo had 6 room blocks (range, 1–42; mode = 3) and 24 pit structures (range, 1–192; mode = 13). Substantial village growth began circa 1220. While the greatest number of centers occurred from 1220 to 1240, villages stayed at their largest size and highest density until the 1260s (see table 5). Most notably, as illustrated by the boxplots of the distribution of community center size in figure 16, there was important variation in community center size in all subregions but especially among McElmo centers. For example, Hedley Pueblo, Yellow Jacket Pueblo, Goodman Point–Shields, Yucca House, Sand Canyon Pueblo, Lancaster Pueblo, Easter Ruin, and Hampton Pueblo were significantly larger than the other McElmo centers and those in much of the rest of the region (see also Glowacki and Ortman 2012:244, fig. 14.3). If size reflects social, political, and ceremonial importance, then these centers played key roles in intraregional social and political relationships not only within McElmo but also across the region.

Mesa Verde Proper centers had an average of 4 room blocks (range, 1–42; mode = 1) and 10 pit structures (range, 1–57; mode = 6). With the exception of those of the Lower San Juan, centers were smaller

TABLE 6. The largest community centers in each subregion based on total number of structures

Totah	Mesa Verde Proper	McElmo	West Central Mesa Verde	Lower San Juan
Aztec	Upper Battleship Rock Pueblo	Hedley	Nancy Patterson	None
Morris 41	Morefield Canyon Great House Village	Yellow Jacket Pueblo	10-Acre Ruin	
Salmon	Long House	Goodman Point–Shields	Montezuma Village	
Holmes Group	Cliff Palace	Yucca House	Monument Village I and II	
Morris 39		Sand Canyon Pueblo		
Kello Blancett		Lancaster		
		Easter		
		Hampton		

Notes: These centers are the outliers identified in the boxplots shown in figure 16, and they are listed in order beginning with the largest center in each subregion. Centers listed in italics have been included because of their ranking based on either the total number of rooms or pit structures rather than the total number of structures.

on average than elsewhere in the region. Here, the greatest number and highest density of centers occurred from 1200 to 1240, and they attained their largest size from 1260 until the region was depopulated. Mesa Verde Proper centers began to grow in 1200. The largest centers in this subregion were Upper Battleship Rock Pueblo, Morefield Canyon Great House, Cliff Palace, and Long House, and they were important influences in the social, ritual, economic, and political interactions on Mesa Verde Proper and beyond (figure 16; table 6). Note that both Long House and Cliff Palace were not outliers for the subregion but were at the extreme end of the size range and given the strong settlement shift to alcove settings in the mid-1200s qualify as being among the largest and most influential on Mesa Verde Proper.

In West Central Mesa Verde, community centers had an average of 3 room blocks (range, 1–26; mode = 1) and 10 pit structures (range, 1–39; mode = 7). Centers were most numerous and occurred with the highest density from 1200 to 1240 (figure 16; table 6). Although centers in West

Central Mesa Verde started increasing in size at 1200, they were at their largest size from 1240 to 1260. Based on size, the most influential large villages in this subregion were Nancy Patterson Village, 10-Acre Ruin, Montezuma Village I and II, and Monument Village.

On average, community centers in the Totah had 4 room blocks (range, 1–29; mode = 1) and 7 pit structures (range, 1–40; mode = 2). The number, density, and average size of centers remained relatively consistent throughout the late 1100s and 1200s. However, this stability is likely, at least in part, a reflection of the dating resolution currently available for these sites. That said, the number and density of Totah centers was highest from 1160 to 1240, and centers were at their largest from 1240 to 1280. The largest and likely most influential of the Totah community centers were Aztec, Morris 41, Salmon, Holmes Group, Morris 39, and Kello Blancett. The number of centers in the Totah reached its peak earlier than elsewhere in the region, which is not surprising, since many of these centers had long histories that became entwined with the establishment of Aztec West in the early 1100s (Brown et al. 2008; McKenna and Toll 1992; Stein and McKenna 1988).

Not only were there fewer community centers in the Lower San Juan than elsewhere in the region, but also they were much smaller. On average, centers had 1 room block (range, 1–3; mode = 1) and 5 pit structures (range, 2–10; mode = 2). The size and low number of centers in the Lower San Juan indicate that they did not operate on the same scale as community centers in the rest of the region. Although the largest villages in the Lower San Juan, such as the Coombs site and Moon House (see figure 11), affected local politics and economics, they were probably not influential beyond the subregion.

These data highlight several important factors necessary for understanding intraregional relationships during the late 1100s and 1200s. First, the differences in when thirteenth-century community centers were the most numerous and largest relate to the histories of each subregion and in turn led to differences in the social and political dynamics among centers. In the Totah, the number of centers peaked early and remained at that level from the late 1100s onward, a circumstance that was likely influenced by the expansion of Aztec in the early 1100s. Elsewhere in the region, the number of large villages increased at different times. On Mesa Verde Proper and in West Central Mesa Verde, the number of centers substantially increased beginning in 1200 and peaked during the 1220–1240 interval. It was not until 1220, however, that centers significantly increased in McElmo, where they ultimately came to dominate the settlement pattern.

Second, in all subregions but the Lower San Juan, there were some community centers that were clearly much larger than the others. This

marked difference in size even among the centers suggests that some villages were more prominent in each subregion than were others. There
were twenty-two centers in the Northern San Juan significantly larger
than the rest of the centers, which suggests that there may have been
some degree of ranked sociopolitical organization that went beyond the
McElmo subregion (Arakawa 2012a; Glowacki and Ortman 2012; Kohler
and Varien 2010; Lipe 2002). This is not to say that other centers were
not religiously and politically influential in regional dynamics, however,
since the presence of specialized architecture, the performance of powerful ceremonies, or the governance of skilled leaders could also make
them important. The sociopolitical relationships among these regionally prominent centers were likely a critical factor in the circumstances
prompting widespread emigration from the region.

Community Center Room-to-Kiva Ratios
(Scale of Social Integration)

Room-to-kiva ratios have long been used to examine the scale of social
integration in the Pueblo Southwest (Lipe 1989; Steward 1937). The
proportion of rooms relative to each kiva can be used to compare the
relative size of basic social groups, assuming that each pit structure had a
similar relationship to the size of the group that was using it (Lipe 1989).
Using this ratio as a comparative measure, however, is complicated by
the fact that not all pit structures were used in the same way, nor did
they have a single intended purpose, since many of them contained evidence of both ceremonial and domestic activities (Ferguson 1989:171;
Lekson 1989, 2008; Lipe 1989). There was also intrasite variation in
room-to-kiva ratios among the room blocks within each village and in
whether or not rooms were closely associated with particular kivas (Bradley 1992, 1993; Lipe 1989; Lipe and Ortman 2000:113–15). Finally, kiva
counts are probably underrepresented in general because they are difficult to identify confidently from surface indicators, since depressions
are obscured by postoccupational deposition processes, especially when
located in floodplains and on talus slopes. Despite these issues, room-to-
kiva ratios likely reflect a modal group size, if not necessarily the specific
size, which can be informative when making broad-scale comparisons
across a region.

The ratios in table 7 were based on the number of habitation sites per
subregion with both room and kiva counts (N = 606 total sites). Great
kivas were obviously used by different and larger groups than small kivas
and were excluded from the kiva counts. The salient pattern in room-to-
kiva ratios among the subregions is that Central Mesa Verde was different from the rest of the Northern San Juan. The ratios of the Central

TABLE 7. Average room-to-kiva ratio of Pueblo III sites in each subregion

Subregion	Number of sites with room and kiva counts	Total number of rooms	Total number of kivas	Average room:kiva ratio	Standard deviation
Totah	120	5,532	397	12.2:1	9.1
Mesa Verde Proper	165	4,121	501	8.6:1	6.2
McElmo	239	9,812	2,011	7.9:1	5.5
West Central Mesa Verde	57	3,170	426	8.6:1	4.2
Lower San Juan	24	291	45	6.5:1	4.7

Mesa Verde subregions showed little difference in the size of the groups potentially associated with each kiva. The highest average room-to-kiva ratio was in the Totah, suggesting that somewhat larger groups of people were using kivas there than elsewhere in the region (provided that kivas were not excessively underrepresented in the archaeological record), whereas the social groups using kivas in the Lower San Juan were smaller than elsewhere in the region. If we take for the moment that the differences in the average room-to-kiva ratios among Central Mesa Verde, the Totah, and the Lower San Juan related to variation in social organization among subregions rather than differences in population levels or vagaries of data recording, then perhaps the ratios highlight cultural differences among these areas. For example, the higher ratio of the Totah is unsurprisingly closer to Chacoan outlier room-to-kiva ratios (i.e., 15.2:1 [Lipe 1989:table 1]), suggesting that the scale of integration in Totah community centers may have been similar throughout much of the thirteenth century. The relatively low average room-to-kiva ratio of the Lower San Juan, however, more closely corresponds with a highly household-based, flexible organization such as found among the Lower San Juan's western neighbors in the Kayenta region (Dean 1996, 2010:342–43).

Civic-Ceremonial Architecture

Architecture that benefited the entire village and was used for either ceremonial or civic purposes informs on village organization because community interactions shaped and were shaped by their buildings. For example, some spaces were more public and were created to promote communal and inclusive group activities, while other spaces were restrictive and intrinsically fostered exclusive and private gatherings. The dichotomy between inclusive and exclusive is particularly germane to Pueblo culture, which has both descent groups and nondescent sodalities in varying configurations depending on the Pueblo community (Adams 1991; Ellis 1964; Ortiz 1969; Plog and Solometo 1997; Ware 2014; Ware and Blinman 2000). The evolution of inclusive and exclusive architecture in ancestral Pueblo villages is central to understanding Pueblo ritual organization across the Northern San Juan and the extent to which it varied among large villages.

To compare civic-ceremonial architecture across the Northern San Juan, I use three categories to delineate the primary use of each structure: group assembly, restricted use, and controlled access (see also Glowacki and Ortman 2012). *Group-assembly* architecture includes buildings that could host large groups of people for both ceremonial and secular activities (i.e., great kivas and plazas). Buildings categorized as *restricted use*, such as great houses and multiwalled structures, were used by smaller groups of people for specific ceremonies and other purposes. *Controlled-access* architecture, such as enclosing walls and towers, directed and defined access within and around the village. I assume that a similar distribution of civic-ceremonial architecture among the subregions indicates participation in similar or related social, ritual, and political activities. However, a shared distribution does not mean that the subregions also constituted a socially or politically integrated entity.

Data pinpointing the construction dates and history of use for most of the civic-ceremonial architecture in each of the community centers across the region are limited. Consequently, the frequency of each type of civic-ceremonial architecture presented in table 8 is the number of community centers with a PIII period component that have a particular architectural type in each subregion. In the case of multicomponent sites, however, the civic-ceremonial architecture itself may not have been built during the PIII period—a situation most germane to great kivas. In those rare instances in which a great kiva may have been present but was clearly no longer in use by AD 1150, it was excluded from the database.

Group-Assembly Architecture

Architecture designated as group assembly created central gathering places for people within the village. The primary forms of group-assembly (or communal) architecture used in the Northern San Juan from AD 1150 to 1300 were great kivas and plazas. The ritual and social activities taking place within these structures not only promoted social integration

TABLE 8. Number of community centers with civic-ceremonial architecture by subregion

	Totah		Mesa Verde Proper		McElmo		West Central Mesa Verde		Lower San Juan	
	N = 59		N = 36		N = 105		N = 46		N = 7	
	N	%	N	%	N	%	N	%	N	%
Centers with civic-ceremonial architecture	46	78	26	72	92	88	30	65	5	71
Great kivas	30	51	7	19	33	31	17	37	1	14
Plazas	12	20	12	33	32	30	13	28	4	57
Great houses	21	36	3	8	19	18	15	32	1	14
Multiwalled structures Total	4[a]	7	5	14	18	17	0	0	0	0
Biwall	4	7	3	8	7	7				
Triwall	1	2	0	0	1	1				
D-shaped	0	0	2	6	10	10				
Towers	5	8	11	31	63	60	13	28	0	0
Enclosing walls	1	2	2	6	40	38	9	19	2	29
Group assembly	39	66	17	47	54	51	26	57	5	71
Restricted use	22	37	8	22	31	30	15	33	1	14
Controlled access	6	10	13	36	66	633	14	30	2	29

Note: These frequencies are the total number of sites and not the total number of a particular architectural form.

[a]Aztec has both triwall and biwall structures and has been included in each of these categories; however, there are only four total centers in the Totah with multiwalled structures.

and cooperation among community members but also provided a political arena where inequalities and social standing were expressed and disagreements were mitigated through competition, sanctions, and negotiation (Adams 1991; Adams and LaMotta 2006; Adler 1990; Chamberlin 2011; Herr 2001; Potter 2000; Potter and Perry 2000; Schachner 2001; Van Dyke 2002; Van Keuren 2011; Vivian and Reiter 1965).

Great kivas are large, semisubterranean circular structures ten to thirty meters in diameter that contain features such as fire pits and floor vaults (Herr 2001). With the exception of the unroofed great kivas in the Cibola region (Kintigh et al. 1996; McGimsey 1980; Schachner 2012), great kivas were usually roofed. Thus, although great kivas were large enough to accommodate many people, potentially the entire village, the rituals, activities, and interactions that occurred in them were private. People who were not inside the great kiva while it was in use were excluded, even if those gatherings benefited the entire village or greater community.

In the Northern San Juan, great kivas have a long history of use that began as early as the late 600s and early 700s (Glowacki and Ortman 2012; Lipe 2006:267; Wilshusen, Ortman, et al. 2012). Although great kivas were a central organizing feature of many large ancestral Pueblo villages throughout the regional occupation, great kivas were most common from the mid-1000s to the mid-1100s (Glowacki and Ortman 2012; Lipe and Ortman 2000). Although the standard form of great kivas remained consistent, there was some experimentation with form in the late 1200s when a few great kivas (e.g., at Sand Canyon and Goodman Point Pueblos) were modified (see Churchill et al. 1998; Lipe 1989; Lipe and Ortman 2000:112). In these cases, the original roof was removed, but the great kiva continued to be used, which suggests that ideas about public versus private community gatherings were changing (Glowacki 2011).

By the PIII period, great kivas were present at many community centers, particularly the long-lived, multicomponent centers established prior to the mid-1100s (see table 8; figure 17). Of the five subregions, the Totah had the highest frequency of centers with great kivas (51 percent), which was notably greater than the frequency in the rest of the subregions (14–37 percent). The high proportion of great kivas in the Totah was likely associated with the direct relationships between Aztec and Chaco (Lekson 1999a, 2008; Van Dyke 2007a) and the occupation history of the Totah. The Totah experienced population growth during the early to mid-1100s (see table 4 and figure 14; see also Brown et al. 2013), the timing of which corresponds with when the number of great kivas and great houses increased in other parts of the region (Glowacki and Ortman 2012) and when Chacoan influence in the region was at its height. After this period of growth, population levels in the Totah remained more or less stable during the 1200s, and coincidentally the architectural forms associated with the thirteenth century, such as plazas, multiwalled structures, towers, and enclosing walls, were less common in the Totah (see table 8; also see below). Similar historical influences may also have affected the social landscape of West Central Mesa Verde, where population also markedly increased in the mid-1100s. Here, the frequency of great kivas (37 percent) was higher than in Mesa Verde Proper and McElmo, where marked population increases occurred later and different architectural

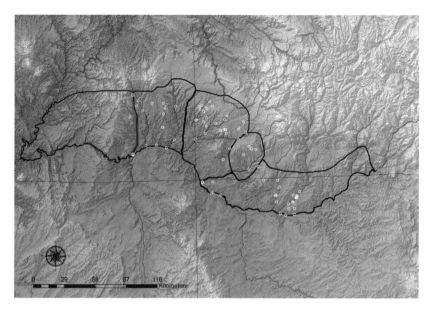

FIGURE 17. Distribution of great kivas at Pueblo III community centers. Illustration by Grant D. Coffey.

forms were constructed at new villages (AD 1200–1220 and AD 1220–1240, respectively).

Activities taking place in plazas were intrinsically more inclusive and visible than those in great kivas and were thus public. In the late thirteenth and fourteenth centuries, plazas—open areas defined by rooms, enclosing walls, or natural features—became increasingly central and formalized spaces in villages across the Pueblo world (Adams 1991; Bernardini 1998; Chamberlin 2011). In the Northern San Juan, plazas became more common at late thirteenth-century community centers and exhibited more variation in their size, shape, demarcation, and location than those in the fourteenth century (Glowacki and Ortman 2012:table 14.2; Lipe and Ortman 2000:111–12). However, two late thirteenth-century plazas, Long House and Fire Temple (Cassidy 1965; Cattanach 1980), are highly formal and evocative of fourteenth-century plazas (figure 18). Thus, the social and ceremonial processes underlying the increasing formalization and centralization of fourteenth-century and later plazas seem to have already begun in the Northern San Juan.

Plazas were present in at least some community centers in all of the subregions at relatively similar frequencies (about 30 percent; see table 8 and figure 19). Technically, the Lower San Juan had the highest frequency of plazas; however, two of the four centers (42SA681 and Fortified Mesa

FIGURE 18. The plaza at Fire Temple, Mesa Verde National Park. Courtesy of Mesa Verde National Park. Photograph taken by Robert D. Jensen.

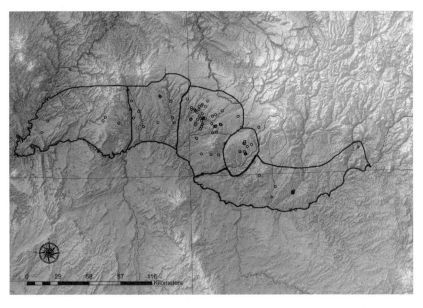

FIGURE 19. Distribution of plazas at Pueblo III community centers. Illustration by Grant D. Coffey.

42SA316) had very few rooms and their associated space was described as a defensive enclosure and/or a ceremonial plaza (e.g., Fast 2012). Therefore, only the plazas at the Et Al site (42SA18431) and Moon House (42SA5005) were comparable to the plazas documented elsewhere in the region.

There was minor variation in the distribution of plazas in that their frequency at Totah centers was slightly lower than that in the other subregions. While it is tempting to suggest that this slight variation was related to historical influences and the primacy of great kivas during the Chaco period described above, the difference is only 10 percent. The temptation to make an association with historical influences increases, however, when one considers that nineteen sites in McElmo were excluded from the analysis because the only criterion for being a community center was the presence of a possible plaza. If these cases were included, the frequency of plazas in the McElmo subregion would increase to 40 percent. Conservatively, the most that can be said is that the distribution of plazas among the subregions hints at temporal variation in the preference for plazas over great kivas at later community centers. This inference is bolstered by trends in McElmo and Mesa Verde Proper, where dating is refined and change during the PIII period can be detected. In these subregions, plazas were more common at post-1220 community centers. For example, in the VEP I study area nearly half of the new centers established after AD 1225 had plazas, but only 20 percent had great kivas (*n* = 27 [Glowacki and Ortman 2012:table 14.2]).

The regional distribution of community centers with group-assembly architecture reveals three important trends. First, if a community center had group-assembly architecture, typically it was either a great kiva or a plaza; only a small subset of the PIII community centers with group-assembly features had both. Moreover, community centers with both great kivas and plazas were found in only three of the five subregions (the Totah had one [3 percent]; McElmo had nine [17 percent]; and West Central Mesa Verde had four [15 percent]). There was no obvious characteristic of the community centers that had both great kivas and plazas, for they occurred at not only multicomponent centers but also late PIII centers. The relatively discrete patterning in the distribution of plazas and great kivas suggests that there were divergent ideas about group assembly among different Pueblo groups across the Northern San Juan. It is unclear whether these differences were due to historical changes in the types of group-assembly architecture used in large villages or to differing cultural traditions among Pueblo groups, or both.

Second, historical changes during the thirteenth century affected the distribution of group-assembly architecture. As noted, great kivas were more commonly associated with centers that had strong connections to Chaco-era dynamics, whereas plazas were more common at post-1220 community centers. The shift to increasingly central and formal plazas for group assembly in the mid-1200s implies that communal rituals, feasts, and other gatherings became increasingly inclusive and visible, and this was part of a broader ritual transformation across the Colorado Plateau (Adams 1991; Bernardini 1998).

Third, data from the VEP I study area in the McElmo subregion showed that during the 1200s group-assembly architecture was more common at the larger centers (Glowacki and Ortman 2012). The regional data show a similar trend but not for all the subregions. Group-assembly architecture tended to be found at the larger community centers in the Eastern Mesa Verde subregions (i.e., McElmo, Mesa Verde Proper, and the Totah) but not in Western Mesa Verde. McElmo centers with group-assembly architecture averaged 173 rooms and 31 kivas, and those without had an average of 88 rooms and 17 kivas. On Mesa Verde Proper the average was 113 rooms and 15 kivas versus 63 rooms and 6 kivas, and in the Totah the average was 125 rooms and 8 kivas versus 53 rooms and 4 kivas. However, in West Central Mesa Verde, community centers with group-assembly architecture averaged 68 rooms and 8 kivas, while those without had an average of 83 rooms and 12 kivas. Group-assembly features were also associated with smaller centers in the Lower San Juan, where centers with group-assembly features had an average of 19 rooms and 2 kivas versus 46 rooms and 7.5 kivas. These differences in the average size of centers with group-assembly architecture point to important variation in social and political organization between Eastern and Western Mesa Verde.

Elsewhere (Glowacki and Ortman 2012:229–30), Ortman and I have suggested that correspondence between group assembly and center size indicated that people at smaller centers either did not require this type of space or may have traveled to larger centers for important dances and ceremonies. If the latter was the case, then it is possible that the smaller centers were part of multiple-center confederacies that were ceremonially and politically interdependent (Lipe 2002). In Western Mesa Verde, however, the prevalence of group-assembly architecture at smaller centers suggests that sociopolitical organization there differed from that of the east, even if the specific differences are unclear. One possibility is that western centers with group-assembly architecture may have integrated small nearby settlements but the centers themselves were more autonomous. Another is that the cultural differences among the villages in Western Mesa Verde were greater than in the east.

Restricted-Use Architecture

Buildings deemed restricted use, such as great houses and multiwalled structures, were integral to village organization, since the interactions within them had implications for everyone in the community. Restricted-use architecture was oriented toward small-scale interactions among people who were members of a specific group (e.g., household, lineage, or nonkin ritual group, depending on how the pueblo was organized). These buildings were inherently exclusionary and associated with differential access to power and specialized knowledge. They embodied foundational attributes of Pueblo ritual organization and were important loci of religious power and authority.

Great houses attained prominence during the late eleventh and twelfth centuries with the rise of Chaco Canyon and the attendant intensification of religious, economic, and sociopolitical networks across the Colorado Plateau. These highly visible buildings had shared characteristics, such as multiple stories, large rooms, enclosed kivas, and stylized construction methods that made them iconic and immediately connected them to Chaco Canyon (Lekson et al. 2006; Powers et al. 1983; Stein and Lekson 1992; Van Dyke 2007b). In the Northern San Juan, great houses were understandably most common during the Chaco period (AD 1060–1140), but they continued to be used throughout the 1200s (Cameron 2009; Ryan 2008, 2010). What is less clear is the extent to which great houses during the post-Chaco period were continuously occupied or had an occupational hiatus followed by reoccupation (Cameron 2005, 2009; Lekson and Cameron 1995; Lipe 2006:303; Lipe and Varien 1999b).

The regional PIII data show that great houses were more common in the Totah and West Central Mesa Verde than in McElmo, Mesa Verde Proper, and the Lower San Juan (see table 8; figure 20). This pattern is similar to the intraregional distribution of great kivas, which were often paired with great houses. It is therefore not surprising that differences in great house frequencies are also associated with the areas that experienced population growth in the mid-1100s. A greater proportion of community centers in McElmo were constructed during the 1200s, and possibly only one new great house was constructed at centers established after AD 1140 (Glowacki and Ortman 2012). Consequently, the frequency of McElmo great houses was lower than that of the Totah and West Central Mesa Verde (see table 8). The frequency of great houses on Mesa Verde Proper was the lowest in the region (see table 8), which is expected since this subregion has long been known for its relative lack of great houses. Formerly, only Far View had been identified as a great house (Cameron 2009; Kantner 2003a; Lekson 1999a); however, there are more great houses in Mesa Verde Proper than has been previously published. Recent fieldwork at MVNP revealed that the propensity to assign site numbers to individual room blocks during the 1950s obscured the presence of a number of large villages and the distinctive buildings associated with them (Glowacki 2012). In addition to

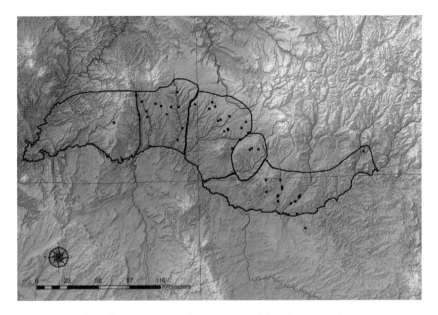

FIGURE 20. Distribution of great houses at Pueblo III community centers.
Illustration by Grant D. Coffey.

Far View, the Upper Battleship Rock Pueblo and the Morefield Canyon
Great House Village—excavated by Colorado University field schools
from 1965 to 1969 under the direction of David Breternitz and Robert Lister (Glowacki 2012; Kleidon et al. 2003)—also have great houses
(Glowacki 2012). The Lower San Juan contained only one great house
with a PIII occupation, the Et Al site, which is the westernmost great
house in the region (Fast 2012; Lipe et al. 2011).

Multiwalled structures were distinctive buildings composed of inter-
connected rooms, most commonly arranged in circular or D-shaped configurations that surrounded one or more central kivas (Fewkes 1916;
Reed 1958; Vivian 1959). Not only did the shape of multiwalled structures vary but also, in the case of circular multiwalled structures, so
did the number of the rows of rooms that surrounded the kiva or kivas:
thus, a biwalled structure had one row of rooms and a triwalled structure had two rows of rooms. Excavation data from these specialized
buildings are limited, but what have been recovered include materials
associated with both domestic and ritual activities (Kuckelman et al.
2009; Lipe and Ortman 2000:110–11; Vivian 1959:85–86). For example, testing in the D-shaped structures at Sand Canyon Pueblo, Hedley
Main Ruin, and Goodman Point Pueblo revealed mealing bins, extended
floor vaults, cooking pots, bone tools, lithics, ground stone, and faunal

bones (Kuckelman et al. 2009; Lipe and Ortman 2000). However, at Sun Temple, the D-shaped structure on Mesa Verde Proper, few features or artifacts were recovered because according to Fewkes (1916) this ceremonial structure was never completed. In another case, animal remains frequently associated with Pueblo ceremonies, such as raptor bones (falcons, eagles, and hawks), were recovered from the Great Tower, a biwall structure at Yellow Jacket Pueblo (Lipe and Ortman 2000:110–11; Muir and Driver 2002).

Although there was a triwall structure at Pueblo del Arroyo in Chaco Canyon (Judd 1959; Vivian 1959; Windes 2010) and biwall structures have been found at Red Willow (Tohatchi Well) near Gallup, New Mexico (Lekson 1983, 2008:308n72; Peckham 1963), in Manuelito Canyon, New Mexico (Lekson 1983:20–21; Weaver 1978:176), and at Kinlichee (NA8022) near Ganado, Arizona (Lekson 1983, 2008:308n72; Osborn 1971:60, fig. 36), multiwalled structures were a decidedly Northern San Juan phenomenon (Glowacki 2010; Reed 1958; Vivian 1959). To date, we know of at least thirty-one multiwalled structures at twenty-seven centers in the Northern San Juan: fifteen circular biwalls, four circular triwalls (three of which were at Aztec), and twelve D-shaped structures. The intraregional distribution of multiwalled structures is also distinctive (figure 21). The westernmost multiwalled structure is the Bitsiel Biwall near Aneth, Utah, which is at the western edge of the McElmo subregion. Since no multiwalled structures are known west of this location, they are a defining characteristic of Eastern Mesa Verde, specifically (figure 21; Lekson 1999a:103; Reed 1958:54; Vivian 1959). Among the eastern subregions, multiwalled structures were most common in the Mesa Verde core (i.e., McElmo and Mesa Verde Proper; see table 8). Multiwalled structures occurred in the Mesa Verde Proper subregion at a frequency similar to that in McElmo (see table 8), but only two of the five centers with multiwalled structures (Sun Temple [5MV352] and Kleidon's Biwall [5MV325]) were on Mesa Verde itself—the rest were to the south and west of the Mesa Verde uplift along the Mancos River (i.e., Kiva Point [5MT2771], Reed 16 [5MT2769], and Morris 33 [5MT2831]).

While only four community centers (Flora Vista [LA2514], San Juan Biwall [LA69891], Holmes Group [LA1898], and Aztec East and West [LA45]) in the Totah had multiwalled structures, Aztec had more multiwalled structures than any other community center in Eastern Mesa Verde. In fact, only two community centers in the Northern San Juan, Aztec and the Goodman Point–Shields complex, had more than one multiwalled structure. The Goodman Point–Shields complex had three multiwalled structures, one D-shaped structure, and two biwall variants (Kuckelman et al. 2009). Aztec, however, had five circular, multiwalled structures, including three triwalled and two biwalled structures (Reed

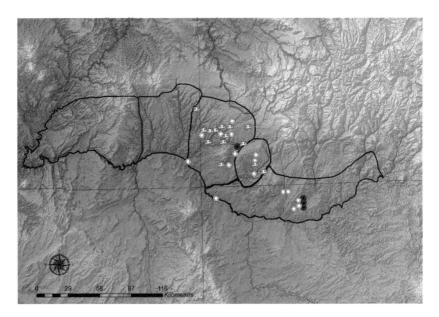

FIGURE 21. Distribution of multiwalled structures at Pueblo III community centers. The circles with black centers are triwall structures, the black circles are biwall structures, and the D-shaped structures are fittingly D-shaped. Illustration by Grant D. Coffey.

et al. 2010; Stein and McKenna 1988; Vivian 1959). Since there are three triwalled structures at Aztec and the only other triwall in the Northern San Juan region is at Mud Springs in McElmo (Holmes 1878), the triwall form is decidedly linked to Aztec and its ritual and sociopolitical organization (Lekson 1983, 2008:308–9n72; Stein and McKenna 1988).

The best-known multiwall structure at Aztec is the Hubbard Triwall, which is just north of the Aztec West great house (Lekson 1983; Vivian 1959). There are, however, four additional multiwalled structures: two biwall structures (Mounds B and C) and two triwall structures (Mounds A and F) (Brown et al. 2008; Reed et al. 2010; Richert 1964; Vivian 1959). The Aztec East portion of the complex, including these four structures, was recently remapped by Reed and his colleagues (2010), and the surface artifacts associated with each architectural feature were analyzed. The Mound A triwall and the Mound B biwall are associated with the Earl Morris ruin, a small great house northeast of Aztec East that was likely built in the mid to late 1100s (Brown et al. 2013; Stein and McKenna 1988). The Mound C biwall is located near the west room block of the Aztec East great house, and the Mound F triwall is situated between the Aztec East and West great houses. In 1953, T. B. Onstott excavated small portions of Mound F (Onstott's Ruin No. 4) and confirmed that it is a triwall structure with two concentric rows of rooms (Vivian 1959:71–73).

Knowing when multiwalled structures were built is integral to understanding their significance across Eastern Mesa Verde. Multiwalled structures, the triwalled form in particular, are considered a defining element signaling participation in a regional religious and political network of which Aztec was the center (Lekson 1999a:103, 2008:308n72; Stein and McKenna 1988). Lekson (1999a, 2008:308n72) connects the symbolic power of triwalled structures, and by extension all multiwalled structures, to Chaco Canyon and supports his case by examining the timing of their construction (Lekson 1983). Drawing on work by Vivian (1959) and Roberts (1927), Lekson proposes that the triwall at Pueblo del Arroyo in Chaco Canyon was the earliest multiwalled structure in the northern Southwest, possibly dating to the early 1100s (Lekson 1983, 2008:308n72). However, the 1109 date used by Lekson (1983:20) to associate the triwall structure at Pueblo del Arroyo with an early 1100s construction most likely came from rooms that were added along the south wall of Pueblo del Arroyo during that time and not from the triwall structure itself (Windes 2010). The triwall is a later addition, as it abuts this early 1100s construction and was also built into postconstruction soil deposited along the back wall of the main building (Vivian 1990:386–87; Windes 2010). The triwall was built using a different masonry style from that of the main building, one associated with the McElmo style, and there was a preponderance of Chaco-McElmo pottery recovered from the excavations. The construction sequence and associated pottery suggest that the triwall was built sometime after 1109, perhaps as late as the mid to late 1100s or early 1200s (Vivian 1959:68–70; Vivian 1990:383–87). Regardless of specifically when the triwall was built and used, the addition of the Pueblo del Arroyo triwall came near the end of the occupation of this great house when the McElmo–Mesa Verde influence was strong in Chaco Canyon and Chaco was in decline (Lekson 1983, 2008; Vivian 1959; Vivian 1990; Windes 2010).

Lekson (1983:16–19, fig. 2) also reanalyzed the pottery and stratigraphy that was documented during Vivian's excavations of the Hubbard Triwall in 1959. Lekson's (1983:21) assessment led him to conclude that the most likely construction date for the Hubbard Triwall was after 1130 and "at the earlier part of this [AD 1125–1175] span" instead of the thirteenth-century Classic Mesa Verde date suggested by Vivian (1959:53). Lekson interpreted the Hubbard and Pueblo del Arroyo data as indicating that triwall structures were probably an innovation initiated in Chaco Canyon to perhaps revitalize a failing Chacoan ceremonial system, which was then promulgated in the Northern San Juan.

Although a high proportion of the Mesa Verde sherds recovered during excavation were associated with postconstruction deposits (Lekson
1983), the Hubbard Triwall was built on the remains of what Vivian
(1959:7, 52, fig. 6) termed the Middle Level occupation, which was
dated to the "McElmo phase" based on the associated pottery (i.e., mid
to late 1100s; Lekson 2006:fig. 1.3). Therefore, the construction of the
Hubbard Triwall necessarily postdates this period (Vivian 1959:52–53;
Vivian 1990:387).

The surface remains for the other multiwalled structures at Aztec
also imply a late 1100s or early 1200s date, since all but the Hubbard Triwall were associated with the eastern portion of the complex.
Although there was some twelfth-century construction at the Aztec East
great house, the majority of the tree-ring dates, and thus the timing of
peak construction and occupation, were from the early and mid-1200s
(Brown et al. 2008; Richert 1964). It therefore stands to reason that
the buildings associated with the Aztec East great house were more
likely contemporaneous with its peak period of construction and occupation than not. Of the four recently remapped multiwalled structures
(Reed et al. 2010), only two, the Mound C biwall and the Mound F
triwall situated between Aztec East and West, had diagnostic pottery
associated with them. In both of these cases, although only few sherds
were present on the surface, the diagnostic pottery was Mesa Verde
Black-on-white indicative of a 1200s occupation. Additionally, in a letter written by Earl Morris to Erik K. Reed on November 12, 1946,
Morris penned, "And I once sunk a pit in a chamber on the east side
of the other mound referred to [Mound F]. There were Mesa Verde
sherds on the floor and a burial from that period beneath it. It would
seem to me that both structures [the Hubbard Triwall and Mound F]
were erected by the Mesa Verde reoccupants of that locality" (quoted in
Vivian 1959:72). Thus, these data suggest that, as with the Mesa Verde
core, most of the multiwalled structures at Aztec were probably associated with the 1200s occupation. This timing makes sense in light of
the tree-ring record for the Aztec complex inasmuch as it followed the
severe drought period from AD 1130 to 1180 when major construction
had ceased at Aztec West and focus had shifted to the Aztec East great
house (Brown et al. 2008; Lipe 2006).

No matter whether the Pueblo del Arroyo and Hubbard Triwall structures were built in the early 1100s or later, this timing would not discount
the idea that at least triwall structures, and probably biwall structures,
emerged as a consequence of Chaco's decline and Aztec's attempt to rees-
tablish its influence and power during a difficult time. After all, there
were five circular, multiwalled structures at Aztec, which clearly indicate
that the circular forms were central to Aztec's sociopolitical and religious

organization and likely originated there. The adoption of multiwalled forms at centers across Eastern Mesa Verde does not necessarily mean that all these buildings signified alignment with an Aztec regional system, however. Multiwalled structures, specifically the biwall and D-shaped forms, proliferated at community centers established after AD 1140 in the Mesa Verde core (Churchill et al. 1998; Glowacki and Ortman 2012:table 14.2; Lipe and Ortman 2000:110–11; Varien et al. 1996:99). The increased frequency of these two forms coincided with the marked population increase during the early 1200s that was especially prominent in the McElmo subregion. Thus, although the circular form may have originated with Aztec, the further elaboration of multiwalled forms was connected to the attendant changes in sociopolitical and religious organization that developed as population and the number of community centers increased in the Mesa Verde core.

The spatial distribution of the different forms of multiwalled structures across Eastern Mesa Verde suggests that they had different cultural and symbolic meanings. Circular multiwalled structures, particularly the biwall form, were built at certain community centers across Eastern Mesa Verde, but the D-shaped structures are found only in the Mesa Verde core (see figure 21 and table 8). To echo Lekson (2008:309n72), this strong pattern means something, but what?

Circular biwalls were related to triwalls and were probably more strongly connected to traditional Chacoan ideology and ritual practice than were the D-shaped structures (Glowacki 2011). In the VEP I study area (McElmo), for example, all but one of the five circular multiwalled structures are at community centers that also have a great house (Glowacki and Ortman 2012). The D-shaped structures are different. They are not found in Chaco or the Totah (Glowacki 2010; Lipe 2006) and were built at community centers established after AD 1140 that had new organizational plans, which did not include great houses (Glowacki and Ortman 2012:table 14.2). For example, nine of the ten centers with D-shaped structures in the VEP I study area lacked great houses. Thus, D-shaped structures seem to have developed as a divergent but related form of restricted-use architecture through the modification of existing practices or the development of completely new ones. The intensification and innovation associated with these structures is perhaps most striking at Goodman Point Pueblo, where there was not only a D-shaped structure but also two biwall variants that elaborated on the conventional forms (figure 22; Kuckelman et al. 2009).

The distinctive distribution of circular multiwalled structures versus D-shaped structures in Eastern Mesa Verde and the absence of multiwalled structures in Western Mesa Verde means that groups across the region differed in their ideas about the role of restricted-use architecture

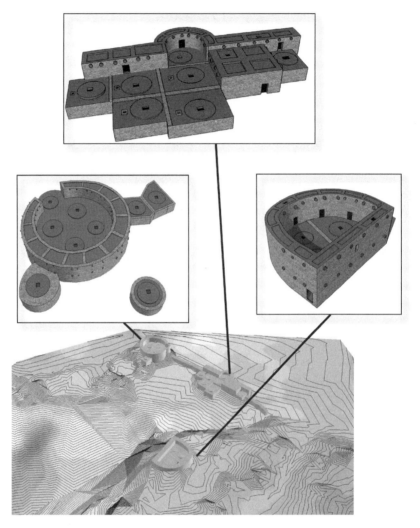

FIGURE 22. The multiwall variants found at Goodman Point Pueblo. Courtesy of Crow Canyon Archaeological Center. Illustration by Grant D. Coffey.

in village and religious organization. The association of circular multi-walled structures with Aztec and great houses, in general, implies some continuity with Chacoan traditions, even if an innovation, and those villages with circular multiwalled structures likely maintained connections with Aztec and the developing Aztec-Chaco ideology (Lekson 1999a, 2008). As such, the distribution of these structures and their variations provides insights into the degree of ideological connectivity with Aztec and how sociopolitical and religious organization changed in the aftermath of the severity of the 1100s.

Not all of the community centers had restricted-use civic-ceremonial architecture (see table 8). In fact, only 22 to 37 percent (that is, one in three or four) of the community centers in each subregion had a great house and/or a multiwalled structure. This too is a striking pattern—one that is not often acknowledged—that means something. Among the possibilities are the following: (1) the religious organization of some community centers did not require a great house or multiwalled structure; (2) if one was required, then it necessitated an alliance with another community center that had a great house or multiwalled structure; and (3) the social landscape involved more cultural diversity than has been previously realized. Restricted-use architecture was clearly important, however, because, of the twenty-two largest community centers in the Northern San Juan (see above), all but three had a great house or multiwalled structure.

Great houses were present in all the subregions; however, multiwalled structures were not. The widespread distribution of great houses indicates that Chacoan influence was pervasive. However, significant changes in the late 1100s and early 1200s reconfigured participation in the traditional Chaco religious system—embodied by great houses—when circular and D-shaped multiwalled structures began to supersede great houses. This change was most dramatic in Western Mesa Verde, where despite the presence of great houses there were no multiwalled structures, indicating that people living in the west did not participate in the religious (revitalization) movements that had developed in Eastern Mesa Verde.

Controlled-Access Architecture

Architecture that regulated access to particular areas within and around Northern San Juan villages included towers and enclosing walls. Towers are typically multistoried, often single-roomed, buildings constructed in a variety of shapes (e.g., circular, square, and D-shaped) and in a variety of settings (e.g., isolated, freestanding within villages, attached to room blocks, and situated on boulders or canyon rims [see Bredthauer 2010; Fewkes 1923; Johnson 2003; Lipe and Ortman 2000; Winter 1977, 1981]). They are often associated with kivas, sometimes referred to as tower-kiva complexes, and some, such as Cedar Tree Tower on Mesa Verde Proper, had features typically found in kivas, such as *sipapus* (Fewkes 1921; Hayes 1964; Rohn 1971, 1977).

The possible functions of towers include defense and protection (Fewkes 1923; Haas and Creamer 1993; Kuckelman 2002), communication (Morley and Kidder 1917), resource monitoring (Bredthauer 2010;

Johnson 2003), storage (Fewkes 1923; Winter 1981), and ceremonial or symbolic purposes (Fewkes 1923; Lipe and Ortman 2000; Van Dyke and King 2010). Probably not all towers were used the same way, and activities taking place in them were likely not mutually exclusive, since a wide variety of artifacts have been found in them (Winter 1977). Unlike the other civic-ceremonial architecture discussed, towers are common at both large and small sites, with the majority being situated in isolated locations or at small pueblos (77 percent, $n = 300$ [of 392 sites with towers]). Although towers have a long history of use in the Northern San Juan region (e.g., Potter and Chuipka 2007), these structures became increasingly common during the late 1100s and 1200s (Glowacki and Ortman 2012; Lipe and Ortman 2000). Towers were present in all of the subregions, but they were most common in Central Mesa Verde, and the McElmo subregion in particular (figure 23; see table 8).

Towers are also strongly correlated with enclosing walls (Glowacki and Ortman 2012; Kenzle 1997; Kuckelman 2000, 2002), which are low walls that delimited boundaries, provided protection, and regulated access (Kenzle 1997). Unfortunately, the available data for this architectural feature are uneven. Kenzle (1997) systematically assessed enclosing walls in the McElmo subregion, but there are not comparable data from the rest of the region. Enclosing walls at MVNP were recorded

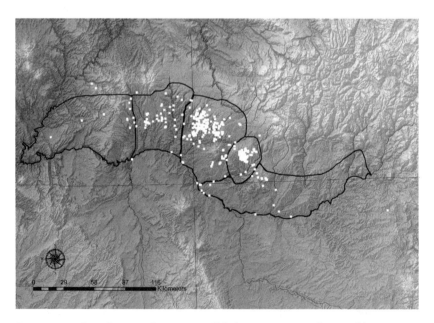

FIGURE 23. Distribution of towers at all habitation sites with a Pueblo III period component. Illustration by Grant D. Coffey.

as retaining walls regardless of whether their function was to delineate space or to shore up talus sediments along the edges of alcoves or on slopes. In other parts of the region, either enclosing walls were not present or they were not the focus of archaeological fieldwork. Thus, the regional data are biased toward the McElmo subregion, a bias that may have happened for good reason, since enclosing walls were most common at community centers built after AD 1140 (Glowacki and Ortman 2012:table 14.2).

The intensification of controlled-access architecture in the Mesa Verde core corresponds with an increase in population and the number and size of community centers in the McElmo subregion. Thus, the construction of enclosing walls and towers was related to a changing sociopolitical landscape that was likely becoming increasingly competitive (Lipe 2002; Varien et al. 2000). In this context, there would necessarily be a heightened emphasis on settlement boundaries, village identity, and protection (Kenzle 1997).

Summarizing Civic-Ceremonial Architecture

Temporal and spatial variation in the types of civic-ceremonial architecture constructed across the region during the late twelfth and thirteenth centuries reveals different types of village organization among community centers. Although the majority of community centers had some type of civic-ceremonial architecture, about one in four did not (see table 8). Some might question whether these pueblos were true community centers since they lacked an obvious centralizing feature like a plaza or a great kiva; yet there was something about their networks, location, organization, and influence that allowed these villages to become larger than the majority of the pueblos in the region. It may be that centers lacking civic-ceremonial architecture had (1) different types of village organization, (2) communal or specialized spaces that were not recognized from surface signatures, or (3) residents who traveled to other centers for specific rituals, dances, and other gatherings (i.e., they were "daughter villages" or maintained interpueblo alliances). Community centers without civic-ceremonial architecture were generally smaller, averaging sixty-seven rooms and eight kivas, than those with it, averaging eighty-seven rooms and eleven kivas, which suggests that there was a size-related social power differential among centers. Similarly, even if civic-ceremonial architecture was present at a center, buildings like great houses and great kivas were not found at every community center. This too indicates important differences in sociopolitical and religious organization among large pueblos that are suggestive of certain community centers having had more power and influence than others.

Variation in civic-ceremonial architecture also highlights fundamental differences in village organization by the early 1200s. During the mid to late 1100s, great houses and great kivas, commonly associated with Chacoan pueblo organization, were the main types of civic-ceremonial architecture. Although great houses and great kivas continued to be used during the 1200s, the newer villages did not tend to have these structures; instead, they had more-formalized plazas and biwalled and D-shaped structures, as well as an increased number of towers and enclosing walls. This change in civic-ceremonial architecture was most pronounced in the Mesa Verde core and coincided with the substantial population increase and consolidation that was happening there (see table 8), which suggests that increased ceremonialism and religious change were important components of this intensified social landscape. The evidence for the modification of communal and exclusionary architectural forms and their associated ritual practices further supports this inference and points to a need to accommodate the changing scales of integration and differentiation required both within and between community centers (see also Lipe 2002:220–24). For example, an increased emphasis on plazas and the use of deroofed great kivas denotes a heightened need to accommodate larger groups during community ceremonies and social activities, whereas variation in the form and distribution of multiwalled structures points to differing ideas about exclusionary religious leadership and connections with Aztec-Chaco ideology.

Summarizing Settlement Trends in the Northern San Juan

This analysis of subregional demography, occupation history, and distribution of community centers and civic-ceremonial architecture reveals a complex picture of the late twelfth- and thirteenth-century social landscape in the Northern San Juan region. In particular, it highlights important spatial and temporal variation in settlement patterns and village organization that expressed marked differences in social histories and affected how circumstances during the 1200s were experienced. As discussed later, these histories also led to differences in the rationale, timing, and rate of emigration from the region.

Broadly speaking, settlement during the 1200s was characterized by increasing population, aggregation, and proximity (Varien 1999; Varien et al. 2007; Wilshusen 2002); however, these dynamics were not uniformly experienced across the region. Intraregional variation was in part due to different modes of population growth and when such growth occurred in each subregion. In those areas where marked population increase happened before 1220, such as the Totah and West Central Mesa Verde, community centers were less concentrated and smaller than in the Mesa Verde core. Correspondingly, the types of civic-ceremonial architecture prevalent were those associated with the eleventh and twelfth centuries and most closely related to Chacoan organization (i.e., great houses and great kivas). In the early to mid-1200s, the most dramatic population growth happened in the Mesa Verde core, principally in the McElmo subregion. That is where community centers attained their greatest number, size, and density. This intensified growth was accompanied by significant changes in village layout and organization, and different forms of civic-ceremonial architecture (such as multiwalled structures) were incorporated into the newer large pueblos. On the western fringe of the region in the Lower San Juan, however, population density was much lower, settlements were smaller, and people were more mobile than in the rest of the region, which made for different types of interactions and concerns. This intraregional spatiotemporal variation corresponds with these important historical landscapes: (1) the deep-rooted differences between Eastern and Western Mesa Verde; (2) the pervasive influence of Aztec and Chaco; and (3) the McElmo Intensification. Unpacking these historical landscapes and their implications for intraregional interactions and sociopolitical complexity is taken up in chapters 5 and 6.

An important outcome of the settlement analysis bears on understanding the nature of sociopolitical complexity in the Northern San Juan during the 1200s. Regional archaeologists use several lines of evidence as indicators of social differentiation and leadership within and among community centers, including (1) restricted-use architecture, (2) kiva-dominated room blocks and nondomestic storage, (3) centralized planning and construction, and (4) ceremonial feasting and ritual (Arakawa 2012a; Lekson 2008; Lipe 2002; Nordby 2001; Ortman and Bradley 2002; Potter 2000; Potter and Ortman 2004). Much of this evidence is drawn from the excavated contexts of a few sites (e.g., Sand Canyon and Yellow Jacket Pueblos).

Lipe (2002), however, has also systematically analyzed regional-scale settlement patterns to examine social power relationships in Central Mesa Verde. Lipe (2002:217–20, fig. 10.3) compared the rank-size distribution of forty-three early PIII centers (AD 1150–1225) and sixty late PIII centers (AD 1225–1290) to assess regional-scale sociopolitical relationships among communities and whether they changed through time. Rank-size analysis examines the relationship between the logarithmic plot of settlement size (in this case, the total number of structures) and rank to evaluate the degree to which settlements were highly integrated into a single, centralized, hierarchical system—indicated by a concave-downward distribution—versus a poorly integrated system of competing polities—indicated by a convex-upward distribution (Johnson 1980). Lipe's (2002:fig. 10.3) log-log plots for early and late PIII showed an increasing trend toward a convex-upward distribution over time. He therefore concluded there was no single, hierarchically organized regional-scale polity in Central Mesa Verde but rather multiple competing polities that became increasingly independent and competitive. A continuing question, however, is whether the trend in rank-size distribution identified by Lipe (2002) would remain the same if Aztec and other Totah centers were included in the analysis, particularly since Lekson (1999a, 2008) and others have suggested that Aztec may have been the primate regional center of the Northern San Juan.

To evaluate this possibility, I analyzed the rank-size distribution of all Northern San Juan community centers occupied from AD 1150 to AD 1290. As with Lipe's analysis, settlement size, and thus rank, was based on the total number of structures (rooms and pit structures/kivas) for each community center ($n = 235$). With Aztec included, the resulting logarithmic plot was a pronounced convex-upward distribution (figure 24), which strengthened Lipe's original assessment of sociopolitical organization in Central Mesa Verde. Thus, at least based on the total number of structures, Aztec was not significantly larger than other centers such that it was the epicenter of a regional-scale, well-integrated polity; rather, the social landscape of the Northern San Juan was highly

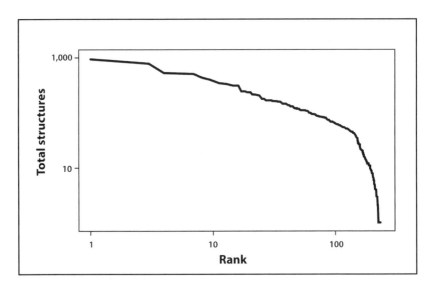

FIGURE 24. Rank-size order of community centers in the Northern San Juan. Settlement size was based on the total number of structures, including both rooms and kivas.

competitive, with a number of sociopolitical entities of different sizes and types of integration.

Nonetheless, these results do not imply that the region was devoid of sociopolitical hierarchy, for, as discussed, there was evidence of central-ized leadership within community centers as well as marked differences in size and the distribution of civic-ceremonial architecture among them. These differences suggest that some community centers had more social power (i.e., religious, economic, or political) than others. For example, the distribution of community center size indicates that there were at least three size classes among them. As described above, there were 4 to 8 community centers in each subregion ($n = 22$), except in the Lower San Juan, that were significantly larger than the remaining 231 centers (see figure 16; table 6). Many of these centers were also located on prime agricultural land or in key geographic locales (e.g., Glowacki and Ort-man 2012) and were linked to important resources. Among the 22 largest centers, 4 were again significantly larger—Aztec, Yellow Jacket Pueblo, Hedley, and Goodman Point–Shields—and thus were the primate centers of the Northern San Juan. Thus, there is an evident site size hierarchy consisting of at least 4 first-order centers and 18 second-order centers that likely played a greater role in regional-scale dynamics than the rest of the community centers (third order) and the many medium-sized and small pueblos across the region (fourth and fifth order).*

The manifestation of distinct size categories implies complex relation-ships among centers that notionally involved varying configurations and degrees of ritual, political, and economic integration among multiple pueblos. In the Mesa Verde core, the two modes of community center aggregation described by Lipe (2002:219–20, 231) are evidentiary of this complexity. Many of the largest centers in the region (see table 6) were self-contained large Pueblo villages that were some distance from other community centers (Lipe 2002:231, table 10.2). An alternative mode was clusters of multiple centers that were more spatially proximate and smaller than the self-contained centers. The implication of this different configuration is that alliance and other formal arrangements among these

---

*The number of primate and secondary centers will change pending updates in structure counts and depending on how different sites are aggregated. For example, the data compiled here are biased toward the PIII period occupation, and at the time the data for Mitchell Springs was compiled, the pit structure count associated with the late occupation was 39 and the room estimate was 200. However, since that time more fieldwork has been done, and there are now 62 total pit structures (some of which are BMIII and PI pit structures). Depending on the ultimate number of late-period pit structures, Mitchell Springs could qualify as a secondary center. In another case, I considered Lowry and its nearby settle-ments as separate sites, but if they were considered in the aggregate, then the Lowry com-plex could also qualify as a higher-order center.

smaller, proximate centers (e.g., clusters in Upper Hovenweep, Wetherill, Chapin, and Upper Squaw) were more likely since it would ensure that they could compete with the largest centers (Lipe 2002:231, table 10.2).

The distribution of the type and number of civic-ceremonial structures also implies power differentials among community centers, as some had multiple great kivas or multiwalled structures and others did not. Smaller community centers often lacked civic-ceremonial architecture, particularly group-assembly and restricted-use architecture, as did the many medium- and small-sized pueblos in the region. The inhabitants of these pueblos may have necessarily been ceremonially and politically connected with larger centers that had these facilities, particularly if certain ceremonies and rituals were centralized. All but one of the twenty-two largest pueblos had great kivas, plazas, great houses, and/or multiwalled structures, making them potential loci for ritual centralization.*

Even among the primate centers, there are tantalizing indications of religio-political differentiation: for example, Aztec and Yellow Jacket Pueblo had circular multiwalled structures and Hedley and Goodman Point–Shields had D-shaped structures. Aztec and Goodman Point–Shields were also the only centers in the Northern San Juan region with more than one multiwalled structure. Aztec had five circular multiwalled structures (three triwalled and two biwalled), and Goodman Point had as many as three, depending on how the variant forms are classified (one D-shaped and two variants [see figure 22]). This distinction suggests that Aztec and Goodman Point–Shields were particularly significant places in the Northern San Juan but may have represented different religious factions, since there were different multiwalled forms at each center.

Broadly speaking, these data add to the growing corpus of evidence for an emergent hierarchy—or perhaps more correctly, hierocracy, as it was religion-based (Lekson 2008:324–34)—in the Northern San Juan region that involved not only intrapueblo social differentiation and leadership but also an amalgam of pueblo confederacies (polities) of varying size, cohesion, and regional influence. Social power and sociopolitical organization among and within community centers and other pueblos were predicated on religion and ritual knowledge and inextricably enmeshed with politics and economics (e.g., Brandt 1994). The strong evidence for communal ritual, public construction, staple food production, and suppressed economic differentiation suggests that corporate-oriented strategies (as defined by Feinman et al. 2000) were the dominant organizational mode (Lipe 2002). However, the evidence for restricted access

---

*The exception is Easter Ruin; however, the possibility exists that either this architecture was obscured by rubble and talus slope wash or else the open areas in the canyon rim complexes between the enclosing wall and room blocks served as plazas.

to storage associated with religious facilities (Lipe 2002; Ortman and Bradley 2002) and the unusual distribution of faunal remains in specific room blocks (Muir and Driver 2002, 2004) at places like Sand Canyon Pueblo suggest also the use of network-based strategies that relied on more-centralized forms of leadership involving key individuals, families, or groups. Evidence for the use of multiple leadership modes belies possible intragroup tensions arising from contradictions and conflicts when both corporate and network strategies were in play (as discussed later). This dynamic may have prevented the multiple Pueblo polities (confederacies) from becoming an integrated regional political system (see also Arakawa 2012a).

The complex relational networks among community centers and associated confederacies (polities) were constantly changing in relation to each other and to fluctuations in climate and environmental conditions and at multiple scales. These places and people were also deeply influenced by the historical landscapes within which they were situated. To better understand these relationships and historical influences requires reconstructing intraregional networks and connections evident through materials exchange and circulation.

CHAPTER FOUR

Reconstructing Intraregional Interaction

Social networks provide not only economic opportunities to exchange goods and to obtain assistance but also avenues for sharing information, building alliances, and recruiting new community members who can bring needed skills, land access, or ritual knowledge (Braun and Plog 1982; Ford 1972; Wobst 1977). The intensity, diversity, and resilience of these networks affect how communities and societies adapt to ever-changing social circumstances and unexpected perturbations. For example, social networks can be used to reduce resource stress during periods of protracted climatic uncertainty such as was experienced during much of the 1200s. Under these circumstances, people often intensify regional social networks to increase access to diverse areas that may have surplus staple crops or other needed resources (Braun and Plog 1982; Colson 1979; Ford 1972; Healey 1990; Minnis 1996; Rautman 1993).

This type of resource buffering may have been an important strategy for ancestral Pueblo people living in thirteenth-century Central Mesa Verde. Van West's (1994) seminal model of agricultural productivity in the McElmo subregion determined that there was always ample productive land such that a "very large population" could have been supported, drought notwithstanding, provided that "mobility and access to productive land was not restricted or that redistribution systems were in place" (Van West 1994:188). This caveat is the crux of the issue. To evaluate the issue of land access, Varien and his colleagues (2000) analyzed the projected agricultural catchments from Van West's initial study for sixty-three of the largest and longest-lived communities in the McElmo subregion and examined how they changed between AD 1050 and AD 1290. Their analysis demonstrated that resource catchments became more constrained as centers became more clustered, which suggests that competition for resources was probably a central concern for at least some McElmo centers.

Recent Village Ecodynamics Project (VEP) analyses of resource catchment, paleoproductivity, and demography extended this line of inquiry by refining Van West's parameters to include new soils data, earlier periods, and more emphasis on the role of temperature in the paleoproductivity model (Kohler 2010) and added new site data to the existing community center database (Glowacki and Ortman 2012). The VEP I paleoproductivity model reinforced Van West's overall conclusions but differed in that projected maize-production levels were much lower, especially for the late 1100s through 1240 period (Kohler 2010). If the refined model is closer to being accurate, then food production and acquisition was likely a greater stress than initially inferred from Van West's model. Relating the VEP I paleoproductivity model to the updated distribution of community centers and their catchments over time shows that not only did catchments increasingly impinge on each other as centers became more concentrated but also the largest centers (Yellow Jacket, Sand Canyon, and Goodman Point pueblos) probably had to achieve maximum production within their catchment (Glowacki and Ortman 2012). In these cases, residents may have been particularly vulnerable to fluctuations in climate and productivity and thereby dependent on food sharing and other redistribution mechanisms.

These model-based studies suggest that agricultural conditions and settlement locations were such that social connections may have been essential for ensuring that villages had adequate access to necessary resources in the event of a shortfall. Yet variation in settlement size and organization across the region, as well as potentially encroaching resource catchments in the McElmo subregion, implies that there was increasing competition even as cooling temperatures and drought were making agriculture in an already marginal zone challenging. Evidently, there were many, sometimes conflicting, demands on intraregional social networks, and understanding the nature of the networks and how they changed during the turbulent twelfth century is essential for elucidating the circumstances leading up to the Mesa Verde diaspora.

Interaction and Exchange Networks in the Northern San Juan

By the turn of the twelfth century, the weakening of Chaco Canyon as the preeminent ceremonial, political, and economic center of the

Pueblo Southwest had far-reaching effects that impelled social and cultural reorganization across much of the Colorado Plateau (Duff and Lekson 2006; Herr 2001; Judge 1989; Kantner and Kintigh 2006; Lekson 2008; Lipe 2006). The shifting social landscape disrupted connections along which exotic and long-distance goods were circulated through Chaco and across the Southwest (Toll 1991, 2006), particularly at the northern extent of the Chacoan system in the Northern San Juan (Arakawa et al. 2011; Lipe 2002, 2006; Varien et al. 1996). Exotic materials that originated in northern Mexico such as copper bells and macaws—rare even during the eleventh and twelfth centuries—were no longer brought into the region (Lipe 2006; Varien et al. 1996:99). Shell too became increasingly rare. The quantities of turquoise and obsidian from sources in New Mexico and Arizona that were more proximate to the region also decreased (Arakawa et al. 2011; Mathien 1997), and only trace amounts of extraregional pottery like White Mountain Red Ware are found at thirteenth-century Mesa Verde villages (Lipe 2002, 2006; Varien et al. 1996; Wilson and Blinman 1995; but see Errickson 1998). Yellow Jacket Pueblo, for example, arguably the largest ancestral Pueblo village in the Northern San Juan (Kuckelman et al. 2003; Ortman et al. 2000), has clear evidence of substantial intraregional exchange (see below; Arakawa 2012b; Ortman 2003), yet only 0.1 percent of the 66,148 sherds recovered from excavation were extraregional red wares (n = 69 sherds [Ortman 2003:table 1]), and the frequency is lower yet at other late Pueblo III (PIII) period centers like Sand Canyon, Castle Rock, and Woods Canyon Pueblos, which had between 0.01 percent and 0.03 percent extraregional red wares (Crow Canyon online database).

Analyses of lithics and pottery assemblages from across the Northern San Juan region show a generally increasing trend in the intensification and localization of intraregional networks through time (Errickson 1998; Ward 2004; Wilson and Blinman 1995), especially within the Mesa Verde core (see below; Arakawa 2012b; Neily 1983; Pierce et al. 2002). The networks maintained among different pueblos were varied and influenced by environmental setting and sociopolitical organization. Neily's (1983) analysis of pottery and lithic assemblages from sixty-five sites on Cow Mesa and Squaw Point in the northwestern portion of McElmo— one of the drier parts of the subregion—is among the earliest Mesa Verde research focused on interaction networks and how they were affected by environmental change from AD 500 to 1300. Neily argues from evidence of decreasing stylistic diversity and a decline in the frequency of exotic and high-quality lithic procurement that interaction networks became more spatially limited (local) and distinct (separate) over time. Neily suggests that the organizational variability and contraction of the Cow Mesa and Squaw Point PIII communities resulted from people reducing contacts with more-distant communities, heightening intracommunity exchange, and increasing territoriality to consolidate resources during an uncertain time.

Using lithic data from seventy-six sites, Arakawa (2012b) examined how energy expenditure to obtain stone raw materials for tool production changed from AD 600 to 1280 in five localities within the Mesa Verde core. He shows that energy expenditure increased during the late PIII and argues that exchange and/or mobility intensified between Mesa Verde Proper and McElmo. Arakawa's (2012b:fig. 12.5) results also show variation in energy expenditures across the study area (i.e., the Mesa Verde core), including low energy expenditure values in the Hovenweep locality in the northwestern corner of the study area, which corresponds with Neily's (1983) study area. The lower energy expenditure values indicate that people in this part of the Mesa Verde core were increasingly relying on local sources during the late PIII period, which corroborates Neily's results.

In their synthesis of pottery production in the Northern San Juan, Wilson and Blinman (1995) highlight trends in pottery production over time, noting that by the PIII period, white ware production involved increasing local demand and standardization that intrinsically decreased the frequency of longer-distance exchanges within the region and beyond. They argue that pottery production and distribution was increasingly localized (Wilson and Blinman 1995:77), an analogous pattern to those suggested for lithic procurement (Arakawa 2012b; Neily 1983). However, variability in pottery production and procurement is also apparent since some areas, such as the Cowboy Wash locality (Errickson 1998), have evidence of increased interregional pottery procurement and interaction during the PIII period.

As population levels increased in the early 1200s, so did white ware production, which also became more specialized. Not only was there a higher demand for white ware, as indicated by higher proportions of white ware to gray ware than in previous periods, but also white ware vessels exhibited a higher degree of polishing and uniform slips that show increasing standardization (Wilson and Blinman 1995). The increased demand fostered changes in pottery firing to enable the production of more pots, because new and larger firing features and trench kilns, appeared in the late 1100s and early 1200s. These kilns could hold sufficient amounts of pottery to supply multiple households, which hints at large-scale production, but whether the kilns were cooperatively used by potters from multiple households or by one or two specialists remains to be demonstrated (Bernardini 2000; Blinman and Wilson 1992:82; Fuller 1984; Wilson and Blinman 1995:76–77).

Northern San Juan Pottery Production and Procurement Networks: A Neutron Activation Analysis Case Study

Pottery circulation among different parts of the Northern San Juan has been well documented (Errickson 1998; Hurst 1991, 1995; Severance 2003; Wilson 1991), but a regional assessment of interaction using comparable data from all parts of the Northern San Juan is needed to better understand intraregional relationships during the PIII period. Not all compositional analytical methods are ideally suited for regional-scale, multiple-ware analyses. For example, petrography is not a viable option in the Northern San Juan, because ancestral Pueblo potters often used sherd temper in decorated pottery (Errickson 1998:58, table 2.33; Pierce et al. 2002:fig. 9.3; Shepard 1939:274–77; Wilson 1991:740–41,748) and distinguishing specific igneous rock sources can be difficult because the source laccoliths (e.g., Sleeping Ute Mountain and the Abajos) were produced from the same magma flow (Errickson 1998:62; Shepard 1939:270). Therefore, Mesa Verde Black-on-white bowls and Mesa Verde Corrugated jars were analyzed using neutron activation analysis (NAA) to delineate patterns of pottery production and procurement across the Northern San Juan.

I selected NAA to chemically characterize the composition of Mesa Verde pottery and potential clay sources for several reasons. First, NAA simultaneously collects compositional data for thirty to thirty-five elements because it has the sensitivity, precision, and accuracy required for measuring trace elements, which are often useful for distinguishing chemical signatures (Glascock 1992). Second, other researchers in the region have successfully used NAA to examine the production and circulation of San Juan red wares and decorated white wares (Errickson 1998:65–70; Hegmon et al. 1995, 1997). Third, regional-scale analyses require a large number of samples to obtain statistically meaningful results (Bishop et al. 1982:278, 312; Plog 1994:148), and amassing adequate numbers of samples often requires multiple phases of data collection due to funding and other constraints. NAA data can be collected at different times or by different labs and then intercalibrated if standards are run with the analytical samples (Glascock 1992; Neff and Glowacki 2002). This capability makes it easier to produce sufficiently large data sets to address large-scale anthropological questions about the organization of pottery production and exchange, identity, social change, and migration, among others (Bernardini 2005; Creel et al. 2002; Duff 2002; Harry et al. 2002; Huntley 2008; Lyons 2003; Peeples 2011; Schachner 2012; Triadan et al. 2002; Zedeño and Triadan 2000).

The Northern San Juan PIII NAA database was assembled in stages. A pilot project, which became the foundation of the regional database, was initiated to determine the viability of the method for discerning compositional groups among different wares and locations within the Mesa Verde core. This study compared 120 Mesa Verde Black-on-white bowls and 60 Mesa Verde Corrugated jars from four sites (Long House, Mug House, Sand Canyon Pueblo, and Castle Rock Pueblo) and 54 clays from four geological formations and other contexts. The analysis identified local production zones for bowls and jars and evidence of pottery circulation not only between Sand Canyon and Castle Rock Pueblos but also between these sites and the cliff dwellings on Mesa Verde Proper (Glowacki 1995; Glowacki et al. 1998; Glowacki et al. 2002; Pierce et al. 2002). The success of the pilot project prompted researchers at Crow Canyon Archaeological Center to obtain funding for the analysis of more than 400 additional samples from excavated contexts, including several small sites in the Sand Canyon locality, Yellow Jacket Pueblo, and Hedley Pueblo, along with associated clay sources, and corrugated jars from Sand Canyon and Castle Rock Pueblos, which had not been done during the pilot project (CHS Grant #95-02-028). Consequently, the regional database is biased toward the McElmo subregion, with a particular emphasis on the Sand Canyon locality.

These data were subsequently augmented by another 350 samples with the support of an NSF-DIG Grant (BCS-012487). This phase of data collection focused on obtaining samples from geographic areas not previously represented in order to extend regional coverage and to ensure comparable sample sizes from the selected subregions. Sample selection was guided by the need to maximize results; therefore, sites in the West Central Mesa Verde subregion were excluded because of the shared geological setting between this area and the McElmo subregions (i.e., Dakota and Morrison Formations). Although this decision posed some interpretive challenges with respect to Central Mesa Verde, it allowed assessment of the pottery from the Lower San Juan and the degree of connectedness between the extreme western portion of the region and the eastern subregions. The Northern San Juan PIII NAA database contains 955 pottery samples from twenty-three sites and 132 clay samples from twelve geologic formations and four subregions ($N = 1,087$) (tables 9 and 10).

TABLE 9. Counts and percentages of local versus extralocal pottery for each site by subregion. Table continued horizontally on facing page.

Subregion	Site	Total local		Local corr.		Local BW	
		N	%	N	%	N	%
Totah	Aztec Ruin	17	85.0	—	—	17	85.0
	Run-Off Ditch Pueblo	37	80.4	19	82.6	18	78.3
	Kin Sin Fin	31	75.6	22	95.7	9	50.0
		85	79.4	41	89.1	44	72.1
MVP	Long House	54	90.0	27	90.0	27	90.0
	Mug House	49	81.6	27	90.0	22	73.3
	Step House	43	86.0	24	96.0	19	76.0
		146	85.9	78	91.8	68	80.0
McElmo	Sand Canyon Pueblo	55	91.7	29	96.7	26	86.7
	Castle Rock Pueblo	55	91.7	29	96.7	26	86.7
	Saddlehorn Hamlet	51	85.0	30	100.0	21	70.0
	Stanton's Site	49	81.7	29	96.7	20	66.7
	Kenzie Dawn	45	90.0	25	100.0	20	80.0
	Lilian's	21	67.7	8	88.9	13	59.1
	Yellow Jacket Pueblo	48	80.0	29	96.7	19	63.3
	Hedley Complex	85	96.6	40	97.6	45	95.7
	Lowry Complex	44	91.7	—	—	44	91.7
		453	87.6	219	97.3	234	80.1
LSJ	Moon House	28	77.8	10	58.8	18	94.7
	B-6-3	7	23.3	0	0.0	7	23.3
	B-17-1	21	70.0	8	47.1	13	100.0
	B-18-3	8	53.3	5	45.5	3	75.0
	B-3-10A	32	64.0	12	48.0	20	80.0
		96	59.6	35	41.2	61	80.3
Regional		780	81.7	373	84.5	407	79.2

Total extralocal		Extralocal corr.		Extralocal BW		Corr.	BW	Total	Unassigned
N	%	N	%	N	%	N	N	N	N
2	10.0	—	—	2	10.0	0	20	20	1
8	17.4	4	17.4	4	17.4	23	23	46	1
8	19.5	1	4.3	7	38.9	23	18	41	2
18	16.8	5	10.9	13	21.3	46	61	107	4
4	6.7	2	6.7	2	6.7	30	30	60	2
10	16.7	3	10.0	7	23.3	30	30	60	1
4	8.0	0	0.0	4	16.0	25	25	50	3
18	10.6	5	5.9	13	15.3	85	85	170	6
2	3.3	1	3.3	1	3.3	30	30	60	3
5	8.3	1	3.3	4	13.3	30	30	60	0
6	10.0	0	0.0	6	20.0	30	30	60	3
8	13.3	1	3.3	7	23.3	30	30	60	3
2	4.0	0	0.0	2	8.0	25	25	50	3
6	19.4	1	11.1	5	22.7	9	22	31	4
8	13.3	1	3.3	7	23.3	30	30	60	4
0	0.0	0	0.0	0	0.0	41	47	88	3
1	2.1	0	0.0	1	2.1	0	48	48	3
38	7.4	5	2.2	33	11.3	225	292	517	26
7	19.4	6	35.3	1	5.3	17	19	36	1
23	76.7	15	100.0	8	53.3	15	15	30	0
8	26.7	8	47.1	0	0.0	17	13	30	1
6	40.0	6	54.5	0	0.0	11	4	15	1
18	36.0	13	52.0	5	20.0	25	25	50	1
62	38.5	48	56.5	14	18.4	85	76	161	4
136	14.2	63	14.3	73	14.2	441	514	955	40

Note: Corr. = Mesa Verde Corrugated; BW = Mesa Verde Black-on-white; MVP = Mesa Verde Proper; LSJ = Lower San Juan.

TABLE 10. Northern San Juan regional NAA clay samples

Clay source	Number of samples	Sample locations	Subregion
Archaeological clay samples	8	Oak Tree House, Sand Canyon Pueblo, Castle Rock Pueblo, Hedley Complex, and Shields Pueblo	Mesa Verde Core
Alluvial clay	7	McElmo drainage; one sample from the Woods Canyon drainage	McElmo
Chinle	11	Comb Ridge, Bears Ears	Lower San Juan
Cliff House Sandstone	1	Chapin Mesa	Mesa Verde Proper
Cutler	3	Bullet Canyon	Lower San Juan
Dakota	44	Sand Canyon, Yellow Jacket Canyon, Lowry Area, Cross Canyon, Spook Point, Clint Swink's modified clays	McElmo
Fruitland	2	Barker Arroyo	Totah
Kirtland	7	Barker Arroyo, Jackson Lake	Totah
Menefee	26	Various locations within Mesa Verde National Park	Mesa Verde Proper
Mancos	14	Mesa Verde National Park and remnant deposits north of the park entrance	Mesa Verde Proper
Moenkopi	1	Base of Bears Ears	Lower San Juan
Morrison	8	Cannonball, McElmo drainage	McElmo
Total clays	132		

Scale of Interpretation of Analytical Samples, and Assumptions

Given what we have to work with in the archaeological record, pottery is a well-suited proxy for reconstructing social networks. Pottery was ubiquitous at most residential sites in the Southwest from about AD 600 onward, which makes obtaining comparable sample sizes from diverse areas easier than it is for other artifact types. Pottery also played a central role in Pueblo society and was not only used for utilitarian functions such as storage, cooking, and serving but also used in ceremonies and feasting. Pottery was circulated within social contexts that were not merely economic (e.g., Sahlins 1972); thus, tracking their circulation informs on a variety of social processes.

Social interaction is multiscalar; consequently, we must often limit our research to a specific scale in order to begin unpacking its complexity. Since my principal concern is with regional-scale dynamics, I focus on pottery production and procurement among people living in different subregions rather than among specific households or communities within them. Evidence of procurement networks at the subregional scale is therefore understood as a composite of individual and group transactions. In a similar vein, the term *local* should be understood as exchanges taking place within a subregion, whereas *extralocal* and *imported* are used interchangeably to refer to pots that came from outside the subregion but within the region as a whole (i.e., intraregional exchange).

The subregional scale is interpretively useful. For one thing, it maximizes the potential for strong compositional separation among samples from different subregions. As described in chapter 2, in most cases subregional boundaries correspond with different geological zones, except of course between McElmo and West Central Mesa Verde. Thus, each subregion approximates a macro-scale resource procurement zone or "manufacturing tract" (Bishop et al. 1982; Blinman and Wilson 1992; Lucius 1982; Wilson 1991:740). Consequently, when pottery circulation between different subregions (i.e., resource zones) is identified, it more clearly represents some type of transaction rather than potters using shared resources. This is an important distinction, since potters from nearby sites likely used the same raw materials to make their respective pots, which makes it difficult to identify instances of pottery exchange between neighboring settlements confidently (Bishop et al. 1982:312). This issue is particularly germane if the geologic setting is similar over a large geographic area, such as in the McElmo and West Central Mesa Verde subregions (e.g., Dakota Formation clays).

Although expansive geologic formations may also have inherent geochemical variation that could allow the detection of distinct compositional signatures, the predilections of potters and other cultural behaviors can either amplify or obscure this variation. For example, even though Dakota clays are geochemically more variable than are clays among the other formations in Central Mesa Verde, ancestral Pueblo potters used only those exposures most suitable for pottery manufacture, which had a homogenizing effect on the compositional signature of pots made with Dakota clays (Glowacki et al. 2002). I am not suggesting that studies focused on households, pueblos, or communities are not feasible but rather, for the task at hand—characterizing regional-scale interaction—that a sub-regional scale makes the most sense and provides necessary context for understanding small-scale interactions as well.

Analytical Samples: Pottery

Mesa Verde Black-on-white (AD 1180–1300) and Mesa Verde Corrugated (AD 1100–1300) pottery was widely produced in the Northern San Juan (Blinman and Wilson 1992; Breternitz et al. 1974; Lister and Lister 1978; Wilson and Blinman 1995). Analyzing both wares informs on different types of interactions because of the distinctive production steps required to make painted and corrugated pots and their specific contexts of use (Abbott 2000; Duff 2002; Zedeño 1994:100–106; Zedeño and Triadan 2000). The production of corrugated jars—typically used for cooking and storage—was a common household activity (Blinman and Wilson 1992; Pierce 1999; Wilson and Blinman 1995:65). Since the only surface treatment is the indentations made when coiling the pot, corrugated jars can be made with relatively few production steps (Feinman et al. 1981). This straightforward production and the widespread availability of corrugated jars suggest that they were utilitarian vessels and potentially less economically valuable than decorated pottery. Ethnographically, utilitarian items are most frequently circulated through generalized exchanges among kin or unrelated people with close ties (Ford 1972; Healey 1990; Sahlins 1972).

Black-on-white bowls were used for both daily activities and formal activities such as rituals, serving, feasting, and burial (Mills 2007; Wilson and Blinman 1995). In addition to shaping the pot, black-on-white pottery production required slipping, polishing, and painting, making these vessels more labor intensive and economically valuable than corrugated jars. Tools such as polishing stones, scrapers, *puki*s, and raw materials associated with making black-on-white pottery are commonly recovered from household contexts (Pierce et al. 2002:198; Wilson and Blinman 1995:76–77), implying widespread production much as with corrugated jars. The effort required when making these bowls and their association with suprahousehold activities, such as feasting, suggest that they were most likely circulated through balanced exchanges with partners beyond the kin network.

The pottery samples used for NAA were obtained from both surface and excavated collections. The sampled sherds were randomly selected from among the available population of rim sherds that were large enough to be nipped without losing diagnostic information. Rim sherds were preferred to ensure that the pottery type was correctly identified; however, in a few cases body sherds were supplemented to achieve the desired sample size. In total, 514 Mesa Verde Black-on-white bowls and 441 Mesa Verde Corrugated jars were analyzed to examine similarities and differences in how these vessel types circulated within the region (see table 9).

The sites selected for this analysis maximized spatial coverage and geological variation across the region and were located in four of the five subregions (i.e., all but West Central Mesa Verde). A minimum of three sites was sampled from each subregion (figure 25; see table 9). Admittedly, three sites are likely not representative of all the variation in production and procurement exhibited by the people living in a particular subregion, but it is a good place to start. The selected sites were also categorized as early (AD 1150–1250) and/or late (AD 1250–1300) PIII with the hope of identifying changes in circulation networks over time. However, the NAA results exhibited no significant temporal differences, indicating that there was no major change in pottery production or procurement networks, that any changes that were made did not significantly alter the compositional chemistry, that NAA was not sensitive enough to detect the changes (Bishop et al. 1982), or that there were sampling issues. Because changes in stylistic and technological attributes occurred during the PIII period (Hegmon 1991; Mills 1999; Wilson 1991), it stands to reason that changes in pottery production and procurement also happened.

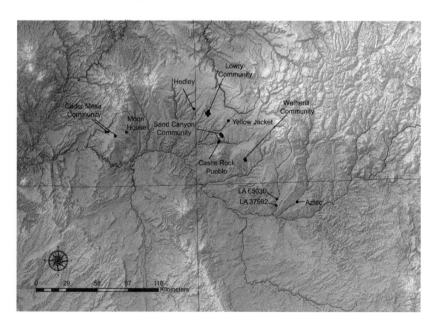

FIGURE 25. Distribution of sites sampled for NAA (see table 11). Illustration by Grant D. Coffey.

Analytical Samples: Clays

Identifying pottery production loci requires linking compositional groups to geographic areas by associating them with particular geologies or resource tracts (Bishop et al. 1982:280, 319). Unfortunately, confidently associating pottery with geologic clays and specific geographic locations can be difficult, because of the widespread availability of clays and the various ways potters affect the geochemistry by mixing different clays, adding a variety of material to serve as tempers, and firing the pot. Nevertheless, some clay composition data are required to make even tenuous claims about provenance because otherwise the only way to infer production locales is by using the "criterion of abundance," that is, identifying the production locale by the site location where the most samples originated in the compositional group (Bishop et al. 1982:301; Rands and Bishop 1980:20). Although much of the time this is a reasonable method for inferring provenance, there are cases where this rule has been contradicted (e.g., Zedeño 1994). Therefore, 132 clays from twelve formations were analyzed to characterize regional clay sources from across the Northern San Juan (see table 10). In addition to those analyzed during the pilot project (Glowacki 1995:26–43), additional clays were subsequently sampled from the Mesa Verde Proper, McElmo, Totah, and Lower San Juan subregions with a particular focus on possible sources in the vicinity of each of the sampled sites.

Clay sampling was guided by the desire to obtain viable clays for making pottery and the need to have adequate numbers of samples to characterize variability within and between formations (Bishop et al. 1982:280–81). C. Dean Wilson collected the Totah clay samples during the La Plata Highway Project in 1990. Archaeological clays of unknown geologic sources from five sites—Oak Tree House, Sand Canyon Pueblo, Castle Rock Pueblo, Shields Pueblo, and the Hedley site complex—were also included. These archaeological samples provided a direct link to clays that were actually used by people living at these sites. Prior to their being tested by NAA, all clay samples were fired to 700 degrees centigrade to emulate firing conditions comparable to those of the pottery samples.

Methods: Neutron Activation Analysis and Compositional Groups

NAA is a mainstream analytical method, and the specific procedures and statistical analyses used in this analysis have been well documented elsewhere (Baxter 1994, 2003; Bieber et al. 1976; Bishop and Neff 1989; Bishop et al. 1982; Glascock 1992; Harbottle 1976; Neff 1994, 2002;

Neff and Glowacki 2002; Sayre 1975). Rather than rehash these descriptions, I briefly describe the rationale underlying the methods used and the resulting compositional groups upon which the subsequent interpretations were based (see Glowacki 2006a).

Transformation, Standardization, and Missing Data

The raw NAA data were transformed to log base-10 values, which scaled these data to a similar order of magnitude, accounting for differences in concentration between the major and trace elements (Baxter 1994:41; Bishop and Neff 1989:63; Glascock 1992:17; Neff 2002). This transformation created comparable variances so that elements with larger concentrations cannot strongly influence the data structure (Baxter 2003:75). A log base-10 transformation also produces a more nearly normal distribution, which is desirable for some of the statistical techniques employed, such as discriminant analysis (Baxter 1994; Neff 2002:16–17). The distributions of many elements are also affected by both natural properties and cultural practices, making it difficult to determine which elements consistently have a normal versus skewed distribution (Neff 2002:16). A log base-10 normalization ameliorates these differential effects. Transformed, but unstandardized, data highlight minor and trace elements, optimizing the ability to identify different recipes within shared resource procurement zones (Baxter 2003:78). Therefore, principal component analysis (PCA) was run on unstandardized data to enhance the potential for identifying multiple production locales within each subregion where potters were using a variety of recipes within a broadly shared resource zone to make their pots.

Elements that occurred in concentrations below detection levels produced missing data, which can deleteriously affect results if used in statistical analyses (Baxter 2003:120). Nickel (Ni) and arsenic (As) were excluded from the analysis because 83 percent of the pottery samples were missing nickel concentrations and 10 percent were missing arsenic. Among the remaining elements, missing data occurred in 2 percent or less of the specimens (usually much less). In these cases, an expectation-maximization (EM) algorithm was used to impute substitutions for the missing data that incorporated both a distance calculation and the established variance-covariance matrix for the data set (Baxter 2003:122–23; Neff 2002:32). Additionally, a corrugated sherd (specimen B7G845) from Site B-17-1 on Cedar Mesa was removed at the outset because it was an extreme outlier and an influential observation (Jolliffe 1986:187). Its unusually high concentration of barium (Ba) inflated the PCA matrix values, strongly skewing the results. The jar is noteworthy, however, because it likely represents long-distance interaction with areas not well sampled,

such as those south and west of Cedar Mesa or outside of the Northern
San Juan altogether.

Identifying Compositional Groups

Using predefined compositional groups to begin analyzing new data may
impose a structure that may not be as strongly present in the new data
(Neff 2002:18); therefore, an inductive, nonexclusive approach was used
to identify compositional groups. To begin, a correlation matrix PCA
(SYSTAT; GAUSS) transformed the amended NAA data into a new set
of uncorrelated variables (principal components) ordered so the first few
components accounted for a majority of variation in the original data
(Baxter 1994; Jolliffe 1986:1). The principal component (PC) scores
were calculated using the pottery compositional data (i.e., the clay samples were not included). A scree plot of the amount of variance explained
by component was used to identify the number of components required
to adequately summarize the entire data set (Baxter 2003:79–80; Jolliffe
1986:96–97). This plot showed that six components (PC1–6) were necessary and explained 80 percent of the total variance present in the data.

A k-means analysis was performed on the standardized PC scores from
components one through six to divide samples into reasonable groups.
The algorithm underlying this analytical method identifies inherent
data structure by eliminating minor covariations that do not account
for substantial differences and partitioning data into representative and
meaningful groups by minimizing intracluster variation and maximiz-
ing intercluster distances (Jolliffe 1986:156; Kintigh and Ammerman
1982:39). Bishop and Neff (1989:72) caution against using discriminant
analysis on k-means clusters derived from the *original* NAA data unless
there is strong natural separation present in the data. In the case of the
Northern San Juan data, the k-means analysis was performed on PC
scores, not the original data. Since numerous geological divisions are represented, there is also strong natural separation in these data. K-means
analysis of the standardized PC scores is equivalent to using Mahalanobis distances on the original variables, which ameliorates the effects of
interelemental correlation since it avoids the elliptical problem inherent in Euclidean distances (Baxter 1994:169; Jolliffe 1986:164; Neff
2002:27). Plotting the resulting log%SSE (sum squared error) against
each clustering stage (Kintigh and Ammerman 1982:39, 43–50) revealed
that the optimum number was the twelve-cluster solution, which identified twelve fairly robust and highly interpretable groups.

These groups were then analyzed to determine group coherence and
to verify group membership using two methods: (1) an inclusive discriminant analysis that maximized the number of samples assigned to

a compositional group and (2) a Mahalanobis distance posterior classification (MDPC), another form of discriminant classification, which
used a conservative threshold for group membership. Neither of these
approaches is completely satisfying. Although the conventional MDPC
method used by researchers at the Missouri University Research reactor (MURR) produces conservatively modeled groups, which gives the
impression that classifications are more accurate, the typical MDPC analysis results in 30 percent or more unassigned cases (Glowacki and Neff
2002:184). This high frequency of unassigned cases is not only extremely
unsatisfying, but also the conservative threshold is probably not realistic given the geochemical variability introduced at all stages of pottery
production, use, and discard. The conservative method, thus, more likely
results in compositional groups that underrepresent the pottery belonging
to a particular group when there are idiosyncrasies among pots made with
the same clays. Conversely, the inclusive method runs the risk of forc-
ing samples into groups and thus overrepresenting the samples associated
with a group. I used the MDPC-based groups as a baseline to evaluate the
reliability of the less rigorously defined groups for a more informed interpretation by allowing for slight variations in recipe. The complementary
use of discriminant analysis and MDPC enabled a higher number of cases
to be assigned to a compositional group, with only 4 percent unassigned
using discriminant analysis versus 41 percent via MDPC.

Discriminant analysis was performed on log-transformed unstandardized compositional data using a jackknifed classification that removed
each case being tested from the compositional group before the probability was calculated, reducing ambiguity with borderline cases (Baxter
2003; Neff 2002:31–33). Discriminant analysis creates rules for group
allocation that minimize the probability of misclassification by displaying
the difference between presumed groups as distinctly as possible (Baxter 1994:186; Jolliffe 1986:156). It is used to assess group validity and
to assign unclassified samples to a group (Baxter 1994:185–88). In this
case, the discriminant analysis was used to examine the groups identified
in the k-means analysis of PC scores by reassigning misclassified samples
to the correct group. After several iterations, all samples had a 90 percent
or better classification rate for group assignment. The resulting groups
were further evaluated by converting the Mahalanobis distances calculated during the discriminant analysis to probabilities, which produced
absolute rather than relative estimates to assess group membership (Baxter 2003:110). The probabilities for each specimen add up to 100 percent
since each specimen has to be a member of one of the groups. If a specimen had a .75 probability or greater of belonging to a particular group, it
was assigned to that group; otherwise it was considered an outlier (table
11; Glowacki 2006a:app. B).

TABLE 11. NAA compositional groups of the Northern San Juan with breakdown by ware and subregion

Group name[a]	N	Corr.	BW	Subregion	N	Corr.	BW	Clay source
Totah Mixed/Corr. (5)	74	42	32	TOTAH	53	35	18	Kirtland; Morrison
				MM	14		14	
				LSJ	7	7		
Totah BW (10A)	38	10	28	TOTAH	32	6	26	Kirtland; Menefee
				MVP	2	1	1	
				MM	4	3	1	
MVP Corr. (11)	91	82	9	MVP	75	74	1	Menefee–Battleship Rock Oak Tree House Sample
				TOTAH	8	5	3	
				MM	7	2	5	
				LSJ	1	1		
MVP BW (4)	96	10	86	MVP	71	4	67	Menefee
				TOTAH	6		6	
				MM	13		13	
				LSJ	6	6		
MM-East Corr. (1)	148	141	7	MM	148	141	7	Dakota-Leander's, County Road 16, Shields unfired corr.
MM-West Corr. (8)	53	51	2	MM	31	29	2	Dakota
				LSJ	22	22		

Analytical group				Source				Notes
MM-A BW (3)	126	16	110	MM	112	14	98	Dakota–Yellow Jacket, Spook Point, Stanton's, Hovenweep; Hedley archaeological sample; Sand Canyon Pueblo archaeological sample
				MVP	4	2	2	
				LSJ	10		10	
MM-B BW (7)	87	16	71	MM	76	8	68	Dakota–Stanton's, Tatum, Hovenweep; Kirtland; Mancos
				MVP	2	1	1	
				LSJ	9	7	2	
McElmo BW (10B)	46	9	37	MM	33	6	27	Mancos; McElmo Alluvial; Menefee; Castle Rock archaeological sample
				TOTAH	4	1	3	
				MVP	6	1	5	
				LSJ	3	1	2	
MM Mixed/BW (6)	61	24	37	MM	53	21	32	Dakota–Wood's Canyon, Shields unfired BW
				MVP	4	2	2	
				LSJ	4	1	3	
LSJ Corr. (9)	24	24		LSJ	24	24		Chinle
LSJ BW (2)	72	11	61	LSJ	72	11	61	Chinle; Bullet; Cutler; Moenkopi; Mancos
Outliers	39	5	34	MM	26	1	25	
				TOTAH	4		4	
				MVP	6	2	4	
				LSJ	3	2	1	

Notes: Corr. = Mesa Verde Corrugated; BW = Mesa Verde Black-on-white; MVP = Mesa Verde Proper; MM = McElmo; LSJ = Lower San Juan.
[a] Numbers in parentheses correspond with the CDA analytical group assignments documented in Glowacki 2006a:app. B.2.

The MDPC conventionally employed at MURR was also used to evaluate group coherence and membership for the twelve groups identified via the k-means clustering. As a more conservative technique, the MDPC groups can be compared with those defined using the more inclusive discriminant analysis, which is a less rigorous technique since it validates reasonable partitions of the data. MDPC calculates the probability of group membership by assessing how far each case is from the centroid of its respective compositional group via a transformed Hotelling's T^2 test value using an F distribution (Bieber et al. 1976; Bishop and Neff 1989; Davis 1986; Harbottle 1976; Neff 2002:30–33; Sayre 1975). With this method, the calculated probabilities do not sum to 100 percent, because they are based on measured distances, not the group assignment. A specimen with a 5 percent probability of group membership means that 95 percent of the presumed compositional group specimens are closer to the centroid than that particular specimen is. The conventional threshold for validating group membership with MDPC is that a specimen must have a probability of 5 percent or greater of belonging to the group and less than a 0.1 percent probability of belonging to any other group (e.g., Bernardini 2005; Duff 2002). Samples were also retained in the group if there was a magnitudinal difference in probabilities for a given specimen (e.g., 65 versus 6.5). The resulting MDPC groups corroborate those achieved using the more inclusive discriminant analysis approach (see Glowacki 2006a:app. B for group assignments for both methods).

The MDPC method identified nine primary compositional groups, and the inclusive discriminant analysis confirmed twelve compositional groups. Three subgroups identified using MDPC correspond with three of the twelve groups identified using discriminant analysis (e.g., one MDPC group became the Totah BW and McElmo BW compositional groups in the discriminant analysis; see Glowacki 2006a:app. B). In these cases, the relaxed group membership criteria of the discriminant analysis increased the sample sizes such that the MDPC subgroups formed their own groups. The inclusive method also enabled the identification of an additional compositional group from the Totah, where geological resources and recipes were more variable than in Central Mesa Verde. Given the correspondence between the results from both methods, interpretation proceeded using the twelve compositional groups defined via discriminant analysis. However, the influence of excessive borderline cases assigned to groups defined by the inclusive method needs to be kept in mind. For example, corrugated jars sampled from sites in the Lower San Juan were members of groups attributed to production sources in the Mesa Verde Proper and Totah subregions. I believe the inclusive analysis assigned these pots to the Mesa Verde Proper and Totah production zones because there was some degree of correspondence between the chemical compositions of the Chinle Formation in the Lower San Juan and the Fruitland Formation in the Totah. Because the majority of the corrugated jars analyzed were produced and consumed within each subregion, it seems unlikely that these jars were transported to the Lower San Juan, which was at the extreme western edge of the region, with two intervening subregions. While this type of travel and potential for exchange is not out of the question, at this juncture the more likely explanation is that these pots represent a source more local to the Lower San Juan that was not adequately sampled for this analysis.

Once the compositional groups were established and validated, they were compared with the analyzed clay samples. To assign clay samples to the most appropriate compositional group, both discriminant analysis and MDPC were again used, but interpretation relied more heavily on the discriminant analysis results. The inclusive method is more forgiving and potentially compensates for the variation introduced by processing the clays and adding tempers (see Glowacki 2006a:app. B for mean elemental concentrations and standard deviations for groups and clays). The clay assignments made with the inclusive method make sense geographically and were corroborated by inferences about compositional group production zones using the criterion of abundance.

Results: Northern San Juan Compositional Groups

Data analysis resulted in 916 assigned (96 percent) pottery samples distributed among twelve compositional groups and 38 unassigned (4 percent) samples (see table 11). The identified compositional groups clearly reflect differences in geographic origin and, to a large degree, wares. Although both wares were often members of the same group (i.e., some corrugated sherds were in a group dominated by black-on-white ware and vice versa), usually one ware was clearly in the majority. Each group was named based on subregion and ware using the criterion of abundance rather than a group number or letter (e.g., Mesa Verde Proper Corrugated). Data presentation is organized geographically from east to west (i.e., Totah, Mesa Verde Proper, McElmo, and Lower San Juan).

Description of Compositional Groups by Subregion

Two compositional groups are dominated by pottery from the Totah: *Totah Mixed/Corr.* and *Totah BW.* Higher concentrations of sodium (Na) and strontium (Sr) and lower levels of titanium (Ti) and antimony (Sb) characterize the Totah Mixed/Corr. group ($n = 74$; see table 11). Of the sherds in this group, 72 percent are from sites in the Totah—Aztec Ruin, Kin Sin Fin (LA37592), and Run-Off Ditch Pueblo (LA65030)—in relatively similar amounts. This compositional group also includes sherds from the McElmo (n = 14, or 19 percent) and Lower San Juan (n = 7, or 9 percent) subregions. There is slightly more corrugated (n = 42) than black-on-white (n = 32). Although the difference is not substantial, the compositional group was interpreted as characterizing corrugated production in the Totah. All but three samples in this group contained similar rock temper regardless of ware. Black-on-white bowls from the La Plata Highway Project area, where two of the sampled sites were located, had unusually high percentages of rock temper in contrast to the typically sherd-tempered bowls from the rest of the region (Wilson 2006). The high proportion of rock temper may have contributed to the compositional similarity among the corrugated and black-on-white wares. The samples in this compositional group are chemically similar to Kirtland and Morrison clay samples, which geologically associated the production of these pots to the Totah. With respect to the Northern San Juan, the Kirtland Formation is found only in the Totah, and although the associated Morrison sample was obtained in southwestern Colorado, sources of Morrison clays are more proximate to the Totah sites (e.g., upstream from Run-Off Ditch Pueblo in Barker Arroyo [C. Dean Wilson, personal communication, 2004]).

The Totah BW compositional group (n = 38) is characterized by relatively high concentrations of cesium (Cs), rubidium (Rb), strontium (Sr), and potassium (K) and low amounts of tantalum (Ta), uranium (U), scandium (Sc), thorium (Th), and aluminum (Al). All samples in this group were either entirely or partially rock-tempered. This group of largely Mesa Verde Black-on-white bowls primarily came from sites in the Totah (84 percent), mainly Run-Off Ditch Pueblo. Other subregions represented include McElmo (11 percent, n = 4) and Mesa Verde Proper (5 percent, n = 2). This compositional group is chemically similar to both Kirtland and Menefee clay. Since the majority of the pottery in this group came from the Totah (only 2 sherds were from sites on Mesa Verde Proper) and the Kirtland clay is specific to the Totah, this compositional group likely represents pots produced in the Totah, perhaps in and around the La Plata sites.

There were two compositional groups assigned to the Mesa Verde Proper subregion: *MVP Corr.* and *MVP BW.* The MVP Corr. compositional group (n = 91) has high concentrations of titanium (Ti), antimony (Sb), scandium (Sc), aluminum (Al), sodium (Na), and vanadium (V), as well as relatively low concentrations of lutetium (Lu), uranium (U), ytterbium (Yb), europium (Eu), hafnium (Hf), thorium (Th), zirconium (Zr), and barium (Ba). This compositional group is characterized by the predominance of rock-tempered Mesa Verde Corrugated jars (90 percent) sampled from Long House, Mug House, and Step House on Mesa Verde

Proper (82 percent). Pottery samples from the Totah (9 percent, $n = 8$), McElmo (8 percent, $n = 7$), and Lower San Juan (1 percent, $n = 1$) are also represented. Menefee clays found in the canyons below these cliff dwellings were used to produce these pots.

The MVP BW compositional group ($n = 96$) is distinguished by relatively high concentrations of europium (Eu), antimony (Sb), rubidium (Rb), and zinc (Zn) plus lower amounts of strontium (Sr), calcium (Ca), iron (Fe), and manganese (Mn). These pots have a variety of tempers including rock, sherd, sandstone, and mixed (rock and sherd). The group is characterized by a predominance of Mesa Verde Black-on-white bowls (90 percent) from sites on Mesa Verde Proper (74 percent). Pottery samples from the Totah (6 percent, $n = 6$), McElmo (14 percent, $n = 13$), and Lower San Juan (6 percent, $n = 6$) are also members of this group. Menefee clays are chemically similar to these pots, linking production to Mesa Verde Proper.

There are six compositional groups associated with the McElmo subregion: *MM-East Corr.*, *MM-West Corr.*, *MM-A BW*, *MM-B BW*, *McElmo BW*, and *MM Mixed*. This subregion had the highest site density and in the analysis was represented by more than eleven sites (see table 9).* Unlike in the other subregions, there are two distinct compositional groups characterizing corrugated production associated with the McElmo subregion. These groups represent localized corrugated production and consumption in the eastern and western portions of this subregion. The MM-East Corr. compositional group ($n = 148$) is defined by relatively high concentrations of hafnium (Hf) and zirconium (Zr) and lower amounts of some of the rare earth elements. It is dominated by rock-tempered Mesa Verde Corrugated jars (95 percent), all sampled from sites in the eastern portion of the McElmo subregion. There are no other subregions represented in this compositional group, implying localized production and consumption of these corrugated jars. Dakota clay samples from the eastern portion of the McElmo subregion are compositionally similar to the pottery samples in this group.

The MM-West Corr. compositional group ($n = 53$) is characterized by high concentrations of the rare earth elements and low amounts of chromium (Cr) and vanadium (V). It is also dominated by rock-tempered Mesa Verde Corrugated jars (95 percent). Most of these came from the Hedley site (42 percent, $n = 22$) in the northwestern portion of the

---

*The data for the Lowry community samples listed in table 9 are from the Mesa Verde Black-on-white sherds analyzed by W. James Judge and James W. Kendrick (Glowacki et al. 2002; Neff and Glascock 1996), consisting of samples from nine sites: 5MT13314 (Turkey House complex); 5MT13435; 5MT13570; 5MT13592 (Casa De Valle); 5MT13596 (Kirby Klein); 5MT13597; 5MT13603; 5MT13606; and 5MT6954.

McElmo subregion and sites in the Lower San Juan (42 percent, $n = 22$).* These samples are predominantly rock-tempered, though a few contain sherd temper. No samples from Mesa Verde Proper and the Totah were assigned to this group, reinforcing the likelihood that it represents the circumscribed production and circulation of corrugated jars that were part of western networks. Dakota clay samples from the McElmo subregion were associated with this compositional group. Even though Dakota clays were used to produce the corrugated jars in both the MM-West and MM-East compositional groups, access to different rock temper sources may have driven the compositional separation. Dakota clays are not available west of Comb Ridge, where the Lower San Juan sites were located. The inference is that this compositional group represents corrugated jars that were produced along the west margin of the McElmo subregion and then transported into the Lower San Juan or were produced in the West Central Mesa Verde subregion;[†] or alternatively, the Dakota clays were transported to the Lower San Juan.

Four compositional groups assigned to the McElmo subregion— MM-A BW ($n = 126$), MM-B BW ($n = 87$), McElmo BW ($n = 46$), and MM Mixed/BW ($n = 61$)—are dominated by Mesa Verde Black-on-white bowls. Both the MM-A and MM-B compositional groups contain more than 80 percent Mesa Verde Black-on-white bowls tempered with a variety of materials. Both of these groups have higher concentrations of rare earth elements and moderate amounts of the remaining elements. These groups also include pottery from Mesa Verde Proper (3 percent, $n = 6$ [in total]) and the Lower San Juan (9 percent, $n = 19$ [in total]). Both groups are compositionally similar to Dakota Formation clay samples procured from locations across the McElmo subregion, but MM-B is also similar to a Mancos and a Kirtland specimen, suggesting more-diverse recipes for body clay or perhaps that the association with these clays was an artifact of the inclusive method for assigning group membership. The

---

*Judge and Kendrick's research (Neff and Glascock 1996) focused on black-on-white pottery production, so no corrugated sherds were sampled from the Lowry community. It would be useful to analyze corrugated sherds from Lowry to determine whether residents of this community participated in the western or eastern corrugated circulation network, or both. Based on the painted pottery sample assignments, I infer that they most likely participated in the western networks.

[†]Remember, no sites were sampled from West Central Mesa Verde for the NAA (e.g., sites from the Cottonwood Wash immediately east of Comb Ridge). Consequently, the patterns of production and procurement may represent interactions between the Lower San Juan and either McElmo or West Central Mesa Verde. Production and exchange occurred between the people in the Lower San Juan and West Central Mesa Verde because pottery with a distinctive black paste originating in the Lower San Juan (some of which was sampled in this study) has been found in West Central Mesa Verde, particularly in the vicinity of Comb Ridge (Severance 2003, 2005).

MM-A compositional group may represent a pottery recipe used in the northwestern portion of the McElmo subregion, since most of the black-on-white bowls sampled from the northern sites of Hedley and the Lowry community (53 out of 92, or 58 percent) fall within this group versus the 28 out of 92 total sherds (30 percent) from these sites in MM-B (see figure 25 for site locations).

Although the McElmo BW ($n = 46$) group also contains 80 percent Mesa Verde Black-on-white bowls with a variety of temper types, it derived from a different resource procurement zone in the southern portion of the McElmo subregion. These pots are compositionally similar to clays from McElmo drainage alluvial deposits and the Mancos and Menefee Formations (perhaps because McElmo Creek flows through these formations). The compositional group is also similar to an archaeological clay specimen from Castle Rock Pueblo (see figure 25), implying that the production loci included this site. The site distribution within the compositional group indicates that these vessels were produced and circulated most frequently among people in the Sand Canyon locality (26 black-and-white bowls out of 37, or 70 percent, were from sites in Sand Canyon).

Although a majority of the sherds in the MM Mixed group ($n = 61$) were Mesa Verde Black-on-white bowls (61 percent, $n = 37$), almost 40 percent of the samples are corrugated jars ($n = 24$). This compositional group has a higher concentration of barium (Ba) and lower amounts of iron (Fe) than the other groups. Various tempers were used to produce the white ware bowls, whereas primarily rock was used to temper the corrugated jars. The pottery was compositionally similar to Dakota clay sampled from the McElmo subregion and likely represented a recipe whose component resources were widely available throughout the subregion and used to make both jars and bowls.

The Mesa Verde Black-on-white compositional groups assigned to the McElmo subregion represent at least four different recipes used to make bowls. These groups suggest a more complex and heterogeneous approach to black-on-white bowl production within the subregion than was the case with corrugated jar production. They also hint at differing circulation networks for bowls produced in the southern and northwestern portion of the McElmo subregion.

Two compositional groups are assigned to the Lower San Juan subregion: *LSJ Corr.* and *LSJ BW*. Both the LSJ Corr. ($n = 24$) and the LSJ BW ($n = 72$) groups contain pottery only from sites in the Lower San Juan. No other subregions are represented. The LSJ Corr. group contains only corrugated jars and was very distinct from the rest of the groups, with the highest concentrations of chromium (Cr), iron (Fe), and scandium (Sc) and the lowest concentrations of other rare earth elements and alkaline and alkali metals of all the compositional groups. These jars were locally produced using Chinle clays and rock tempers in combinations that were not used to produce black-on-white bowls.

The LSJ BW group is distinguished by relatively high concentrations of cobalt (Co), calcium (Ca), potassium (K), and manganese (Mn), with lower amounts of hafnium (Hf), zirconium (Zr), tantalum (Ta), thorium (Th), and aluminum (Al). Of these samples, 85 percent ($n = 61$) are Mesa Verde Black-on-white bowls with a variety of tempers. The remainder are rock-tempered corrugated jars. These vessels are similar to clays sampled from the Chinle, Cutler, and Moenkopi Formations, which were all specific to the Lower San Juan subregion. Thus, potters exploited the spectrum of viable clays available in the Lower San Juan to produce decorated bowls.

Summary of Compositional Groups

The majority of the Mesa Verde Black-on-white bowls and corrugated jars were produced using locally available clay sources within each subregion and typically those nearest to their residences. Thus, generally speaking, jars and bowls in the Totah were produced using Kirtland clays (and other unsampled formations such as Nacimiento), Menefee clays were used on Mesa Verde Proper, Dakota clays were used in McElmo, and Chinle clays were used in the Lower San Juan. In most subregions, corrugated jars and black-on-white bowls were produced using the same clays; the exception is the Lower San Juan, where black-on-white bowl production involved several different clay sources (Chinle, Cutler, and Moenkopi Formations), but more than half the corrugated jars were made using Dakota clay, and Chinle clays were used less frequently (see table 11). Much of the elemental separation between compositional groups with black-on-white bowls and corrugated jars within each subregion, therefore, was driven by differences in the temper used for these wares. For example, corrugated pots were almost exclusively tempered with igneous rock, whereas temper in the black-on-white bowls was more varied.

Within the McElmo subregion, differences among compositional groups for each ware indicate that there were specific intraregional production zones and associated pottery circulation networks. Not only were there apparent differences in eastern and western corrugated jar production in the McElmo subregion, but also there were Mesa Verde Black-on-white bowl production zones specific to the northern, southern, and western portions of the subregion. These intra-subregional differences in pottery production and distribution are associated with variation in resource availability and show evidence of important social boundaries.

Intraregional Interaction Networks

Within each subregion, most pottery was locally produced and consumed (82 percent of the total sample, $n = 779$) and 14 percent ($n = 136$) was extralocal (see table 9). Corrugated jars were not generally imported from beyond the subregion in the Mesa Verde core, which suggests that these utilitarian vessels were often exchanged short distances among kin and close associates. As discussed below, however, people in the Totah obtained a relatively high proportion of jars from Mesa Verde Proper, and people in the Lower San Juan procured a majority of their jars or the clays to make them from beyond the subregion, implying that different contexts were involved in the circulation of these jars and resources. The proportions of local and extralocal Mesa Verde Black-on-white bowls were similar among the subregions tested.

Among the eastern subregions, people in the Totah obtained extralocal pottery at slightly higher frequencies than did people in McElmo and Mesa Verde Proper (figure 26; see table 9). A chi-squared test on

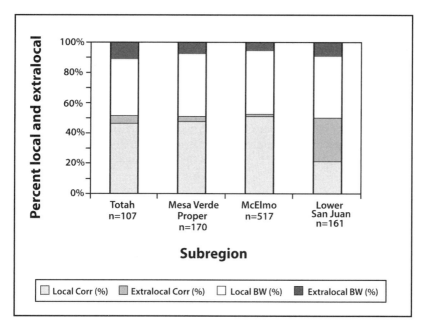

Figure 26. Percentage of local versus extralocal pottery by ware for each subregion (n = number of sherds sampled from each subregion). Unassigned sherds are not shown, but the percentages are based on the total, including unassigned specimens.

the frequency of extralocal bowls among the eastern subregions indicated that the differences were not significant, however (χ^2 = 4.41 < 5.99, df = 2, α = 0.05). Thus, in the east, no one subregion obtained more pottery from outside the subregion than did the others, and everyone was participating to some degree in the networks and activities that enabled the procurement of extralocal bowls. The slightly higher frequencies in the Totah may derive from the more eastern location of the La Plata sites (Run-Off Ditch Pueblo and Kin Sin Fin) within the subregion, which may have afforded more contact with people living in Mesa Verde Proper.

In the far western subregion, pottery production and procurement was markedly different (figure 26). Jars were more frequently obtained from extralocal sources than were bowls in the Lower San Juan, a pattern opposite that of the eastern subregions, where bowls were more frequently procured from beyond the subregion. Thus, it appears that the natural or cultural circumstances in the far western part of the region required obtaining either corrugated jars or the clays to make them from outside of the Lower San Juan rather than using local resources or procurement networks (see below; Glowacki et al. n.d.).

I used the heuristic categories *sporadic connections* (less than 2 percent), *weak connections* (2–10 percent), and *strong connections* (more than 10 percent) to discern patterns in intraregional networks maintained through pottery import and export among the subregions (table 12). Sporadic transactions are chance or rare encounters between people that happened regardless of the social and political climate. Although these transactions represent individual intraregional interactions, the low-level frequencies of sporadic bowl procurement also create statistical "noise" that obscures key patterns of interaction. In the following discussions, the greatest emphasis is placed on the robust trends evident via the strong connections among subregions, with some weight on the weak connections.

I assume that the presence of an extralocal pot in a particular subregion represents some form of direct or indirect interaction with the people living in the subregion where the vessel originated. Differences in population size and density can affect pottery production and circulation because factors such as the level of demand, productive capacity, and frequency of transactions are intrinsically linked to the number and distribution of the people making and using the pots (Arnold 1985:128, 166; Ford 1972; Rice 1987; Sahlins 1972:131). Site size and density varied demonstrably among each subregion (see tables 2–4), and undue influences from demographic variation on pottery production and procurement are of particular concern for these analyses.

TABLE 12. Counts and percentages of imported pottery by subregion and ware

	Totah					Mesa Verde Proper			
	Corr. (N)	Corr. (%)	BW (N)	BW (%)		Corr. (N)	Corr. (%)	BW (N)	BW (%)
Totah	*41*	*89.1*	*44*	*72.1*	Totah	1	1.2	1	1.2
MVP	5	10.9	9	14.8	MVP	78	*91.8*	68	*80.0*
McElmo	0	0.0	4	6.6	McElmo	4	4.7	12	14.1
LSJ	0	0.0	0	0.0	LSJ	0	0.0	0	0.0
	McElmo					Lower San Juan			
	Corr. (N)	Corr. (%)	BW (N)	BW (%)		Corr. (N)	Corr. (%)	BW (N)	BW (%)
Totah	3	1.3	15	5.1	Totah	7	8.2[a]	0	0.0
MVP	2	0.9	18	6.2	MVP	7	8.2[a]	0	0.0
McElmo	*219*	*97.3*	*234*	*80.1*	McElmo	34	40.0	14	18.4
LSJ	0	0.0	0	0.0	LSJ	35	41.2	*61*	*80.3*

Notes: Italicized numbers = local pottery. Percentages do not add up to 100 percent, because the unassigned sherds are not shown in this table. Corr. = Mesa Verde Corrugated; BW = Mesa Verde Black-on-white; MVP = Mesa Verde Proper; LSJ = Lower San Juan.

[a] These jars are likely statistical vagaries that resulted from weak compositional correspondence among clay formations (that is, Kirtland, Fruitland, Menefee, and Chinle).

Imported Pottery

In middle-range societies, obtaining pots and other goods from elsewhere implies an intentional effort not only to acquire an object but also to have social connections to those places and with those people (Sahlins 1972). Tracking the frequency and source of extralocal Mesa Verde bowls by subregion reveals important differences in the relationships among the residents in each of the subregions (figures 27, 28, and 29; see table 12). Among the eastern subregions, the frequencies of imported pottery indicate that people living in the Totah had strong connections with those in Mesa Verde Proper and weak connections with McElmo, whereas people living in Mesa Verde Proper had strong connections with those in McElmo and sporadic connections with the Totah residents. Thus, while people in the Totah obtained most of their extralocal pottery from Mesa Verde Proper, people in the cliff dwellings that were sampled on Mesa Verde Proper were obtaining nearly all of their extralocal bowls from McElmo (figure 29).

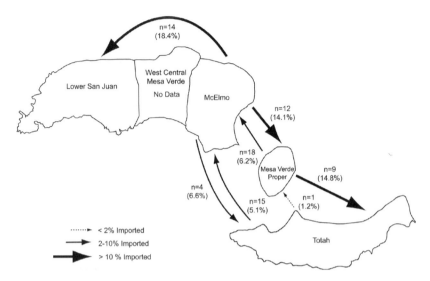

FIGURE 27. Schematic map of intraregional Mesa Verde Black-on-white bowl circulation in the Northern San Juan during the Pueblo III period (AD 1150–1300). Illustration by Grant D. Coffey.

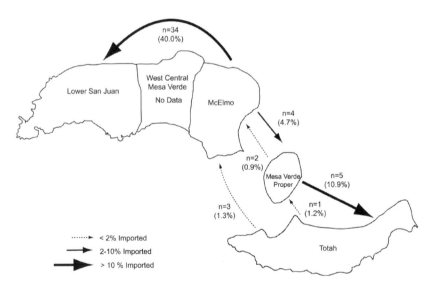

FIGURE 28. Schematic map of intraregional Mesa Verde Corrugated jar circulation in the Northern San Juan during the Pueblo III period (AD 1150–1300). Illustration by Grant D. Coffey.

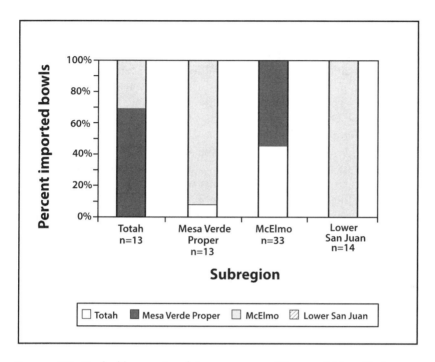

FIGURE 29. Stacked bar graphs of the percentage of imported Mesa Verde Black-on-white bowls found in each subregion (*n* = the total number of imported vessels in each subregion).

The asymmetry of these relationships is significant in light of the presumed intraregional prominence of Aztec. When pottery was imported from beyond the subregion, the strongest connections that people in the Totah had were with those living in Mesa Verde Proper. Not only were most extralocal bowls obtained from there but also notable frequencies of corrugated jars were acquired from Mesa Verde Proper sources. The evidence of strong connections via corrugated jars in the Totah differed markedly from the Mesa Verde core, where the utilitarian jars were most often locally circulated. The higher frequency of extralocal jar procurement from Mesa Verde Proper suggests that social behaviors besides transactions among kin or close associates may have been involved in circulating these jars. For example, it may be that these jars, perhaps filled with seed corn or beans, were carried and deposited as people emigrated from the Mesa Verde core. However, since all of the extralocal jars in the Totah were from the La Plata sites, which are closer to Mesa Verde Proper, people living at these two pueblos may have had closer connections to those living in Mesa Verde Proper or some access to the Mancos and Menefee clays.

McElmo has the lowest frequency of extralocal pottery of all the sub-regions (i.e., 10.6 percent; see table 9), which is to be expected since it also has one of the highest site densities in the region (see table 2). With more people and potters concentrated in the McElmo subregion, satis-fying bowl consumption needs from primarily local sources was likely easier than in the other, less dense, subregions. As well, population pres-sure and the attendant settlement changes intensified local dynamics, which may have further suppressed the amount of pottery obtained from other subregions. Nonetheless, people in the McElmo subregion did import pottery from other subregions, albeit at frequencies that indicate weak pottery procurement connections with those living in Mesa Verde Proper and the Totah. What is of interest here is not the strength of the connections per se but rather that people in McElmo maintained a different pattern of intraregional connections through pottery procure-ment than the other eastern subregions even though similar frequencies of extralocal pottery were consumed (see table 9 and figure 26). Unlike both the Totah and Mesa Verde Proper, where one of the eastern sub-regions was favored over the other, pottery in the McElmo subregion was imported at similar frequencies from both Mesa Verde Proper and the Totah (6.2 percent and 5.1 percent, respectively; see table 12 and figures 27–29). Thus, there was something qualitatively different about the McElmo subregion and the intraregional networks in which people participated compared with those associated with the Totah and Mesa Verde Proper. One possibility is that these connections reflect the cen-trality of McElmo to regional dynamics and geography, since neither was favored. Remember too that although there are no NAA data to support this inference, bowls were also likely imported from West Central Mesa Verde. Yet no pottery was imported from the Lower San Juan (see table 12). This clear difference between the eastern and far western subre-gions suggests that interaction between them may have been limited and that if there were commodity exchanges people in the Lower San Juan were using materials other than pottery.

Pottery procurement in the Lower San Juan also differed from that in the eastern subregions because of the high frequency of extralocal corrugated jars (see tables 9 and 12). A majority of these imported jars were made with Dakota Formation clay, which is not available in the Lower San Juan. Consequently, people living in the subregion were either transporting Dakota clays from the east because they were better suited for making corrugated jars than the locally available clays, which were used to make bowls, or they were importing most of their corru-gated jars (see also Glowacki et al. n.d.). If they were importing Dakota clays, then people in the Lower San Juan were traversing Comb Ridge or otherwise traveling to Dakota clay sources in West Central Mesa Verde that were at least eight to twelve kilometers away to obtain the necessary clays to make their jars. If importing vessels, then people were carrying jars, again either over Comb Ridge or by other longer routes, and were maintaining strong connections with people in the western half of the McElmo subregion as well as in West Central Mesa Verde. It is also possible that some of the corrugated jars made from Dakota clays were transported by Mesa Verde ancestral Pueblo people when they expanded into the Lower San Juan after the Kayenta tradition populations withdrew from the area in the mid to late 1100s (Lipe 1970). Although the NAA results indicate that small numbers of corrugated jars may have been imported from the Totah and Mesa Verde Proper (see table 12), these cases were more likely speciously assigned to these compositional groups because of the weak chemical compositional correspondence between Chinle clays (from Utah) and the Kirtland and Fruitland clays (from New Mexico).

Mesa Verde Black-on-white bowls in the Lower San Juan were imported at frequencies similar to those in the eastern subregions; however, no bowls were obtained from the Totah or Mesa Verde Proper. The main source for extralocal bowl procurement was the McElmo subregion and West Central Mesa Verde, though the latter remains to be demonstrated via NAA. These data suggest that pottery procurement networks in the Lower San Juan were western-specific with some connections to the western margins of the McElmo subregion.

Exported Pottery

Because they are different sides of the same transaction, to fully understand the degree of connectivity between areas requires close examination not only of the amount of pottery imported and its source but also of the quantity and destination of exported pottery. A comprehensive assessment also requires accounting for population size differences among interacting groups because the number of people affects the frequency and relative importance of transactions within the group. It takes fewer transactions among members of a small group to have a significant impact on the population than it does in large groups (Blau 1977:19–30; Duff 2002:14–17). This consideration is of particular concern in the Northern San Juan if using subregions as an analytical unit, because of the marked intraregional differences in population (see chapter 3).

The peak number of momentary room counts in each subregion (see table 4) suggests that community center population in the McElmo subregion was three times that of the Totah, five times that of Mesa Verde Proper, four times that of West Central Mesa Verde, and sixty-five times that of the Lower San Juan. The potential effect can be illustrated by assuming that the total population for each subregion is approximated by the peak momentary room count (see table 4). Further assume that each person owned one pot and that inhabitants of the Lower San Juan and McElmo subregions each imported 10 percent of their total pots from the other subregion. In the Lower San Juan, 10 percent represents just five McElmo pots that ended up in the far western subregion (10 percent of the peak population of fifty). Obtaining these pots would have required five transactions that involved 10 percent of the Lower San Juan population. In contrast, if these same five transactions happened in the McElmo subregion, they would affect only 0.1 percent of the McElmo population. Conversely, importing 10 percent of the McElmo pottery from the Lower San Juan would require 409 acquisitions, which would entail more than eight transactions per person in the Lower San Juan. This asymmetry is important. It means that even though importing large quantities of pottery is expected to impact the importers significantly, this does not mean that there is a similar impact from the perspective of the exporters if there are substantial population imbalances between the two areas, as is the case here. The proportion and directionality of pottery export can and do differ from those evident from the frequencies of imported vessels.

The magnitude of bowl export cannot be evaluated by simply look-ing at the proportion of pots from each composition group that was found outside its source area, because the total population from which the exported pottery came is unknown. As a result, it is not possible to directly gauge the relative impact and frequency of export in this manner. To examine pottery export, therefore, requires modeling the total uni-verse of pots in each subregion, which is assumed to be directly related to subregion population, to estimate the quantities of pots exported to each of the subregions (table 13). The underlying assumptions of the model are as follows: (1) each person owned one pot; (2) the population of each subregion is proportionate to its maximum momentary room count of community centers; and (3) the compositional samples from each sub-region reasonably represent the proportions of the sources of their pots. Thus, first, the percentage of the total Northern San Juan population that resided in each subregion was calculated using the peak momen-tary room count for each subregion (see table 4). For example, the peak momentary room count for the McElmo subregion is 4,094 rooms at AD 1260, which is 56.6 percent of the total number of peak momentary room counts for all subregions (7,239 rooms). To facilitate conceptual-ization of the model, the total population for the region was assumed to be 10,000 people, which is within the range of existing regional popula-tion estimates, albeit at the low end of this range (Duff and Wilshusen 2000:181–83; Lipe 1995:143; Varien et al. 2007; Wilshusen 2002:101).

TABLE 13. Estimated total population of pottery exported from each subregion

			Proportions of black-on-white bowl sources					
Subregion where found	% subregion population	Model subregion population	Sourced to Totah	Sourced to MVP	Sourced to MM	Sourced to LSJ	Unassigned source	Total
Totah	17.0	1,700	0.72	0.15	0.07	0.00	0.07	1.01
MVP	10.6	1,060	0.01	0.80	0.14	0.00	0.05	1.00
MM	56.6	5,660	0.05	0.06	0.80	0.00	0.09	1.00
WMV	15.1	1,510	0.00	0.00	0.00	0.00	0.00	0.00
LSJ	0.7	70	0.00	0.00	0.18	0.80	0.01	0.99
Total	100	10,000						

	Estimated bowls by source (proportions)					
Subregion where found	Sourced to Totah	Sourced to MVP	Sourced to MM	Sourced to LSJ	Unassigned Source	Total
Totah	1,224 (.81)	255 (.18)	111 (.02)	0	111	1,701
MVP	11 (.01)	848 (.59)	148 (.03)	0	53	1,060
MM	283 (.19)	340 (.24)	4,528 (.94)	0	509	5,660
WMV	0	0	0	0	0	0
LSJ	0	0	13 (.003)	56 (1.0)	1	70
Total	1,518	1,443	4,800	56	643	7,817
Total pot population produced	19%	18%	61%	1%	8%	100%
Exported	19%	41%	6%	0%		

Note: Numbers in italics equal frequency of local consumption. MVP = Mesa Verde Proper; MM = McElmo; WMV = West Central Mesa Verde; LSJ = Lower San Juan.

This means 5,660 people (56.6 percent of the 10,000 total) are estimated to have lived in the McElmo subregion based on the modeled expectations (table 13). Although the total population estimate was selected for heuristic purposes, the resulting export percentages are numerically independent of the choice of this number.

Next, the number of people living in each subregion (remember, each has one pot) was multiplied by the percentage of pots from the different source zones in each subregion to calculate an estimated total population of pots in that subregion from each source. For the McElmo example, the projected total number of Mesa Verde Black-on-white bowls that came from Mesa Verde Proper was estimated by multiplying 0.06 (the proportion of bowls in McElmo that came from Mesa Verde Proper) by 5,660 (the McElmo population estimate), which resulted in 340 Mesa Verde Proper bowls in McElmo sites. This calculation was performed for each subregion to create a matrix of the estimated number of bowls from each source zone (see the second half of table 13).

The estimated numbers of pots from each source zone were summed, and the percentages of the source total were then calculated. To follow the same example, a total of 1,443 bowls is estimated to have been *produced in* Mesa Verde Proper, which represents 18 percent of the pots with known sources. (West Central Mesa Verde was not included, because source data are lacking.) Finally, the percentage of exported pots from each source was calculated by subtracting from the pottery production total for each source the number of pots that are estimated to have been used within the source subregion and then dividing by the source total. For the 1,443 bowls sourced to Mesa Verde Proper, 848 were *found in* Mesa Verde Proper and were thus not exported. The export percentage is then 41 percent, or (1,443–848)/1,443. While the assumptions of this model may not be perfectly realistic, they are surely far better estimates than can be made without considering the relative populations.

The resulting bowl export frequencies highlight several important dynamics among the eastern subregions. First, a surprisingly high proportion of the Mesa Verde Black-on-white bowls produced in Mesa Verde Proper were exported (i.e., 41 percent; see table 13). This proportion of estimated vessel export was significantly higher than those estimated for both the Totah and the McElmo subregion and suggests that people on Mesa Verde Proper were very involved with interaction networks and activities that circulated bowls in both subregions. This was an unexpected result, particularly since traveling from cliff dwellings on Mesa Verde Proper can be difficult and requires traversing canyons and mesas, with substantial changes in elevation. Of the exported bowls, slightly more than half went to McElmo (i.e., one in four of all the bowls produced), and the remaining fraction was exported to the Totah (i.e., one in six bowls). Although exporting to McElmo was slightly favored, people on Mesa Verde Proper were clearly engaged in social interaction networks with people in both subregions.

Second, maintaining connections with people and pueblos in the McElmo subregion through the exchange of bowls was an important component of interaction networks among the eastern subregions. Mesa Verde Black-on-white bowls were exported to McElmo from the Totah and Mesa Verde Proper in relatively similar quantities (i.e., proportions of 0.19 and 0.24, respectively; see table 13). However, the reverse was not true, since only a minor fraction of the bowls produced in McElmo was exported beyond the subregion (see table 13). This difference suggests that participating in the activities underlying the circulation of Mesa Verde Black-on-white bowls, such as attending ceremonies and feasting events, was most pronounced in the McElmo subregion.

When people did export bowls from McElmo, the majority was transported to the east rather than to the far western portion of the region (see table 13). Conversely, people in the Lower San Juan did not export bowls to any of the eastern subregions. Thus, connections with the far western portion of the region through the circulation of bowls was minimal, and it seems that people living in the Lower San Juan were not participating to the same degree as those living in the east in the behaviors and social gatherings that promoted the circulation of bowls.

A Comment on Site Size and Network Diversity

Although subregional-scale interaction networks are the main analytical focus, important differences in the frequency of extralocal bowl procurement among the individual pueblos within each subregion related to site size are also present (see table 9). Of the sites sampled for NAA, the small to medium-sized sites (*n* = 12 [the Lowry Community is counted as 1 site]) have higher frequencies of extralocal procurement than the larger pueblos (i.e., community centers, *n* = 8), regardless of the distance between each small to medium-sized pueblo and the nearest community center. In the Totah, given its prominence as a ceremonial and political center, I expected Aztec to have higher frequencies of pottery from elsewhere in the Northern San Juan (extralocal). However, the two La Plata sites, Run-Off Ditch Pueblo and Kin Sin Fin, had higher frequencies of extralocal bowl procurement than did Aztec West. Their more western location in the La Plata drainage, which is somewhat closer to Mesa Verde Proper than Aztec is, may have facilitated greater access to pots made from Menefee and Mancos clays or the clays themselves. The NAA sample size from Aztec West is small compared with that of the La Plata sites, plus the samples are associated with one of several main buildings in the Aztec complex. Therefore, the samples from Aztec West may not be representative of pottery production and procurement networks for Aztec, generally. However, recent analyses by Lori Reed (2013) of pottery paste and temper for the assemblage from the West Ruin Fill Level Adjustment Project ($n =$ 5,221) found similarly low frequencies of extralocal pottery (i.e., 15 percent nonlocal, including both red ware and white ware). In Mesa Verde Proper, extralocal bowl procurement is notably higher at Mug House, a small community center with 8 kivas and 87 rooms (Rohn 1971), than at either Step House, a small cliff dwelling, or Long House, which was one of the largest centers in the subregion (21 kivas and 150 rooms [Cattanach 1980]). In McElmo, three of the small sites in the Sand Canyon locality and Yellow Jacket Pueblo, one of the primate centers of the Northern San Juan (195 kivas and 600 rooms [see chapter 3]), have the highest frequencies of extralocal bowl procurement. However, the frequency of extralocal bowls at the other large community centers sampled in McElmo (i.e., Sand Canyon Pueblo and Hedley) is low. Castle Rock Pueblo, a medium-sized community center (16 kivas and 60 rooms [Kuckelman 2000]), has slightly higher frequencies (13.3 percent [see table 9]) than these two large centers but lower frequencies than Yellow Jacket Pueblo (23.3 percent). In the Lower San Juan, the small sites on Cedar Mesa have high frequencies of extralocal bowls (this is particularly evident for Site B-6-3, where the majority of the vessels are extralocal); the largest site sampled (Moon House) has the lowest frequency of extralocal bowls.

These data suggest that people living in small to medium-sized pueblos across the Northern San Juan maintained networks that more frequently involved obtaining bowls from beyond the subregion than was the case for people living in community centers. The correspondence of extralocal bowl procurement with site size could simply be a function of population size because larger pueblos had more potters to satisfy their needs. Community centers were also important social, religious, political, and economic hubs, however, which facilitated pottery procurement from the surrounding community and neighboring centers. I believe that the difference in procurement patterns is related to organizational variability or other social factors more than to population size differences, and therefore that people living in small to medium pueblos had diverse networks for pottery procurement that were independent from centers. Differences in setting and timing of occupation also influenced access to pottery from beyond the subregion. For example, in the Lower San Juan, seriation of the pottery found at Site B-6-3 indicates that it was among the first settlements established after the post-1100s drought (Matson et al. 1990). Thus, the high frequency of extralocal pottery likely reflects a residential population who brought pots with them when they relocated to the area. In contrast, Moon House (see figure 11) was primarily occupied during the 1240s through the late 1260s. It was one of the few centers west of Comb Ridge and by the late 1200s was the latest and largest settlement in the Lower San Juan (Bloomer 1989; Lipe et al. 2010). In this case, the low frequency of extralocal pottery is more likely related to the short occupation span of Moon House and the relative lack of nearby neighbors with whom to trade.

Arakawa (2012b:191) noted a similar pattern in his study of tool stone procurement in the Mesa Verde core, finding that energy expenditure values for Yellow Jacket, Sand Canyon, Shields, and Castle Rock Pueblos were all lower than those for the small sites in the Sand Canyon locality (i.e., people went farther from the small sites than from the community centers to obtain stone for making tools). As commodities, Mesa Verde Black-on-white bowls and lithic materials for tool making have different manufacturing requirements and social circumstances for exchanges. That the same procurement patterns are evident in two different media suggests that the variation among the large and small pueblos is not due to pottery-specific issues and highlights important differences in village organization and interaction networks. Given the presumed nodal importance of community centers, the difference in procurement patterns of pottery was an unexpected outcome.

The primary exception to this procurement pattern is Yellow Jacket Pueblo, which has the highest frequency of extralocal bowl procurement of all the sampled community centers (see table 9). This is an important distinction since Yellow Jacket Pueblo is also one of the largest community centers in the entire region (see chapter 3), yet it is unexpected since lithic procurement patterns showed a high reliance on local materials (Arakawa 2012b). However, Ortman's (2003) comparison of nonlocal assemblages from beyond Central Mesa Verde among three community centers (i.e., Woods Canyon, Castle Rock, and Yellow Jacket Pueblos) found that Yellow Jacket Pueblo had a higher relative abundance of nonlocal materials than the other two, smaller, community centers. The frequency of nonlocal material and bowls from outside McElmo suggests that Yellow Jacket Pueblo held a prominent socioeconomic, and thus religious and political, status within the Mesa Verde core, if not the Northern San Juan, and differed organizationally from Aztec in the degree to which nonlocal pots were imported to the pueblo.

Summarizing Intraregional Pottery Procurement and Interaction

For the most part, people across the region were producing and obtaining pottery through localized interactions at distances that typically did not exceed the limits of the subregion as defined. When pottery was obtained from beyond the subregion, there was variation in the directionality and intensity of pottery procurement networks, particularly between the eastern and far western subregions. Pottery production and procurement patterns and inferred interaction networks in the Lower San Juan differed from those in the eastern subregions in two main ways.

First, people living in the westernmost subregion had a different mode of corrugated jar production and procurement than people in the rest of the region. As discussed above, residents of the Lower San Juan either made their own jars from Dakota clay procured in West Central Mesa Verde (east of Comb Ridge) or transported jars from West Central Mesa Verde (inferred) and McElmo. A recent analysis of corrugated jars from the Comb Wash great house community, west of Comb Ridge, supports this finding, identifying several different recipes using Dakota clays, found only east of Comb Ridge, to make corrugated jars among those analyzed (Glowacki et al. n.d.). Some of these jars may represent local production using transported clay, but the small sample sizes make it difficult to be certain about this interpretation. However, even if we find a smoking gun, such as corrugated wasters found in Lower San Juan kilns that were made from Dakota clays, both behaviors likely contributed to the high frequencies of extralocal corrugated jars at sites in the Lower San Juan (i.e., 35 to 100 percent; see table 9).

Long-distance transport of either utilitarian pottery or the raw materials for their manufacture is required when the local clays are inadequate for producing the desired ware (e.g., prone to spalling) (Arnold 1985). In the Southwest, this circumstance was particularly prevalent for potters using the geological resources in what we know today as Arizona (Abbott 2009; Harry et al. 2013; Van Keuren et al. 1997). Carter and Sullivan (2007), for example, similarly found that the raw materials used to make Tusayan and San Francisco Mountain Gray Wares were not locally available in the Upper Basin of the Grand Canyon. In this case, too, it was impossible to determine whether it was the vessels or the materials that were transported to the Upper Basin. Interestingly, the complex geological environment of the Upper Basin/Grand Canyon/Coconino Plateau includes the Chinle Formation, as does the geology west of Comb Ridge. This shared geological context suggests that locally available high-iron clays were not suitable for cooking jars in both areas.

If the residents of the Lower San Juan were importing corrugated jars rather than the clays, then they must have exported materials other than pottery, since little Lower San Juan pottery was found farther east (none was detected via NAA, but see below). Highly valued commodities like cotton, salt, deer, and bighorn sheep were available in places like Cedar Mesa and Glen Canyon but either were absent or access was more limited in the rest of the region. Climatic conditions in most of the Northern San Juan were not conducive for growing cotton, except in southeastern Utah, where cotton was grown and used in textiles (Kent 1983; Ortman 2000a, 2008). Salt was also available in the canyons of southern Utah but not in other parts of the region (Kinnear-Ferris et al. n.d.), and bighorn sheep were more common in the canyon country of the Lower San Juan than elsewhere in the region. Although deer were found across the Northern San Juan, there may have been a shortage of artiodactyls in the Mesa Verde core, particularly in the mid to late 1200s (Muir and Driver 2002). In a recent study comparing numbers of projectile points and artiodactyl ratios between the Mesa Verde core and Western Mesa Verde, Arakawa and his colleagues (2013) found that people in Western Mesa Verde had more projectile points and hunted more large game than did people in the Mesa Verde core. In exchange for cotton, salt, and big game, residents of the Lower San Juan—a dry, agriculturally marginal area—may have particularly needed not just corrugated jars but ones filled with corn or beans to safeguard against poor crop yields (i.e., commensal, interdependent exchanges like Plains-Pueblo interactions [see Spielmann 1991]).

If the inferred primary context for corrugated jar circulation is generalized, kin-based transactions involving short distances, which seemed to be the case in the Mesa Verde core and elsewhere in the Southwest (Abbott 2000; Ford 1972; Zedeño and Triadan 2000), then extralocal corrugated jars may have been transported longer distances through other types of relationships and mechanisms. For example, a high frequency of extralocal utilitarian jars could represent people moving with jars rather than exchanging them. If we assume that this inference is true, then another possible explanation for the high frequency of extralocal jars in the Lower San Juan is that Mesa Verde ancestral Pueblo populations brought corrugated jars, perhaps filled with seed corn or beans, with them when the population shifted in the late 1100s and early 1200s (Lipe 1970; Lipe et al. 2010; Matson et al. 1988). Although migration does not account for all the extralocal jars in the Lower San Juan, the movement of people is an important consideration for understanding pottery circulation in the Southwest (Zedeño 1998) and likely was a factor, given the Kayenta–Mesa Verde population movements integral to the history of the Lower San Juan.

Second, people in the Lower San Juan did make pots from locally available clays, particularly bowls, but did not exchange them long distances (i.e., beyond the subregion). Instead, they participated in localized interaction networks concentrated in the western portion of the region, and perhaps they exchanged pottery with Kayenta people to the west and south. Residents of the Lower San Juan were evidently not well connected with the far eastern portion of the region, at least through pottery procurement, since NAA results showed no evidence of the circulation of bowls with people in the Totah and Mesa Verde Proper.

Interaction via bowl procurement between McElmo and the Lower San Juan, though evident, was limited (see tables 12 and 13). Although people in the Lower San Juan imported roughly 18 percent of the bowls sampled from there, most of these bowls sourced to compositional groups MM-B and MM-West, which were associated with Hedley Pueblo and the western part of the McElmo subregion (i.e., there were fewer connections with Yellow Jacket Pueblo and the other, more eastern, McElmo pueblos). From the eastern perspective, only trace amounts of Mesa Verde Black-on-white bowls were exported from McElmo to the Lower San Juan (see table 13), and rarely has pottery from the Lower San Juan been found in the McElmo subregion. Thus far, the only evidence of the latter are Mesa Verde Black-on-white bowls with a distinctive dark-colored, nearly black, paste found in high frequencies at sites in the Lower San Juan and inferred to have been produced there (Hurst 1991, 1995, 2006; Severance 2003, 2005). The NAA results support this inference because several pottery samples with this distinctive paste were members of the black-on-white bowl compositional group that sourced to Chinle clays in the Lower San Juan (see table 11; see also Glowacki et al. n.d.). Serving as evidence of export is the fact that this distinctive pottery has been mainly found in West Central Mesa Verde, immediately east of Comb Ridge in Cottonwood Wash (Severance 2003, 2005), and only a few sherds have been found at Albert Porter Pueblo, a medium-sized community center in the northwestern quadrant of the McElmo subregion.

In sum, patterns of pottery circulation suggest that people in the Lower San Juan maintained networks that were primarily focused on interactions among people in Western Mesa Verde, as well as beyond the Northern San Juan region. Thus, it may be inferred that they were also not actively participating in the demographic, ceremonial, and political intensification happening among the eastern subregions, at least with respect to pottery procurement. This inference is supported by the western-specific interaction networks and differences in corrugated jar production, which, given their utilitarian use and predominantly generalized exchange mechanisms, point to a pronounced social and cultural boundary between the eastern and western portions of the region.

Pottery production and procurement networks among the eastern subregions differed from those in the far west in degree of connectivity. Mesa Verde Black-on-white bowls were exchanged among all the eastern subregions; thus, people in McElmo, Mesa Verde Proper, and the Totah had bowls from the other two subregions. However, the frequencies and directionality of these connections suggest that there were asymmetrical relationships among the eastern subregions. McElmo bowls were imported by all the subregions, which was not the case for any other subregion with assemblages that were analyzed using NAA. Only people in McElmo had evident connections with both eastern and western portions of the region.

Pottery production and procurement in the McElmo subregion primarily involved local interactions, given the lower frequencies of extralocal pottery import and export there than in the other eastern regions. This inference from the NAA data is also corroborated by the comparison of design attribute data from six Late PII communities (AD 1080–1140) and eight Late PIII communities (AD 1250–1280) in the McElmo subregion to infer how readily ideas about pottery designs were transferred among communities and how this information flow changed through time (Glowacki and Ortman 2001). The Monte Carlo–adjusted Euclidean distance coefficients for pairs of communities occupied during Late PII range from 0.1 to 0.4 with a mean of 0.25, and those for Late PIII communities range from 0.01 to 0.2 with a mean of 0.14. These results suggest that designs used among Late PII communities were more variable than those in Late PIII. Essentially, pottery designs became more similar through time, indicating increased face-to-face interaction and information sharing among communities in the Late PIII period.

The high quantity of local consumption in McElmo resulted from a number of social processes, including the marked increase in population and aggregation, an increased number of community centers, and intensified ceremonialism and sociopolitical interaction. The dynamic social and political environment and high number of people and potters concentrated in the McElmo subregion apparently suppressed the number of extralocal pots brought into the region. Evident variation among the McElmo community centers that were sampled indicates the development of individualized interaction networks with a varying degree of connectivity depending on the geographic location and occupation history of the center. One of the largest community centers in the region, Yellow Jacket Pueblo, was also long-lived and located in some of the best agricultural lands in the McElmo subregion and correspondingly had the highest frequency of extralocal bowl consumption (23.3 percent; see table 9 and figure 27). Sand Canyon Pueblo, with a shorter occupation, had one of the lowest frequencies of extralocal bowls (3.3 percent; see table 9) in the Sand Canyon locality. Hedley Pueblo, also among the largest community centers in the region, is located on the northwestern boundary of the McElmo subregion and the periphery of the Mesa Verde core. There was no extralocal pottery identified among the Hedley assemblage, and the pottery produced in this area had strong western associations (compositional groups MM-B and MM-East). Thus, people living at Hedley

Pueblo were more frequently participating in local interactions that likely involved people in West Central Mesa Verde.

In the Totah, people exported the majority of their bowls to McElmo, but they obtained more bowls from Mesa Verde Proper than from McElmo. This asymmetry suggests that people in the Totah had different types of relationships with people on Mesa Verde Proper versus those in McElmo. The differences in pottery procurement patterns noted here may have been influenced by idiosyncrasies of the specific pueblos sampled and the behaviors of their residents. For example, extralocal McElmo bowls produced in the McElmo Creek resource tract were found at Kin Sin Fin, but only two extralocal bowls were found in the Aztec West assemblage and both were sourced to Mesa Verde Proper. Nonetheless, there are other factors such as the proximity to Mesa Verde Proper and the high-density occupation of the eastern portion of the Mesa Verde cuesta in the eleventh and beginning of the twelfth centuries that may have also affected social networks and pottery procurement.

Mesa Verde Proper was situated between the Totah and McElmo, and pottery production and distribution reflect this juxtaposition. People on Mesa Verde Proper imported Mesa Verde Black-on-white bowls from McElmo rather than the Totah, even though people in the Totah were importing more from Mesa Verde Proper. Yet people on Mesa Verde Proper were also invested in connections with the Totah because they likely exported a high proportion of the bowls they made (41 percent; see table 13) to both the Totah and McElmo, in similar amounts. Thus, people on Mesa Verde Proper were strongly connected with the eastern subregions and actively participating in sociopolitical and ceremonial networks that promoted bowl circulation.

In sum, the clear differences in exchange networks depended on where people lived in the region. These differences were multiscalar, encompassing social and cultural divisions between the eastern and western parts of the region, interactions among the eastern subregions, and variation in pottery procurement patterns among small to medium-sized pueblos and community centers within subregions. Integrating these important dimensions with settlement histories enriches our understanding of the social circumstances preceding widespread migration from the region by identifying the degree of connectivity among disparate populations and their historical landscapes across the region.

CHAPTER FIVE

Interpreting the Historical Landscapes

As noted at the outset of this book, history matters, yet we often forget just how influential it is. History is fundamental to how we understand our place in the world, forming the foundation for how identity is constructed, social power is garnered, and connections are forged. It shapes our perceptions and therefore our actions and decision making in the present, even if it is a past present. The migrations and eventual regional depopulation at the end of the 1200s did not take place in a vacuum; they were historically situated, contingent occurrences created and influenced by the conditions and actions that came before (Beck et al. 2007; Pauketat 2001; Sewell 2005:248–57). To understand what happened in the 1200s requires a historical perspective.

Place also matters. Everything people do and experience is spatially situated (Casey 1996; Van Dyke 2007a:38–39); thus, place, like history, is central to how we construct knowledge about the world and ourselves. We imbue landscapes with meaning through personal experiences past and present, relived through memory, stories, and visits, and we ascribe powerful symbolism to landforms, drawing from their essence, both beautiful and practical, which can transcend the natural into the supernatural. Dudley Patterson, an elder Western Apache horseman, voiced an oft-cited statement that expresses the essential connections that individuals and cultures have with place: "Wisdom sits in Places. It is like water that never dries up. You need to drink water to stay alive don't you? Well, you also need to drink from places. You must remember everything about them" (Basso 1996:70). The places we live in and know affect the manner in which we go about our daily lives, including the shape and substance of our homes, how we get our food, the people we interact with, and the pathways we travel.

History and place are inextricably entwined and constitute a powerful and requisite framework for understanding large-scale societal change. Historical landscapes—"stable and elastic configurations of mutually reinforcing traditions which form partial social orders" (Robb and Pauketat 2013a:25)—were long-lived and tied to specific places, social configurations, and/or ways of life (e.g., technological innovations). They were created by the intersection of particular cultural practices, resources, economies, and environmental settings and the agency of individuals as they lived their lives. Genealogies of practice, the recursive relationships between people, objects, actions, and traditions and how they evolved further defined the character of historical landscapes (Mills and Walker 2008:12–13; Pauketat and Alt 2005; Robb and Pauketat 2013b). In the Northern San Juan, historical landscapes can be related to geography, settlement patterns, and shared architecture, such as great houses and multiwalled structures. They are also anchored by community centers with particularly strong religious, political, and/or economic influences: important nodes that influenced settlement and social networks in relation to them. Aztec and Yellow Jacket Pueblo, for example, were among the largest ancestral Pueblo centers in the Northern San Juan, with long histories of occupation lasting more than two centuries (Brown et al. 2008; Varien et al. 2008). Both became important focal points that played major roles in the occupational history of the region. Historical landscapes were not mutually exclusive or discretely bounded entities, however. They had pervasive and often overlapping influences that differentially affected people living in them.

Armed with the detailed intraregional patterns of settlement histories and interaction networks presented in the previous two chapters, I now turn to discussing several historical landscapes of the Northern San Juan to examine how ancestral Pueblo populations with diverse histories, social organizations, networks, and environmental settings came to the same conclusion by the end of the thirteenth century. The following are three examples of instances in which historical landscapes particularly influenced the lives of ancestral Pueblo people during the late 1100s and 1200s: (1) the marked cultural differences between Eastern and Western Mesa Verde; (2) the broad-reaching influence of Aztec and Chaco; and (3) the short-lived impact of the McElmo Intensification.

Eastern and Western Mesa Verde

The oldest historical landscapes are evident in the deep-rooted cultural differences between Eastern and Western Mesa Verde, apparent as early as the eighth century, if not before (Matson 1991; Potter and Chuipka 2007:425–26; Wilshusen, Schachner, and Allison 2012). Though not the only evidence of cultural diversity within the region (e.g., Wilshusen and Ortman 1999), this social boundary was mutable, becoming more or less pronounced over time and shifting across space. Potter and Chuipka (2007, 2010; Potter et al. 2012) infer a strong cultural boundary between Eastern Mesa Verde, which for the Pueblo I (PI) period (AD 750–900) is defined as the upper reaches of the San Juan River (i.e., the Piedra, Pine, Animas, and La Plata drainages), and the rest of the region.* These differences were most evident in village organization and architecture (Potter et al. 2012). East of the La Plata drainage, pit structures at large villages like Sacred Ridge, Morris 23, and Sambrito Village had variable shapes with vent holes constructed in equally variable configurations (i.e., one, two, or bifurcated). Pit structures were typically associated with single-row room blocks with no evidence of shared room blocks or middens, implying that households were relatively autonomous, if loosely aggregated. Pottery assemblages contained high proportions of glaze-painted pottery and low frequencies of the red wares that characterize western assemblages. Variation in pit structure shape, biological differences, and the treatment of human remains indicate that several cultural groups intermixed in Eastern Mesa Verde (Potter and Perry 2011). The presence of enclosures and evidence of extreme perimortem processing at Sacred Ridge, Sambrito Village, and Burnt Mesa attest to intergroup violence and social conflict among these multicultural populations (Potter and Chuipka 2010; Potter and Perry 2011; Potter et al. 2012).

West of the La Plata drainage, cultural groups and their settlement patterns, though not homogenous, were more similar to each other than were those in the east (Allison et al. 2012; Wilshusen and Ortman 1999). Large PI villages like McPhee Village (McElmo) and Alkali Ridge No. 13 (West Central Mesa Verde) had rectilinear pit structures with single-hole vent openings and double-row room blocks, as well as evidence of communal areas with high proportions of red ware pottery (Blinman 1989; Hegmon et al. 1997; Potter et al. 2012; Wilshusen, Ortman, et al. 2012). Differences remained, however, for in West Central Mesa Verde, there were fewer large villages, a greater tendency for villages to be situated in defensible locations, and more fluctuation in population levels than in the Mesa Verde core (Allison et al. 2012), and in the Lower San Juan, Mesa Verde ancestral Pueblo population density was extremely low (Allison et al. 2012).

---

*Regional differences during the PI period can be further divided into Central and West Mesa Verde (Allison et al. 2012; Wilshusen, Ortman, et al. 2012). For the sake of the broader discussion, however, I focus on generalized attributes rather than specific details.

We know much less about the nature of an eastern and western cultural boundary during the Chaco period (i.e., Pueblo II, AD 900–1150). Although great house communities have been well studied (e.g., Cameron 2009; chapters in Reed 2008c), there has not yet been a systematic, synchronic analysis of Chaco period settlement patterns across the Northern San Juan that would allow us to more fully address this topic. Nevertheless, we do know that great house communities were established across most of the region reaching just west of Comb Ridge (i.e., Et Al and Owen great houses [Fast 2012]), which suggests that either the eastern and western cultural divisions among the Mesa Verde pueblo people were less pronounced during the Chaco period or else the cultural boundary was farther west.

To the west of Comb Ridge, beyond the westernmost great houses, Kayenta immigrants moved into Western Mesa Verde, settling in areas like Cedar Mesa and the Red Rock Plateau (i.e., the Lower San Juan) during the 1000s and early 1100s, when climate and precipitation were relatively stable (Lipe 1970; Matson et al. 1988). This Chaco period expansion of Kayenta populations into the Northern San Juan increased interactions among culturally distinct pueblo groups including Mesa Verde, Virgin Branch, and Fremont. The high frequency of Kayenta pottery types at Mesa Verde settlements indicates regular interactions among these populations (Lipe 1970; Lipe and Glowacki 2011), particularly in the western portion of the region. However, substantial quantities of Kayenta pottery were also transported farther east to places like the Bluff Great House (Cameron 2009:40, 291) and in lesser amounts to sites in Eastern Mesa Verde, including Aztec West in northwestern New Mexico. These interaction networks were altered in the mid-1100s when the Kayenta ancestral Pueblo people withdrew from the western margins of the Northern San Juan region and consolidated in their original homelands (Arizona). This emigration and contraction of Kayenta populations coincided with the severe drought of the mid-1100s, but other stressors, such as the intense violence happening in the Mesa Verde core at this time (Cole 2012; Kohler et al. 2014; Kuckelman et al. 2000), may have also contributed to causing the Kayenta ancestral Pueblo people to leave the Northern San Juan. As the Kayenta people departed and the severe drought conditions of the mid-1100s subsided, Mesa Verde populations expanded into the Lower San Juan (Lipe 1970; Matson et al. 1988).

By the early 1200s, the mutable boundary had shifted again, as cultural differences between populations in the McElmo and West Central Mesa Verde subregions increased. Social and cultural changes in West Central Mesa Verde point to increasing localization that lessened participation in eastern social, ceremonial, and political dynamics (see below). Thus, by the thirteenth century, Western Mesa Verde comprised West Central

Mesa Verde and the Lower San Juan. In Eastern Mesa Verde, there was heightened social interaction and ceremonial intensification between the Totah and the Mesa Verde core (see chapters 3 and 4; see also Diederichs et al. 2011). These dynamics created further social separation from Western Mesa Verde. As discussed in the concluding section of the book, the differences between Eastern and Western Mesa Verde affected the processes and migration pathways that resulted in the regional depopulation (Cordell et al. 2007; Glowacki 2010; Lipe et al. 2010), which ultimately contributed to the histories of the Eastern and Western Pueblos of today (Ortman 2012; Ware 2014).

Eastern Mesa Verde

Because Eastern Mesa Verde looms large in the ensuing discussion, I simply present here a few salient details to begin drawing the contrasts between the eastern and western portions of the region during the late twelfth and thirteenth centuries. As described in chapter 2, Eastern Mesa Verde contains some of the most productive agricultural land in the region (Adams and Petersen 1999). The higher elevations, enriched soil quality, and sufficiently watered areas made farming at many locales in the eastern subregions a better proposition than in the western portion of the region (e.g., Morefield Canyon in Mesa Verde Proper [Benson 2011]). At least twice as many people lived in Eastern Mesa Verde, and the number of community centers was quadruple that of Western Mesa Verde (*n* = 200). Eastern villages were larger, having five room blocks and fourteen pit structures on average (compared to three room blocks and ten kivas), and more concentrated than in Western Mesa Verde, especially in the McElmo subregion (see chapter 3; Glowacki 2010; Varien 1999). Since there were more large villages, there were also higher frequencies of all the major types of civic-ceremonial architecture, including great houses, great kivas, plazas, circular and D-shaped multiwalled structures, towers, and enclosing walls (see chapter 3). Following the hardships of the 1100s, significant social and cultural changes occurred, including increased aggregation into large pueblos (Glowacki and Ortman 2012; Varien et al. 2007), intensification of ceremonialism (Glowacki 2011), and increasing settlement proximity that prompted cooperation and alliances as well as conflict over territory and resources (Lipe 2002; Varien et al. 2000) that did not happen to the same extent in Western Mesa Verde.

Western Mesa Verde

By the late 1100s and early 1200s, the geographic area encompassed by Western Mesa Verde corresponded with what we know today as southeastern Utah, which is much lower and drier than the eastern portion of the region (see chapter 2). The median annual rainfall in Western Mesa Verde was the lowest in the northern Southwest, even if that amount was less variable over the years than in the Mesa Verde core (Wright 2010:fig. 4.4). Although water was, and is, a healthy preoccupation for everyone living in the region, it was an overriding concern and especially strong influence on settlement patterns and daily life for ancestral Pueblo people in Western Mesa Verde. The frequency of tower complexes positioned at canyon heads and well-watered drainages—such as Cave Towers (42SA1725), a multiroom and kiva complex with enclosing walls and five towers, and Dry Wash Overlook Ruin (42SA5024), with four towers connected by enclosing walls—stresses the importance of ensuring access to water (Bredthauer 2010).

Not only is the area notoriously hot and dry, but also the red rock canyons and outcrops, though stunning, are not ideal for farming except in the wide-bottomed canyons, like Montezuma Canyon, or perhaps in washes like Comb and Butler. The resultant patchy distribution of agricultural land precluded extensive dryland farming (Lipe 1970:91–92), and diverse subsistence strategies were required for living in Western Mesa Verde, especially in the Lower San Juan. Projectile point frequencies and artiodactyl ratios (e.g., deer and mountain sheep) indicate that large game hunting was more common in Western Mesa Verde than in the Mesa Verde core (Arakawa et al. 2013). Although not a food crop, cotton was cultivated in the lower San Juan drainage (Lipe 1970; Webster 2008) and was used to make sandals and other textiles (Bellorado et al. 2012; Cameron 2009; Kent 1983; Ortman 2000a, 2008). Big game and both the raw cotton and finished cotton products, as well as salt, were highly valued and were likely exchanged throughout the region and beyond to obtain necessary goods (e.g., seed corn and/or corrugated jars [see chapter 4]) to supplement subsistence in this marginal environment.

Given the environment, not surprisingly, population density in Western Mesa Verde was about half that of the eastern portion of the region (see chapter 3 and table 2). The western frontier of the Mesa Verde occupation had a mix of settlement strategies, with some groups retaining flexibility and other groups investing in place and establishing relatively large pueblos at permanent water sources. The majority of those who lived in this demanding, yet captivating, landscape were highly mobile and lived in small and dispersed pueblos, especially farther west in areas like Cedar Mesa and the Red Rock Plateau (Lipe 1970; Matson et al. 1988). An extended household-based social organization allowed families to readily move as needed to adjust to environmental challenges or social change (Dean 1996, 2010). This mode of settlement organization, which was shared by the Kayenta populations, typified the occupation of the Lower

San Juan and was a predominant strategy in West Central Mesa Verde (see chapter 3 and table 3).

Fewer community centers (i.e., a 1:4 ratio; *n* = 53) were established in Western Mesa Verde, and they were smaller and more dispersed than the centers in Eastern Mesa Verde (see chapter 3). The ratios of centers to habitation sites and rooms to kivas in West Central Mesa Verde are more similar to those of the east, whereas those for the Lower San Juan are significantly different, reflecting smaller group and settlement sizes. Unlike the rest of the region, centers were not integral to sociopolitical organization in the western margins of the Northern San Juan (see chapter 3 and tables 3 and 6). Not only were community centers less common in the Lower San Juan (*n* = 7) but also they were smaller than elsewhere in the region. Only two centers met the size criteria, while the rest had specialized features like excess storage or large plaza-like enclosures. The majority of the western centers (*n* = 46, or 87 percent) were located in West Central Mesa Verde and in this way had more affinity with the Mesa Verde core, which is why this area is often considered part of Central Mesa Verde. However, as I have noted, this association changed in the early 1200s, when increased localization reoriented western social, ceremonial, and political dynamics.

Most of the West Central Mesa Verde centers, including Monument and Coalbed Villages, were multicomponent, with occupations spanning from the late PI through PIII periods, and many were depopulated by the mid-1200s. Only seven of the forty-six centers were single-component PIII settlements. Thus, the settlement history and organization of the largest villages in Western Mesa Verde were significantly influenced by the social and political climate of the Chaco period (AD 950–1150). Correspondingly, the dominant civic-ceremonial architecture was great houses and great kivas (see chapter 3 and table 8). Chacoan influences were less evident in the Lower San Juan, where interaction with Kayenta populations, who also show little evidence of Chacoan interaction (Dean 1996, 2010), was a major influence.

The four largest community centers in West Central Mesa Verde— Montezuma Village I and II, 10-Acre Ruin complex, Monument Village, and Nancy Patterson—were positioned along the Montezuma drainage (Hurst and Till 2009:fig. 4.3). This location and correlation with community center size was not an accident, given the well-watered and wide canyon bottom suitable for farming: it was the best agricultural location in Western Mesa Verde. In chapter 3, I describe three size classes of community centers and suggest that the sociopolitical organization of the region involved settlement size hierarchy and interpueblo alliances. These four western centers were classified as second-order centers (see table 8), implying that they were among the more influential centers in the Northern San Juan. They were not the only community centers in Montezuma Canyon, for Coalbed Village and Greasewood Flats Ruin, which were also large centers, even if not the largest, were located there as well. The number and size of community centers in the Montezuma drainage suggest that this was a politically important locale within Western Mesa Verde and elsewhere in the region. Unlike the Mesa Verde core, and the McElmo subregion in particular, the major centers of Montezuma drainage were regularly spaced along the canyon, typically at the confluence of a tributary and the main drainage, except 10-Acre Ruin complex, which was at the head of a tributary (Hurst and Till 2009).

By AD 1225, important social and cultural changes in Western Mesa Verde were evident in a variety of media and suggest that the ancestral Pueblo people who lived here were altering their social and religious organization and the ways they identified with other groups (Bellorado et al. 2012; Glowacki 2010, 2011). These changes followed a difficult drought period in the mid to late 1100s and corresponded with a period of population growth and aggregation in West Central Mesa Verde between AD 1200 and 1220 (see table 4 and figure 14), ultimately leading to a disengagement from Eastern Mesa Verde practices and interactions.

Changes in sandal technology and the iconography depicted on murals and in rock art imply widespread reorganization in Western Mesa Verde influenced in part by changing relationships with and perceptions of Chaco and Aztec that altered local interactions and practices. For example, twined sandals, made of finely woven yucca with raised geometric designs on the tread or designs that were painted or dyed after production, were used until the early 1200s, subsequently being replaced by plaited sandals (Webster 2008). Webster (2008:183) suggests that twined sandals were specifically used as ceremonial dance footwear, given the amount of labor and specialized knowledge needed to make them, the intricacies of the unique geometric designs on the tread, and the impracticality of wearing finely twined fiber sandals for daily use (figure 30). Twined sandals were primarily found in great houses (Webster 2008), but in Western Mesa Verde, twined sandals and their images appeared in a variety of contexts, including domestic structures like small kivas, habitation rooms, and small to mid-sized habitation sites, near potential agricultural fields, and along restricted routes of travel (Bellorado et al. 2012). Preservation and sampling issues may help explain why twined yucca sandals were found in more-varied contexts in Western Mesa Verde, where the drier climate and numerous alcoves afforded better preservation and more research has been directed at non–great house contexts. Nevertheless, the high frequency of sandal imagery in Western Mesa Verde and the depiction of sandals on rock art panels near habitations and on the inside and outside walls of rooms and kivas (Bellorado et al. 2012) suggest that

FIGURE 30. A twined yucca sandal with brown and tan interlocking diamond design from Grand Gulch, Utah. Field Museum, Catalog Number 1468.164834, Photographer, Laurie D. Webster.

twined sandals had a different role in Western Mesa Verde culture than in other parts of the region.

The frequency of cotton textiles, twined yucca sandals, and iconography of these items in Western Mesa Verde, particularly in the Cedar Mesa and Comb Ridge locality (Bellorado et al. 2012), is especially intriguing in light of Webster's (2008:183, 186) suggestion that cotton cordage, cloth, and finished textiles and possibly twined yucca sandals may have been imported by residents of Aztec, Salmon, and the Chaco Canyon great houses from communities in southeastern Utah and northeastern Arizona (but see Teague 1998 for a discussion of the Hohokam being the source of Chaco cotton). If this was the case, then those living in Western Mesa Verde may have relied on the exchange of raw cotton and/or finished cotton and yucca products with Chacoan ritual specialists and others to obtain corn or other needed commodities (see chapter 4). This could potentially help explain why sandal iconography was commonly depicted in or near domestic settings. Twined yucca sandals fell into disuse across the northern Southwest coincident with both the decline of Chaco and the extreme drought conditions of the mid-1100s. The exceedingly dry conditions certainly would have negatively impacted sandal production. If suppliers and producers in Western Mesa Verde were no longer able to leverage cotton, finished cotton products, and twined yucca sandals as a buffering mechanism to acquire supplementary food and other resources, it would have been a true economic hardship for them. Locally, however, sandal production and iconography remained an important part of western identity, particularly for those living in the Cedar Mesa and Comb Ridge localities (Bellorado et al. 2012).

Textile imagery in other media also became less complex and bolder by the early thirteenth century, especially in Western Mesa Verde. Overall, textile imagery on rock art panels decreased and depictions of large shields, which may have been associated with the development of warrior sodalities (societies), became more common (Bellorado and Mills 2014; Schaafsma 2000). Sodalities are corporate groups that crosscut lineages, so it is interesting that sandal iconography with unique sandal designs associated with individuals was phased out and symbolism likely associated with non-kin groups appeared (Bellorado et al. 2012; Schaafsma 2000). Similarly, murals incised in the plastered walls of kivas and rooms commonly depicted woven textile iconography; however, by the early to mid-1200s painted murals that portrayed banded pottery designs and landscape representations were more common (Bellorado et al. 2012; Ortman 2008). Ortman (2008) hypothesizes that this shift in mural imagery and technology represented fundamental changes in how ancestral Pueblo people conceived of their architecture and worldview.

Other lines of evidence also indicate that people living in Western Mesa Verde were reorganizing and becoming increasingly removed from the intensifying social dynamics in the east. For example, highly visible exterior bowl designs became more common in Eastern Mesa Verde (Hegmon 1991; Mills 1999; Ortman 2000b, 2002), particularly at the large, aggregated villages with public architecture (Robinson 2005). The increased frequency of these designs co-occurred with significant population aggregation and changes in plaza layouts across the Pueblo Southwest. Since visible designs painted on bowl exteriors have been known to symbolically communicate affiliations and group identity (e.g., Bowser 2000), this co-occurrence suggests that the scale of feasting and other communal activities increased and may have involved signaling social or religious identities within and among larger groups of people (Chamberlin 2011; Mills 1999, 2007; Ortman 2000b; Potter 2000; Spielmann 1998, 2004). However, exterior bowl designs are nearly absent on western bowls, indicating that this kind of symbolic display was less important in western communal ritual practices (Robinson 2005:70–75, fig. 5.7).

There are also no multiwalled structures in Western Mesa Verde. As further discussed later, thirteenth-century religious intensification in Eastern Mesa Verde prompted the proliferation of multiwalled structures in the early 1200s (see also chapter 3). These specialized religious buildings were part of differing religious movements and revitalization efforts originating in Aztec and the largest ancestral Pueblo villages in the Mesa Verde core. The absence of these buildings is a clear indication that people living in Western Mesa Verde were not participating in these new institutions and rituals (Glowacki 2011). Instead, settlement and architectural changes in community centers suggest that in the aftermath of the severe, mid-twelfth-century drought, there were differing coping strategies as western Pueblo groups either "stayed the course" or shifted settlement locations to canyon-rim and spring settings in the early to mid-1200s (Hurst and Till 2009). Some of these differences had to do with the extent to which Pueblo groups were adhering to traditional Chacoan practices and beliefs. In some cases, such as the Bluff Great House (Cameron 2009), groups continued to live in their well-established great house communities until the mid-1200s. Current evidence suggests the great house communities were depopulated earlier than the canyon-rim community centers, a trend that hints at the possibility that groups more aligned with traditional Chacoan ideals may have needed to leave the region before other groups. The Comb Wash great house community may be an example of a particularly conservative and traditional group of Pueblo people who were committed to Chacoan prescripts, for they built what may be the only new great house in the region constructed after the mid-1100s (Hurst and Robinson 2014). Those cultural groups that settled in canyon-rim settings did not build great houses or multiwalled structures, but also they did not completely abandon past Chacoan practices and connections. As Hurst and Till (2009:77–78) point out, many of these new, canyon-rim community centers were ritually connected to earlier great houses and roads. For example, Five Acre Ruin on Mustang Mesa was connected to a late PIII period canyon-head complex by an unmistakable road. These linkages through time are similar to those noted by Fowler and Stein (1992) in Manuelito Canyon in New Mexico.

The frequency of Kayenta pottery (e.g., Tsegi Orange Ware) in the Mesa Verde core also sharply decreased by AD 1225 (Errickson 1998:73; Wilson and Blinman 1995) as the Kayenta populations contracted into their homelands (Dean 1996, 2010). In prior years, when the frequency of Kayenta-style pottery was higher, not all the pottery that came into the Mesa Verde core was directly exchanged, for some of it was procured from Mesa Verde populations in Western Mesa Verde who lived between the Kayenta areas and the Mesa Verde core. Therefore, the decrease in Kayenta pottery after AD 1225 may also reflect changing relationships between groups living in Western Mesa Verde and the Mesa Verde core, as well as a decrease in the availability of Kayenta pottery. Although the Kayenta withdrawal changed western interaction networks, some connections between Mesa Verde and Kayenta Pueblo people were maintained, particularly in Western Mesa Verde (e.g., Bluff Great House [Cameron 2009:305]).

An emphasis on generalized exchange networks among kin and other contacts is also evident in the production and circulation of Mesa Verde Corrugated jars in western-specific networks (see chapter 4). In the Lower San Juan, Mesa Verde Black-on-white bowls also had a relatively limited circulation. Although pottery from West Central Mesa Verde was not analyzed for the NAA study presented in chapter 4, the analyses of the pottery and lithic assemblages from the Bluff Great House (Cameron 2009; Ward 2004) and recent NAA from great house communities in the Comb Ridge locality (Glowacki et al. n.d.) suggest that exchange was generally becoming more localized than in previous periods.

The cultural and historical trajectory of the ancestral Pueblo people who lived in Western Mesa Verde was complex. Situated between two major cultural populations, Eastern Mesa Verde and Kayenta, Western Mesa Verde was always culturally diverse and a frontier for one group or another. Many factors contributed to this cultural diversity, from the "ebb and flow" of Kayenta population movements, to being the northwestern edge of the distribution of Chaco great houses, to forming the western portion of Central Mesa Verde. All of these factors resulted in intermixing not only between Mesa Verde and Kayenta Pueblo groups, but also with Virgin Branch and Fremont groups, as well as Chaco affiliates, and non-Chaco groups. Many of these groups were highly mobile and living in small villages, while others were more sedentary and lived in large, aggregated villages. These various groups were probably also multilingual and perhaps not just between the Kayenta and Mesa Verde populations, for the Mesa Verde Pueblo groups living in the Lower San Juan had markedly different settlement patterns and pottery procurement networks than those in the rest of the Northern San Juan (see chapters 3 and 4). This cultural diversity, and its history in this part of the region, was a major influence on the divergence between Eastern and Western Mesa Verde in the early to mid-1200s. It is an important key to understanding the process of detachment from place and the ensuing emigrations, which are further explored in the final chapter.

Aztec-Chaco

The most pervasive historical landscapes in the Southwest emerged during the late 900s and 1000s when Chaco Canyon, nearly one hundred kilometers south of the Northern San Juan region, became a preeminent ceremonial, political, and economic center for the northern Southwest.* The far-reaching influence of Chaco and subsequent developments were variably layered into the deep historical landscapes of Eastern and Western Mesa Verde (see also Cameron 2005). Much has been written about the renowned great houses of Chaco Canyon (AD 900–1150), the influence of their inhabitants across the northern Southwest, and their role in ancestral Pueblo society (e.g., chapters in Lekson 2006; Vivian 1990). The distinctive position of Chaco Canyon in Pueblo history has been studied from multiple, interrelated perspectives: economic (Cameron 2001; Judge 1979; Sebastian 1992; Toll 1991), religious and ceremonial (Crown and Wills 2003; Judge 1989; Mills 2002; Plog 2011; Renfrew 2001; Stein and Lekson 1992; Van Dyke 2007a), astronomical (Sofaer 1997), political (Earle 2001; Lekson 1999b, 2008; Plog and Heitman 2010; Wilcox 1999), and regional (Crown and Judge 1991; Kantner 2003b; Kantner and Kintigh 2006; Marshall et al. 1979; Powers et al. 1983; Roney 1992). Since this book is about Mesa Verde and what happened in the 1200s, I do not attempt a comprehensive discussion of Chaco, particularly when

---

*Some might view the use of the "Aztec-Chaco" label as neglecting to acknowledge the unique identity of Aztec and the local history of the Totah (Middle San Juan), which is of course not my intention. I do not use "Aztec-Chaco" to refer to the place; instead, I use it to refer to the ideological and religious complex associated with Aztec, which had a long history of development and was deeply rooted in that of Chaco.

many others have written much more knowledgeably and eloquently on the topic. Nonetheless, the occupants of the twelve iconic great houses in Chaco Canyon had extensive influence across much of the northern Southwest for nearly two centuries—influence that decidedly affected the inhabitants of the Northern San Juan.

Chaco Canyon was central to an extensive multiscalar network (i.e., the Chacoan regional system [Judge 1991; Judge and Schelberg 1984]) that variably influenced ancestral Pueblo people across the Colorado Plateau and other cultural groups farther south. The distribution of more than 250 great house communities that architecturally reference great houses in Chaco Canyon (Chaco Research Archive 2013; Kantner 2003b:table 1; Powers et al. 1983) indicates widespread connections to Chaco across the northern Southwest. As noted in chapter 4, the people and rituals of Chaco Canyon also facilitated the circulation of utilitarian goods and exotic items like copper bells, macaws, and turquoise across the Southwest and into northern Mexico (Betancourt et al. 1986; Cameron and Toll 2001; Cordell et al. 2008; Toll 1991; Windes and McKenna 2001:124, 134–36). Whatever else Chaco Canyon may have been, it was a religiously powerful place that played key roles in economic, ceremonial, and political relationships across the northern Southwest. Thus, when Chaco began to decline and social cohesion weakened, there were wide-ranging impacts across the Pueblo Southwest that disrupted religious and economic networks while everyone figured out "life after Chaco." These repercussions were most direct in the Northern San Juan, for it was there, along the Animas River, that Aztec, a new ceremonial and political center and progeny of Chaco, was established in the late 1000s and early 1100s (Brown et al. 2008; Lister and Lister 1987; Morris 1928). Thus, in the north, figuring out "life after Chaco" also meant negotiating "life with Aztec." The founding of Aztec was a major regional development that eventually resulted in reinventing the ceremonial and political power of Chaco ideology in the north (Brown et al. 2008; Cameron and Duff 2008; Judge 1989, 2002; Lekson 1999b, 2008; Lipe 2006; Van Dyke 2008). This conversion did not happen overnight, however, nor was Aztec the only game in town.

Aztec North, the earliest building in the Aztec complex, was established in the late 1000s during a period of widespread immigration in the Northern San Juan. Population in the Totah began to increase in the mid-1000s and had increased by more than 80 percent by the late 1000s and early 1100s, coincident with the establishment of great houses including Salmon, Aztec North, and Aztec West (Brown et al. 2013; Reed 2011). The extent to which population increased after AD 1060 in the Totah and McElmo subregions can be accounted for only by the arrival of new people to these areas (Brown et al. 2013; Reed 2011;

Varien et al. 2007, 2008). In the McElmo subregion, for example, this period had the highest rate of population growth for the entire ancestral Pueblo occupation of the Village Ecodynamics Project I (VEP I) study area (2.0 percent [Varien et al. 2007, 2008:358]). This influx of people coincided with the proliferation of Classic Chaco-style (Bonito) great house communities across the Northern San Juan (Brown et al. 2013; Brown et al. 2008; Cameron 2005, 2009; Reed 2011; Varien et al. 2007). In addition to Aztec North, great houses like Jaquez, Morris 41, and Salmon were all established in the Totah between AD 1060 and 1100 (McKenna and Toll 1992; Reed 2008a; Van Dyke 2008). Numerous great houses were also established in Central Mesa Verde sites, including Yellow Jacket Pueblo, Lancaster, Albert Porter, Lowry, Bluff Great House, Et Al, and Owen (Cameron 2009; Fast 2012; Glowacki and Ortman 2012; Martin 1936; Ryan 2008, 2010; Varien et al. 2008). Many of these great houses, including Salmon and Aztec North, were constructed between AD 1075 and the 1090s (Brown et al. 2008; Reed 2006b, 2008b; Varien et al. 2008).

The Chacoan expansion across the northern Southwest in the mid to late eleventh century coincides with the most intensive period of great house construction and modification in Chaco Canyon (i.e., AD 1020–1120 [Lekson 1991, 1999b; Vivian 1990:234]). Paradoxically, this intensified construction and the spread of great houses beyond Chaco Canyon also corresponded with dry conditions and low agricultural productivity that were particularly acute during the 1080s and 1090s (Sebastian 1992). These conditions would have proved challenging for the residents of Chaco Canyon and their religious leaders, particularly if religious authority was founded on the ability to maintain balance and provide bountiful harvests. As Sebastian (1992:135–38) notes, there are two explanations for a Chacoan expansion in the midst of climatic downturns at the end of the eleventh century. Either it was a product of the Chacoan leadership using uncertainty and the promise of stability to expand their power and influence through increased hierarchical organization and diaspora, or it was the result of the ritual and political power of the Chacoan leaders being undermined by this uncertainty, creating social instability that was ameliorated as people moved away and new great house centers were established (see also Van Dyke 2008:336).

Importantly, climatic conditions elsewhere in the Southwest were not much better than those at Chaco Canyon, for there was also drought during the 1090s in the Northern San Juan region (Van West and Dean 2000; Wright 2010). Another important consideration is that settlement data for McElmo and the Totah currently suggest that population was likely increasing before the climatic downturns and poor agricultural yields of the 1080s and 1090s in Chaco Canyon (i.e., AD 1060–1100

[Varien et al. 2007]). If this population growth in the Northern San Juan was the result of emigrants from Chaco Canyon and the central San Juan Basin, the motivations for leaving these areas had more to do with social dynamics and politics than environmental factors, at least at the beginning. Therefore, another possibility is that both hegemony and factionalism were involved in the Chaco expansion. The initial impetus may have come from the Chaco leadership and groups within Chaco Canyon (Brown et al. 2008; Irwin-Williams 2008; Lekson 1999b; Reed 2008a; Sebastian 1992; Wilcox 1999), but once the climatic hardships of the 1090s settled in, their leadership and strategies were called into question and there may have been more dissension by the time Aztec was being established (Van Dyke 2008). Regardless of the degree to which factionalism or hegemony was responsible for the Chaco expansion, when and how great houses and their canons were adopted and incorporated into communities in the late 1000s and early 1100s was locally negotiated in varied social contexts that differed on a case-by-case basis in the extent to which there was resistance or acceptance of these new ideals.

Regardless of the motivations involved, the Northern San Juan may have been particularly attractive to people living in Chaco Canyon and other parts of the San Juan Basin for several reasons. During the mid-1000s, farming conditions in the region were good, with two prolonged periods of above-average precipitation, AD 1047–1066 and AD 1069–1080 (Wright 2010). Demographically, in the late 900s, population had declined, particularly in the McElmo subregion, where population density remained low until AD 1060, with the majority of the population living in small pueblos (Glowacki and Ortman 2012; Varien et al. 2007). Thus, there was social and geographic space for immigrants to move into the region and establish brand-new villages, as well as opportunities to join existing ones. Furthermore, people living in the Northern San Juan region were already predisposed to Chacoan ideologies, because several early, Classic Chaco-style great houses (pre-1060) had been established at Sterling, Morris 41, Chimney Rock, the Lakeview Group (Wallace, Ida Jean, and Haynie), the Reservoir Ruin Group, and Morefield Canyon (Glowacki 2012; Glowacki and Ortman 2012; McKenna and Toll 1992; Reed 2008a, 2008b). Therefore, the Northern San Juan may have been familiar territory to people living in Chaco Canyon and elsewhere in the San Juan Basin. These connections could have been particularly deeply rooted if, as Wilshusen and Van Dyke (2006) have proposed, the large PI pueblos in Central Mesa Verde, like McPhee Village, were proto–great houses and when ancestral Pueblo people left the Mesa Verde region at the end of the 800s and early 900s they moved to the areas in and around Chaco Canyon (see also Windes 2004). In addition to these early great houses, new syntheses of settlement patterns on Mesa Verde Proper indicate that although population declined there in the 900s, much as in the rest of the region, it did not decrease as dramatically. Not only that, population levels on the Mesa Verde uplift rebounded more rapidly after this depopulation than elsewhere in the region, particularly between AD 1020 and 1060 (Glowacki 2012; Kleidon et al. 2003; Schwindt et al. 2014). Thus, Mesa Verde Proper was an important locale during this period and may have had strong ties to Chaco Canyon. One of the largest ancestral Pueblo villages on the Mesa Verde uplift was Morefield Canyon Great House Village (AD 920–1140), with twenty-nine room blocks, forty-eight pit structures, a great house, a plaza, and two great kivas (Glowacki 2012; Kleidon et al. 2003). This community center was well established, with at least one great kiva, by the end of the tenth century (McLellan 1969), even if the great house was not built until the mid to late 1000s. It was well positioned to be an important locale in the region—one that may have been well-known to those living in Chaco Canyon.

Although many great houses were established in the late 1000s, Aztec North and Salmon were clearly different. The groups that immigrated to these places brought potent ritual knowledge with them either at the behest of Chaco leadership or in spite of it. Van Dyke's (2003) comparative architectural study of 188 great houses across the Southwest found that the attributes and layout of Aztec and Salmon were highly similar to those in Chaco Canyon. Our understanding of Salmon and its broader social context has been greatly advanced by the recent synthesis of a decade of research by Cynthia Irwin-Williams and the San Juan Valley Archaeological Program (SJVAP) in the 1970s (Reed 2006a). Salmon was a planned endeavor built in a location where there was no prior residential use and enough space to build one of the largest great houses outside of Chaco Canyon (Reed 2006a, 2008b). The significant cluster of tree-ring dates between AD 1087 and 1090 indicates stockpiling and a concerted, rapid construction episode at the end of the eleventh century (Windes and Bacha 2008). The initial Chacoan-phase building had 250 rooms, and in its final form, Salmon had an estimated 300 rooms with as many as three stories in places. With core-and-veneer masonry, a symmetrical layout, a great kiva, and an elevated "tower" kiva, Salmon was an important residential and ritual Chacoan regional center with clear ties to Chaco Canyon (Irwin-Williams 2008; Reed 2008b; Van Dyke 2008).

The proximity, size, Chacoan formality, and construction episodes suggest there were also strong connections between Salmon and Aztec, which has led some to suppose that Salmon and Aztec were built by the same group of Chaco migrants (Lekson 1999b; Stein and McKenna 1988). Yet Windes and Bacha (2008) noted technological and stylistic differences in construction methods between the two centers that make it more likely that different groups were responsible for the construction of Salmon and Aztec. Though it remains difficult to demonstrate, this understanding does not preclude the possibility that individuals or families initially residing at Salmon later moved to Aztec, as suggested by Reed (2008b), especially post-1120 and during the expansion of Aztec East.

We may never know definitively whether Salmon and Aztec were established because of a coordinated effort initiated by Chaco leadership or whether a splinter group of religious leaders left Chaco Canyon with an idea to begin anew. As noted, these prospects may not have been mutually exclusive, especially if one considers the potential for a Rashomon effect, since there were likely differing interpretations about why these great houses were established, depending on social status and whether one lived in Chaco Canyon or in the Totah and elsewhere in the Northern San Juan. What we do know is that, first, both Salmon and Aztec were established in areas with little evidence of prior occupation (Lekson 1999b; McKenna 1998; Reed 2008b; Stein and McKenna 1988; Van Dyke 2008). The tabula rasa approach to locating these new and ritually charged buildings has been interpreted as an intentional strategy that allowed implementation of large-scale planned construction and symbolized a new beginning. Second, the establishment of Salmon and Aztec involved migrant groups from Chaco Canyon with specific and detailed knowledge of Chaco architecture and ritual, who also had to work and live with local populations (Reed 2008a; Van Dyke 2008; Windes and Bacha 2008); and third, both Salmon and Aztec involved duplicating specific configurations found in Chaco Canyon. The bracket-shaped layout of Salmon, for example, is often compared to Hungo Pavi (Reed 2008b; Van Dyke 2008).

The case of Aztec is most striking, as there are clear connections between the groups involved in its founding and the religious and political leaders in Chaco Canyon (Lekson 1999b; Reed 2008b, 2011; Stein and McKenna 1988). Not only did the founders have specific and potent ritual knowledge, but also they had a long-term plan to reproduce the core ritual landscape of Chaco Canyon in the Animas Valley (Lekson 1999b; McKenna and Toll 1992; Stein and McKenna 1988; Van Dyke 2008:341–44). First noted by Stein and McKenna (1988), the planned, symmetrical arrangement of the great houses of Aztec North, West, and East and associated buildings (e.g., Mound F Triwall) replicated the relationships among Pueblo Alto, Pueblo Bonito, and Chetro Ketl, respectively (figure 31). Their locations relative to nearby major drainages were also similar, though the Animas River was potentially a more reliable water source than the Chaco Wash. The emulated ritual landscape was clearly intended to imbue Aztec with the power and authority of the Chaco ritual-ideological complex, which inextricably linked Aztec to the legacy of Chaco.

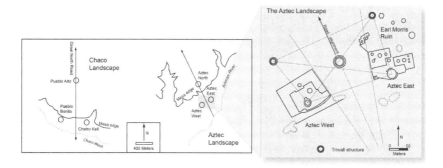

FIGURE 31. *Left*, the ritual landscapes of Aztec and Chaco compared. After Van Dyke 2007a:10, fig. 8.4, which was originally drafted by Catherine Gilman (Archaeology Southwest). *Right*, the ritual landscape of Aztec and association among buildings. After McKenna and Toll 1992:136, fig. 11-4. Illustration by Grant D. Coffey.

Aztec North, the first great house to be built, is the least understood of the Aztec great houses. Built by the 1090s and possibly earlier (Brown et al. 2013), Aztec North, with more than one hundred rooms, was situated on the mesa top overlooking the Animas floodplain. It was constructed using adobe, which is unusual for Chaco-style construction; however, adobe was more frequently used for large-scale construction in the Animas Valley (Brown and Paddock 2011). The use of adobe in Aztec North may be an indication that local groups were involved in its construction. The rest of the buildings in the Aztec complex were all sited in relation to the location of Aztec North (Stein and McKenna 1988).

Aztec West, the largest great house outside of Chaco Canyon, is southwest of Aztec North. Since much of Aztec West has been excavated, we know much more about its construction history than the rest of the Aztec complex (Lister and Lister 1987; Morris 1928). Aztec West was built as a Classic Chaco-style great house in five major episodes between AD 1100 and 1290 (Brown et al. 2008). Most of it was built during the Chaco phase (pre-1130) over the course of three major episodes using formal Chaco-style core-and-veneer masonry as well as local materials and methods such as adobe and cobble construction (Brown et al. 2008:238). Later construction episodes used the blockier McElmo- and Mesa Verde–style masonry, and although rooms were added in the later period, construction at this time primarily involved reorganization and renovation of the existing structure (Brown et al. 2008:table 12.2). By the end, the E-shaped building of Aztec West had approximately five hundred rooms, sixteen kivas, a great kiva, and an enclosed plaza.

Much of our information about the construction sequence and use of Aztec East derives from Richert's (1964) test excavations, which have been supplemented by recent stabilization, documentation, and tree-ring dating (Brown et al. 2008; Reed et al. 2010). Although there is evidence for an initial small-scale building episode around AD 1120, the tree-ring record suggests that most of Aztec East was built in the mid to late 1200s using McElmo-style masonry and a layout reminiscent of the later great houses in Chaco Canyon, like Kin Kletso (Brown et al. 2008:242–45, fig. 12.2; Richert 1964). By the end, Aztec East contained 350 rooms, nineteen kivas, a great kiva, and a plaza. The plaza at Aztec East was smaller than the large, front-oriented one at Aztec West, and Brown and his colleagues (2008, 2013) suggest that this may be due to a greater emphasis on using the blocked-in kiva courtyards in Aztec East. The construction, layout, and size of Aztec East differed from those of Aztec West, and its architecture more closely reflects the substantial social, political, and ceremonial changes of the thirteenth century. Nearby and north of Aztec East, the Earl Morris ruin is a small McElmo-style great house with 85–100 rooms (Brown et al. 2013). As more fully described in chapter 3, the Aztec complex also contains five multiwalled structures including the Hubbard Triwall, two other triwalls (the central Mound F and Mound A), and two biwalls, Mounds B and C (Reed et al. 2010; Richert 1964; Vivian 1959).

At the turn of the twelfth century, the establishment of the great house complex at Aztec dramatically altered the social, political, and ritual landscape, locally and regionally. In the Totah, population continued increasing into the late 1100s, and at least seven new community centers were established (see chapter 3; table 5). Of the fifty-nine community centers identified in the Totah, 70 percent ($n = 41$) were multicomponent, with long histories of occupation beginning in the late PI (AD 750–950) or early PII (AD 950–1150) period. Therefore, the history of Chaco and the establishment of Aztec were strong influences on the histories of these ancestral Pueblo villages. This influence is evident in the high frequency of great houses and great kivas at Totah community centers and the high room-to-kiva ratios (12:1 [see table 7]) that were more similar to those found in Chacoan great house community organization. Aztec was, of course, one of the primate centers in the Northern San Juan, and there were also five second-order community centers in the Totah: Morris 41, Salmon, the Holmes Group, Morris 39, and Kello Blancett (see chapter 3), located along the La Plata, Animas, and San Juan drainages where these rivers converge (figure 32).

The distribution of great houses across the Northern San Juan is a manifestation of the traditional Chaco historical landscape that included and was eventually transformed by Aztec (i.e., became Aztec-Chaco).

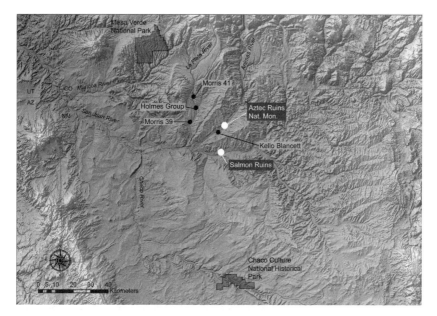

FIGURE 32. Distribution of the largest community centers in the Totah. Illustration by Grant D. Coffey.

Great houses were built and used in all of the subregions ($n = 59$ at sites with a PIII component [see figure 20 and table 8]); thus, Chaco-based ideologies and practices were elements of both the eastern and western historical landscapes. To some degree, the Chaco expansion was a unifying force among different Pueblo cultural groups, but these circumstances changed after Aztec was established, altering local and regional politics and relationships that were then tested by new climatic and environmental hardships that could not be ignored.

The Chaco to Post-Chaco Transition: The Forging of Aztec-Chaco

The beginning of the Chaco to Post-Chaco transition (AD 1130–1180) was manifested by the establishment of Aztec in the early 1100s and the subsequent dynamics as Chaco declined. This period of concentrated sociopolitical upheaval and violent conflict occurred during particularly harsh climatic and environmental conditions and was a pivotal point— one that demanded significant cultural change and created contingencies that forever altered the nature of the ancestral Pueblo occupation of the Northern San Juan. The primary stimulus for this turmoil was the onset of the AD 1130–1180 megadrought (Cook et al. 2004). This was no ordinary drought. As the most severe drought between AD 900 and AD 1300, its severity, intensity, and duration were such that cultural groups across the Southwest were ill-prepared to cope with the harsh conditions, having never experienced a similarly severe event in their recent past. People everywhere were forced to make drastic changes. In the Central Mesa Verde region, the effects of this severe drought were compounded by additional environmental challenges including low water tables, stream entrenchment, and degraded floodplains (Van West and Dean 2000:37), which made farming, an already besieged endeavor, even more difficult. This combination of drought and environmental hardship was a game changer, one that recast the social landscape by causing people to make substantial changes in long-established practices.

In Chaco Canyon, the process of decline, despite the severe drought, was slow, taking place over at least a generation or more, depending on how you define its end as an important ceremonial center (Van Dyke 2008). Here, as in the Mesa Verde core during the mid to late 1200s, social and cultural change preceded the drought, and in the early 1100s, new McElmo-style great houses—small, rectangular or square structures with blocky masonry and blocked-in kivas, but no plazas—as exemplified by Kin Kletso, Casa Chiquita, and New Alto (Lekson 1986; Vivian and Mathews 1965) were constructed during one of the best periods for agricultural production in the history of the occupation of Chaco Canyon (Sebastian 1992:134). This new style of great house construction has been interpreted as representing Mesa Verde immigration into Chaco Canyon, since the blocky masonry used is similar to that found in the Northern San Juan (e.g., Vivian and Mathews 1965), and also as a local innovation initiated by Chaco leaders, perhaps in an effort to renew confidence in their authority after the 1090s drought (Lekson 1986; Van Dyke 2004). In either case, the construction of McElmo-style great houses signaled a pronounced organizational change, since these structures housed smaller groups of people and required less labor and fewer resources, including timbers, than did the Classic Chaco-style great houses. These characteristics suggest some level of sociopolitical reorganization and a diminished capacity for marshaling the labor and resources to build large great houses using the intensive core-and-veneer construction with tabular masonry, which had been so iconic.

At roughly the same time as McElmo-style great houses were built in Chaco Canyon (i.e., early 1100s), Aztec West—a large and clearly Classic Chaco-style great house—was built in the Totah. The strong adherence to replicating the core of the Chaco ritual landscape at Aztec seems contradictory given the architectural changes in Chaco Canyon, lending some support to the possibility that social disruptions in Chaco Canyon may have caused a traditionalist splinter group to relocate and establish Aztec (Van Dyke 2008). As the megadrought of the mid-1100s gained traction, dynamics in Chaco Canyon continued to shift. Connections to Aztec reinvigorated social networks toward the north, while existing relationships with those to the west in the Chuskas dwindled. For example, the organization of pottery production changed, as the frequency of organic painted pottery with northern influences that required less fuelwood to make increased and the frequency of Chuska pottery decreased, which corresponded with a decline in the Chuskan population (Toll 2001; Vivian 1990:382).

The combination of severe drought and societal change appears to have weakened the ceremonial, economic, and political system centered on Chaco Canyon, and Aztec was well positioned to be its successor. The ascendancy of Aztec was not without its own challenges, however, for a number of changes also happened in the Northern San Juan region during the mid-1100s megadrought. First, settlement patterns during the severe drought conditions changed as more people began living in smaller residential sites that were increasingly located in canyon settings rather than aggregating in larger ones on mesa tops and ridges (Glowacki and Ortman 2012; Lipe 1995:153; Lipe and Varien 1999b:303, 312; Varien 1999:149). In the VEP I study area (McElmo), for example, in those areas with full-coverage survey, only an estimated 30 percent of the population lived in community centers during the mid-1100s. The dispersed settlement pattern comprising small habitations favored in the mid-1100s differs from those of the 800s and late 1200s, when we see evidence of intensified aggregation during serious droughts followed by differing levels of depopulation (Glowacki and Ortman 2012; Varien et al. 2007). It is an important difference, one that may have allowed for more flexibility and a quicker rebound, because subsequent to the mid-1100s drought, population increased (as opposed to decreased).

The shift to canyon settings was a virtually region-wide trend occurring on canyon rims, at canyon heads, on talus slopes, and in alcoves in Mesa Verde Proper (Hayes 1964:109–10; Lipe 1995:153; Nickens 1981:39), the Lower San Juan (Bedell 2000; Lipe 1970:123; Matson et al. 1988:254–55), and McElmo and West Central Mesa Verde (Lipe and Ortman 2000; Ortman et al. 2000; Varien 1999). The topography of the Totah precluded canyon-oriented sites; instead, settlements in that subregion became increasingly concentrated in the river valleys (McKenna 1998; McKenna and Toll 1992:134; Stein and McKenna 1988). The shift to canyon settings has long been associated with the need for defense and access to water in the 1200s (e.g., Varien et al. 1996). However, new studies indicate that the timing of this marked change in settlement locations happened earlier, coincident with the drought and social contexts of the Chaco to Post-Chaco transition. Recent analysis of VEP community center data (Glowacki and Ortman 2012:table 14.1) shows that centers were predominantly built in canyon-rim and spring settings after AD 1140. In the Upper Cliff Canyon locality on Chapin Mesa (Mesa Verde Proper), which includes Cliff Palace, ceramic seriation of 2,600 sherds from 107 sites also shows a gradual shift in settlement location toward the head of Cliff Canyon (figure 33; Kleidon et al. 2007). From AD 1025 to 1140, habitations were situated in primarily upland settings, particularly just west of Cliff Canyon in a persistent community cluster that was occupied since at least the AD 800s. Between AD 1140 and 1180, settlement locations changed dramatically when this persistent community disappeared, and new residences, including the cliff dwellings known as Three Clan Dwelling (5MV514) and Mummy House (5MV520), were built near drainages and on canyon rims. In West Central Mesa Verde, however, sites dating to the mid to late 1100s were primarily located on mesa tops and ridges, and the shift to canyon settings did not happen until the 1200s (Hurst and Robinson 2014; Hurst and Till 2009). This difference in timing may relate to demographic trends, as population levels in this much drier part of the region were low during the mid to late 1100s, when people were also likely leaving the area because of the drought, and the population began to increase by AD 1200, when canyon rim settlements also increased.

Situated on canyon rims, settlements were near seep springs and drainages where the use of check dams would enhance agricultural productivity—a definite advantage during severe drought. Moving to canyon settings affected land use practices and likely led to increased territorialism. Canyon settings, and their presumed advantages, continued to be increasingly important for the remainder of the regional occupation,

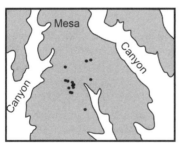
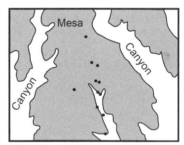

AD 1025 – 1140   AD 1140 – 1180

FIGURE 33. Site location changes in the Cliff Canyon locality in Mesa Verde National Park, showing the shift to canyon-rim and spring locations. Illustration by Grant D. Coffey.

particularly in Mesa Verde Proper, where cliff dwelling construction peaked in the mid-1200s (Brisbin et al. 2007; Fiero 1999; Glowacki 2006b; Nordby 2001).

The second dynamic affecting the Northern San Juan region during the mid-1100s drought was unprecedented levels of violence that testify to the extreme severity of this period. The comparison of the incidence of skeletal trauma (violence) with population growth from AD 600 to 1300 indicates atypically high levels of violence in McElmo during the 1100s for the number of people living there (Cole 2012; Kohler et al. 2014), a pattern driven in part by the high incidence of dismemberment and postmortem processing that characterized violence during this period (Billman et al. 2000; Kuckelman et al. 2000:table 1). Figure 34 shows the locations of sites with evidence of violent deaths during the 1100s and identifies nine sites in McElmo, two sites in Mesa Verde Proper, and one in the Totah (Billman et al. 2000; Kuckelman et al. 2000:table 1, fig. 1; Lipe 2006; Morris 1939:105; Toll 1993). The distribution and intensity of this violence suggests that fighting and conflict were widespread in Eastern Mesa Verde during the mid-1100s, though perhaps most prevalent in McElmo.

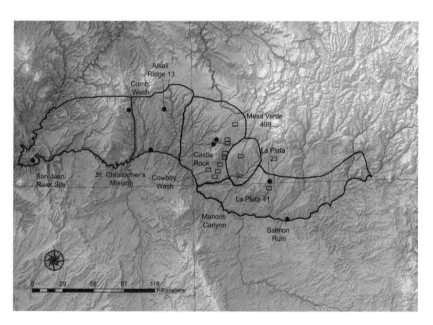

FIGURE 34. Distribution of evidence of violence during the Pueblo II and Pueblo III periods. Sites indicated by open boxes were occupied from the late Pueblo II to early Pueblo III period, and those indicated by filled circles were occupied in the mid to late 1200s. After Kuckelman et al. 2000:fig. 1; illustration by Grant D. Coffey.

Among the likely reasons for this manifest violence were raiding for much-needed resources, personal vendettas, territorial disputes, and sociopolitical conflict as the leadership at Aztec asserted itself in the region—all of which were exacerbated by the stress and uncertainty produced by the extreme drought. In a particularly gruesome case, in the Montezuma Valley west of Ute Mountain, twenty-four residents of the southern Piedmont community of Cowboy Wash were brutally killed and butchered in a single catastrophic event (Billman 2008; Billman et al. 2000). Excavation of four of the ten small habitations in this community uncovered not only human remains of men and women of all ages but also evidence that these people were butchered, roasted, and consumed (Billman et al. 2000). This and the presence of floor assemblages with numerous artifacts including whole pots, metates, baskets, and a blanket, plus evidence of burning in some of the pit structures, indicates that the occupation of the Cowboy Wash community ended suddenly when the residents were overcome by an outside group. That the evidence of extreme violence and postmortem processing was pervasive in all of the excavated habitations, and possibly more was present in the unexcavated habitations, indicates that the residents of Cowboy Wash were victims of a coordinated, large-scale attack. Significantly, the Cowboy Wash community pottery assemblages contained among the highest frequency of Chuskan pottery in the Mesa Verde core, ranging from 1.5 to 30 percent (Billman 2008:57; Errickson 1993), implying that either the residents of this community were Chuskan immigrants themselves or they had strong and active connections with those living in the Chuskas. This is an important point, for the implication is that this attack was perpetrated against a community whose history differed from that of many others in the Mesa Verde core—one that was directly or indirectly associated with the Chacoan diaspora in the late eleventh century.

Billman (2008) concluded that the Cowboy Wash attack was likely motivated by psychosocial stress that was heightened as agricultural productivity continued to be dangerously low with no end to the drought in sight, which undermined faith in sociopolitical and ceremonial relationships, particularly with Chaco in decline. These difficulties caused neighboring groups to raid each other, and since the Cowboy Wash community was smaller and more isolated than other communities and was more connected with groups outside the region, it was vulnerable to attack. These dynamics were most certainly at play, but I would also suggest that the attack on Cowboy Wash may have been evidence of warfare between groups motivated by growing ideological and political differences. As conditions continued to deteriorate, many people would have become increasingly distrustful of Chacoan leadership and ceremonialism. Those more closely tied to traditional Chaco ideologies and having strong connections to Chaco and Aztec, as its proxy, may have become targets.

The Cowboy Wash community was one of several communities along the Montezuma Valley with evident violence during the mid-1100s (see figure 34). This important corridor into the Mesa Verde core was apparently a much-contested landscape during the Chaco to Post-Chaco transition and may very well have become a political boundary, particularly if ideological schisms had formed and groups were rebelling against Aztec in light of perceived ritual failure. It is likely no accident that a series of large, late community centers, including Yucca House, were established in the Montezuma Valley subsequent to this contentious time.

With the seemingly relentless drought and widespread violence, as a newly established ceremonial and political center, Aztec had much to overcome. The trying social and climatic conditions that lasted throughout the mid to late 1100s significantly curtailed the ability of the Aztec leadership to replicate Chaco (Lekson 1999a:159, 2008; Lipe 2006), if that was in fact their goal. The extensive labor and economic networks that seemed a hallmark of the established Chacoan social order were not maintained at Aztec after AD 1130. Large-scale, planned construction episodes also ceased (Brown et al. 2008; Lipe 2006), and the construction that was undertaken increasingly used local juniper wood rather than more-distant large timbers, such as ponderosa pine (Windes and Bacha 2008). The frequency of long-distance, imported ceramics and lithics also markedly declined (Brown et al. 2008; Lipe 2006), and intraregionally the frequency of imported bowls was low compared with that in Chaco Canyon (see below). These differences in regional interactions and the lack of organized resource procurement and large-scale construction post-1130 imply that Aztec had to scale back, creating increased parity with the other large community centers of the Mesa Verde core (Lipe 2006). In short, "life with Aztec" was different from "life with Chaco."

Another key difference was that much of the resources and possibly labor to construct and sustain Chaco came from the Chuskas. There was not, however, necessarily a correlate for Aztec. Although Lekson (1999a:102) draws a parallel relationship between Aztec and the Montezuma Valley (a part of the McElmo subregion), my analyses suggest that the relationships between Aztec (Totah) and McElmo were not like those between Chaco and the Chuskas. First, the organization of pottery production and procurement differed. NAA data show that imported pottery more frequently came into the Totah from Mesa Verde Proper rather than McElmo. Toll (2001:59) estimated that nearly 50 percent of the white ware in Chaco was imported, whereas NAA results indicate that only 10 percent of the bowls sampled from Aztec were imported (see table

9), thus, much more was locally produced (see also Reed 2008b). The differences in sample size between these two studies, which were significant, may account for this variance. However, recent temper and paste analyses of Aztec pottery assemblages by Lori Reed (2013), based on two analyses with more than 7,000 sherds primarily from Aztec West, identified similar frequencies of nonlocal white wares (i.e., about 15 percent). Pottery was not exported from Chaco Canyon to the Chuskas, or elsewhere for that matter; in contrast, residents of Aztec and La Plata sites exported an estimated 19 percent of their bowls to McElmo and a small amount to Mesa Verde Proper (see table 13). Second, settlement patterns also differed. The territory between Chaco Canyon and the Chuskas had a low population density and dispersed settlement pattern, but Mesa Verde Proper, which had a high population density (see table 2), was situated between Aztec and the McElmo subregion. Finally, community centers in the McElmo subregion during the 1200s were a major force driving sociopolitical and ceremonial organization and interaction in the Northern San Juan. Although there were some similarly large sites in the Chuskas, such as Skunk Springs (Lekson 1999b; Powers et al. 1983; Stein and Fowler 1996; Vivian 1990), the McElmo subregion had a much higher population density and more large centers than the Chuska region.

This does not mean that Lekson's suggestion is completely without merit, however, for it may be that the population of Mesa Verde Proper was more analogous to the Chuskan population than the McElmo population was. Current evidence suggests that the ancestral Pueblo population living in Mesa Verde Proper may have had stronger connections with Aztec and the Totah, at least for a time. Population density was particularly high on Mesa Verde Proper during the PII period (AD 950–1150), especially along the eastern portion of the Mesa Verde uplift (Glowacki 2012; Kleidon et al. 2003). The closer proximity of this major population center to the Totah and Aztec would suggest higher frequencies of interaction among people living in these two areas. This inference is supported by the NAA data, which shows the Totah having higher frequencies of pottery circulation with those living in Mesa Verde Proper than those living in the McElmo subregion (see chapter 4). There were clearly strong social networks between these populations, and the nature of these connections needs to be better understood. However, the relationship between these two areas still differed from that of Chaco and the Chuskas, for the strongest ties that people living in Mesa Verde Proper had through pottery circulation were with those in McElmo (see chapter 4), and by the 1200s, changes in settlement created increasing social and spatial separation from the Totah (see also chapter 7).

Further evidence that the severity of social and climatic conditions impinged on the influence of the Aztec leadership is the cessation of great house construction at villages established after AD 1140 (Glowacki and Ortman 2012; Lipe 2006:276, 293; Lipe and Varien 1999a:260). Certainly the megadrought made new construction, especially major projects like a new great house, difficult. The low number of tree-ring dates in the mid-1100s supports this inference, provided that the sampling is not terribly skewed (Lipe 2006:276; Lipe and Varien 1999b; Varien 1999). Not everyone was stymied by these conditions, however, for recent evidence indicates that there was some mid-1100s construction at large sites, such as Albert Porter and Woods Canyon Pueblo (Glowacki and Ortman 2012; Ortman et al. 2000; Ryan 2010; Varien et al. 2007). Nonetheless, when conditions improved, Classic Chaco-style great houses were still not constructed at new aggregated villages (but see chapter 6 for possible exceptions; see also Glowacki and Ortman 2012). The cessation of new great house construction signifies a significant change in ideas about maintaining traditional Chacoan ideologies and ritual organization that emerged during this incredibly difficult period as Chaco declined and Aztec struggled (Glowacki 2010, 2011; Lipe 2006:276). Although existing great houses continued to be used and modified throughout the 1200s (Cameron 2009; Lekson and Cameron 1995; Ryan 2010), as people moved past the challenging social and climatic contexts of the mid to late 1100s, new ways of organizing villages and religious practices developed.

Revitalization and Rebound

After the severe drought subsided, the turn of the thirteenth century was a period of recovery and rebound for everyone, which also brought major social and cultural changes. In some sense, this was when Aztec became the driving force behind Aztec-Chaco ideology, as Chaco's influence had waned. Dramatic changes at the Aztec complex in the 1200s indicate that reinvestment in construction and reorganization was among the post-drought strategies employed by the Aztec-Chaco leadership. First, there was a dramatic shift in the way the Aztec West great house was occupied in the early 1200s (Brown et al. 2008; Diederichs et al. 2011). The number of people living in Aztec West increased because of either in situ population growth or immigration (Brown et al. 2008). New construction at Aztec West included the Annex, which added seven room blocks and sixteen kivas. This addition was not preplanned; it was tacked on and did not adhere to the Chacoan blueprint used to build the rest of the great house. Another change is that first- and second-story rooms at Aztec West were plastered with bichrome dado schemes in which the lower half of the wall was painted red and the upper half a lighter color such as tan

(Diederichs et al. 2011; Morris 1928). These schemes are common at cliff dwellings, such as Spruce Tree House, suggesting shared cultural conventions between those living at Aztec and Mesa Verde Proper (Diederichs et al. 2011).

Most of Aztec East was built during the thirteenth century (with major construction episodes in AD 1200–1220 and AD 1240–1250); thus, Aztec East played a central role in the revitalization of Aztec in the aftermath of the devastating mid-1100s. Aztec East was likely established before the peak construction periods, however, for there is a cluster of earlier dates between AD 1110 and 1120 (Brown et al. 2008:fig. 12.2; Richert 1964). Richert (1964:12–13) noted that Gladwin interpreted the eight earlier dates obtained during Richert's excavation as reuse beams that were scavenged from Aztec West, and Richert believed that the rooms he excavated (i.e., Rooms 8–14 and 24 and the kiva above Room 1) were built sometime after AD 1200. However, on the basis of both the tree-ring dates obtained through Richert's excavation and additional dates obtained from standing architecture and intact roofs (a total of 297 dates), Brown and his colleagues (2008) concluded that the cluster of dates between AD 1115 and 1120 represents initial construction at Aztec East, not reused beams. This claim is bolstered by the identification of rooms that contained only dates in the 1100s (assuming that the sample from the room is representative) and rooms where the primary beams dated to the 1100s but lintels and roofs may have been repaired in the 1200s. The initial construction of Aztec East at roughly the same time as Aztec West also makes more sense given what seems to be the intentional emulation of the configurations found at Chaco Canyon (see figure 31; Stein and McKenna 1988; Van Dyke 2007a).

Regardless of when initial construction began, Aztec East and Aztec West had clearly different histories. The history of Aztec West was predominantly influenced by the contexts of the initial establishment of Aztec, whereas the history of Aztec East was much more related to revitalization and Chacoan revival in the 1200s. The new, thirteenth-century construction at Aztec East was rooted in traditional tenets, for there were clear examples of Chacoan-style masonry and a conventional great house layout was followed; however, this was not the case for the 1200s construction at Aztec West (Brown et al. 2008:245). This conspicuous difference between Aztec East and West in the style and types of construction in the 1200s may relate to practical considerations, but another possibility is that there were multiple groups at Aztec with differing ideas about what they should be doing. Elsewhere in the Northern San Juan, there was also evidence of remodeling or expansion of existing great houses (Cameron 2009; Lekson and Cameron 1995; Ryan 2010), as well as of divergence since most large villages established after the mid-1100s did not include a great house (see chapter 3; see also Glowacki and Ortman 2012).

The Aztec-Chaco religious leaders—no strangers to revitalization as a strategy, since Aztec itself may have been established with this purpose in mind—also built a brand-new type of religious building, presumably as part of a new religious movement to affirm the potency of Aztec-Chaco ideology. Multiwalled structures—specialized buildings with a row or rows of contiguous rooms, typically circular or D-shaped in form, surrounding one or more kivas—began appearing at community centers in the late 1100s or early 1200s (see chapter 3). That Aztec had five circular, multiwalled structures (Reed et al. 2010; Stein and McKenna 1988) and nearly every other large pueblo in Eastern Mesa Verde with multiwalled structures had only one implies that the circular form was strongly associated with Aztec-Chaco religio-political organization (Lekson 1983, 2008; Stein and McKenna 1988).

As described in chapter 3, evidence for the timing of the construction of circular multiwalled structures is inconclusive. Given what we know, these buildings were constructed after the severe drought, at the very end of the 1100s or, more likely, during the early 1200s. Lekson (1999a, 2008) suggests, because of the triwall constructed at Pueblo del Arroyo, that the impetus for these structures came from Chaco Canyon. However, given the inconclusive dating of both the triwall at Pueblo del Arroyo and those at Aztec, it is equally plausible to me that these structures were originally built at Aztec by the Aztec-Chaco leadership and subsequently, or perhaps in tandem, the one at Pueblo del Arroyo was built to reinforce the symbolic connections with Chaco.

The changing influence of the Aztec-Chaco ideological complex in Mesa Verde society and its associated historical landscape can be inferred by the shift from great houses that signaled connections to traditional Chaco to circular multiwalled structures indicative of an Aztec-Chaco revitalization movement (see chapter 3; Lekson 2008; Stein and McKenna 1988). The distribution of villages with great houses indicates that during Chaco's prime there was widespread participation in its broader sociopolitical and ceremonial organization across the Northern San Juan region. The distribution of multiwalled structures was more limited, however. Multiwalled structures were built only in Eastern Mesa Verde and were most common in the McElmo subregion, where there were both circular and D-shaped forms (see below). Despite the presence of great house communities in Western Mesa Verde, there were no multiwalled structures there. This strong pattern suggests that the influence of Aztec-Chaco was not as pervasive across the Northern San Juan as that of Chaco.

Aztec, as a historical landscape, had a powerful influence that was deeply connected with Chaco, even if much had changed by the thirteenth century. At its inception, Aztec was poised to be the New Chaco of the North, but Chaco's decline and the severity of the social and climatic conditions in the mid-1100s had repercussions for Aztec. Although there were evident efforts to revitalize the strength and influence of Aztec, the regional response to these efforts to perpetuate the system was varied; evidence suggests that Western Mesa Verde was disengaging from Aztec and its new religious movements and that the Mesa Verde core was balkanizing (see chapters 6 and 7).

The McElmo Intensification, AD 1220–1260

The most intense, if short-lived, historical landscape of the ancestral Pueblo occupation of the Northern San Juan can be seen in the rapid population growth and attendant social and cultural changes in the Mesa Verde core during the early 1200s. Much of this growth and intensification centered on the McElmo subregion, where the rapid increase in the size and density of community centers transformed social, ritual, and political relationships, which apparently resulted in factionalization and schisms among villages and cultural groups. Of the many factors leading to the Mesa Verde migrations, the McElmo Intensification and the ensuing social upheaval was probably one of the main catalysts behind widespread emigration from the region.

In large part, the severe social and climatic conditions of the mid to late 1100s set the stage for intensified population aggregation and ceremonialism in the 1200s. Among other factors, the relocation to canyon-rim settings and reactions to the intense violence and evident warfare during the Chaco to Post-Chaco transition (discussed above) reconfigured social networks and settlement patterns in ways that promoted aggregation and increased residential proximity. In McElmo, ancestral Pueblo villages that would become among the largest in the region were well established prior to the mid-twelfth century drought (i.e., Yellow Jacket Pueblo, Goodman Point–Shields, Lancaster, and Hedley; see table 8). These community centers were situated on or near optimal agricultural land, which likely afforded their residents greater stability than their neighbors experienced during the dire drought conditions in the late twelfth century. Many of these centers had stable occupations or even grew, if only slightly, during the mid to late 1100s (Ryan 2010; Varien et al. 2008). The stability provided by these key community centers may have made the McElmo area, and living in larger villages, seem an attractive alternative, because when the drought conditions abated after AD 1180, at least thirteen new community centers were established, and twenty-six more were founded between AD 1220 and 1240 (see table 5). In the end, the scale and degree to which aggregation and residential proximity occurred in the McElmo subregion far exceeded what happened elsewhere in the region (see chapter 3), such that by the mid to late 1200s, much of the population was living in large, aggregated villages (Glowacki and Ortman 2012; Varien et al. 2007).

Aggregation has both advantages and disadvantages. In the uncertain contexts of the late 1100s, living in large villages could have been advantageous because larger social groups could provide mechanisms for buffering agricultural yields during difficult periods, for protecting residents against external threats, for mitigating access to resources, and for resolving disputes (Adler 1994, 1996; Cordell 1996:230–33; Cordell et al. 1994; Kintigh 1994; Kohler 1992; LeBlanc 1999; Orcutt 1991; Stone 1994; Van West and Kohler 1996). However, aggregation, particularly if it happens rapidly, also affects interpersonal relations within and between villages. Integrating new groups of people, whether they are local or immigrants from elsewhere, can be a difficult process, one that often creates social tensions as people renegotiate relationships, cultural identities, and practices. Resolving tensions created during acculturation and syncretism can also lead to substantial organizational change within communities to accommodate diverse perspectives and ideals (Adler 1996; Bernardini 1996; Crown and Kohler 1994), which can have both good and bad consequences. Another disadvantage is that aggregated communities can become too large and unwieldy, making their residents more susceptible to vulnerabilities because they are unable to quickly respond to problems when they arise (Hegmon et al. 2008).

During the first half of the 1200s, as population increased and the available land filled up, community centers were not only larger and more aggregated but also more concentrated than ever before (Varien 1999). As distances between pueblos of all sizes decreased, mobility and access to productive farmland required negotiation among more and larger groups—interactions that would be further complicated during environmentally unfavorable periods. These dynamics became strong social stressors when resource catchments used by villages and households began to encroach on others, engendering an increasingly contested landscape (Varien et al. 2000).

Organizational Change and Religion

The changes that happened in the aftermath of the mid to late 1100s were significant and ultimately stimulated the reconceptualization of fundamental aspects of Pueblo culture, with long-lasting implications. Pauketat (2011:232) summarized this transformation as a "notable shift away from the outward-looking, all-encompassing visual culture of Chaco and its Pueblo III period descendants toward the inward-turned, centripetal visual culture of the Pueblo IV period." The cultural and organizational changes that took place during the McElmo Intensification were part of the kinetic chain of events and processes that cascaded across the pre-Hispanic Pueblo world and resulted in the transformation of a culture predicated on a Chacoan ideology that was vertically oriented to one that was more horizontally oriented and inward-looking. Momentous change like this does not happen overnight; it unfolded over the course of several generations across the Colorado Plateau, continuing well into the fourteenth century. Nor was it uniformly experienced, for each village, household, and individual had different needs, perceptions, social connections, resources, and personal histories, which had to be accommodated and negotiated at various social scales.

The McElmo Intensification was a crucial period in this transformation: it was when many people began to realize that they wanted to do things differently but did not know entirely how they wanted to do them. The rapid growth of McElmo community centers brought together diverse groups of people who had different traditions and probably spoke different languages (e.g., Ortman 2012). Analysis of demographic data in the VEP I study area (McElmo) shows that low to modest amounts of immigration likely contributed to the population growth that is evident after AD 1225 (Varien et al. 2007:fig. 5b). Thus, the amalgamation of people in these large villages included members of the local community who had previously lived in smaller, nearby pueblos, individuals and households from elsewhere in the McElmo subregion, and immigrants from other parts of the region, particularly Western Mesa Verde (Glowacki 2010). Elsewhere, I have suggested that individuals and groups were leaving the western part of the region in greater numbers than in the Mesa Verde core, and given the concurrent, significant population increase in the McElmo subregion, at least some of the people leaving the west were moving into the eastern community centers (Glowacki 2010:208–9). An increase in the frequency of pottery design attributes derived from loom-woven cotton cloth thought to have originated in Western Mesa Verde (Ortman 2000a) lends support to this inference—provided that the increased frequency was related to the movement of people rather than ideas or pots. The west-to-east movement of people during the early to mid-1200s contributed to community center growth in the Mesa Verde core, and McElmo in particular; however, the new settlement data presented in chapter 3 suggest two important differences from my previous work. One, the overall numbers of people who may have been moving from Western Mesa Verde to McElmo were lower than my earlier assessments; and two, people emigrated from all subregions between AD 1240 and 1260, but people were leaving West Central Mesa Verde at a higher frequency than in the McElmo subregion (see table 4 and figure 14). Thus, as emigrants from Western Mesa Verde joined communities in McElmo, the McElmo community centers were also losing people.

The 1200s brought a quickly shifting social landscape, and each village had varied solutions for accommodating these changes. An obvious indicator of the fundamental changes in organization during this period was that community centers established after the 1220s differed from existing, long-lived pueblos. As discussed by Lipe (2006), for centuries the basic unit of social, ceremonial, and political organization was the household, which was readily identifiable in the settlement footprint. The basic San Juan Pattern consisted of residential units with a small block of four to eight rooms to the north and a kiva and midden placed south of the room block; this arrangement is also called a "Prudden Unit" after T. Mitchell Prudden, who first noted the pattern in 1903. The north-south axis was symbolic and was referenced at multiple architectural scales. Beyond the individual residential unit, this axis was also used to orient features within the kivas as well as the entire village layout. In addition to the household kivas, village- and community-scale great kivas were another key characteristic of the San Juan Pattern. Archaeologically visible as early as the AD 600s and 700s, the San Juan Pattern was the traditional core of village organization in the Northern San Juan until sometime after AD 1225. Two classic examples of the conventional San Juan Pattern layout are Yellow Jacket Pueblo and Lancaster, which have multiple, linear room blocks containing two or more household units that are front-oriented along a north-south axis (figure 35). The conventional San Juan Pattern embodied deeply held Pueblo religious ideologies and symbolism that was broadly shared among ancestral Pueblo groups across the San Juan Basin. This shared understanding may have allowed groups to move easily between the central and northern San Juan Basin, such as at the end of the 800s (Wilshusen and Van Dyke 2006). Additionally, as suggested by Lipe (2006), the long-held organizational tenets of the San Juan Pattern were foundational to the legitimization of the new social order established by Chaco because they provided historical connections and symbolic support to bolster the new Chacoan canons.

Although community centers with this conventional layout persisted throughout the Pueblo occupation of the region, a new type of village organization appeared after AD 1225. The new spatial layout (e.g., Sand Canyon Pueblo, Seven Towers, and Yucca House) was more aggregated,

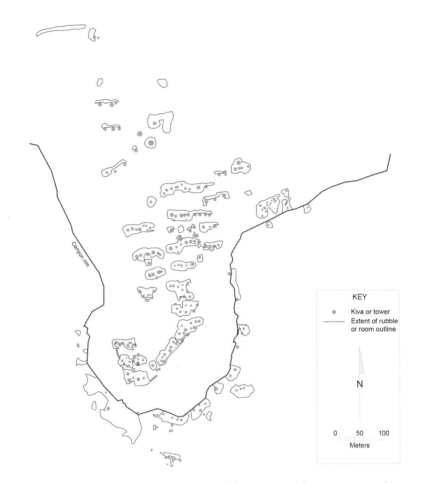

FIGURE 35. Plan map of Yellow Jacket Pueblo. Drawing after Ortman et al. 2000:fig. 2. Illustration by Grant D. Coffey.

was inwardly focused, conformed to topography, and exhibited a bilateral layout (Glowacki 2011; Lipe 2006; Lipe and Ortman 2000; Ortman 2012; Varien et al. 1996). This fundamental change in village layout reconfigured household arrangements and identity within the village. Architectural configurations convey social and cultural meanings (Glassie 2000). The distinctiveness of households in the San Juan Pattern indicates that they had substantial autonomy within the village. In the new village configurations with inward-focusing, aggregated blocks, such as at Sand Canyon Pueblo, individual households are more difficult to identify, which suggests that households had become more integrated and the relationships between households and village-level institutions changed.

This organizational change within Pueblo villages likely accompanied a heightened emphasis on village-level needs and institutions, such as religious sodalities, over kin-based ones (Bernardini 1996; Ware 2014; Ware and Blinman 2000).

This fundamental change in village organization was a widespread phenomenon throughout the Mesa Verde core, despite happening in different ways and to different degrees. More than fifteen community centers with these new spatial arrangements were established post–AD 1225, primarily in canyon settings. These new villages contained newly aggregated groups of people with new ways of doing things. Importantly, this cultural reorganization also happened in existing community centers with long histories such as Yellow Jacket Pueblo and Goodman Point–Shields (Kuckelman et al. 2009; Ortman et al. 2000; Varien et al. 2008). At Yellow Jacket Pueblo, for example, the Great Tower Complex at the head of the canyon and the larger room blocks at the southern end of the village were more aggregated, even though much of the village had conventional, linear room blocks. Additionally, the northern portion of Goodman Point–Shields consisted of multiple, linear room blocks, but the later occupation of the village was consolidated along the canyon rim. Finally, preliminary analysis of room configurations at Spruce Tree House cliff dwelling show similar village reorganization in which pre-1230 individual households were readily apparent, but as population increased throughout the mid-1200s, rooms became increasingly connected and households more difficult to define (Brisbin et al. 2007).

The impetus for this change in village layout may have been the arrival of new cultural or ethnolinguistic groups that moved into the Mesa Verde core; however, the social and cultural processes involved were probably not attributable to this one factor alone. External pressures stemming from the mid-1100s drought, such as the need to secure reliable access to water typically found at canyon heads or to heighten village defensibility, may have also prompted local groups to reconfigure their villages to better conform to the topography when they relocated to the canyon settings. Changing cultural attitudes in the wake of the decline of Chaco may also have caused certain groups of people to move away from the traditions associated with it, which may have included the conventional San Juan Pattern.

Intrinsic to this new village organization was evidence of differential distributions of social power (i.e., social inequality), particularly in the Mesa Verde core. For example, the new community centers often had bilateral divisions either created by natural features, such as drainages or buttes, or constructed with masonry walls and structural arrangements, which often separated residential areas from the civic-ceremonial architecture (Fiero 1999; Glowacki 2001; Lipe and Ortman 2000:108–9;

Nordby 2001; Parks and Dean 1998; Rohn 1971). There was not a corresponding difference in the distribution of material goods within and
among thirteenth-century Mesa Verde villages, however (Lipe 2002),
which is markedly different from what can be seen at Chaco Canyon.
Instead, status and social power in Mesa Verde society was reflected in
the architecture through access to key buildings and resources within
community centers, which was presumably enabled by the possession of
ritual and other specialized knowledge or being a member of an important family or founding clan (Arakawa 2012a; Lipe 2002). The bilateral
division in Mesa Verde villages separated civic-ceremonial architecture
from residential architecture, intimating a strongly ordered internal organization that created social and political inequality depending on location of residences relative to civic-ceremonial buildings, such as at Sand
Canyon Pueblo (Lipe 2002; Lipe and Ortman 2000:109), and may have
connoted a cultural emphasis on dual organization (Lipe and Ortman
2000:108–9; Nordby 2001:107–9).

Other aspects of the new village layout point to an increasing consolidation of power by individuals or groups within these community centers
(i.e., clans, lineages, descent groups, or sodalities). In the mid to late
1200s, as community centers grew, access to resources and spaces within
villages became increasingly restricted; not everyone had equal access to
them. This aspect of village organization is most visible in the cliff dwellings on Mesa Verde Proper, where the well-preserved architecture shows
extensive remodeling and new construction to create reduced access to
storage rooms, special-use areas, and seep springs (Fiero 1999; Nordby
2001; Parks and Dean 1997). For example, the only known access to the
large storage rooms in the upper alcove ledge at Cliff Palace was through
the Speaker Chief Complex, a central three-storied portion of the cliff
dwelling (Nordby 2001:109). Fewkes (1911:28) observed that this section of Cliff Palace was likely the oldest part of the cliff dwelling and that
it contained the most rooms and the most varied types of architecture
with well-laid masonry. In his estimation, this area was likely the most
important place in Cliff Palace, in part because it was so central to the
dwelling and well protected, and he hypothesized that members of the
founding clans may have lived in this area.

Large villages with late occupations in the McElmo subregion also
have evidence of controlled access and centralized leadership. Sand
Canyon Pueblo, for example, has evidence of a centralized block of
thirty storage rooms associated with the D-shaped structure and plaza
on the west side of the village, implying a reliance on network-based
strategies that required centralized forms of leadership involving key
individuals, families, or groups (Lipe 2002; Ortman and Bradley 2002).
Additionally, Bradley's (1992, 1993) analysis of the perimeter wall

surrounding Sand Canyon Pueblo concluded that it was built in a single construction event, suggesting coordinated planning and a level of centralized leadership that was not architecturally apparent at earlier large pueblo villages in the region (Ortman and Bradley 2002:48–49, 52–53). Another example of controlled access and centralized leadership is the Great Tower Complex at Yellow Jacket Pueblo, an important religious precinct with a biwall structure and a block of eleven enclosed kivas, situated at the head of Yellow Jacket Canyon, where it was associated with a series of check dams and effectively controlled access to the spring at the canyon head.

The Role of Religion in Village Reorganization

In Pueblo culture, social and cultural reorganization that fundamentally changed village layouts could happen only through religious changes and revitalization movements initiated by religious leaders or others with prominent standing. These types of changes likely involved a variety of initiatives and processes, including the development of new religious societies, the creation or importation of new rituals and practices, the modification of existing ones, and the revival of traditional ways. The contexts specific to each village or group would influence the way changes were incorporated into the social life of each community and the degree to which they were successfully adopted.

Elsewhere I have suggested that religious change and revitalization movements were a central cause of social unrest during the mid to late 1200s and an important stressor contributing to the Mesa Verde migrations (Glowacki 2011; see also Ortman 2012). Conflict, social tension, and resistance are intrinsic to religious change because differing, and often contradictory, beliefs and intentions can be held among the individuals and groups involved, even if overarching goals and guiding principles might be shared. Politics, contested power, and personal aspirations further complicate these dynamics and contribute to the uncertainty and tension associated with realizing religious change. The uncertainty that comes with initiating new religious movements and other ritual change creates a period of social instability that also heightens vulnerability to additional crises or problems (Wallace 1956). These difficulties can make it challenging for religious movements to coalesce and gain momentum, creating new problems in addition to existing ones (i.e., social movements can fail), which can be socially, politically, and economically disruptive as well (Harkins 2004). Moreover, both failed and successful movements have ramifications and unintended consequences with which to contend.

Periods of religious change can be difficult during the best of times but are even more so during periods of extreme uncertainty. These conditions present an interesting contradiction, for the natural tendency when faced with disruption is to seek stability, and religion provides one means of achieving it. Yet changing ritual practices or even intensifying existing ones can be further destabilizing. During prolonged stresses, opposition and resistance become heightened, which can force people to take extreme actions that they would not have normally done (Vokes 2007; Wallace 1956). The McElmo Intensification was such a period.

Ceremonial intensification in the early to mid-1200s was characterized by widespread experimentation in light of a growing need for different forms of integration within community centers and differentiation among them (Glowacki 2011). The diversity in the manifestations of religious change across the region, especially in the Mesa Verde core, underscores the point that there was not one prescribed "way," but many. The diverse modifications and innovations in ritual and religious change affected both communal activities and exclusionary rituals controlled by small groups within each village. As described in chapter 3, different forms of group-assembly architecture were incorporated into community centers to accommodate larger groups of people with different histories. With increasing aggregation in the 1200s, at some large villages, there was also increased importance placed on public, community-scale ritual, particularly at plazas. Roughly half of the community centers had group-assembly features, and among those that did, the majority of the centers had either a great kiva or a plaza. Whether a village contained a great kiva or plaza is potentially attributable to different cultural traditions; however, there is also a temporal component to consider. Great kivas are most commonly associated with Chaco-era occupation, and plazas, although present in great houses, took on increasing importance in the large, aggregated villages established after AD 1225. In addition to the increase in the number of plazas at late, aggregated villages, the need to accommodate more people in communal gatherings was also achieved in innovative ways, including the removal of existing great kiva roofs (e.g., Sand Canyon Pueblo) and the construction of a few highly formalized plazas that were more akin to those of the fourteenth century (i.e., Long House and Fire Temple).

Circular multiwalled structures, discussed above (see also chapter 3), were primarily built at the late large villages in Eastern Mesa Verde that did not subscribe to the traditional San Juan Pattern. These buildings represent a new religious organization presumably linked to Aztec that appeared concurrently with the changes in the overall village layout. D-shaped multiwalled structures, though based on a similar concept, were something different. These buildings were unique to the Mesa Verde core and were not built at Aztec or in the Totah, Chaco Canyon, or Western Mesa Verde.* They were also not built at community centers with existing great houses, but circular multiwalled structures were (Glowacki and Ortman 2012). Thus, it seems to me that the construction and use of D-shaped structures was an intentional expression of difference from Aztec-Chaco ideologies. If so, the distinctive distribution of D-shaped structures would be an indication of symbolic and ideological conflict (*sensu* Chamberlin 2006) among cultural groups with varying degrees of connectedness to Aztec and its ideologies, since both circular and D-shaped multiwalled structures were present in the Mesa Verde core. Moreover, there is at least one example of further modifications to the circular multiwalled form at Goodman Point–Shields, which had two new-style buildings inspired by the concept in addition to a D-shaped structure (see figure 22; see also Kuckelman et al. 2009). The use of D-shaped structures and experimentation with formal principles during the latest construction at one of the primate regional centers just prior to its depopulation are clear examples of increasingly divergent ideas about religious organization and the variety of ways that religious change was experienced in the 1200s.

The McElmo Intensification was more than a period when population increased and consolidated in the Mesa Verde core, resulting in the formation of large aggregated villages and more communities in closer proximity that had difficulties making ends meet when faced with drought and cooler-than-normal temperatures. It was also a time when the way people organized themselves—religiously, politically, and socially—and interacted with each other changed. This change happened quickly, and there were many different ideas about how to do it. This social landscape was complicated by both cultural diversity and increasing social inequality, and emergent hierarchy as social power became concentrated within and among the largest pueblos in the Mesa Verde core (see chapter 3). Each of the historical landscapes—Eastern and Western Mesa Verde, Aztec-Chaco, and the McElmo Intensification—was compelling and all-encompassing for those who lived within them. How these landscapes intersected and how people were positioned within them are what make up the history of "leaving Mesa Verde."

---

*Lekson (2008:308–9n72) suggests that the enclosed plaza at Aztec West made it a D-shaped structure, implying that it was symbolically equivalent to the D-shaped multiwalled structures (e.g., Sun Temple). However, in plan view, Aztec West is more rectangular than D-shaped (e.g., Brown et al. 2008:fig. 12.3). Moreover, it remains to be demonstrated that all buildings in the shape of a "D" were necessarily symbolically or functionally equivalent (i.e., rooms, towers, multiwalled structures, and great houses with defined plazas).

CHAPTER SIX

Envisioning the Sociopolitical Landscape

One of the principal domains in which the influences of differing social histories and their landscapes intersected is through sociopolitical organization and social networks. If the longevity of the San Juan Pattern is any indication, social organization and the different ways social power was distributed within and among pueblo villages were largely household based and relatively stable. This pattern changed dramatically after the mid-1100s (see chapter 5).

Much of what happened in thirteenth-century Mesa Verde related to pueblo organization being in a state of flux as villages, households, and individuals reacted differently to the decline of Chaco and the rise of Aztec, coped with integrating new groups of people as village sizes and numbers increased in the Mesa Verde core, and adjusted to a rapidly shifting social and political landscape during a prolonged period of difficult climatic conditions in the 1200s. Consequently, religious organization and authority (sociopolitical organization) changed in different ways for different groups within and between pueblo villages across the region: some tightly held to convention, others revived old traditions, and still others modified established rituals or brought in members of different cultural groups with new rituals (Glowacki 2011). The diverse manifestations of change and accommodation in the wake of the Chaco to Post-Chaco transition ultimately led to a fragmented social landscape that did not hold.

Central to this period of flux were changing ideas about the communal and hierarchical components of social and religious organization among the pueblos. In the 1980s, the extent to which ancestral

Pueblo organization was hierarchical (ranked) or egalitarian (communal) became a contentious topic in the context of the Grasshopper–Chavez Pass debates (e.g., Reid 1989; Upham and Plog 1986). Academically, the intensity of these debates caused some young Southwest archaeologists coming up through the ranks in the 1990s (such as myself) to shy away from the topic, even as the issues were being reframed using relational constructs focused on inequality and social power (e.g., McGuire and Saitta 1996; Mills 2000; Plog 1995). Social hierarchy is also not emphasized in contemporary Pueblo organization, which is predominantly characterized as steadfastly communal (a cultural more that perhaps developed in part because in the Pueblo past the more hierarchically oriented institutions could not maintain balance). Yet there were, and are, differences in status among Pueblo people (e.g., Brandt 1994). Today, these differences are largely knowledge based and are mediated through ceremonial cycles requiring different ritual knowledge at different times. There are also specific families and clans with long-standing positions of leadership that take on primary roles in making key decisions for the pueblo, often because their ancestors were among the putative earliest arrivals (as with the Bear Clan among the Hopis).

Nearly all cultures and societies simultaneously use some combination of network-oriented strategies that restrict access and promote social inequalities among specific people or groups (ranked) and corporate strategies that promote integration and benefit the entire community (communal). Hierarchical and egalitarian, much like religion and politics, are not mutually exclusive or oppositional categories; they are dialectic, existing in relation to each other (Blanton et al. 1996; Feinman 2000; McGuire 2011; McGuire and Saitta 1996). What differs in each case is the extent to which each is emphasized, for there are always elements of both. Blanton and his colleagues (1996) termed this *dual processualism*, which they described as a continuum wherein a society trends more toward network or corporate strategies depending on their configuration. A relational approach to the multiscalar processes involved in sociopolitical organization promotes a more-nuanced examination of the interrelationships among these constituents and recognizes that they are not essential categories (e.g., Heitman and Plog 2005). This conceptualization also acknowledges the mutability of these modes, underscoring that the dialectic between them constantly changes, which reminds us that sociopolitical organization was not as fixed as it might seem in the archaeological record. A relational approach also allows us to better examine the inherent contradictions that inevitably occur when both modes are used and the resulting tensions that often drive cultural change (McGuire and Saitta 1996). Dialectical change in sociopolitical organization happens for many reasons but often coincides with substantial population increases and decreases. For example, communal institutions might have been preferred until population levels increased such that network-based strategies and social ranks were increasingly relied on to apportion social, material, and ritual resources among larger groups of people (McGuire and Saitta 1996:212).

At different points in Pueblo history, social organization was more dependent on hierarchical institutions and network-based strategies than on egalitarian and corporate ones, and vice versa. When the dialectic between these modes changed, regardless of the impetus, it created periods when inherent contradictions and tensions in the community were exposed and required resolution. These periods underlie many of the major cultural transitions noted in Pueblo history. For example, during the late 700s and 800s, as population increased dramatically in the Northern San Juan, social inequality became more pronounced in conjunction with the formation of large aggregated villages.

The presence of large U-shaped room blocks with well-constructed rooms, large storage areas, oversized pit structures with ritual features, and ceramic and faunal evidence indicative of feasting and ritual intensification suggests that network-based strategies promoting key individuals or households over others had become more prominent at some villages (Potter 1997; Schachner 2001; Wilshusen, Ortman, et al. 2012; Wilshusen and Van Dyke 2006; Windes 2004). However, many of the early community centers also had great kivas, which are associated with communal and corporate modes of organization. In the Village Ecodynamics Project I (VEP I) study area, six of the twenty-six community centers dating to the AD 725–980 period had a U-shaped room block and oversized pit structure, eleven community centers had great kivas, and three of them had both a U-shaped room block and a great kiva (Glowacki and Ortman 2012:table 14.3). Thus, during this early period of aggregation, villages were being organized in different ways as groups, likely with different cultural backgrounds, aggregated and experimented with ranked leadership and communal systems (Wilshusen and Ortman 1999; Wilshusen, Ortman, et al. 2012). By the turn of the tenth century, regional population had declined markedly (Glowacki and Ortman 2012; Schlanger 1988; Wilshusen, Ortman, et al. 2012). Among other factors, discontent with the emergence of increased social inequality (i.e., households with more social power) and the social changes that came with it induced the depopulation of at least some villages. For example, at McPhee Village, which had a U-shaped room block, the oversized pit structure was burned, apparent violence occurred in some of the small, household pit structures, and there was evidence of a failed attempt to construct a great kiva (Schachner 2001; Wilshusen, Ortman, et al. 2012).

The nature of sociopolitical complexity—the degree to which egalitarian and hierarchical institutions were emphasized—at Chaco Canyon also changed over the course of its rise and fall (Lekson 1999a, 2008; Van Dyke 2007a; Ware 2001; Wilcox 1999). The overall trend was seemingly toward a gradually increasing emphasis on hierarchy as some individuals, households, and/or lineages gained more social and ritual power than others until insurmountable difficulties were encountered in the mid-1100s. Occupation in Chaco Canyon started in the late 800s with several small villages—Una Vida, Pueblo Bonito, and Peñasco Blanco (proto–great houses), which were roughly the same size. These first Chaco great houses, which may have had ancestral connections to the Northern San Juan (Van Dyke 2007a; Wilshusen and Van Dyke 2006; Windes 2004), were established by different households and lineages that gained differential access to social power and resources, resulting in varied historical trajectories. By the end of the occupation, Pueblo Bonito had expanded to 695 rooms arranged in its iconic D-shape, Peñasco Blanco had 215 rooms with a curved, oval configuration, and Una Vida had 160 rooms in an L-shaped room block with enclosed plaza (room counts from Van Dyke 2007a:table 5.1).

As population in Chaco Canyon increased throughout the 1000s, so did social differentiation, which became more materially apparent at multiple scales. First, by the 1100s, there were thirteen great houses in Chaco Canyon, each with differing size, layout, material goods, and longevity, which implies corresponding differences in social and ritual power among them. Pueblo Bonito was unquestionably the largest, with more rooms, kivas, objects, and elite burials than any other great house. The arrangement of great houses within Chaco Canyon also suggests ranked difference, for Pueblo Bonito, Chetro Ketl, and Pueblo Alto formed a concentrated locus of religious power among the families and clans housed there (see figure 32). Second, there were both great houses and small pueblos in Chaco Canyon. Their obvious size differences and specific placement on opposite sides of the canyon with great houses on the north and small pueblos on the south denote social and cultural differences that were evident in their use. The occupants of these disparate buildings had access to different resources that resulted in apparent dietary and nutritional differences (Akins 2003), and different activities took place within them (e.g., turquoise production at small pueblos and ritual use of turquoise at great houses [Mathien 1997]). Finally, the religious leadership and families housed in Chaco Canyon great houses had different levels of social power and types of ritual knowledge than those associated with the typically smaller, outlying great houses across the Colorado Plateau. Chaco ideology and organization had various hierarchical configurations that consolidated aspects of ritual and social power, creating inequality within the Chaco system.

Corporate institutions and communal practices were not absent; rather, they were likely the foundation from which these ranked configurations developed. The construction of the great houses required a collective and coordinated effort that integrated different social segments within and beyond the community to harvest and transport construction timbers, to obtain the stone and clay, and to construct the buildings (Lekson et al. 2006; Wills 2000). Communal ceremonies and other large-scale gatherings, such as feasting events (e.g., Windes 1987), were held in the great kivas and plazas associated with these great houses. Other crosscutting changes were associated with the emergence of sodalities and the social tensions arising as elements of religious and sociopolitical organization became independent from the previously dominant corporate kinship groups (Ware 2001, 2014; Wilcox 1999).

Chacoan pueblo organization was not fully stratified, nor was it entirely egalitarian; rather, it embodied elements of both and its composition changed over time. McGuire and Saitta (1996:201) refer to the simultaneous use of hierarchical and egalitarian modes of organization as indicative of a "complex communal society," which seems a useful heuristic for the moment. In the case of the Chaco Canyon complex communal society, ceremonialism and sociopolitical organization were evidently becoming increasingly dependent on ranked leadership and social inequalities, even if the corporate ethos remained central. The dialectic between these elements of pueblo organization was an ongoing source of social tension that affected community cohesion and continued to be a central factor shaping social interaction and relational networks in thirteenth-century Mesa Verde.

Sociopolitical Intensification and Fragmentation in the Northern San Juan

In the late 1000s, the relatively rapid adoption of central elements of Chacoan pueblo organization evidenced by the construction of great houses at many pueblo communities across the northern Southwest testifies to the powerful and far-reaching impact of the Chacoan expansion and its attendant religious movement. This transformative movement, founded on the advancement of Chacoan ideology and its associated political and economic advantages and obligations, was a broadly integrating force that forged multifarious connections, both direct and nebulous, across the Pueblo world. The canons associated with the Chaco expansion were not uniformly adopted across this vast area, even at those communities with great houses. Nonetheless, they became a key element of sociopolitical and ceremonial organization across the Southwest (Lekson 1999a; Sebastian 1992; Wilcox 1999) and in the Northern San Juan, in particular.

As great houses proliferated across the region, Chacoan sociopolitical organization became the foundation of many of the long-lived community centers, variably linking them to the institutions of the Chaco and eventually the Aztec-Chaco ceremonial complex. In a few cases, great houses were built de novo (e.g., Escalante, Bluff Great House). However, most great houses were built at existing villages, incorporating new, if familiar, tenets that formalized social inequalities by creating prominent spaces where ritual and resource access was restricted (e.g., Morefield Canyon Great House Village, Yellow Jacket Pueblo, Mitchell Springs). The presence of these buildings and the way they were used enabled certain pueblos and communities to become much larger or more prominent than others, particularly if they were situated on or near good farmland and water.

In the Northern San Juan, roughly one in four community centers with a Pueblo III period (PIII) occupation had a great house (*n* = 59; see table 7). All but three of the centers with great houses had long histories of occupation that began in the eleventh century or earlier. The three exceptions are Yucca House (McElmo), Comb Wash Great House (West Central Mesa Verde), and Flora Vista (Totah). Of these, Comb Wash Great House is the only one that has been clearly associated with construction in the PIII period (Hurst and Till 2009). Recent testing at Flora Vista, which has multiple adobe and cobble room blocks and three towers associated with a plaza, indicates that this community center was built and occupied in the 1200s, and it is now believed that Flora Vista did not contain a great house (P. Reed, personal communication, 2013).

The founding of Yucca House is often presumed to have been in the mid to late 1100s or early 1200s (e.g., Glowacki and Ortman 2012; Ortman 2012) based on the preponderance of Mesa Verde Black-on-white pottery and three tree-ring dates (1163vv, 1229vv, and 1263vv) from the southeast corner room of the Upper House. However, the presence of at least ten PII period sherds, including Deadmans Black-on-red, recorded during in-field analysis at the West Complex, the evidence of earlier buried architecture in remote-sensing imagery, the lack of pottery and tree-ring data from the Lower House, and anecdotal accounts from local members of the community about finding substantial amounts of red ware south of the Lower House suggest that Yucca House may have been built before the mid-1100s (Glowacki 2001). When systematic in-field pottery analysis was conducted at Yucca House, there were no visible sherds associated with the Lower House (Glowacki 2001), presumably because it is nearest to the entrance trail for the national monument. Because of the paucity of information, it is impossible to know whether the Lower House was a new pueblo configuration established in the context of increasing aggregation in the 1200s (e.g., Ortman 2012) or, as has also been proposed, an earlier, Chacoan component of Yucca House, as suggested by its L-shaped room block and low wall enclosing a plaza with a great kiva, which some take to be reminiscent of a great house plan. Future test excavations are required to better understand the historical development of Yucca House to more securely date its occupation. Thus, there may have been only one new great house built during the post-Chaco era.

Notably, most PIII community centers (more than 70 percent) did not have great houses. Yet those centers that contained great houses were often, if not always, larger than community centers without them. Of the twenty-two largest PIII community centers in the region (i.e., first- and second-order centers [figure 36; see table 8]), all but six had great houses.* Conspicuously, all four of the settlements that became primate regional centers by the thirteenth century—Aztec, Yellow Jacket Pueblo, Goodman Point–Shields, and Hedley—had great houses established in the late 1000s. Great kivas, emblematic of communal ritual, were also commonly associated with great house communities (i.e., thirty-one of the fifty-nine community centers with great houses also had great kivas; see chapter 3). Only seven of the largest community centers (*n* = 22) lacked a great kiva, including Hedley, one of the four noted primate centers.

The correlation between the presence of great houses and the largest villages in the region implies that great houses and their affiliated leaders and institutions became an important foundation of sociopolitical and religious organization that concentrated social power and enabled growth and increasing influence within and among villages. These circumstances, interwoven with other factors such as access to resources, created inequalities among villages and community centers that undergirded Mesa Verde sociopolitical organization (see chapter 3). The extent to which a hierarchical difference in size translates to more or less social, political, and economic power among villages is debatable. Yet the evident site size hierarchy is an important dimension of differentiation that had implications for the distribution of social power—intrinsically founded on religious institutions and rituals—and access to resources, which may have heightened competition among

*One of the six centers is Monument Village, which has not yet been adequately mapped (Hurst and Till 2009:61).

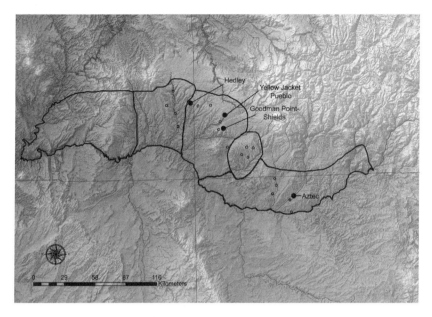

FIGURE 36. Distribution of Pueblo III period primate (filled circles) and second-order (open circles) centers in the Northern San Juan. Illustration by Grant D. Coffey.

certain villages and centers. Another dimension of sociopolitical and thus religious differentiation among ancestral Pueblo villages is the presence and absence of particular civic-ceremonial architecture at community centers. For example, that great houses were present only at certain pueblos suggests that either great house communities were key nodes that attracted people from surrounding villages and nearby centers (thereby forming loose confederacies and alliances), or there were different cultural groups and modes of pueblo organization, or some combination of both.

By the late 1000s and early 1100s, the increasing differences in village sizes and their social and religious organization suggest that there were complex relationships among the villages, with varying configurations of interpueblo alliances as well as fracture lines along which competition and warfare developed. Although not directly demonstrable beyond proximity and exchange networks, the loose confederacies or polities that developed throughout the 1100s and 1200s had rich and varied histories of how they prospered, struggled, intensified, and dissolved (see also Lipe 2002). Though many confederacies of varying sizes and cohesion likely existed, the largest community centers, and most certainly the primate centers, were central villages in the most influential polities in the region.* The key to characterizing Mesa Verde sociopolitical organization and how it relates to what transpired in the years preceding widespread emigration from the region is to better understand the relationships among these villages and their affiliates.

If the fortunes of fate had not intervened, the momentum attained during the Chacoan expansion and the ascendancy of Aztec could have coalesced into a centralized sociopolitical system, but for the two generations of severity that changed everything (see chapter 5). Times of extreme galvanize people to make significant changes, for they lay bare contradictions and make it impossible to ignore what is not working. In Pueblo culture, the domain for social and political change is religion. During periods of social stress and climatic uncertainty, people become especially inclined to initiate operational changes in religious organization and practice through revitalization movements and other means (Harkins 2004:xxiii; Vokes 2007; Wallace 1956). From the sociopolitical perspective, changes in religious organization reconfigured the balance of integrative, communal practices and restrictive, ranked religious institutions. McGuire and Saitta (1996:212) suggest that in complex communal societies, "any factor that increased production (e.g., environmental change, agricultural intensification) would support communalism, while drought or agricultural failure would expose the full force of hierarchy. With plenty there is more to share and strengthen the position of high-ranked clans through communal ideals, and with want high-ranked clans justify the expulsion of others for the survival of the whole."

The dynamics theorized by McGuire and Saitta may help explain the evident social tensions and sudden increase in the number of new, large aggregated villages during the McElmo Intensification (see chapter 5). After AD 1180, at least forty-seven new community centers were established in Central Mesa Verde (see table 5), with the majority of them located in the Mesa Verde core. The number of community centers increased for a variety of reasons and through different processes. In some cases, families may have become more disposed to pooling resources through aggregation after a difficult period or their desire to relocate to an area with better farmland and water had increased, and the Mesa Verde core was a prime locale. Regardless, much of this expansion occurred when climatic and environmental factors were generally good, especially compared with what preceded. The subsequent extended

---

*Lipe (2002), who also discusses the likelihood of pueblo polities, identified the primate and second-order community centers in the Mesa Verde core, describing them as "isolated" large villages with some distance between them and other centers.

period of uncertainty, however, may have exposed fracture lines within villages, resulting in a heightened proclivity toward fissioning when conflicts could not be resolved.

The new types of villages established after AD 1200 exemplified an increased emphasis on corporate organizing principles and village-level identities with inward-oriented pueblo layouts and an intensified focus on group-assembly architecture (e.g., formalized plazas, unroofed great kivas [see chapters 3 and 5]). Regardless of whether these new cultural ideals in village organization happened in response to the failure of a specific type of ranked leadership, because the increasing number of people required new ways of integrating and enhancing community cohesion, or as an outcome of acculturation as diverse cultural groups aggregated, these changes reinforced communal ritual and organization—as did the mechanisms that promoted the suppression of economic differentiation, for social rank and religious power were not evident in the distribution of material goods among community members.

This does not mean that social rank and inequality were absent, however. The complex communal society of Chaco, and inherently Aztec, had become increasingly dependent on various hierarchical institutions that created social rank and inequality, and in many ways the sociopolitical organization of the Mesa Verde core was contingent upon them. As described in chapters 3 and 5, interpueblo sociopolitical inequalities are evident in the community center size hierarchy and the variable distribution of public architecture among and within community centers. Intrapueblo social inequalities and centralized forms of leadership involving key individuals, families, or groups were also evident in the planned construction of some villages, the distinct distribution of residential and public architecture within the new villages, and the restricted access to storage associated with religious facilities (Arakawa 2012a; Lipe 2002; Ortman and Bradley 2002). There is also bioarchaeological evidence of potential status differences within communities. For example, Martin and her colleagues (2010) found high frequencies of skeletal trauma, including depression fractures, broken ribs, broken long bones, and occupational stress markers, on a specific group of women in the Jackson Lake and Barker Arroyo communities in the La Plata Valley of the Totah. Unlike the rest of the population, these women were also buried in haphazard positions without grave goods, which suggests the presence of a subclass of women, possibly indentured servants or laborers obtained through raiding, who experienced differential treatment, including physical abuse.

Moreover, not all of the religious organizational changes implemented after AD 1180 were corporate, for multiwalled structures were restricted-access civic-ceremonial architecture analogous to great houses.

Multiwalled structures, likely implemented by the Aztec-Chaco religious leadership (circular form), were adopted by at least fifteen community centers in Eastern Mesa Verde (see table 7). Multiwalled structures were also conceptually reinvented as a D-shaped structure by twelve community centers in the Mesa Verde core (see table 7). Only a few thirteenth-century pueblos (11 percent) had multiwalled structures, which were primarily components of religious organization at the largest community centers. Thus, at least some new villages were retaining elements of ranked sociopolitical and religious organization even as it was being restructured.

There were diverse manifestations of how the new arrangements of communal and ranked organization were configured at villages established in the 1200s. Each of the five largest new thirteenth-century community centers in the Mesa Verde core had a distinct pueblo organization. Long House had a formalized plaza in the center of the village (Cattanach 1980). Cliff Palace was tightly aggregated in the alcove, with evidence of restricted storage access associated with central religious facilities but no large, group-assembly architecture within the village itself. However, Cliff Palace residents could have used the Sun Temple D-shaped structure and plaza at Fire Temple, which are both located across Cliff Canyon, provided that traversing the steep canyon was not too much of an impediment (Rohn 1977). Sand Canyon Pueblo contained a great kiva and a D-shaped structure (Ortman and Bradley 2002). Recent mapping of Easter Ruin during the VEP community center survey in 2003 (Glowacki and Ortman 2012) documented informal plaza and courtyard spaces but no great kiva or multiwalled structure. Finally, Yucca House had two great kivas and a circular biwall structure (but see above regarding dating; see also Glowacki 2001).

New cultural ideals regarding pueblo organization were not limited to only those villages established in the 1200s; they were also incorporated into the long-lived large community centers, such as Yellow Jacket Pueblo and Hedley (see below). In these villages, any organizational and religious changes taking place in the 1200s had to be negotiated and adapted to accommodate existing arrangements and religious practices. This presented rather different social circumstances for the residents of these community centers than for those in villages established in the thirteenth century, with a village layout that physically embodied the contemporaneous cultural changes taking place. Hypothetically, the former may have caused more discord within the community, as differences among conservative and progressive members of the village would need to be negotiated, whereas the latter may have contributed to increased discord between community centers, if political and cultural differences between residents of these villages with manifestly different histories created conflict.

Growing political and cultural differences are evident in thirteenth-century villages (see also Ortman 2012). A majority of the centers built in the 1200s ($n = 122$) were smaller than those established earlier, did not have great houses or multiwalled structures, and were spatially clustered (Lipe 2002). These shared differences, and the clustered arrangement in particular, suggest that there may have been some degree of political and ceremonial integration among them. Aggregating their room counts suggests that the clustered centers potentially created a social and political grouping that rivaled the primate and second-order centers, which were the largest singular centers in the region (Lipe 2002:220). These clusters were potentially a new formulation of pueblo polity that developed out of the social and political contexts of the 1200s that would have either been in competition with the largest centers or joined their coalitions participating in rituals and other activities. Thus, a major factor underlying the McElmo Intensification was the competing social, political, and ritual networks that developed with the emergence of pueblo polities of varying size, cohesion, and regional influence and the resulting social instability as individuals and villages adjusted to the cascading effects of changing sociopolitical organization and networks.

Much of the resulting social and political change and effort to gain social power and influence was implemented in the religious realm, in which new religious movements and ritual innovation reconfigured sociopolitical organization. These types of changes likely exposed fracture lines both within and between villages along which schisms were likely to form, especially when traditional and progressive viewpoints came into conflict. Much of the dissension may have related to the extent to which villages and groups wanted to break with "the establishment" (i.e., Aztec-Chaco), bringing into conflict those seeking to retain their current power and status and those seeking to change their circumstance. As a consequence, the sociopolitical tensions between ranked leadership and communal ethos were inextricably ingrained in these conflicts and their resolution. Sometimes the clash of ideals was overt, and at other times it was embroiled in family or individual rivalries over issues such as potential marriage partners (e.g., Malotki 2002). These conflicts were not limited to within villages and likely played a major role in social dynamics among villages, even among those that were allied. The factionalized social environment produced by competing sociopolitical entities that emerged from Aztec-Chaco and the McElmo Intensification in Eastern Mesa Verde was ultimately what led to the Mesa Verde migrations (see also Arakawa 2012a).

Aztec-Chaco and the McElmo
Intensification Collide

We can see these competing ideals in the social histories of the primate centers. Each of them was established at roughly the same time, had at least one great house, and was situated in a prime location with good access to water and productive farmland, the latter of which allowed each to develop and expand into primate centers, twelfth-century drought and violence notwithstanding. Subsequent to the Chaco to Post-Chaco transition, however, their trajectories diverged, in part depending on the strength of connections with Chaco and Aztec. Aztec was obviously entrenched in traditional Chacoan ideology, even if its religious leaders also developed derivative institutions and ritual practices. Yellow Jacket Pueblo was also largely traditional in its organization and for much of its history, yet its residents clearly accommodated their changing ideals into their existing village structure. Both Hedley and Goodman Point–Shields were also established with traditional conventions but were more dramatically adapted to the marked culture change of the 1200s, when entirely new pueblos and civic-ceremonial architecture were built in the same vicinity.

Aztec

Aztec has already been described in some detail (see chapters 3 and 5); therefore, only a few salient points will be recapped here to facilitate comparison with the other primate centers. Aztec represented the Chaco establishment in the Northern San Juan, and the reproduction of the Chaco ritual core facilitated Aztec's ascendancy to a primate center. This rising trajectory was further augmented by the Chacoan great house diaspora, which may have expanded relational networks for the primate center, at least for a while (e.g., Arakawa et al. 2011).

When the severity of the mid-1100s hit, however, Aztec's sociopolitical momentum was quashed. The residents of Aztec no longer sustained large-scale, planned construction efforts, long-distance exchange declined, and fewer residential sites were occupied in the Totah, in general (Brown et al. 2013; Brown et al. 2008; Lipe 2006). Aztec's historical connections to Chaco and location along the Animas River enabled it to endure this difficult period, even if in a diminished capacity. In its prime, Chaco was an integrative force, but by the late 1100s its precariously dry locale was compromised by severe drought conditions, which contributed to undermining the religious authority of the Chaco Canyon elite. The loss of faith in the supremacy of Chaco became extensive enough that what cohesion it had attained was lost, and other places, particularly in the Northern San Juan, gained social power and influence in its stead.

It was in this context that Aztec reinvented itself through investment in new construction and revitalization movements, including the development of circular multiwalled structures that retained elements of the restricted access and ranked religious leadership associated with great houses (see chapters 3 and 5). If the distribution of circular multiwalled structures represented the Aztec-Chaco sphere of influence after the Chaco to Post-Chaco transition, it was, unlike Chaco's more extensive influence, confined to Eastern Mesa Verde (see figure 21). The westernmost circular biwall structure was Yellow Jacket Pueblo. The only other community center with a triwall structure was Mud Springs, located in the Montezuma Valley (Colorado), south and slightly east of Yellow Jacket Pueblo.* The frequencies of pottery imported from elsewhere in the region suggest that Aztec and the Totah had the strongest ties with residents of Mesa Verde Proper, but Aztec's social networks and sphere of influence appear to have weakened farther west. For example, the lack of multiwalled structures in Western Mesa Verde and the development of the D-shaped structures suggest disengagement from Aztec-Chaco religious institutions (Glowacki 2011).

Yellow Jacket Pueblo

Yellow Jacket Pueblo was an august Mesa Verde establishment with an occupation of more than 220 years beginning in the mid-1000s (Kuckelman 2003; Ortman et al. 2000; Varien et al. 2008). It was the largest community center in the Northern San Juan, with 195 kivas, thirty-five room blocks (estimated 600–1,200 rooms), nineteen towers, a great house, a great kiva, a circular biwall at the Great Tower Complex, a reservoir, and possible road segments (Kuckelman 2003). Centrally situated and located on some of the most productive land in McElmo, Yellow Jacket Pueblo was a large community center from its inception and was likely one of the most religiously and politically powerful centers in the Mesa Verde core (Ortman et al. 2000). The location and size of Yellow Jacket Pueblo allowed it to persist, and even slightly expand, during the Chaco to Post-Chaco transition.

*The location of this triwall is interesting in that Mud Springs is one of several large community centers, including Yucca House, situated in the gap between the eastern slopes of Ute Mountain and the western escarpments of the Mesa Verde uplift. Mud Springs is among the sites that may have been part of a contested cultural and political boundary during the Chaco to Post-Chaco transition resulting from conflict that may have related to the degree to which groups and villages were aligned with Aztec-Chaco or not (see chapter 5).

Yellow Jacket Pueblo has a classic San Juan Pattern organization with a strong north-south orientation (see figure 35). With a great house, great kiva, and circular biwall structure, Yellow Jacket Pueblo was ideologically aligned with Chaco and Aztec-Chaco canons, even if the strength of this connection may have waned by the end of the 1200s. Yellow Jacket Pueblo was not necessarily a subordinate of Aztec, however, for architectural variation and patterns of intraregional exchange imply that it was relatively autonomous. Architecturally, there was deviation from the Aztec-Chaco conventional biwall structure, often an isolated building, which seems a blending of religious organizational ideals. Built in the mid to late 1200s, the Great Tower Complex was an unconventional architectural block with eleven kivas, ten rooms, four towers, several dams, and the large biwall structure (Kuckelman 2003) that concentrated religious activities within the village. This architectural block was also highly aggregated and situated at the head of Yellow Jacket Canyon, traits that conform to those exhibited by thirteenth-century community centers. The residents of Yellow Jacket Pueblo and Aztec also had differing social networks (see chapter 4; Arakawa 2012b; Ortman 2003). For example, obsidian-sourcing studies show that residents of Yellow Jacket Pueblo obtained obsidian through distinct long-distance networks (Arakawa et al. 2011; Shackley 2009, 2010) and also imported pottery at higher frequencies than not only Aztec but also several other large community centers (see chapter 4).

Hedley Site Complex

Located just west of the Colorado-Utah border in a tributary of Monument Canyon (Utah), Hedley was the northernmost and westernmost of the primate centers. This part of the McElmo subregion was drier than elsewhere, but Hedley was situated in a well-watered location with a reservoir, which likely contributed to encouraging aggregation and helped the residents of Hedley to withstand the harsh drought conditions during the Chaco to Post-Chaco transition.

This primate center contained more than 160 kivas and 700 rooms in three residential clusters (West Hill, Middle Ruin, and Main Ruin), two great houses, and a D-shaped structure (figure 37; Ortman et al. 2000). The focus of the occupation at Hedley changed over time. The earliest occupation was likely West Hill, where there was a buried late PI village (Wilshusen and Ortman 1999). After a hiatus (AD 950 to the mid-1000s), a great house and cluster of room blocks were also built here following the traditional canons of the San Juan Pattern (Ortman et al. 2000). The population at Hedley expanded in the early to mid-1100s,

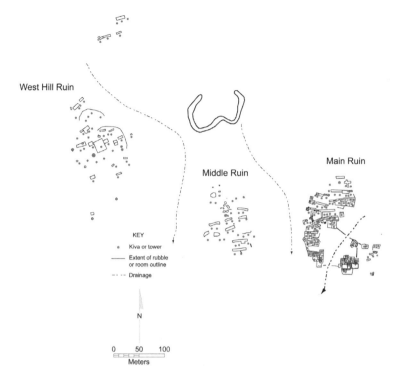

FIGURE 37. Map of Hedley site complex showing the relationships between West Hill, Middle Ruin, and Main Ruin. Drawing after Ortman et al. 2000:fig. 3. Illustration by Grant D. Coffey.

when Middle Ruin, which had as many as 29 kivas and 12 room blocks, was established and occupied until at least the early 1200s (Ortman et al. 2000). Middle Ruin also generally conformed to the principles embodied by the San Juan settlement pattern. Also at this time, a second great house was constructed at Main Ruin and was connected to the Middle Ruin residential cluster by a causeway.

There was another growth period in the mid-1200s, when much of Main Ruin was constructed (Ortman et al. 2000). By the end of its occupation, Main Ruin contained 85 kivas, at least 20 room blocks with an estimated 400 surface rooms, a remodeled great house, an enclosed plaza, and a D-shaped structure. The organizational layout of Main Ruin was more reflective of the changing cultural ideals of the 1200s and is reminiscent of Sand Canyon Pueblo, even if a north-south orientation and household units are more architecturally visible (figure 37; Ortman et al. 2000). In the Mesa Verde core, most of the community centers with a D-shaped structure did not have an associated great house (see chapter 3; see also Glowacki and Ortman 2012); thus, Hedley is a notable exception to this pattern, especially since it had two, one of which was remodeled late in the occupation. Residential structures were added to the Main Ruin great house in the mid to late 1200s, several doors were sealed, and an associated kiva was modified. These renovations were contemporaneous with the construction of the D-shaped structure, the establishment of the southwest and central plazas, and the addition of enclosing walls (Ortman et al. 2000). Thus, significant reorganization and redirection occurred in the last decades of the occupation of Hedley that likely embodied changing ideas about traditional connections to Aztec-Chaco. That those living in Hedley may have been less involved with eastern dynamics and elements of the Aztec-Chaco religious complex is also evident in the pottery and lithic procurement patterns they maintained, which were relatively localized and more oriented toward Western Mesa Verde (see chapter 4; Arakawa 2012b; Neily 1983).

Goodman Point–Shields Complex

The Goodman Point–Shields complex comprises two different areas of concentrated settlement within the larger Goodman Point community (figure 38; see Duff and Ryan 2000; Kuckelman et al. 2009): Shields Pueblo was the older and more northern, mesa-top settlement (Duff and Ryan 2000; Duff et al. 2010); Goodman Point Pueblo was the short-lived, late canyon-rim complex (Kuckelman et al. 2009). Although Shields and Goodman Point Pueblos are often treated as separate sites, here, because of their proximity and overlapping occupation histories, I consider them part of the same large community center that transformed over time (see also Lipe 2002).*

Shields Pueblo was primarily occupied from AD 1050 through the 1200s, but there is some evidence of a late 700s occupation. It was a largely San Juan Pattern settlement that contained an estimated ninety kivas and nineteen linear room blocks with a north-south orientation, a possible great house, and road segments (Duff et al. 2010). The possible great house (Architectural Block 100) was a prominent and centrally located room block with oversized surface rooms, evidence of tabular banded masonry, nearby road segments, and an associated oversized kiva

*In addition to Shields, Lupine Ridge, an early PIII period residential settlement with about twenty kivas, is situated just north of Goodman Point Pueblo (Coffey and Copeland 2011). Lupine Ridge is close enough that it has an associated midden that probably extends under the northern enclosing wall for Goodman Point Pueblo; it may have been the more immediate precursor to the canyon-rim complex.

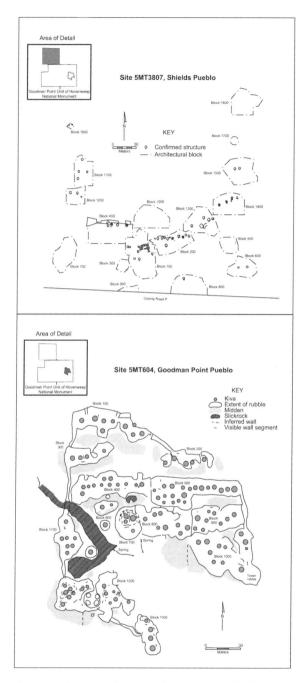

Area of Detail

Goodman Point Unit of Hovenweep
National Monument

Site 5MT3807, Shields Pueblo

Block 1800

Block 1600

N

KEY

0   50
Meters

○ Confirmed structure
— Architectural block

Block 1700

Block 1100

Block 1500

Block 1200

Block 1000

Block 1300

Block 1400

Block 400

Block 500

Block 200

Block 600

Block 700

Block 300

Block 100

Block 900

Block 800

County Road P

Area of Detail

Goodman Point Unit of Hovenweep
National Monument

Site 5MT604, Goodman Point Pueblo

KEY

○ Kiva
Extent of rubble
Midden
Slickrock
- - Inferred wall
~ Visible wall segment

Block 100

Block 300

Block 200

Block 500

Block 400

Block 600

Block 900

Block 1100

Block 800

Block 700   Spring

Spring

Block 1000

Block 1200

Tower
rubble

Block 1300

N

0   30
Meters

FIGURE 38. Map of the Goodman Point–Shields
complex. Courtesy of Crow Canyon Archaeological
Center. Illustration by Grant D. Coffey.

dating to the early 1100s (Duff and Ryan 2000). Although there was not a great kiva at Shields Pueblo, residents may have been using the Harlan great kiva to the south (Coffey 2014).

An additional nearby Chaco period building was Monsoon House, a north-south-oriented pueblo that had blocked-in kivas with subfloor vents and enclosing walls along the east and west (Coffey and Copeland 2011). Current data suggest that occupation was from around AD 1100 to the mid-1200s, at which time at least two of the kivas were burned and the buildings were dismantled and potentially reused to build the canyon-rim complex (Coffey and Copeland 2011). Monsoon House was the largest pueblo near the Harlan great kiva, which was to the east, and was situated along a connecting road that runs near this great kiva and Shields Pueblo to the north.

The occupation of the Goodman Point–Shields complex started with the deeply rooted canons of the traditional San Juan Pattern and elements of Chacoan organization, but this changed dramatically in the mid-1200s when some Chaco period settlements, such as Monsoon House and portions of Shields, were decommissioned, and the occupation of the community center shifted from the mesa top to the canyon rim and spring. Goodman Point Pueblo contained at least 114 kivas, thirteen multistoried room blocks with an estimated 450 rooms, one great kiva, several multiwalled structures, and extensive village-enclosing walls (Kuckelman et al. 2009). The number of kivas suggests that an estimated 570 to 800 people occupied the canyon-rim complex. Based on tree-ring dates and pottery type frequencies, Goodman Point Pueblo was constructed and occupied from the late AD 1250s until regional depopulation about 1280. Further evidence of a short-lived occupation are the relatively shallow middens, the lack of trash-filled rooms, and the absence of cultural material underlying the architecture (Kuckelman et al. 2009). It is impressive that the occupation of Goodman Point Pueblo barely lasted a generation, considering its size and the amount of architectural innovation that happened there.

As one of the primate centers, the Goodman Point–Shields complex was further distinguished in that the canyon-rim complex contained three multiwalled structures: one D-shaped and two biwall variants that elaborated on the conventional form (see figure 22; Kuckelman et al. 2009). This distinction is significant because there were only two centers in the Northern San Juan region with more than one multiwalled structure; the other one was, of course, Aztec. It is also significant because none of the Goodman Point multiwalled structures conform to the Aztec-Chaco architectural canon, a difference I interpret as signifying a conclusive break from the Aztec-Chaco establishment and evidence of the revolutionary changes that were happening at Goodman Point–Shields and elsewhere in the Mesa Verde core. The history of Goodman Point–Shields represents a significant reconceptualization of pueblo village life and major social, political, and ceremonial transformation at one of the most prominent locales in the Mesa Verde core.

The Primate Centers and the Mid-1200s

The divergent histories of the long-lived primate centers reflect differing trajectories of how the residents of each one coped with their circumstances, the complexities of which eventually led to redefining pueblo organization. Contending with differing and perhaps contradictory ideas about the evolving sociopolitical and ceremonial role of Aztec through the prism of local politics and in the context of increasing population aggregation and difficult farming conditions was bound to generate disagreement and tension within and between villages. These tensions reached critical mass in the mid-1200s, prompting extensive reorganization and innovation at each of the primate centers that rippled across the region. The different modes of reorganization among these four centers reflect a changing balance of power as population in the Mesa Verde core, and McElmo in particular, increased. A critical dimension of this shift in the regional center of gravity—riddled with uncertainty and strife—is that Aztec went from being an integrative force in the region to one that engendered increasing autonomy.

These sociopolitical dynamics and dramatic cultural changes, most evident at the primate centers, were pervasive, and each community center contended with them depending on its own unique circumstances. Upheavals at the large villages also had implications for those living in small or medium-sized villages, and the insecurity caused by changes at the centers likely prompted adjustments in their social networks to buffer these uncertainties, which may be why there are higher frequencies of extralocal pottery and lithics at small villages than at many community centers (see chapter 4; see also Arakawa 2012b), or led to people leaving these villages to join the larger ones. The increasing ethos of "every man for himself" (and village for itself), further amplified by climatic hardships, created a highly competitive and acrimonious social climate, as the increased emphasis on enclosing walls and towers at these and other community centers may attest (see chapter 3; Glowacki and Ortman 2012).

Evidence for shifting alliances and growing competition between Aztec and the centers in the Mesa Verde core is most apparent in Mesa Verde Proper, which was stuck in the middle of these competing entities. As discussed in chapter 5, unlike elsewhere in the region, population density was high on Mesa Verde Proper in the late 900s and 1000s (Kleidon et al. 2007; Kleidon et al. 2003; Schwindt et al. 2014), and the social histories of this population were fundamentally affected by Chaco Canyon, the great house expansion period, and, in due course, Aztec. Settlement during this period and throughout the 1100s was highly concentrated in the canyons and mesas of the eastern portion of the Mesa Verde uplift, which was more proximal to both Aztec and Chaco Canyon than other areas were. The largest community centers at this time had great houses (i.e., Morefield Canyon Great House Village, Farview, and the Battleship Rock complex [Fewkes 1921; Glowacki 2012; Kleidon et al. 2003]). There were also two large community centers with possible great houses in Whites and Prater Canyons, both wide-bottomed, well-watered canyons on the eastern side of the Mesa Verde uplift (Glowacki 2012; Kleidon et al. 2003). The concentrated occupation and evident ideological connections to Chaco and Aztec-Chaco suggest that Mesa Verde Proper ceremonial and social networks were, at this time, predominantly oriented toward Aztec and other settlements in the Totah, and likely Chaco Canyon.

During the early to mid-1200s, however, the eastern canyons and mesas of Mesa Verde were depopulated and settlement shifted to the central and western portions of the uplift, areas that were more interior with steeper canyons (Glowacki et al. 2010). This shift coincided with intensified occupation in the alcoves, as it occurred when the majority of the construction in the cliff dwellings took place (Brisbin et al. 2007; Cattanach 1980; Fiero 1999; Glowacki 2006b; Nordby 2001). Although relocation to alcove settings—part of the broad, regional pattern of moving to canyon settings—happened for a variety of reasons, including increased control of water sources and defense, it also entailed a realignment of sociopolitical and ceremonial networks and pueblo reorganization, drawing on new canons found in late PIII McElmo centers. Consider, for example, the organization of Cliff Palace and the broader Chapin community (Rohn 1971), which included both Sun Temple—a large D-shaped structure—and Fire Temple (Fewkes 1916; Vivian and Reiter 1965). Strong connections with McElmo settlements were also evident in both pottery and lithic procurement sources and networks (see chapter 4; Arakawa 2012b). Thus, it seems that in the 1200s, people living on Mesa Verde Proper reoriented social and ceremonial networks to become more associated with McElmo centers, consolidating the Mesa Verde core perhaps more than it had been during previous periods.

In summary, changes in sociopolitical and ceremonial organization were a critical component of the social landscape that prompted widespread emigration from the region. These changes were a reflection of modifications stemming from growing disaffection with Aztec-Chaco that reconfigured ranked and communal organizations, ceremonial and political alignments, and social and economic networks, as well as other pragmatic concerns, such as agricultural production, territoriality, and water rights. These changes were most intense in the mid-1200s, producing a highly contentious social climate that was worsened by an increasingly aggregated population coupled with climatic hardships, which created problems that could ultimately be overcome only by leaving.

CHAPTER SEVEN

Leaving Mesa Verde

Emigration from the Northern San Juan region happened for reasons as varied as the individuals and groups that left, especially those leaving at the forefront of the migrations in the late 1100s and early 1200s. For some, the process of detachment and leaving Mesa Verde was long, potentially involving much of the thirteenth century, but for others it was an abrupt and rapid transition. The manifold reasons for leaving were influenced by how people were situated in the politically charged, multicultural, and presumably multilingual, social landscape. With the historical contingencies and diverse circumstances established, a more considered examination of the regional depopulation is possible.

The extent to which the complete depopulation of the Northern San Juan was protracted or rapid has received much attention, with most of the deliberation focused on the Mesa Verde core and its rapid depopulation, which involved the exodus of potentially more than 10,000 people in less than a generation (Lipe 1995:152; Lipe and Varien 1999b:312; Rohn 1989:166; Varien 1999:202, 2010:table 1.1; Varien et al. 1996:103–4; Varien et al. 2007:289; Wilshusen 2002:118). Some consideration has also been given to the long-term processes involved, including the gradual emigration of individuals and households beginning in the late 1100s and early 1200s (Ahlstrom et al. 1995; Duff and Wilshusen 2000). All recognize, implicitly if not explicitly, that the regional depopulation was a complex process comprising both rapid and gradual phases, which were further complicated by spatial and temporal variation and ongoing short-distance migrations by individuals and households.

The last century and a half of the Mesa Verde occupation of the Northern San Juan is characterized by three phases of regional emigration and intraregional population movement with different character, intensity, and duration: (1) strategic emigration and relocation during the severity of the drought and violence in the mid to late 1100s; (2) situational emigration and relocation during the comparative stability of the early to mid-1200s; and (3) mass exodus and refuge during the volatile mid to late 1200s. As described, the Chaco to Post-Chaco transition was truly difficult (see chapter 5). The critical stressors of extreme violence and severe drought prompted strong responses including both aggregation and emigration— responses that varied across the region. In McElmo, both increasing aggregation and emigration were evident (Glowacki and Ortman 2012; Ryan 2010; Varien et al. 2007:table 3). In Mesa Verde Proper (Glowacki et al. 2010) and the Totah (Brown et al. 2013), population declined. In Western Mesa Verde, Kayenta populations left the region to concentrate in well-watered locations with arable land in the Kayenta heartlands (e.g., Klethla Valley and Navajo Mountain uplands [Dean 1996, 2010]). The Mesa Verde groups occupying areas such as Cedar Mesa and the Red Rock Plateau had a mixed response, for while some groups stayed, others emigrated from the region (Matson et al. 1988; Varien et al. 1996).

The different ways people responded to the severity of the Chaco to Post-Chaco transition had a major influence on how the next century unfolded. In some cases, the severe conditions became an enabler galvanizing aggregation, which promoted a trajectory of increasing village size that particularly took hold in Eastern Mesa Verde. The uncertainty of this period also changed attitudes about the steadfastness of Chacoan institutions and religious practices, which enabled factions and new religious movements and practices to form, creating new stressors. Those who instead chose to emigrate from the region demonstrated the effectiveness of relocation and established connections between their homelands and destinations that may have facilitated future migratory pathways.* The turmoil of the Chaco to Post-Chaco transition became ingrained in social memory through the recounting of oral histories, which informed perspectives and influenced actions in the years to come.

Compared to what preceded it, AD 1200 to 1240 was a more stable period, despite the episodes of prolonged below-average temperatures (Wright 2010) and substantial social change as population and aggregation continued to increase, especially in the McElmo subregion. People still migrated, however. Much of this population movement was intraregional, involving short distances within communities (e.g., the Goodman

*Return migration probably accompanied these emigrations, as it is a common component of migration (Anthony 1990). There is little evidence of these connections via exchange networks, however, since long-distance exchange decreased subsequent to this period (Wilson and Blinman 1995). It is unclear whether the lack of exchange evidence was the result of social reasons or whether the proportion of people leaving the region was too low to have much of an influence on potential exchange networks.

Point and Sand Canyon communities [Varien 1999]) or moves to a neighboring subregion, which contributed to the apparent population consolidation in the Mesa Verde core. Under these circumstances, enabling
factors may have played a greater role than stressors, since joining an
existing village often required familial or other personal connections or
the possession of specialized knowledge.

Population in all parts of the region, except the Lower San Juan,
increased between AD 1220 and 1240; however, the increase was most
dramatic in the McElmo subregion, where populations living in the centers increased five times more than in centers in West Central Mesa
Verde and the Totah (see table 4). A proportion of this increase was local
aggregation into community centers, but demographic change in the
VEP I study area in McElmo indicates that some immigration was also
involved (Varien et al. 2007:fig. 5b), with migrants most likely moving
in from West Central Mesa Verde (Glowacki 2010). The formation of
new types of villages and religious organization promoted a social environment conducive to change, which further enabled increasing population movement and immigration. The Aztec-Chaco revitalization, village
reconfiguration including the construction of enclosing walls and towers,
and the initial benefits of heightened aggregation all promoted stability,
at least for a time—an inference supported by a recent analysis by Kohler
and his colleagues (2014) showing that violence during much of the early
1200s was lower than would be expected given the prevailing conditions.

The mid-1200s were clearly a tipping point, however, one that apparently involved too much change, too fast, during an uncertain time.
The conditions under which people emigrated were extreme, especially
socially. Stressors stemming from social upheaval and conflict, which
were compounded by worsening climate and agricultural capacity, over-
whelmingly motivated emigration. Between AD 1240 and 1260, people
across the region were leaving, but the highest frequency of emigration
was from Western Mesa Verde and on Mesa Verde Proper. After AD 1260,
the highest frequency of emigration was from McElmo and the Totah
(see chapter 3). The different processes involved in the detachment from
place and the timing and rate of emigration were intimately connected to
the historical landscapes in which people were ingrained, albeit in complex ways. The most pronounced differences in emigration and detachment were between Eastern and Western Mesa Verde.

Leaving Western Mesa Verde

Several enabling factors, not shared by those living in the eastern part
of the region, influenced the nature, timing, and pathways of emigration

from Western Mesa Verde. To begin with, people in Western Mesa Verde were more predisposed to moving and leaving than were those in the east, since the majority of the population of Western Mesa Verde lived in dispersed, small, multihousehold pueblos and were highly mobile, especially in the far western areas like the Lower San Juan. This settlement pattern, unlike the large, aggregated community centers to the east in the Mesa Verde core, readily enabled household fissioning and relocation (see chapter 5; Dean 1996, 2010) and was an important means of coping with the dry and harsh environment and low agricultural potential.

Western Mesa Verde was also a multicultural frontier where different Mesa Verde Pueblo groups, with varying Chacoan influences, and Kayenta Pueblo people intermixed (see chapter 5). These groups also had interactions with the nearby Virgin and Fremont populations who lived to their north and west (Allison 2010). Even though cultural diversity was also present in Eastern Mesa Verde (Ortman 2012; Schillaci et al. 2001; Schillaci and Stojanowski 2002), the context and degree of diversity among the Western Mesa Verde cultural groups differed markedly. In the west, the low population density and high mobility enabled a higher proportion of the population to have more direct interaction with diverse cultural groups than in the highly concentrated population of the Mesa Verde core. Western Mesa Verde populations were also more affected than their counterparts in the east by the expansion and contraction of Kayenta populations in the eleventh and twelfth centuries (Cameron 2009; Dean 1996, 2010; Matson et al. 1988). The historically situated and culturally diverse social networks in Western Mesa Verde provided connections with people possessing knowledge of different social and natural geographies, enabling different migration pathways and destinations than in Eastern Mesa Verde.

Another important difference is that people living in Western Mesa Verde were at the northwestern extreme of the Chacoan sphere of influence and also more distant from Aztec than were the Mesa Verde Pueblo groups in the eastern part of the region. The frontier nature of Western Mesa Verde meant the social landscape was a mosaic of interspersed groups where some villages were more tied to Chacoan influences than others were, and these influences increasingly diminished in the western extremes. Thus, from the outset, the residents of Western Mesa Verde were not as well integrated into the ceremonial and political networks stemming from Chacoan practices as were those in the east.

All but one of the sixteen great house communities in Western Mesa Verde (i.e., Et Al Great House [Fast 2012]) were either in the immediate vicinity of Comb Ridge or located to the east of it (see figure 20). Thus, more than half of Western Mesa Verde lacked great houses, and in the Lower San Juan, there is little to no evidence of Chacoan influences

(Dean 1996, 2010). In short, Comb Ridge, though not a physical impediment, was an ideological boundary, and west of it people were minimally involved in the social, political, and religious dynamics of Chaco and Aztec. The Pueblo people living west of Comb Ridge blended Mesa Verde and Kayenta traits, making them distinct from groups living in Central Mesa Verde and the Totah (see chapters 3 and 5).

Those living in the eastern portion of Western Mesa Verde, however, had stronger connections with Aztec and the Mesa Verde core, at least prior to the early 1200s. Yet their peripheral location relative to both "things Chaco" and Aztec meant a greater degree of independence and physical distance from the dynamics stimulated by the Aztec-Chaco revitalization and McElmo Intensification in the Mesa Verde core. This independence enabled people and communities in Western Mesa Verde to easily dissociate when difficulties and dissension occurred to the east, which appears to have happened in the early to mid-1200s, since no multiwalled structures were built. It made leaving Western Mesa Verde easier, as well.

The process of detaching from place, or at least an increased proclivity toward moving and leaving, had strong roots in the Chaco to Post-Chaco transition. As insecurities heightened with increasing violence and worsening drought and were exacerbated by the decline of Chaco and the ensuing turmoil as Aztec campaigned and the McElmo Intensification began, people in Western Mesa Verde became disaffected. There were enough challenges "at home" that they did not have the time or the resources to invest elsewhere. Since they were living in marginal climes to begin with, the drought was especially hard felt. Not only did the terribly dry conditions affect their already limited ability to grow corn, beans, and other crops, but it also disrupted access to cotton and other materials that may have been integral to their subsistence (see chapters 4 and 5). At the turn of the thirteenth century, when conditions improved, rather than re-engaging with those in the east, people in West Central Mesa Verde became more localized and consequently peripheral to the Mesa Verde core. Their distancing from eastern dynamics—evidenced by the absence of multiwalled structures—does not mean that there was no interaction with the east or that Chacoan-affiliated ideologies were utterly rejected. Western community centers with great houses continued to be occupied into the mid-1200s, and the Comb Wash Great House is the only clear example of a new great house being built after the mid-1100s (Hurst and Till 2009). Thus, there were pockets of conservatism where some villages maintained their traditional (Chacoan) ceremonial practices. This entrenchment seems to have extended to other realms, including the persistence of sandal production and iconography at post-Chaco sites (Bellorado et al. 2012). If these villages were strongly traditionalist, they may have also resisted Aztec-Chaco revitalization by eschewing the construction of multiwalled structures. Regardless of their underlying reasons, a growing majority of the West Central Mesa Verde population had dissociated from eastern politics and ceremonialism, which had become contentious. To paraphrase Voltaire at the end of *Candide*, they were cultivating their own gardens and staying out of it. This distancing created new ideological and political boundaries that socially separated those who remained in West Central Mesa Verde from eastern dynamics, such that Western Mesa Verde dynamics became most germane. This was not the case for everyone, however, because more people left centers in West Central Mesa Verde during the early to mid-1200s than in the Totah or McElmo subregions (see table 4). Some of this emigration resulted from people leaving the region altogether, but in other cases, people who wanted to maintain their connections with Eastern Mesa Verde and actively participate in the revolutionary changes happening at the McElmo centers left to join them. Still others, those who had become completely disenfranchised, used emigration from the region as a means of detaching from Mesa Verde society altogether.

Emigration from West Central Mesa Verde in the mid-1200s was part of a broader regional trend in which the Northern San Juan generally emptied out from west to east (see chapter 3; Glowacki 2010; Lipe 1995); a trend that Dean (1996) also notes for the Kayenta region. Tree-ring data support this inference, since the distribution of known dates shows a sharp reduction in construction timbers by the late 1260s (Lipe 1995; Lipe et al. 2010), which suggests that much of the Western Mesa Verde ancestral Pueblo population had departed by AD 1270, before the so-called Great Drought began. Not only were more people leaving sooner, but also emigration from Western Mesa Verde accelerated faster than from other parts of the region. By AD 1260–1280, twice as many people were leaving West Central Mesa Verde as in the McElmo subregion and as many as ten times more people than in the rest of the subregions (see table 4). Why, then, were more Pueblo people leaving the west sooner than in the east?

That Western Mesa Verde is generally drier and a marginal environment for growing corn and other crops means people would be more susceptible to climatic difficulties such as cooling temperatures and below-average precipitation (Kohler et al. 2007; Wright 2010). Consequently, Western Mesa Verde residents may have been more impacted by climatic perturbations sooner than those living in the east, particularly populations in the Lower San Juan, an area that received half the amount of precipitation and had higher local variability than Central Mesa Verde, which includes West Central Mesa Verde (Wright 2010:93). Climatic concerns across Western Mesa Verde therefore were not uniformly experienced, nor were they necessarily extreme enough to explain why Pueblo people began leaving Western Mesa Verde in the mid-1200s, since climatic trends such as below-average precipitation do not clearly correlate with population loss until the 1270s (Lipe et al. 2010). Climatic factors alone cannot fully account for why so many people left Western Mesa Verde, particularly since a majority emigrated before the extended drought beginning in the late 1270s, and they relocated to areas in Arizona that were just as dry and difficult, if not more so.

Although people living in West Central Mesa Verde were no longer as closely aligned with sociopolitical dynamics in Eastern Mesa Verde, there were still repercussions. When significant changes happened in the east, such as the Aztec-Chaco revitalization movement and the responding Mesa Verde reformation, it also generated social change in West Central Mesa Verde as people reacted by localizing (hunkering down), leaving to join villages in the Mesa Verde core, or leaving the region entirely. These responses altered the social, political, economic, and ceremonial networks of those who stayed in West Central Mesa Verde, which had cascading effects for those in the Lower San Juan. For example, ties with those to the east may have diminished as exchange became more localized (see chapter 4), and networks that provided access to needed food or commodities and were particularly relied on for buffering during difficult times became disrupted. The shifting social landscape heightened insecurity, which was further accentuated by the challenging climatic factors.

Another, perhaps more unsettling, factor adding to a heightened sense of insecurity is the possibility that Pueblo cultural groups from farther west (including not only the Kayenta but also those living in the Northern Periphery, the Virgin and Fremont populations) were moving into and through Western Mesa Verde. All of these people were farmers who were having their own difficulties. At the western and northernmost limits of the environments that could support maize agriculture, those living in and beyond the Lower San Juan more acutely felt the periods of below-average precipitation and cooling trends during the early to mid-1200s. When these challenges became too great, mobility and relocation were key coping mechanisms. Current radiocarbon data suggest that Virgin farming ended by the late 1200s and for the Fremont ended around AD 1300 (Allison 2010). But recent radiocarbon dates taken directly from maize samples suggest that the Fremont may not have farmed maize after AD 1250 (Allison 2014). Although the sample size is small ($N = 50$) and more research is required to fully assess the implications, these exciting new data suggest that Fremont populations were struggling by the mid-1200s and small-scale migration and relocation would have been a means of coping with these difficulties. The circumstances of the Virgin populations may have been similar, since radiocarbon data suggest that they may have departed by the end of the 1200s (Allison 2010). Though scant, evidence of Pueblo and Fremont interactions has been found at the Bluff Great House, where two of the ten Bull Creek points—a western triangular projectile point found across southeastern Utah in both Pueblo and Fremont areas—recovered were long enough to have likely been from the Fremont area (Cameron 2009:306).

Growing evidence also suggests that Athabaskan population movements may have been affecting groups living in the Northern Periphery and Western Mesa Verde by the mid to late 1200s (e.g., Seymour 2012). Ives (2014) recently analyzed thirty-nine perishables from the Promontory Caves collection made by Julian Steward in the 1930s using AMS radiocarbon dating, which produced a two-sigma date range from AD 1167 to 1395 with central tendencies in the 1200s. These results—when paired with other lines of evidence including oral histories, genetic data, and the appearance of Promontory pottery—suggest that Athabaskan groups had moved into the Salt Lake area by the 1200s and were intermixing with neighboring groups, including the Fremont. Finally, the timing of the Numic expansion into the area is also debated, but evidence suggests that Numic people were in northwestern Colorado by AD 1100 and may have moved into the Northern San Juan region and affected Pueblo settlement dynamics in the thirteenth century (Ambler and Sutton 1989; Madsen 1994; Reed 1994). The corpus of the existing and new data indicates that the Fremont, Virgin, Athabaskan, and Numic people were all moving into new areas that likely included Pueblo territory; a better understanding of these histories is required to understand what happened in the Northern San Juan and Western Mesa Verde, in particular.

Pressured from both the east and the west and, if resources were constrained, locally as well, people living in Western Mesa Verde had plenty of reasons to be concerned about their security. Settlement patterns reflect this concern, for most sites in the Lower San Juan—probably the most impacted by population movements if new groups were coming into the region—and many sites in West Central Mesa Verde have defensive characteristics. Their relatively small habitations were positioned in highly defensible locations along cliff edges or tucked into alcoves of all sizes in places like Cedar Mesa, Natural Bridges, and Grand Gulch (Bedell 2000; Dean 1996; Lipe 1970; Matson et al. 1988). The presence of defensive refuge enclosures at difficult-to-reach locations (e.g., Fortified Mesa [Fast 2012]) and defensive walls running along the perimeter of alcoves (e.g., Moon House [Bloomer 1989]) also underscore a perceived need for protection. As noted in chapter 5, shield rock art, highly visible to identify group affiliation and possibly an indication of membership in a warrior sodality, was also associated with alcove sites (Bellorado and Mills 2014; Schaafsma 2000). The prevalence of these sites and architecture

and the investment required to build and live in them implies that violence and warfare—or at least the threat of violence—were widespread
(Solometo 2006).

At first glance, the drier climate and rugged terrain of Western Mesa
Verde make it easy to assume that compounding climatic hardships in the
1200s simply made living here untenable. While this certainly mattered,
leaving Western Mesa Verde was more complicated than that in being
prompted by stressors beyond climate and drought. Although less directly
impacted by the collapsing sociopolitical and religious institutions in
Eastern Mesa Verde, people still faced repercussions from these changes
and had to figure out where they stood, which was especially difficult
for those living in West Central Mesa Verde. Some clung to convention
and entrenched their Chacoan traditionalism (e.g., Comb Wash great
house), even as they dissociated from the east. Most, however, became
increasingly autonomous as social distances among groups increased,
which would have made encounters with displaced groups from beyond
the Northern San Juan potentially even more troubling. Given settlement
locations, violence and conflict emerging from these contexts played a
key role in prompting emigration from Western Mesa Verde. Being part
of the western frontier and living in small, independent social groups
(i.e., not integrated into larger sociopolitical entities) were enablers that
allowed people to readily emigrate. Thus, when circumstances became
too inhospitable in Western Mesa Verde, it was easier for more people to
leave faster than it was in the east.

Leaving Eastern Mesa Verde

Leaving Eastern Mesa Verde was another matter entirely. Although the
episodes of emigration paralleled those in the west, the numbers of
people leaving (intensity) and the combination of stressors and enablers
underlying each episode differed. Emigration during the harsh Chaco to
Post-Chaco transition period entailed not only long-distance moves out
of the region but also intraregional relocation and aggregation into large
community centers in the Mesa Verde core as well as expansion into
Western Mesa Verde (see chapter 3; Glowacki and Ortman 2012; Matson
et al. 1988; Varien et al. 1996; Varien et al. 2007). The consequences
of how people coped with the difficulties of the mid-1100s created new
challenges and contingencies that affected Mesa Verde for generations
and culminated in regional depopulation.

Thirteenth-century emigration from Eastern Mesa Verde was largely
the result of sociopolitical upheaval stemming from opposition and religious reformation that increased conflict and warfare and ultimately

collapsed the emergent Aztec-Chaco religious and sociopolitical system. Calamitously, these circumstances were worsened by difficult agricultural conditions brought on by prolonged cooling periods and, for those still in the region in the late 1270s and 1280s, severe drought. The intensity and diversity of stress factors, both external and emergent, played out in various ways among the eastern subregions, even if the outcome was the same. Therefore, I consider each of them in turn to compare their contexts and processes of emigration.

I begin by discussing Mesa Verde Proper because it was caught between two powerful centers of gravity that were both reaching critical mass. More people may have been leaving Western Mesa Verde sooner than in the east, but in this regard Mesa Verde Proper was an important exception. Between AD 1240 and 1260, more people were leaving Mesa Verde Proper centers than anywhere else in the region (see table 4). This emigration differed from that in the west, however, in that it was followed by a brief period of aggregation from AD 1260 to 1280, when people sought refuge in the cliff dwellings. The frequency of emigration from Mesa Verde Proper in the mid-1200s was significantly higher than the other eastern subregions (i.e., a 23 percent decrease in population, as opposed to 3 percent and 4 percent in McElmo and the Totah, respectively [see table 4]). Counterintuitively, this was the same period in which cliff dwelling construction and occupation peaked at places such as Cliff Palace, Balcony House, Long House, and Spruce Tree House (Brisbin et al. 2007; Cattanach 1980; Fiero 1999; Nordby 2001). This contradictory pattern implies that aggregation into the cliff dwellings and other late villages involved social conflict and displacement that resulted in significant numbers of people leaving the subregion.

Settlement patterns in Mesa Verde Proper dramatically changed in the mid-1200s as people depopulated the eastern portion of the cuesta and concentrated in the more interior mesas and canyons. In some ways, this change is counterintuitive in that people left some of the most agriculturally productive and well-watered places in the region (e.g., Morefield Canyon [Benson 2011]) to move to relatively less productive locales on the cuesta, a disparity they ultimately remedied through the intensified use of check dams along canyon and talus slope drainages, which significantly increased potential yields (see chapter 2; Hayes 1964; Kleidon et al. 2007; Kleidon et al. 2003; Rohn 1963). If, however, relocating to alcoves and other canyon rim settings was their primary concern, it is the more interior canyons, like Soda, Long, and Navajo, where alcove formation is more prevalent. The eastern canyons of Whites, Morefield, and Prater are wide-bottomed canyons with more gradual talus slopes lacking habitable alcoves. Relocation to the more rugged, interior canyons of the cuesta suggests a perceived need to heighten security by living in places that were more protected and difficult to access (Hayes 1964; Lancaster et al. 1954; Rohn 1977)—an inference further supported by the coincidence of this settlement shift with the dramatic changes in sociopolitical and religious organizations and networks happening in Eastern Mesa Verde.

The depopulation of the eastern canyons and mesas increased travel distances to Aztec and elsewhere in the Totah and implies that proximity to these areas became less important than local concerns, including protection. To me, it also implies an ideological and sociopolitical reorientation as ideas about connections with Aztec and the Aztec-Chaco sociopolitical system changed (see chapter 6). If this is true, then among those people leaving Mesa Verde Proper in the mid-1200s were those more aligned with Aztec-Chaco ideologies who wanted to be in the Totah. Population growth in Aztec and Salmon in the mid-1200s (Brown et al. 2013; Reed 2006a) and the new construction at Aztec East and West incorporating Mesa Verde–style masonry and murals (see chapter 5; Brown et al. 2008; Brown and Paddock 2011; Diederichs et al. 2011; Lipe 2006; Lister and Lister 1987:91–95; Morris 1928) correspond with when a substantial number of people were leaving Mesa Verde Proper. Because migration pathways from Mesa Verde Proper inevitably passed through the Totah, these emigrants contributed to the local population growth and social changes happening at Aztec and in the Totah during the mid-1200s.

Those who stayed in Mesa Verde Proper, despite the increased distance and changing orientations toward Aztec, remained involved with the religious and sociopolitical networks but became more aligned with McElmo centers. As described in chapter 4, strong connections between residents of Mesa Verde Proper and both McElmo and the Totah are evident via pottery procurement frequencies (see chapter 4), and there are multi-walled structures in Mesa Verde Proper (see chapter 3). The presence of both circular and D-shaped structures suggests that allegiances were divided if the different forms in fact indicate affinity with Aztec-Chaco revitalization (circular) versus the Mesa Verde reformation centered in McElmo (D-shaped). That people living in the Chapin community, which included Cliff Palace, built the largest D-shaped structure in the region, Sun Temple (Fewkes 1916), at the end of the occupation suggests the religious and sociopolitical changes happening on Mesa Verde Proper paralleled those happening in McElmo at the largest centers like Goodman Point Pueblo. Changes such as these likely entailed contentious social conflict and negotiation, as did aggregating into the cliff dwellings, especially the largest ones, for it required people to learn how to live in close quarters. For example, households would necessarily lose autonomy when the entire village is constrained by an alcove.

Evidence of conflict within the cliff dwellings comes from a detailed architectural documentation study of Spruce Tree House, which revealed that two religious rooms and a tower were burned after AD 1250 (Brisbin et al. 2007; Glowacki 2006b). Some or all of this destruction could have been done by outside attackers, particularly given the defensive aspect of the tower. However, the ceremonial rooms that were targeted suggest a purgative decommissioning due to a changeover in religious authority and are indicative of underlying internal social conflicts. Significantly, these ceremonial rooms and at least one of the towers (the Main Street Tower) did not fall into disuse, for subsequent to their burning all three were remodeled and reroofed. Because the latest tree-ring date at Spruce Tree House is 1278v—a noncutting date from a secondary beam in Room 6—these structures were likely used for almost another generation after they burned. Notably, the timing of the events surrounding the burning and reuse of these structures seems to correspond with the AD 1260 to 1280 period when population increased as people sought refuge in the cliff dwellings. This evidence suggests that the accommodation of new groups was at times contentious.

Other episodes of burning also happened at Spruce Tree House, since at least three of the kivas were burned (Kivas A, E and H), most likely upon abandonment in the last decades of occupation, because there is no evidence of remodeling (Brisbin et al. 2007). Interpreting the motive behind these conflagrations is difficult, because of multiple equally plausible explanations, including ritual closure when families moved voluntarily, a purgative decommissioning if families were forced out, or violent invasion. Not all kivas were burned, however, so either the ritual closure hypothesis is unlikely or the rituals were unneeded in these cases or those associated with the other kivas left too quickly to perform any closing rituals or no one remained who could perform them. At least two other cliff dwellings, Mug House and Long House, also have burned kivas, some of which were remodeled and reused (e.g., Kivas C and D in Mug House [Rohn 1971]).

Despite all this, the cliff dwellings were good places to be, in troubled times, that allowed people to stay until the very end. All of the major cliff dwellings have noncutting dates in the 1270s, and Balcony House, Square Tower House, and Long House have an AD 1280 noncutting date, making these sites among the last places occupied in the region (Lipe 1995; Varien 2010:table 1.3). That the cliff dwellings were likely refuges of last resort is also implicated in Nordenskiöld's (1990:170) description of unburied human remains in all the dwellings he investigated, which implies that no one may have been left to inter them.

Meanwhile, leaving Aztec (Totah) and McElmo was probably particularly volatile and wrenching. The decline of Chaco and the severe drought conditions in the mid-1100s compromised Aztec's power and exposed weaknesses that ultimately proved difficult to overcome. By the mid-1200s, with people in West Central Mesa Verde seceding and the Mesa Verde core splintering (see chapters 5 and 6), Aztec was clearly struggling. Despite their efforts to revitalize (see chapters 5 and 6) and continued regional presence (Cameron and Duff 2008; Lekson 2008), the religious and sociopolitical institutions of Aztec ultimately collapsed as political centers in McElmo increasingly undermined its power through reformation, factionalization, and competition.

Provided that the Totah data are not overly influenced by the more limited chronological resolution in this part of the region, they suggest that by AD 1180 some people were always leaving (see figure 14 and table 4; see also Brown et al. 2013:fig. 6), but the overall rate of emigration was slower than in other subregions and many people remained until the last decades of occupation (i.e., the 1250s through the 1270s). The latest cutting date from Aztec East is AD 1269, which also has noncutting dates in the 1270s, and the latest dates from Aztec West are in the 1260s. Thus, at least some people lived at Aztec until the late 1270s, if not 1280s, and Aztec West may have been depopulated before Aztec East (Brown et al. 2008:figs. 12.1 and 12.2).

Although deteriorating climatic conditions and lower agricultural productivity contributed to their difficulties, most people had left Aztec and the Totah before the onset of the drought in AD 1276. The social stressors were what forced most people to leave the Totah; obviously, chief among these was strident ideological and sociopolitical conflict involving violence and warfare. Both the Hubbard Triwall at Aztec and the triwall at Pueblo del Arroyo in Chaco Canyon (Vivian 1959) had gouged-out floors and were dismantled either in a ritualized decommissioning event or through intentional eradication. In either case, these triwalls—iconic of Aztec-Chaco ideologies—were destroyed and no longer an active part of the ritual landscape. Additionally, Salmon, a great house strongly associated with Aztec (see chapter 5), was destroyed in a catastrophic fire in the late 1200s (Reed 2006a). Evidence of violence and warfare is difficult to interpret, but in the context of an event such as the collapse of a major religious and sociopolitical system, these two examples of intentional destruction suggest that they did not "go gentle into that good night" (to borrow the words of Dylan Thomas).

If possible, leaving McElmo was even more acute and contentious than leaving the Totah, for the rapid buildup in McElmo had a correspondingly calamitous and precipitous end. Social upheaval and ceremonial intensification during the mid-1200s caused strife and other circumstances that marginalized individuals and families who emigrated earlier than everyone else (see table 4). Most of the emigration from McElmo, however, was back-loaded, and the lion's share happened post-AD 1260 (see chapter 3; Varien 2010; Varien et al. 2007). The religious and sociopolitical upheaval in the mid-1200s was catastrophic, rending long-standing social networks and undermining long-held ideological tenets that had antecedents harkening back to the AD 800s and 900s, if not before. The social landscape was likely even more factionalized than we realize, because identity and religion are not necessarily reflected in material culture. For example, on First Mesa, the villages of Sichomovi (Hopi) and Okeowangi (Hopi-Tewa) are indistinguishable from each other based on pottery and architecture despite strong ethnic differences (Dongoske et al. 1997; Kroskrity 1993).

Specifically what transpired in McElmo is difficult to divine because the nature of the politics and confederacies that existed among the centers and other pueblos is poorly understood, as is the degree to which McElmo centers were connected to or independent from Aztec. Yet, as this book has detailed, signs of a complex combination of multiple competing centers enmeshed in different alliances are evident. Variation in settlement size and civic-ceremonial architecture among the community centers suggests that hierarchical inequalities in social, economic, and religious power existed among them (see chapters 3 and 6). Many of the largest centers were long-lived establishments, founded when great houses were first being built across the northern Southwest and were affiliated to varying degrees with Chaco ideologies. The religious authority base of the Chaco system that undergirded McElmo sociopolitical and religious organization was compromised by the severe climatic and social conditions during the mid-1100s. This opened the door for changes in social, political, and religious organization and increasing competition among the centers.

When the leadership at Aztec attempted to fill this void with an Aztec-Chaco revitalization movement at the turn of the thirteenth century, not everyone joined the new movement. It was in this context, coupled with dramatically increasing population size and density, that new types of villages, like Sand Canyon Pueblo, were established, creating new political entities that disrupted or altered existing, and likely long-standing, social networks. In this new social milieu, opposition to the establishment and religious reformation developed. Great houses were not constructed at the new villages, and although multiwalled structures were built at some of them, in some cases these structures were D-shaped or other variations instead of the circular form promoted via Aztec-Chaco ideologies. These social changes were divisive, and the manifold fracture lines along which factions developed included (1) long-lived, multigenerational centers versus the late centers; and (2) those that were pro-Aztec-Chaco (establishment) versus those wanting change (progressive). These and other dimensions created massive social ruptures, which increased competition, autonomy, and violence among people and villages, and were accentuated by agricultural hardships that unbeknownst to them included imminent severe drought. Emigration during this turbulent period (i.e., 1250s and 1260s) gained momentum, becoming a full-blown exodus by the 1270s.

This social chaos imbalanced not just individual villages but all of Mesa Verde society. A central tenet of Pueblo cosmology, balance is expressed through directionality, symmetry, and ceremony (e.g., Malotki 2002; Ortiz 1969; Van Dyke 2007a). When things are not right, something or, more often, someone is to blame for the ensuing social chaos. Most often, these problems must be corrected through ritual and other religious practices, and in the mid-1200s, religious organization itself was in flux. If, during this liminal period, religious practices were changed such that certain ritual specialists were no longer necessary and they subsequently emigrated, it could have been impossible to bring back prior rituals should the new ones be deemed ineffectual. By the mid to late 1200s, balance clearly needed to be restored even if extreme measures were required (e.g., the village destroyed, as in Awatovi [Fewkes 1893]) and it ultimately meant starting over somewhere else.

If deposing Aztec was the goal, the residents of the McElmo centers may have won the metaphorical war, but they lost the battle. The Mesa Verde reformation and changes in religious and social organization at villages like Goodman Point–Shields and Yucca House could have succeeded in gaining traction and stability were it not for the onset of the late 1270s drought, which made an already divisive and unstable social landscape even more so. Those remaining in McElmo had to contend with compounding hardships as not only farming conditions deteriorated but also warfare increased insufferably, as evidenced by the violent clashes that led to the abandonment of Sand Canyon and Castle Rock Pueblos (Kuckelman 2010; Kuckelman et al. 2003). These new challenges came at a precarious time in the founding of the new organizational canons of the Mesa Verde reformation, leaving these villages vulnerable and unable to endure this crucible, such that the remaining Pueblo populations left.

Leaving Eastern Mesa Verde was the culmination of growing schisms within Pueblo society and a physical manifestation of the ultimate rejection of overt ideological and political links to Chaco and Aztec, if not their historical connections. It involved rebuffing not only Aztec-Chaco but also, as discussed below, the hierarchical power structures upon which it was founded (see also Arakawa 2012a). People left Eastern Mesa Verde because the Aztec-Chaco religious and sociopolitical system collapsed and the Mesa Verde reformation was unsuccessful. Although the buildup of change and tension was long in the making, the transformation happened quickly in the latter half of the 1200s, and in less than a generation the revolutionary tides of change and emigration could not be stemmed. The collapse was precipitous, turbulent, and beset with endemic warfare (Kohler et al. 2014; Kuckelman 2010; Kuckelman et al. 2000). Leaving Eastern Mesa Verde meant leaving this chaos behind and shedding most of the cultural signatures associated with Aztec-Chaco and the Mesa Verde reformation, such as kiva jars, mugs, iconic architectural forms, and types of religious organization that emphasized hierarchical power structures (Arakawa 2012a; Lipe 2010). Many Eastern Mesa Verde migrants ended up in the Rio Grande region, perhaps because despite the Pueblo populations living there during the Chaco era, there was little Chacoan influence in the region (Fowles 2004).

How Complete Was the Depopulation?

Varien (2010:21–25, table 1.3) analyzed the distribution of 2,322 cutting dates using binomial probability and found that the likelihood of going five years without a cutting date was minimal. He therefore infers that the region was most likely completely depopulated by AD 1285, since the latest known tree-ring date is AD 1280, an inference further supported by evidence of drought in AD 1280, 1283, and 1284. For the vast majority of the Pueblo population, this proposed timing was probably true; people either had moved away or had died by AD 1285. However, scattered families and small groups of Pueblo people could have remained in the region for a number of years without being archaeologically visible, especially if they were living in the cliff dwellings. Pueblo people today have stories about those who stayed behind, and archaeological evidence suggests that at least some people continued living in villages even after others had emigrated. In Spruce Tree House cliff dwelling, for example, midden accumulation in the plaza space in the back of the alcove (Nordenskiöld 1990) and in the Main Street Tower (noted in 1903 by Thomas McKee, a professional photographer) suggest that a smaller population continued to live in Spruce Tree House at the end of its occupation. Even though many people may have been gone by AD 1285, a remnant Pueblo population may have continued to live in the region into the 1290s or later.

Another important line of evidence pointing to an extended Pueblo presence in the Northern San Juan is the occurrence of sites with Hopi yellow ware in Western Mesa Verde. This distinctive ware can be made only from resources mined from the Hopi mesas and started being made around AD 1300. To assess the nature and timing of the Pueblo depopulation of the Four Corners region, Adams and Adams (1993) compiled a database of all known sites (N = 62) with Hopi yellow ware or rock art in southern Utah and northern Arizona; nineteen of these sites are within Western Mesa Verde. They argue that although visitation may account for some of the evidence, it was most likely, based on their pottery assemblages and site locations, that these sites were permanent Pueblo occupations. Among the Western Mesa Verde sites in their sample, eight were associated with pre-1200s pottery, nine with pottery assemblages dating to the 1200s, and two with post-1300 pottery assemblages. These distributions imply that people living in Western Mesa Verde had connections with the Hopi mesas through trade or return migrations and that some Pueblo people may have been in the area after AD 1300, perhaps staying on longer than those in Eastern Mesa Verde.

Other evidence of continued Pueblo presence in the region includes postabandonment use of Shields Pueblo (Ryan n.d.), where in some cases kiva roofs collapsed and people returned to build circular shrines with masonry walls no more than seven courses high in the footprint of the kivas. Ryan (n.d.) interprets these postabandonment structures as evidence of ritual decommissioning performed within several years of their original use by those who had formerly used the kivas. These shrines were built to maintain definitive ties to this place and past, even after the inhabitants had moved elsewhere. There are no dates associated with these shrines; soil deposition after the kiva roofs collapsed indicates that some unknown amount of time had elapsed before the shrines were constructed. Thus, we do not really know when these shrines were built. Was it by people who had once lived on the mesa top and then moved into Goodman Point Pueblo or by people who had left altogether and came back to maintain claims to their ancestral homelands?

Given evidence of continued Pueblo presence in the Northern San Juan, it is even more curious to me that Pueblo people did not return to this area once the social dynamics had been diffused by the exodus and the climate improved around AD 1300 (Wright 2010). As is often suggested, the collective memory of what happened in Mesa Verde may have kept ancestral Pueblo people from returning to live in the Northern San Juan again: what happened there was just too terrible, and they did not want history to repeat itself. With the significant changes to Pueblo culture in the fourteenth century, subsequent to the catastrophic collapse of Aztec-Chaco and the failed Mesa Verde reformation, that past must have been a powerful deterrent. However, these sentiments were probably not as keenly felt by those who had lived in Western Mesa Verde, yet none of them returned to live year-round, even if they may have stayed on longer (Adams and Adams 1993). Therefore, the only way it makes sense to me that Pueblo people did not come back to live in some part of the Northern San Juan is if there were also other groups of people in the region, making it more difficult to return.

As discussed above, there is growing evidence that not just Numic and Athabaskan peoples but also the Fremont and Virgin populations may have been in and through the region by the mid to late 1200s and 1300s (Allison 2010, 2014; Cameron 2009; Ives 2014; Seymour 2012). In addition to the archaeological record, the oral histories of the Utes and Navajos also describe interactions with Pueblo people. For example, when the Hayden Expedition stopped to document Castle Rock in AD 1875, their local guide, John Moss, an Indian agent for the Hopis (1864–1868), recounted a story he had heard about the area. It described how the Pueblo people who were living there had been visited by strangers from the North and how they were forced into the cliffs because of raiding by the neighboring Utes (Kuckelman 2000). Oral histories also describe interactions between Navajos and Pueblo people in the Northern San Juan (McPherson 2014). Understanding how the population movements of Pueblo groups from the Northern Periphery and the Ute and Athabaskan groups affected the Mesa Verde Pueblo populations is an important area of study, one that is necessary to better understand not only their histories but also what happened at the end of the 1200s.

Where Did They Go?

As turbulent and complex as the social histories of the Pueblo people in the Northern San Juan were, the migration histories and what happened on the way to and at destinations were equally complex, if not more so. Since this particular book is about leaving place—as opposed to going and what happened when they went, topics explored by several recent books (e.g., Ortman 2012; Ware 2014)—I next present a few insights about where they went, gained from the perspective of leaving.

When thousands of people, likely tens of thousands, left the Northern San Juan region, they caused a ripple effect across the Pueblo world. Differences between Eastern and Western Mesa Verde historical landscapes structured migration routes from the region: for example, many though not all of those who lived in the eastern subregions moved into northern New Mexico and those in the western subregions into northern Arizona (Borck 2012; Cordell et al. 2007; Dean 1996, 2010; Ortman 2012; Roney 1995). The contexts from which Mesa Verde Pueblo people emigrated shaped their beliefs, motivations, and actions and affected what happened at their destinations.

When Pueblo groups from Western Mesa Verde left the region, many likely headed south, but whether that was southwest toward Black Mesa, down the Chinle Wash, or toward the Chuska Mountains varied greatly depending on personal circumstance and connections and was heavily influenced by whether one lived in the Lower San Juan or West Central Mesa Verde. People who left the region from Western Mesa Verde were more socially and physically distant from the sociopolitical upheaval and reformation in Eastern Mesa Verde. Their contexts of emigration therefore stemmed more from local concerns, such as security and subsistence, circumstances that did not entail abandoning cultural practices, especially for those living in the Lower San Juan. This important distinction may be why it seems easier to archaeologically track Western Mesa Verde and Kayenta Pueblo people who migrated south to places like Goat Hill, Reeve Ruin, and Point of Pines, than those leaving the east (Lyons and Clark 2008; Woodson 1999).

Although some Western Mesa Verde migrants may have ended up going east or southwest, most went south into and through Kayenta areas (Dean 1996, 2010). By the late 1200s, contact between Mesa Verde and Kayenta groups had increased, for Mesa Verde types are the most common extralocal pottery at Tsegi period sites. Kayenta settlement patterns also changed substantially at this time in ways reminiscent of those in Central Mesa Verde, including the formation of large, central pueblos, the construction of towers and cliff dwellings, and the use of Mesa Verde–style masonry and kiva features (Dean 1996, 2010). These settlement changes were prompted by local circumstances including pressure from non–Mesa Verde groups but also developed because of increased interactions with people from Mesa Verde, which likely included not only cooperation and conflict but also cohabitation, if Mesa Verde households sought refuge by joining Kayenta settlements. Throughout Pueblo history, seeking refuge among different indigenous groups during times of famine, disease, or strife has been a common recourse (e.g., Hopi-Tewas, Dinetah and Pueblitos, Hopis and Navajos in Canyon de Chelly, Jemez and Navajos [Jett 1964]). Given the circumstances, some Western Mesa Verde families may have joined Kayenta settlements, but similarities in material culture between the two groups would make detecting these instances difficult.

Among other routes, when Pueblo groups left the region from Eastern Mesa Verde, many headed southeast through the Gallina (Borck 2012)—especially those leaving the Totah and Mesa Verde Proper—or south along the Chaco Wash along the east side of the Chuskas. The turbulence of leaving and migrating is clear in the Gallina, where evidence of direct skeletal violence, burned structures, towers, and defensible cliff dwellings are widespread. In a recent analysis of least-cost migration pathways from the Northern San Juan to the Northern Rio Grande, Borck (2012) found a strong correlation between the proposed pathways and sites with evidence of violence. The Gallina is thought to have been depopulated shortly after AD 1275, and some of the sites with violence along the proposed migration routes have post-1250s and post-1260s dates. Thus, many of the Mesa Verde migrants moving into and through this area were those leaving in the mid-1200s, and most of the emigrants leaving the region at this time were leaving Mesa Verde Proper. As with the Kayenta populations, we often talk about Mesa Verde migrants moving through the Gallina, but perhaps some migrants tried to stay. The familiar canyon settings with defensible locations might have been attractive to the migrants, despite putting them in a position of having to contend with the local Gallina population. Other potential evidence of Mesa Verde migrants moving south into New Mexico comes from Pinnacle Ruin, which was founded in the late 1200s. This site, situated on a defensible butte, has architecture and pottery that are distinct from those of the surrounding local settlements, with a preponderance of Magdalena Black-on-white pottery, which is similar in layout and style to Mesa Verde Black-on-white (Lekson et al. 2002).

Those leaving Eastern Mesa Verde were more forcefully uprooted and escaping the religious and political strife as their sociopolitical system collapsed. These experiences strongly conditioned their worldview as they moved into new locations and were integrated into communities in the late 1200s and early 1300s. As a result, the natural tendency would be to work against the more integrated and top-down, hierarchical components of the sociopolitical and religious organization that characterized Eastern Mesa Verde society by promoting communal solutions, adopting corporate strategies, and increasing village autonomy. These new canons were likely reinforced at their destinations, where local populations had to adjust to increasing numbers of people and negotiate integrating diverse groups of people (or not). The Mesa Verde migrants and their descendants were active contributors to the pervasive cultural changes, including the intensification of the Katsina religion, in the early 1300s. The simultaneously cooperative and contentious processes of syncretism and acculturation as the Mesa Verde migrants and their histories melded into those of the inhabitants of their destination dramatically transformed Pueblo society over the course of the fourteenth century (see chapter 1, figure 2).

The histories of the ancestral Pueblo occupation of the Northern San Juan have a strong correspondence with the historical trajectories of the Eastern and Western Pueblos of today. For example, the Hopis (with an emphasis on matrilineal households, clans, and lineages that is distinct from Eastern Pueblos) have oral traditions that are strongly connected with the Kayenta populations and people of the Western Mesa Verde region (e.g., Gilpin et al. 2002; Ware 2014). The Keresan and Tanoan Pueblo groups with social organizations emphasizing crosscutting, integrative groups (sodalities and moieties) have strong connections to Eastern Mesa Verde (Cordell et al. 2007; Gilpin et al. 2002; Ortman 2012; Roney 1995; Ware 2014). The Mesa Verde migrations did not form the Eastern and Western Pueblos as we know them today, for there were yet centuries of change to come, including the Contact period. They were, however, a watershed moment creating historical contingencies that influenced the long arc of transformation, syncretism, and innovation involved in the development of the modern pueblos (e.g., Ware 2014).

The Depopulation of a Region: Lessons Learned

I begin this book by noting our fascination with societal collapse. It seems enigmatic, yet we know what happened. Some combination of shifting population levels, changing climate, conflict, breakdown in governance, religious strife, economic hardships, and individual actions created an untenable situation that required a monumental, societal-scale reconfiguration—a reset. At some times and places, a reset can be achieved through a peaceful changeover in leadership, the implementation of new, broad-sweeping policies, ground-breaking innovations in some sector of society, or some combination of these mechanisms. In these cases, at least some key factors, be they economic, demographic, sociopolitical, or environmental, are in an upswing, making societies robust enough to have the flexibility to make the required changes. But in other cases, a catastrophic convergence of challenging, crosscutting factors exacerbates vulnerabilities and undermines a society's ability to respond. The necessary changes are too slow in coming; they are "on the verge" when some tipping point—environmental calamity, revolution, or invasion—induces a systemic, societal breakdown that can be overcome only by a complete overhaul, one best achieved, when possible, by leaving and starting over. To understand "when and why collapse?" requires knowing how the social histories of places and people unfolded, the lived experience, and the complex and historical interrelationships among variables and how they differed across time and space.

As a case study, the Northern San Juan depopulation has important insights to offer for understanding how interrelated factors can have differential impacts because of situational and historical variation, yet the large-scale outcome is the same. Part of the reason it was so difficult for Nordenskiöld to understand what happened in the cliff dwellings at Mesa Verde is that he did not fully realize the complexities of the cliff dwellers' histories and their cascading ramifications (i.e., what came after). The idea that "history matters" is not merely a platitude; it influences everything. The historical landscapes in which we live and the climatic and social histories linked to us through them affect, in both direct and indirect ways, our cognitive and cultural frameworks and ultimately our actions, which not only impacts immediate circumstances but also intrinsically influences future options (Hassan 2002; Hoffman and Smith 1999). The varied histories of the Pueblo people living in the Northern San Juan—their Eastern and Western identities and the degree to which they were connected to Chaco and Aztec—affected what people did when they faced shared challenges, and different responses resulted.

Spatial variation is another key dimension. Different local influences, such as size of the local population, climate, and distance from a major center, affect how people manage the more broadly shared circumstances and the types of stressors or enablers that affected them on a daily basis. People in Western Mesa Verde were farther away from Aztec and the Mesa Verde core and the social and ideological conflict and change in Eastern Mesa Verde, but they were more likely to have been impacted by new cultural groups moving into the region and climatic shocks than were those in the east. The impact of spatial variation is intrinsically a multiscalar issue; to gain a more nuanced understanding of the lived experience will require going beyond the Eastern/Western and subregional scales I address here to compare localities, drainages, communities, and villages.

The temporality of how circumstances were experienced is another key element for understanding processes of collapse, depopulation, and transformation. Emigration and change in the mid-1200s were different from emigration and change in the late 1200s. People leaving Mesa Verde Proper in the mid-1200s, for example, were leaving for a variety of reasons related to the dramatic changes in settlement and organization happening on the cuesta and across Eastern Mesa Verde. Yet by the late 1200s, everyone was leaving for similar reasons: to escape the intense violence and drought. The temporal and spatial variation of large-scale processes affects our perceptions of the nature and timing of them. When viewed from Western Mesa Verde and Mesa Verde Proper, the process of emigration was protracted, as more people were leaving earlier than in McElmo and the Totah, but emigration was rapid in the linchpin areas when the sociopolitical and religious organization in Eastern Mesa Verde collapsed, despite evident emigration prior to the collapse.

Leaving is an event, but detaching from place has its own, often multigenerational, history. It takes a long time for changes to manifest and for people to realize their implications, and by the time they do, new changes are under way. There is often a long buildup preceding big change, which is engendered by a flashpoint—events or people—that precipitates rapid social transformations, causing cascading effects that cannot be stopped. Revolutions, such as what happened at the end of the 1200s, happen quickly. In less than five years after the storming of the Bastille in 1789, for example, the French monarchy, which had endured for more than a thousand years, ended. The specific events sparking the mid-1200s upheaval in the Northern San Juan likewise happened quickly, even if they remain archaeologically undetectable, and here too, a social order that had lasted for centuries ended and a new one began. Although long-term historical contingencies, which unfolded over more than a century and a half, shaped these circumstances, it was the immediate, short-term conditions and the small things, the everyday actions and reactions of individuals, that precipitated the eventful responses culminating in regional depopulation.

The Northern San Juan case study also highlights that intrinsically, social factors are paramount for understanding collapse and transformation. Although the "standard trio" of environmental change, population growth, and resource stress certainly played an important role in the circumstances shaping the lives of ancestral Pueblo people in the Northern San Juan, the reasons they left, particularly in Eastern Mesa Verde, were largely due to social problems—problems that involved religion and politics and emerged from historically embedded relationships that unfolded over generations.

We cannot ignore climatic or environmental factors, because they too matter, testing our abilities to adapt and respond. However, climate as an explanation unto itself doesn't cut it. Like the Mayas, who depopulated areas that were more agriculturally suitable to move to drier areas, Pueblo people living in the Northern San Juan left areas with more-reliable rainfall and better agricultural potential than some of them found at their destinations (Wright 2010), especially the migrants who relocated to the Hopi mesas and other locales in northeastern Arizona, which were just as dry as or drier than the places they left.

People living in Eastern Mesa Verde did not have to leave because of the "standard trio"; they had to leave because the way they were organized did not work for their times. It was not good for them. There was too much baggage (historical), it was too controlled, and their ability to respond to changing circumstances was too constrained. They were out of balance, religiously and sociopolitically, for the dialectic between the communal and hierarchical components of Mesa Verde pueblo organization had become too imbalanced, creating vulnerabilities that could not be overcome. The sociopolitical organization, overly dependent on the overtly hierarchical institutions, was too fragile, and its leaders could not adapt quickly enough to prevent the social order from disintegrating; it was too entrenched. Given the complex, interrelated, and multicenturial histories of Chaco, Aztec, and the Northern San Juan, it would have been difficult to completely break from the Chacoan ritual and ideological complex without a major cataclysm so they could start over.

APPENDIX

Northern San Juan Pueblo III Community Center Data

Site number	Site name	Subregion[a]	Date	Rooms	Room blocks
42SA22760	Hedley site complex	A	1060–1280	700	40
5DL27	Ansel Hall site	A	1080–1200	175	26
5DL492	Spook Point Pueblo	A	1225–1260	23	1
5DL506	Brewer Well	A	1225–1280	60	8
5DL554		A	1060–1260		3
5DL578	Brewer Mesa Top	A	1100–1280		12
5DL717, 488	Lower Squaw Village	A	1140–1280	75	6
5DL859	Hampton (Squaw Point) Ruin	A	1060–1280		13
5DL861, 860, 863	Upper Squaw Village	A	1140–1260	60	4
5MT1000	Seven Towers Pueblo	A	1225–1280	175	
5MT10438	Ruin Canyon Rim Pueblo	A	1225–1280	45	3
5MT10566		A	1150–1280	40	1
5MT107		A	1020–1280	4	1
5MT10853	Jackson's Hovenweep Castle	A	1225–1260	48	2
5MT10991	Mitchell Springs	A	600–1280	200	20
5MT11055	Rincon Keep	A	1150–1225		3
5MT11601	Cottonwood Ruin	A	1180–1280	80	1
5MT11842	Woods Canyon Pueblo	A	1140–1280	200	28
5MT121	Rohn 84 (Farmer Pueblo)	A	1225–1280	100	3
5MT123	Albert Porter Pueblo	A	1100–1225	80	11
5MT13041	Maxwell Community	A	980–1280		19
5MT13314	Turkey House complex	A	1225–1280	38	7
5MT136	Bass site complex	A	1060–1280	100	27
5MT14874		A	1225–1260	46	3
5MT1541		A	1180–1280	60	2
5MT1566	Lowry Ruin	A	1060–1280	37	1
5MT1647	Gardner Pueblo	A	1225–1280	200	4
5MT1648	Hovenweep Mesa Top	A	1225–1280		1
5MT1655	Thompson site	A	1180–1280		7

Kiva/Pit structures	Towers	Great houses	Great kivas	Multiwalled structures			Plazas	Enclosing walls
				D-shaped	*Biwall*	*Triwall*		
160	1	2		1			2	1
35	3	1	1					
8								1
21	1							1
			1					
19								
19	1							1
95	4		1					1
13	1							1
44	16		1	2			1	1
17	5							1
1	1							
			1					
14	1		1				1	
39	3	2	2	1				
	1						1	
14	1							
49	10			1			1	1
24	4							1
51	3	1						
11		1						
15	1						1	1
49		1						
2								
9	1							
8		1	1					
41	6							1
12	1							
12	4						1	1

Site number	Site name	Subregion[a]	Date	Rooms	Room blocks
5MT16789		A	1180–1280		8
5MT16805	Harlan great kiva	A	1020–1260		1
5MT16808		A	1180–1280	25	2
5MT16844		A	1060–1280		4
5MT1692		A	1150–1250	4	1
5MT17259		A	1060–1225		11
5MT1825	Castle Rock Pueblo	A	1260–1280	60	2
5MT18419		A	1150–1280		
5MT1905	Haynie Ruin	A	1140–1225	80	2
5MT207	Rohn 150	A	1225–1280	75	8
5MT2299	Beartooth Ruins	A	1175–1275	150	7
5MT2347	Ute Canyon site	A	950–1250		5
5MT245	Sandstone Canyon Mesa Top	A	1225–1280		6
5MT2516	Herren Farms complex	A	1140–1280	100	1
5MT2681	Airstrip site	A	1060–1225		3
5MT2766		A	1060–1280		4
5MT3325		A	1150–1280		1
5MT338	Cannonball Ruins	A	1225–1280	90	3
5MT35	Stevenson Ruin	A	1100–1280	150	1
5MT36		A	600–1280		
5MT3793	Easter Ruin	A	1180–1280	270	7
5MT3807	Shields Pueblo	A	980–1280		19
5MT3925	Casa Negra	A	1060–1225	60	4
5MT4126	Ida Jean/North McElmo 8	A	1100–1260	55	2
5MT4329	Isleta de Vaca Pueblo	A	1180–1280		2
5MT4388	Bement site	A	1060–1280		5
5MT4421	Kristie's site	A	1140–1280	100	5
5MT4447	Emerson/Sundial Ruin	A	1060–1280		4
5MT4450	Reservoir Ruin Group	A	980–1260		8

				Multiwalled structures				
Kiva/Pit structures	*Towers*	*Great houses*	*Great kivas*	*D-shaped*	*Biwall*	*Triwall*	*Plazas*	*Enclosing walls*
21	1							
			1					
10							1	
9	1							
1					1			
8								
16	1			1			2	1
			1					
7		1						
9	2							1
10								
9								
8	1							1
32	1						1	
3			1					
3			1					
							1	
32	5			1				
15								
1				1				
60	3							1
90		1						
5		1						
3		1	1				1	
11	1						1	1
4	3		1				1	
12	1		1					
6								
14	2	1	1	1				

Site number	Site name	Subregion[a]	Date	Rooms	Room blocks
5MT4466	Mud Springs	A	1140–1280	150	9
5MT4474	Moqui Spring Pueblo	A	1250–1280	150	1
5MT4575	Pedro Point	A	1225–1280	40	3
5MT4700	Rich's Ruin	A	1180–1280	80	2
5MT4802	Pock/Pigge site	A	1175–1225	56	7
5MT4803	Lancaster/Pharo Ruin	A	1060–1280	350	22
5MT4813	Lower Cow Canyon	A	1225–1260		3
5MT5	Yellow Jacket Pueblo	A	1060–1280	600	42
5MT5006	Yucca House	A	1140–1280	450	2
5MT502	Painted Hand Pueblo	A	1150–1300		3
5MT532	Kearns' Site	A	1140–1280		6
5MT5498		A	1020–1180		4
5MT601	Hackberry-Horseshoe Ruins	A	1180–1260	100	2
5MT603	Cut Throat Castle	A	1180–1280		3
5MT604	Goodman Point Pueblo	A	1260–1280	400	13
5MT6359	Yellowjacket Floodplain site	A	1225–1280	50	3
5MT6768		A	1225–1280		
5MT697	Wild Goose Pueblo	A	1225–1280		1
5MT6970	Wallace	A	1020–1280	82	1
5MT699		A	1060–1280		1
5MT7088	Big Spring Ruin	A	1225–1260	150	3
5MT717	Ruin Canyon Mesa Top	A	1225–1260		1
5MT7414		A	1060–1225		1
5MT751	Big Ruin site	A	1140–1260		6
5MT7575	Hidden Spring	A	1225–1260		4
5MT765	Sand Canyon Pueblo	A	1240–1280	420	16
5MT7656	Hibbets Pueblo	A	1225–1260	100	2
5MT7740	Cowboy Wash Pueblo	A	1225–1275	40	1
5MT797	Cow Mesa 40	A	1150–1300	30	3

Kiva/Pit structures	Towers	Great houses	Great kivas	Multiwalled structures D-shaped	Biwall	Triwall	Plazas	Enclosing walls
19	5					1		
20	1		1		1		1	1
18	5						1	1
6			1					
10	1							
75	4	1	1				1	
5	3		1				1	1
195	18	1	1		1		1	1
79		1	2		1		2	1
3	2						2	1
15	4		1					1
10								
20	1				1			
16	6							1
86	5	1	1		1		2	1
6	2						1	
							1	
11	1							1
7		1						
			1					
32							1	1
14								
1			1					
2	1						1	
11	3							1
101	14		1	1			1	1
15	2						1	
13	1			1			1	1
9	2						2	1

Site number	Site name	Subregion[a]	Date	Rooms	Room blocks
5MT7984		A	1060–1260		1
5MT8092		A	1225–1280		1
5MT835	Little Cow Canyon	A	1225–1280	200	4
5MT839	North Lowry Great House	A	1100–1250	65	4
5MT863		A	1180–1280		2
5MT875	Miller Pueblo	A	1225–1280	80	2
5MT8888	Hartman Draw	A	920–1225		1
LA69897		A	1150–1280		1
LA69909		A	1150–1280		
NSF-CCS 2	Bear Paw Pueblo	A	1225–1260		1
NSF-CCS 9	Brewer Canyon Pueblo	A	1180–1280	50	7
Rohn Y-149	Griffey site	A	1180–1260	150	
NSF-CCS 4	Harris Pueblo	A	1225–1280		4
NSF-CCS 3	McVicker's Site	A	1225–1260		4
NM A-1-8	Tonache Tower	A	1150–1300	50	1
Unrecorded	Bitsiel Ruin (biwall)	A	1150–1280		4
Unrecorded	Morley-Kidder 1917	A	1225–1280	100	1
Unrecorded	Papoose Canyon Pueblo	A	1250–1280	50	1
5MT2150	Hoy House	B	1100–1225	60	1
5MT2156	Lion House	B	1060–1260	46	1
5MT2769	Reed Site 16	B	1060–1280		3
5MT2771	Kiva Point	B	1020–1290	100	1
5MT2831	Morris 33	B	1100–1225	14	1
5MT2832	Morris 38	B	1225–1290	10	3
5MV00034	Thirty-Four-Plex/Soda Canyon Pueblo	B	920–1260	104	8
5MV00325	Kleidon's Biwall	B	1020–1225	28	1
5MV00352	Sun Temple	B	1225–1290	24	1
5MV00520	Fire Temple complex	B	1225–1290	6	1
5MV00523	Oak Tree House	B	1180–1225	55	1

				Civic-ceremonial architecture				
Kiva/Pit structures	*Towers*	*Great houses*	*Great kivas*	*Multiwalled structures*			*Plazas*	*Enclosing walls*
				D-shaped	*Biwall*	*Triwall*		
9	1							
			1					
51	7						2	1
15	5	1						1
3	1		1					
29	6							1
3		1	1					
1			1					
	1		1					
14	2						1	1
32	3		1					1
20								
27	1							1
18	2							1
2								
12					1			
11								
6								
6								
6								
			1		1			
8			2		1			
1				1			1	
2	1		1					
17	2							
1					1			
3	1			1			1	
2							1	
6								

Site number	Site name	Subregion[a]	Date	Rooms	Room blocks
5MV00625	Cliff Palace	B	1225–1290	141	1
5MV00640	Spruce Tree House	B	1200–1290	130	1
5MV00650	Square Tower House	B	1180–1260	60	1
5MV00782		B	1225–1260	40	1
5MV00808.2	Far View House/Gila Pueblo 139	B	1060–1260	55	1
5MV00821	Gila Pueblo 48	B	1020–1225	40	1
5MV00840	Gila Pueblo 51 or 52?	B	1060–1260	50	1
5MV00907	Juniper Flats	B	1180–1290	130	5
5MV01031	Thirty-Four-Plex Isolated Great Kiva	B	1100–1290	4	1
5MV01067	Morefield Canyon Great House	B	700–1260	350	31
5MV01073	Moccasin Mesa Reservoir Village	B	1060–1225	125	14
5MV01157	Head of Long Canyon complex	B	1060–1290	90	7
5MV01200	Long House	B	1225–1290	150	1
5MV01201	Ceremonial Cave	B	1180–1260	3	
5MV01212	Kodak House	B	1225–1280	67	1
5MV01229	Mug House	B	1180–1280	87	1
5MV01241	Nordenskiold Ruin No. 16	B	1225–1290	39	1
5MV01385	Double House	B	1060–1290	60	1
5MV01406	Spring House	B	1180–1290	85	1
5MV01449	Site 20½	B	1200–1280	48	1
5MV01560	Wetherill Mesa possible great kiva	B	1060–1200		
5MV03622	Park Mesa (lone PII)	B	1140–1225	100	2
5MV03633	Park Mesa North Canyonhead	B	1060–1200	45	4
5MV03749	Upper Battleship Rock Pueblo	B	880–1260	400	42

Civic-ceremonial architecture								
Kiva/Pit structures	Towers	Great houses	Great kivas	Multiwalled structures			Plazas	Enclosing walls
				D-shaped	Biwall	Triwall		
21	2						1	
9	2						1	
8	1							
2	1							
5		1						
5								
2	1							
8							1	1
			1				1	1
48		1	2				1	
22							1	
8	3							
21							1	
2							1	
8								
8	2							
7	1							
5								
7								
3								
			1					
6								
7								
57		1					1	

Site number	Site name	Subregion[a]	Date	Rooms	Room blocks
5MV03808	School Section Canyon Pueblo	B	1020–1225		7
42SA1	Brew's #1	C	1200–1260	85	1
42SA11087	Five Acre Ruin	C	1200–1260	120	9
42SA11181		C	1060–1290	15	1
42SA11203		C	1060–1225	12	1
42SA14275	Radon Spring Ruin	C	1250–1290	50	1
42SA14430	Gravel Pit	C	1060–1290	50	1
42SA14631	Deadman's Canyon Head (early PII)	C	1100–1225	65	2
42SA15206	10-Acre Ruin	C	1150–1250	275	12
42SA16005		C	1060–1290	27	1
42SA16017	Horse Canyon Ruin	C	1060–1290		1
42SA16459	Five Acre E Spring complex	C	1150–1280	40	10
42SA16962	Decker Ruin	C	1200–1260	60	1
42SA17347	Moki Island #8	C	980–1280		3
42SA18100	Greasewood Flat	C	1160–1260	40	5
42SA20393	Wetherill's Chimney Rock	C	1100–1290	40	6
42SA2110	Nancy Patterson Village	C	800–1290	325	7
42SA2117		C	1060–1290	63	2
42SA21325	Five Acre E Ridgetop	C	1100–1290	30	1
42SA22674	Bluff Great House	C	1060–1225	50	1
42SA23616	Hammond Great House complex	C	1060–1290	10	1
42SA24756	Comb Wash Great House	C	1150–1260	50	3
42SA259	Red Knobs	C	1060–1225	150	9
42SA28206	O'Grosky Ruin	C	1150–1290	30	5
42SA29509	Linda's Kiva	C	1080–1225		1
42SA3208	Ruin Spring Ruin	C	1150–1290	75	1
42SA3217	Sacred Mesa	C	980–1260		1

				Civic-ceremonial architecture				
Kiva/Pit structures	Towers	Great houses	Great kivas	Multiwalled structures			Plazas	Enclosing walls
				D-shaped	Biwall	Triwall		
6			1					
16								
27		1	2					
1			1					
			1					
4	2							
5								
9								
39		1						
4	1						1	1
1			1				1	
7	3							1
9							1	
5		1						
5		1	1					
10	3							
21		1					1	
7	2						2	
9								
4		1	1					
1	1	1	1				1	1
7	4	1						1
15		1	1					
6	3						1	1
			1					
8	5							1
8			1					

Site number	Site name	Subregion[a]	Date	Rooms	Room blocks
42SA3680	Fortified Mesa	C	1100–1260	20	5
42SA4998	Bradford Canyonhead Ruin	C	1225–1290	100	1
42SA5222	Cottonwood Falls Great House	C	1080–1240	100	2
42SA5271	Arch Canyon Great House	C	1080–1240	50	2
42SA5278	Brew's Site #13	C	600–1225	15	2
42SA5647	Rincon Great Kiva complex	C	1060–1225		3
42SA6671	Jackson's Montezuma Creek Bench Ruin #2	C	1060–1290	100	1
42SA700	Edge of Cedars	C	1080–1225	75	7
42SA7123	Aneth Archaeological District	C	1100–1260	55	1
42SA7215	Deadman's Canyonhead Ruin	C	1160–1290	50	1
42SA822	Montezuma Village I and II	C	1060–1260	200	1
42SA8455	Parker site	C	1200–1260	50	1
42SA920	Coalbed Village	C	1200–1290	125	26
42SA971	Monument Village	C	980–1260	150	3
Other	Tsitah Wash complex	C	1060–1280	50	1
Unrecorded	Black Mesa Ruin/ Quartzite Pueblo	C	1060–1225	20	3
Unrecorded	Phil Hall site	C	1060–1225		1
Unrecorded	Ute Gravel Pit site	C	1200–1260	75	1
Unrecorded	Waving Wand/Kiva Cave	C	1160–1290	15	1
Unrecorded	Whiskers Ruin	C	1100–1260	80	3
5AA83	Chimney Rock Pueblo	D	1090–1200	45	1
5LP1264		D	1060–1280		14
ENM5007- 5014	Aztec Terrace	D	1060–1280	36	8

Civic-ceremonial architecture								
Kiva/Pit structures	Towers	Great houses	Great kivas	Multiwalled structures			Plazas	Enclosing walls
				D-shaped	Biwall	Triwall		
1							3	
20								
12		1	1					1
5	1	1					1	1
2							1	
1			1					
13			1					
10		1	1					
7	1							
10	1							
20	1	1	1				1	1
10	1							
20	1	1	1				1	1
30								
5		1					1	
			1					
10								
1			1				1	
7								
2		1					1	
2								
			1					

Site number	Site name	Subregion[a]	Date	Rooms	Room blocks
ENM5091		D	1060–1280	40	3
ENM5096		D	1060–1280	45	1
LA122652	Sterling	D	1020–1260	40	1
LA13112	West Water	D	1150–1280	75	1
LA13433	Farmer (Arroyo) complex	D	1060–1280	40	3
LA13434	Dein Ruin	D	1060–1280	50	1
LA15185	Estes Arroyo Bridge	D	1150–1300	75	1
LA1897	Morris 39	D	600–1300	300	29
LA1898	Holmes Group	D	1150–1250	325	36
LA1921	Jackson Lake	D	1150–1200	49	1
LA1932		D	1060–1280	40	1
LA1988	Squaw Springs–Morris 40	D	1000–1225	20	1
LA20266	Fiedler site	D	1060–1280	80	5
LA2514	Flora Vista	D	1200–1280	125	3
LA2520	Upper Barker Draw	D	1060–1280	60	1
LA2609	Jaquez Ruin	D	1060–1300	100	8
LA27498	Barker Arroyo Great House	D	1060–1280	150	6
LA27948		D	1150–1280		8
LA29441		D	1060–1280	35	9
LA29442		D	1060–1280	12	2
LA3131	East Side Rincon	D	600–1280		
LA3376		D	1150–1280	20	2
LA37601		D	1060–1280	20	1
LA45	Aztec East and West	D	1110–1280	950	11
LA50158	Cobblestone Mountain	D	1060–1225	17	1
LA50337		D	1150–1280	36	2
LA5603	Aztec North	D	1100–1225	110	1
LA5626	East Mesita	D	1150–1300		1

				Multiwalled structures				
Kiva/Pit structures	Towers	Great houses	Great kivas	D-shaped	Biwall	Triwall	Plazas	Enclosing walls
3								
1								
5		1						
8								
3		1					1	
		1	2					
16		2	5					
22	2	2	4		2			
3		1					1	
3		1						
2		1						
15								
6		1	1		1			
2								
11		1	1					
15		1	1				1	
6								
6			2					
1			1					
			1					
1							1	
2		1						
21		3	3		2	3	1	
2							1	
2								
2		1	2					1
1			2					

Site number	Site name	Subregion[a]	Date	Rooms	Room blocks
LA5631	Morris 41	D	800–1280	490	4
LA5642	Twin Angels/Kutz Canyon	D	1060–1280	25	
LA59211		D	800–1280		8
LA59967	Kello Blancett	D	1150–1300	200	4
LA60002		D	1060–1280	7	1
LA60006		D	1060–1280	8	1
LA60010		D	1060–1280	20	1
LA60018		D	1060–1280	20	3
LA60019		D	1060–1280	60	2
LA60020		D	1060–1280	80	2
LA60021		D	1060–1280		
LA60022		D	1060–1280	65	2
LA60024		D	1060–1280		
LA60746		D	1060–1280		1
LA61051	Old Fort	D	1150–1280	60	1
LA6286	Gillentine site	D	1150–1300		3
LA65029		D	1060–1280	10	3
LA685	El Malpais	D	1100–1200	20	3
LA69891	San Juan Biwall	D	1150–1225		
LA69892	Canal Creek Great Kiva	D	1150–1300	4	1
LA69925	Twin Towers Pueblo	D	1150–1280	50	1
LA80316		D	1060–1280		
LA8619	Shannon Bluff (Point site)	D	1150–1280	150	7
LA8620	Fruitland Pueblo	D	1150–1250	80	1
LA8846	Salmon	D	1060–1280	330	1
LA9050	Old Indian Racetrack	D	1150–1280		4
NM A-1-29	Holmes Great Kiva	D	1225–1280		
Other	Tse Taak'a	D	1150–1280	100	
42GA34	Coombs site	E	1060–1220	70	1
42SA1726	Tower Canyon complex	E	1060–1270	12	1

				Civic-ceremonial architecture				
Kiva/Pit structures	Towers	Great houses	Great kivas	Multiwalled structures			Plazas	Enclosing walls
				D-shaped	Biwall	Triwall		
40		1	2					
2		1						
8								
10		1	1					
			2					
1			1					
1							1	
2			2					
3							1	
4							1	
			1					
2			3					
			1					
			1					
8		1						
1			2					
			1					
8			2					
			1	1				
			1					
5	2						1	
20								
8		1	1					
2	1							
30	1	1	2				1	
1								
	1		1					
1								
10								
			1					

Site number	Site name	Subregion[a]	Date	Rooms	Room blocks
42SA18431	Et Al site	E	1100–1270	27	1
42SA316	Fortified Mesa (fortress)	E	1150–1240	4	
42SA5005	Moon House	E	1240–1290	42	3
42SA5114		E	1100–1270	22	1
42SA681	Rehab Center	E	1150–1270	2	1

[a] A = McElmo; B = Mesa Verde Proper; C = West Central Mesa Verde; D = Totah; E = Lower San Juan.

Civic-ceremonial architecture								
Kiva/Pit structures	Towers	Great houses	Great kivas	Multiwalled structures			Plazas	Enclosing walls
				D-shaped	Biwall	Triwall		
2		1					1	1
							1	
2							1	1
5								
							1	

REFERENCES CITED

Abbott, David R. 2000. *Ceramics and Community Organization Among the Hohokam*. Tucson: University of Arizona Press.

———. 2009. Extensive and Long-Term Specialization: Hohokam Ceramic Production in the Phoenix Basin, Arizona. *American Antiquity* 74:531–57.

Adams, E. Charles. 1991. *The Origin and Development of the Pueblo Katsina Cult*. Tucson: University of Arizona Press.

———. 1994. The Katsina Cult: A Western Pueblo Perspective. In *Kachinas in the Pueblo World*, edited by Polly Schaafsma, 35–46. Albuquerque: University of New Mexico Press.

———. 1996. The Pueblo III–Pueblo IV Transition in the Hopi Area, Arizona. In *The Prehistoric Pueblo World, A.D. 1150–1350*, edited by Michael A. Adler, 48–58. Tucson: University of Arizona Press.

Adams, E. Charles, and Jenny L. Adams. 1993. Thirteenth Century Abandonment of the Four Corners: A Reassessment. Paper presented at the 92nd Annual Meeting of the American Anthropological Association, Washington, DC.

Adams, E. Charles, and Vincent M. LaMotta. 2006. New Perspectives on an Ancient Religion: Katsina Ritual in the Archaeological Record. In *Religion in the Prehispanic Southwest*, edited by C. S. VanPool, T. L. VanPool, and D. A. Philips Jr., 53–66. London: AltaMira.

Adams, Karen R., and Kenneth L. Petersen. 1999. Environment. In *Colorado Prehistory: A Context for the Southern Colorado River Basin*, edited by William D. Lipe, Mark D. Varien, and Richard H. Wilshusen, 14–50. Denver: Colorado Council of Professional Archaeologists.

Adams, Robert McC. 1981. *Heartland of Cities: Surveys of Ancient Settlement and Land Use on the Central Floodplain of the Euphrates*. Chicago: University of Chicago Press.

Adams, William Y., and Nettie K. Adams. 1959. *An Inventory of Prehistoric Sites on the Lower San Juan River, Utah*. Glen Canyon Series 1, Museum of Northern Arizona, Bulletin 31. Flagstaff: Northern Arizona Society of Science and Art, Inc.

Adler, Michael A. 1990. Communities of Soil and Stone: An Archaeological Investigation of Population Aggregation Among the Mesa Verde Anasazi, A.D. 900–1300. PhD diss., Department of Anthropology, University of Michigan, Ann Arbor.

————. 1994. Population Aggregation and the Anasazi Social Landscape: A View from the Four Corners. In *The Ancient Southwestern Community*, edited by W. H. Wills and Robert D. Leonard, 85–101. Albuquerque: University of New Mexico Press.

————. 1996. Land Tenure, Archaeology, and the Ancestral Puebloan Social Landscape. *Journal of Anthropological Archaeology* 15 (4): 337–71.

Adler, Michael A., and Mark D. Varien. 1994. The Changing Face of the Community in the Mesa Verde Region, A.D. 1000–1300. In *Proceedings of the Anasazi Symposium 1991*, compiled by Jack E. Smith and Art Hutchinson, 83–97. Mesa Verde National Park, CO: Mesa Verde Museum Association.

Ahlstrom, Richard V. N., Carla R. Van West, and Jeffrey S. Dean. 1995. Environmental and Chronological Factors in the Mesa Verde–Northern Rio Grande Migration. *Journal of Anthropological Archaeology* 14 (2): 125–42.

Akins, Nancy J. 2003. The Burials of Pueblo Bonito. In *Pueblo Bonito: Center of the Chacoan World*, edited by Jill E. Neitzel, 94–106. Washington, DC: Smithsonian Books.

Allison, James R. 2010. The End of Farming in the "Northern Periphery" of the Southwest. In *Leaving Mesa Verde: Peril and Change in the Thirteenth-Century Southwest*, edited by Timothy A. Kohler, Mark D. Varien, and Aaron M. Wright, 128–55. Tucson: University of Arizona Press.

————. 2014. The Chronology of Fremont Farming in Northern Utah. Paper presented at the 79th Annual Meeting of the Society for American Archaeology, Austin, TX.

Allison, James R., Winston B. Hurst, Jonathan D. Till, and Donald C. Irwin. 2012. Meanwhile in the West: Early Pueblo Communities in Southeastern Utah. In *Crucible of Pueblos: The Early Pueblo Period in the Northern Southwest*, edited by Richard Wilshusen, Gregson Schachner, and James R. Allison, 35–52. Los Angeles: Cotsen Institute of Archaeology Press, UCLA.

Ambler, J. Richard, and Mark Q. Sutton. 1989. The Anasazi Abandonment of the San Juan Drainage and the Numic Expansion. *North American Archaeologist* 10 (1): 39–53.

Anderson, Orin J., Barry S. Kues, and Spencer G. Lucas, eds. 1997. *Mesozoic Geology and Paleontology of the Four Corners Region*. Guidebook, 48th Annual Field Conference, Four Corners. New Mexico Geological Society.

Anthony, David W. 1990. Migration in Archeology: The Baby and the Bathwater. *American Anthropologist* 92 (4): 895–914.

Arakawa, Fumiyasu. 2012a. Cyclical Cultural Trajectories: A Case Study from the Mesa Verde Region. *Journal of Anthropological Research* 68:35–69.

————. 2012b. Tool-Stone Procurement in the Mesa Verde Core Region Through Time. In *Emergence and Collapse of Early Villages: Models of Central Mesa Verde Archaeology*, edited by Timothy A. Kohler and Mark D. Varien, 175–96. Berkeley: University of California Press.

Arakawa, Fumiyasu, Jamie Merewether, and Christopher Nicholson. 2011. Evaluating Chaco Influences in the Central Mesa Verde Region Using Material Culture during the Pre-A.D. 1150 and Post-Chaco Periods. Paper presented at the 76th Annual Meeting of the Society for American Archaeology, Sacramento, CA.

Arakawa, Fumiyasu, Christopher Nicholson, and Jeff Rasic. 2013. The Consequences of Social Processes: Aggregate Populations, Projectile Point Accumulation, and Subsistence Patterns in the American Southwest. *American Antiquity* 78:147–65.

Arnold, Dean E. 1985. *Ceramic Theory and Cultural Process*. Cambridge: Cambridge University Press.

Baars, Donald L. 1983. *The Colorado Plateau: A Geologic History*. Albuquerque: University of New Mexico Press.

Barnes, F. A. 1978. *Canyon Country Geology for the Layman and Rockhound*. Salt Lake City, UT: Wasatch Publishers.

Basso, Keith H. 1996. Wisdom Sits in Places: Notes on a Western Apache Landscape. In *Senses of Place*, edited by Steven Feld and Keith H. Basso, 53–90. Advanced Seminar Series. Santa Fe, NM: School of American Research Press.

Baxter, Michael J. 1994. *Exploratory Multivariate Analysis in Archaeology*. Edinburgh: Edinburgh University Press.

———. 2003. *Statistics in Archaeology*. London: Arnold.

Beck, Robin A., Jr., Douglas J. Bolender, James A. Brown, and Timothy K. Earle. 2007. Eventful Archaeology: The Place of Space in Structural Transformation. *Current Anthropology* 48:833–60.

Bedell, Melanie L. 2000. Late Pueblo II and Pueblo III Cliff Dwellings and Community Patterns in Grand Gulch, Southeastern Utah. Master's thesis, Department of Anthropology, Washington State University, Pullman.

Bellorado, Benjamin A. 2013. An Introduction to Recent Research in the Eastern Mesa Verde Region. *Kiva* 78 (4): 339–75.

Bellorado, Benjamin A., and Barbara J. Mills. 2014. The Ties That Bind: Textile Imagery, Social Proximity, and Communities of Practice in the Northern Southwest. Paper presented in A Gift for Passion and Detail: Linda Cordell, Archaeology, and Beyond at the 79th Annual Meeting of the Society for American Archaeology, Austin, TX.

Bellorado, Benjamin A., Laurie D. Webster, and Thomas C. Windes. 2012. Footsteps of Identity: The Context of Pueblo III Sandal Imagery in the Northern Southwest. Paper presented at the 78th Annual Meeting of the Society for American Archaeology, Honolulu, HI.

Benson, Larry V. 2011. Factors Controlling Pre-Columbian and Early Historic Maize Productivity in the American Southwest, Part 2: The Chaco Halo, Mesa Verde, Pajarito Plateau/Bandelier, and Zuni Archaeological Regions. *Journal of Archaeological Method and Theory* 18:61–109.

Bernardini, Wesley. 1996. Transitions in Social Organization: A Predictive Model from Southwestern Colorado. *Journal of Anthropological Archaeology* 15:372–402.

———. 1998. Conflict, Migration, and the Social Environment: Interpreting Architectural Change in Early and Late Pueblo IV Aggregations. In *Migration and Reorganization: The Pueblo IV Period in the American Southwest*, edited by Katherine A. Spielmann, 91–114. Anthropological Research Papers 51. Tempe: Arizona State University.

———. 2000. Kiln-Firing Groups: Inter-household Economic Collaboration and Social Organization in the Northern American Southwest. *American Antiquity* 65:365–78.

———. 2005. *Hopi Oral Tradition and the Archaeology of Identity*. Tucson: University of Arizona Press.

———. 2008. Identity as History: Hopi Clans and the Curation of Oral Tradition. *Journal of Anthropological Research* 64:483–509.

———. 2011. North, South, and Center: An Outline of Hopi Ethnogenesis. In *Religious Transformation in the Late Pre-Hispanic Pueblo World*, edited by Donna M. Glowacki and Scott Van Keuren, 196–220. Tucson: University of Arizona Press.

Berry, Michael S. 1982. *Time, Space, and Transition in Anasazi Prehistory*. Salt Lake City: University of Utah Press.

Betancourt, J. L., Jeffrey S. Dean, and H. M. Hull. 1986. Prehistoric Long-Distance Transport of Construction Beams, Chaco Canyon, New Mexico. *American Antiquity* 51:370–75.

Bieber, A. M., D. W. Brooks, Garman Harbottle, and Edward V. Sayre. 1976. Application of Multivariate Techniques to Analytical Data on Aegean Ceramics. *Archaeometry* 18 (1): 59–74.

Billman, Brian R. 2008. An Outbreak of Violence and Raiding in the Central Mesa Verde Region in the 12th Century AD. In *Social Violence in the Pre-Hispanic American Southwest*, edited by Deborah L. Nichols and Patricia L. Crown, 41–60. Tucson: University of Arizona Press.

Billman, Brian R., Patricia M. Lambert, and Banks L. Leonard. 2000. Cannibalism, Warfare, and Drought in the Mesa Verde Region During the Twelfth Century A.D. *American Antiquity* 65:145–78.

Bishop, Ronald L., and Hector Neff. 1989. Compositional Data Analysis in Archaeology. In *Archaeological Chemistry IV*, edited by Ralph O. Allen, 57–86. Advances in Chemistry Series 220. Washington, DC: American Chemical Society.

Bishop, Ronald L., Robert L. Rands, and George R. Holley. 1982. Ceramic Compositional Analysis in Archaeological Perspective. In *Advances in Archaeological Method and Theory*, vol. 5, edited by Michael B. Schiffer, 275–330. New York: Academic Press.

Blanton, Richard, Gary Feinman, Stephen Kowalewski, and Peter Peregrine. 1996. A Dual-Processual Theory for the Evolution of Mesoamerican Civilization. *Current Anthropology* 37:1–14.

Blau, Peter M. 1977. *Inequality and Heterogeneity: A Primitive Theory of Social Structure*. New York: Free Press.

Blinman, Eric. 1989. Potluck in the Protokiva: Ceramics and Ceremonialism in Pueblo I Villages. In *The Architecture of Social Integration in Prehistoric Pueblos*, edited by William D. Lipe and Michelle Hegmon, 113–24. Occasional Papers 1. Cortez, CO: Crow Canyon Archaeological Center.

Blinman, Eric, and C. Dean Wilson. 1992. Ceramic Perspectives on Northern Anasazi Exchange. In *The American Southwest and Mesoamerican Systems of Prehistoric Exchange*, edited by Jon E. Ericson and Timothy G. Baugh, 65–94. New York: Plenum.

Bloomer, William W. 1989. Moon House: A Pueblo III Period Cliff Dwelling Complex in Southeastern Utah. Master's thesis, Department of Anthropology, Washington State University, Pullman.

Borck, Lewis. 2012. Patterns of Resistance: Violence, Migration, and Trade in the Gallina Heartland. Master's thesis, School of Anthropology, University of Arizona, Tucson.

Bowser, Brenda J. 2000. From Pottery to Politics: An Ethnoarchaeological Study of Political Factionalism, Ethnicity, and Domestic Pottery Style in the Ecuadorian Amazon. *Journal of Archaeological Method and Theory* 7:219–48.

Bradley, Bruce A. 1992. Excavations at Sand Canyon Pueblo. In *The Sand Canyon Archaeological Project: A Progress Report*, edited by William D. Lipe, 79–97. Occasional Papers 2. Cortez, CO: Crow Canyon Archaeological Center.

———. 1993. Planning, Growth, and Functional Differentiation at a Prehistoric Pueblo: A Case Study from SW Colorado. *Journal of Field Archaeology* 20:23–42.

Brandt, Elizabeth A. 1994. Egalitarianism, Hierarchy, and Centralization in the Pueblos. In *The Ancient Southwestern Community: Models and Methods for the Study of Prehistoric Social Organization*, edited by W. H. Wills and Robert D. Leonard, 9–23. Albuquerque: University of New Mexico Press.

Braun, David P., and Stephen Plog. 1982. Evolution of Tribal Social Networks: Theory and Prehistoric North American Evidence. *American Antiquity* 47:504–25.

Bredthauer, Allison. 2010. A Towering Enigma: An Examination of Pueblo II and Pueblo III Towers in the Northern San Juan Region. Master's thesis, Department of Anthropology, University of Colorado, Boulder.

Breternitz, David A., Arthur H. Rohn, and Elizabeth A. Morris. 1974. *Prehistoric Ceramics of the Mesa Verde Region*. Museum of Northern Arizona Ceramic Series 5. Flagstaff: Northern Arizona Society of Science and Art.

Brisbin, Joel M., Donna M. Glowacki, and Kay E. Barnett. 2007. Spruce Tree House 2007 Summary of Architectural Documentation: Structures and Social Organization in a Thirteenth Century Cliff Dwelling, Mesa Verde National Park, Colorado. Archeological Site Conservation Program. Manuscript on file at Mesa Verde National Park, Colorado.

Brown, Gary M., and Cheryl I. Paddock. 2011. Chacoan and Vernacular Architecture at Aztec Ruins: Putting Chaco in Its Place. *Kiva* 77:203–24.

Brown, Gary M., Paul F. Reed, and Donna M. Glowacki. 2013. Chacoan and Post-Chaco Occupations of the Middle San Juan Region: Changes in Settlement and Population. *Kiva* 78 (4): 417–48.

Brown, Gary, Thomas C. Windes, and Peter J. McKenna. 2008. Animas Anamnesis: Aztec Ruins or Anasazi Capital? In *Chaco's Northern Prodigies: Salmon, Aztec, and the Ascendancy of the Middle San Juan Region After A.D. 1100*, edited by Paul F. Reed, 231–50. Salt Lake City: University of Utah Press.

Cameron, Catherine M. 1993. Abandonment and Archaeological Interpretation. In *Abandonment of Settlements and Regions: Ethnoarchaeological and Archaeological Approaches*, edited by Catherine M. Cameron and Steve A. Tomka, 3–10. Cambridge: Cambridge University Press.

———. 2001. Pink Chert, Projectile Points, and the Chacoan Regional System. *American Antiquity* 66:79–102.

———. 2005. Exploring Archaeological Cultures in the Northern Southwest: What Were Chaco and Mesa Verde? *Kiva* 70:227–53.

———. 2009. *Chaco and After in the Northern San Juan: Excavations at the Bluff Great House.* Tucson: University of Arizona Press.

Cameron, Catherine M., and Andrew I. Duff. 2008. History and Process in Village Formation: Context and Contrasts from the Northern Southwest. *American Antiquity* 73:29–57.

Cameron, Catherine M., and H. Wolcott Toll. 2001. Deciphering the Organization of Production in Chaco Canyon. *American Antiquity* 66:5–13.

Carter, Sidney W., and Alan P. Sullivan III. 2007. Direct Procurement of Ceramics and Ceramic Materials, "Index Wares," and Models of Regional Exchange and Interaction. In *Hinterlands and Regional Dynamics in the Ancient Southwest*, edited by Alan P. Sullivan III and James M. Bayman, 139–62. Tucson: University of Arizona Press.

Casey, Edward S. 1996. How to Get from Space to Place in a Fairly Short Stretch of Time: Phenomenological Prolegomena. In *Senses of Place*, edited by Steven Feld and Keith H. Basso, 13–52. Santa Fe, NM: School of American Research Press.

Cassidy, Francis. 1965. Fire Temple. In *The Great Kivas of Chaco Canyon and Their Relationships*, edited by Gordon R. Vivian and Paul Reiter, 73–81. Monograph 22. Albuquerque: School of American Research and University of New Mexico Press.

Cattanach, George S. 1980. *Long House, Mesa Verde National Park, Colorado.* Publications in Archaeology 7H, Wetherill Mesa Studies. Washington, DC: National Park Service, U.S. Department of the Interior.

Chaco Research Archive. 2013. Chaco Outlier Query. www.chacoarchive.org (accessed August 3, 2013).

Chamberlin, Matthew. 2006. Symbolic Conflict and the Spatiality of Traditions in Small-Scale Societies. *Cambridge Archaeological Journal* 16 (1): 39–51.

———. 2011. Plazas, Performance, and Symbolic Power in Ancestral Pueblo Religion. In *Religious Transformation in the Late Pre-Hispanic Pueblo World*, edited by Donna M. Glowacki and Scott Van Keuren, 130–52. Tucson: University of Arizona Press.

Chuipka, Jason P. 2009. Exploring Ethnic Diversity and Sociopolitical Strategies of Early Pueblo I Villages in the Northern San Juan Region, AD 750–840. In *Animas–La Plata Project*, vol. 13, *Special Studies*, edited by James M. Potter, 43–83. SWCA Anthropological Research Paper 10. Phoenix: SWCA Environmental Consultants.

Churchill, Melissa J., Kristin A. Kuckelman, and Mark D. Varien. 1998. Public Architecture in the Mesa Verde Region, A.D. 900 to 1300. Paper presented at the 63rd Annual Meeting of the Society for American Archaeology, Seattle, WA.

Coffey, Grant D. 2014. The Harlan Great Kiva Site: Civic Architecture and Community Persistence in the Goodman Point Area of Southwestern Colorado. *Kiva* 79 (4). Forthcoming.

Coffey, Grant D., and Steve R. Copeland. 2011. *Report of 2010 Goodman Point Community Testing, Montezuma County, Colorado*. www.crowcanyon.org/good manpoint2010 (accessed September 3, 2013).

Cole, Sarah M. 2012. Population Dynamics and Warfare in the Central Mesa Verde Region. In *Emergence and Collapse of Early Villages: Models of Central Mesa Verde Archaeology*, edited by Timothy A. Kohler and Mark D. Varien, 197–218. Berkeley: University of California Press.

Colson, Elizabeth. 1979. In Good Years and in Bad: Food Strategies of Self-Reliant Societies. *Journal of Anthropological Research* 35:18–29.

Colton, Harold S. 1955. *Pottery Types of the Southwest: Wares 8A, 9A, 9B, Tusayan Gray and White Ware, Little Colorado Gray and White Ware*. Museum of Northern Arizona Ceramic Series 3A. Flagstaff: Northern Arizona Society of Science and Art.

———. 1956. *Pottery Types of the Southwest: Tsegi Orange Ware, Winslow Orange Ware, Homol'ovi Orange Ware, Jeddito Yellow Ware, Awatovi Yellow Ware*. Museum of Northern Arizona Ceramic Series 3C. Flagstaff: Northern Arizona Society of Science and Art.

Cook, Edward R., Connie A. Woodhouse, C. Mark Eakin, David M. Meko, and David W. Stahle. 2004. Long-Term Aridity Changes in the Western United States. *Science* 306:1015–18.

Cordell, Linda S. 1996. Big Sites, Big Questions: Pueblos in Transition. In *The Prehistoric Pueblo World, A.D. 1150–1350*, edited by Michael A. Adler, 228–40. Tucson: University of Arizona Press.

————. 2000. Aftermath of Chaos in the Pueblo Southwest. In *Environmental Disaster and the Archaeology of Human Response*, edited by Garth Bawden and Richard M. Reycraft, 179–93. Maxwell Museum of Anthropology, Anthropological Papers 7. Albuquerque: University of New Mexico.

Cordell, Linda S., David E. Doyel, and Keith W. Kintigh. 1994. Processes of Aggregation in the Prehistoric Southwest. In *Themes in Southwest Prehistory*, edited by George J. Gumerman, 109–33. Santa Fe, NM: School of American Research Press.

Cordell, Linda S., and Fred Plog. 1979. Escaping the Confines of Normative Thought: A Reevaluation of Puebloan Prehistory. *American Antiquity* 44:405–29.

Cordell, Linda S., H. Wolcott Toll, Mollie S. Toll, and Thomas C. Windes. 2008. Archaeological Corn from Pueblo Bonito, Chaco Canyon, New Mexico: Dates, Contexts, Sources. *American Antiquity* 73:491–511.

Cordell, Linda S., Carla R. Van West, Jeffrey S. Dean, and Deborah A. Muenchrath. 2007. Mesa Verde Settlement History and Relocation: Climate Change, Social Networks, and Ancestral Pueblo Migration. *Kiva* 72:379–405.

Cowgill, George L. 1988. Onward and Upward with Collapse. In *The Collapse of Ancient States and Civilizations*, edited by Norman Yoffee and George L. Cowgill, 244–76. Tucson: University of Arizona Press.

Creel, Darrell G., Tiffany C. Clark, and Hector Neff. 2002. Production and Long-Distance Movement of Chupadero Black-on-White Pottery in New Mexico and Texas. In *Geochemical Evidence for Long-Distance Exchange*, edited by Michael D. Glascock, 109–32. Westport, CT: Bergin and Garvey.

Crown, Patricia L. 1994. *Ceramics and Ideology: Salado Polychrome Pottery*. Albuquerque: University of New Mexico Press.

————. 1998. Changing Perspectives on the Pueblo IV World. In *Migration and Reorganization: The Pueblo IV Period in the American Southwest*, edited by K. Spielmann, 293–301. Anthropological Research Papers 51. Tempe: Arizona State University.

Crown, Patricia L., and W. James Judge. 1991. *Chaco and Hohokam: Prehistoric Regional Systems in the American Southwest*. Santa Fe, NM: School of American Research Press.

Crown, Patricia L., and Timothy A. Kohler. 1994. Community Dynamics, Site Structure, and Aggregation in the Northern Rio Grande. In *The Ancient Southwestern Community*, edited by W. H. Wills and Robert D. Leonard, 103–17. Albuquerque: University of New Mexico Press.

Crown, Patricia L., and W. H. Wills. 2003. Modifying Pottery and Kivas at Chaco: Pentimento, Restoration, or Renewal? *American Antiquity* 68:511–32.

Davis, Emma Lou. 1964. Anasazi Mobility and Mesa Verde Migrations. PhD diss., Department of Anthropology, University of California–Los Angeles.

Davis, John C. 1986. *Statistics and Data Analysis in Geology*. 2nd ed. New York: John Wiley and Sons.

Dean, Jeffery S. 1969. *Chronological Analysis of Tsegi Phase Sites in Northeastern Arizona*. Papers of the Laboratory of Tree-Ring Research 3. Tucson: University of Arizona Press.

———. 1996. Kayenta Anasazi Settlement Transformations in Northeastern Arizona, A.D. 1150–1350. In *The Prehistoric Pueblo World, A.D. 1150–1350*, edited by Michael A. Adler, 29–47. Tucson: University of Arizona Press.

———. 2010. The Environmental, Demographic, and Behavioral Contexts of the Thirteenth-Century Depopulation of the Northern Southwest. In *Leaving Mesa Verde: Peril and Change in the Thirteenth-Century Southwest*, edited by Timothy A. Kohler, Mark D. Varien, and Aaron M. Wright, 324–45. Tucson: University of Arizona Press.

Dean, Jeffery S., William H. Doelle, and Janet D. Orcutt. 1994. Adaptive Stress, Environment, and Demography. In *Themes in Southwest Prehistory*, edited by George J. Gumerman, 53–86. Santa Fe, NM: School of American Research Press.

Dean, Jeffery S., Robert C. Euler, George J. Gumerman, Fred Plog, R. H. Hevly, and T. N. V. Karlstrom. 1985. Human Behavior, Demography, and Paleoenvironment on the Colorado Plateaus. *American Antiquity* 50:537–54.

Demarest, Arthur. 2004. *Ancient Maya: The Rise and Fall of a Rainforest Civilization*. Cambridge: Cambridge University Press.

Demarest, Arthur A., Prudence M. Rice, and Don S. Rice, eds. 2004a. *The Terminal Classic in the Maya Lowlands: Collapse, Transition, and Transformation*. Boulder: University Press of Colorado.

———. 2004b. The Terminal Classic in the Maya Lowlands: Assessing Collapses, Terminations, and Transformations. In *The Terminal Classic in the Maya Lowlands: Collapse, Transition, and Transformation*, edited by Arthur A. Demarest, Prudence M. Rice, and Don S. Rice, 545–71. Boulder: University Press of Colorado.

deMenocal, Peter B. 2001. Cultural Responses to Climate Change During the Late Holocene. *Science* 292 (5517): 667–73.

Diederichs, Shanna, Gary M. Brown, and Kay E. Barnett. 2011. Thirteenth-Century Social Identities in the Middle San Juan Region: A Comparison to Mesa Verde. Paper presented at the 67th Annual Meeting of the Society for American Archaeology, Sacramento, CA.

Di Lernia, Savino. 2006. Building Monuments, Creating Identity: Cattle Cult as a Social Response to Rapid Environmental Changes in the Holocene Sahara. *Quaternary International* 151 (1): 50–62.

Dongoske, Kurt E., Michael Yeatts, Roger Anyon, and T. J. Ferguson. 1997. Archaeological Cultures and Cultural Affiliation: Hopi and Zuni Perspectives in the American Southwest. *American Antiquity* 62:600–608.

Dorigo, Guido, and Waldo Tobler. 1983. Push Pull Migration Laws. *Annals of the Association of American Geographers* 73 (1): 1–17.

Douglass, Andrew E. 1929. The Secret of the Southwest Solved by Talkative Tree-Rings. *National Geographic* 56:736–70.

Dozier, Edward P. 1954. *The Hopi-Tewa of Arizona*. Berkeley: University of California Press.

———. 1964. The Pueblo Indians of the Southwest: A Survey of the Anthropological Literature and a Review of Theory, Method, and Results. Papers in Honor of Melville J. Herskovits. *Current Anthropology* 5:79–97.

———. 1970. *The Pueblo Indians of North America*. New York: Holt, Rinehart, and Winston.

Drèze, Jean, and Amartya Sen. 1989. *Hunger and Public Action*. Oxford, UK: Clarendon Paperbacks.

Driver, Jonathan C. 2002. Faunal Variation and Change in the Northern San Juan Region. In *Seeking the Center Place: Archaeology and Ancient Communities in the Mesa Verde Region*, edited by Mark D. Varien and Richard H. Wilshusen, 143–60. Salt Lake City: University of Utah Press.

Duff, Andrew I. 1998. The Process of Migration in the Late Prehistoric Southwest. In *Migration and Reorganization: The Pueblo IV Period in the American Southwest*, edited by Katherine A. Spielmann, 31–52. Anthropological Research Papers 51. Tempe: Arizona State University.

———. 2002. *Western Pueblo Identities: Regional Interaction, Migration, and Transformation*. Tucson: University of Arizona Press.

Duff, Andrew I., Karen R. Adams, and Susan C. Ryan. 2010. The Impact of Long-Term Residential Occupation of Community Centers on Local Plant and Animal Resources. In *Leaving Mesa Verde: Peril and Change in the Thirteenth-Century Southwest*, edited by Timothy A. Kohler, Mark D. Varien, and Aaron M. Wright, 156–79. Tucson: University of Arizona Press.

Duff, Andrew I., and Stephen H. Lekson. 2006. Notes from the South. In *The Archaeology of Chaco Canyon: An Eleventh-Century Pueblo Regional Center*, edited by Stephen H. Lekson, 315–37. Santa Fe, NM: School of American Research Press.

Duff, Andrew I., and Susan C. Ryan. 2000. *The Shields Pueblo Research Project Annual Report, 1999*. www.crowcanyon.org/shieldspueblo1999 (accessed September 3, 2013).

Duff, Andrew I., and Richard H. Wilshusen. 2000. Prehistoric Population Dynamics in the Northern San Juan Region, A.D. 950–1300. *Kiva* 66:167–90.

Duwe, Samuel G. 2011. The Prehispanic Tewa World: Space, Time, and Becoming in the Pueblo Southwest. PhD diss., Department of Anthropology, University of Arizona, Tucson.

Earle, Timothy. 2001. Economic Support of Chaco Canyon Society. *American Antiquity* 66:26–35.

Eddy, Frank W. 1977. Archaeological Investigation at Chimney Rock Mesa, 1970–1972. Memoirs of the Colorado Archaeological Society 1. Boulder: Colorado Archaeological Society.

Eggan, Fred. 1950. *Social Organization of the Western Pueblos*. Chicago: University of Chicago Press.

Eisenstadt, Shmuel N. 1988. Beyond Collapse. In *The Collapse of Ancient States and Civilizations*, edited by Norman Yoffee and George L. Cowgill, 236–43. Tucson: University of Arizona Press.

Ekren, E. B., and F. N. Houser. 1965. *Geology and Petrology of the Ute Mountains Area, Colorado*. Geological Survey Professional Paper 481. Washington, DC: U.S. Government Printing Office.

Ellis, Florence Hawley. 1964. *A Reconstruction of the Basic Jemez Pattern of Social Organization, with Comparisons to Other Tanoan Social Structures*. University of New Mexico Publications in Anthropology 11. Albuquerque: University of New Mexico Press.

Ericson, Jonathon E., and Timothy G. Baugh. 1993. *The American Southwest and Mesoamerica: Systems of Prehistoric Exchange*. New York: Plenum.

Errickson, Mary. 1993. Archaeological Investigations on Reach III of the Towaoc Canal. Four Corners Archaeological Project, Report 21. Cortez, CO: Complete Archaeological Service Associates.

———. 1998. Ceramic Material Culture. In *The Puebloan Occupation of the Ute Mountain Piedmont*, vol. 6, *Material Culture Studies*, edited by Brian R. Billman, 3–74. Soil Systems Publications in Archaeology, vol. 22, no. 6. Phoenix, AZ: Soil Systems.

Euler, Robert C. 1988. Demography and Culture Dynamics on the Colorado Plateau. In *The Anasazi in a Changing Environment*, edited by G. J. Gumerman, 192–229. Cambridge: Cambridge University Press.

Fast, Natalie. 2012. How Great Were Cedar Mesa Great House Communities, A.D. 1060–1270? Master's thesis, Department of Anthropology, Washington State University, Pullman.

Feinman, Gary M. 2000. Dual-Processual Theory and Social Formations in the Southwest. In *Alternative Leadership Strategies in the Prehispanic Southwest*, edited by Barbara J. Mills, 207–24. Tucson: University of Arizona Press.

Feinman, Gary, Kent Lightfoot, and Steadman Upham. 2000. Political Hierarchies and Organizational Strategies in the Puebloan Southwest. *American Antiquity* 65:449–70.

Feinman, Gary, Steadman Upham, and Kent Lightfoot. 1981. The Production Step Measure: An Ordinal Index of Labor Input in Ceramic Manufacture. *American Antiquity* 46:871–84.

Ferguson, T. J. 1989. Comment on Social Integration and Anasazi Architecture. In *The Architecture of Social Integration in Prehistoric Pueblos*, edited by William D. Lipe and Michelle Hegmon, 169–73. Occasional Papers 1. Cortez, CO: Crow Canyon Archaeological Center.

Fewkes, Jesse Walter. 1893. A-wa'-to-bi: An Archeological Verification of a Tusayan Legend. *American Anthropologist* 6:363–76.

————. 1911. *Antiquities of the Mesa Verde National Park, Cliff Palace*. Smithsonian Institution Bureau of American Ethnology, Bulletin 51. Washington, DC: Government Printing Office.

————. 1916. Excavation and Repair of Sun Temple, Mesa Verde National Park. Washington, DC: Department of the Interior.

————. 1921. Fieldwork on the Mesa Verde National Park, Colorado. In *Explorations and Fieldwork of the Smithsonian Institution in 1920*. Smithsonian Miscellaneous Collections 72 (6): 75–94.

————. 1923. The Hovenweep National Monument. *American Anthropologist* 25:145–55.

Fiero, Kathleen. 1999. *Balcony House: A History of a Cliff Dwelling*. Mesa Verde National Park Archeological Research Series 8A. Mesa Verde National Park, CO: Mesa Verde Museum Association.

Fish, Suzanne K., and Stephan A. Kowalewski, eds. 1990. *The Archaeology of Regions: A Case for Full-Coverage Survey*. Washington, DC: Smithsonian Institution Press.

Force, Eric R., and Wayne K. Howell. 1997. *Holocene Depositional History and Anasazi Occupation in McElmo Canyon, Southwestern Colorado*. Arizona State Museum Archaeological Series 188. Tucson: University of Arizona.

Ford, Richard I. 1972. Barter, Gift, or Violence: An Analysis of Tewa Intertribal Exchange. In *Social Exchange and Interaction*, edited by Edwin N. Wilmsen, 21–45. Anthropological Papers 46. Ann Arbor: Museum of Anthropology, University of Michigan.

Fowler, Andrew P., and John R. Stein. 1992. The Anasazi Great House in Space, Time, and Paradigm. In *Anasazi Regional Organization and the Chaco System*, edited by David E. Doyel, 101–22. Maxwell Museum of Anthropology, Anthropological Papers 5. Albuquerque: University of New Mexico.

Fowles, Severin M. 2004. Tewa Versus Tiwa: Northern Rio Grande Settlement Patterns and Social History, A.D. 1275 to 1540. In *The Protohistoric Pueblo World, A.D. 1275–1600*, edited by E. Charles Adams and Andrew I. Duff, 17–25. Tucson: University of Arizona Press.

Fox, Robin. 1967. *The Keresan Bridge: A Problem in Pueblo Ethnology*. Monographs on Social Anthropology 35. London: Athlone.

Fuller, Steven L. 1984. *Late Anasazi Pottery Kilns in the Yellowjacket District, Southwestern Colorado*. CASA Papers 4. Cortez, CO: Complete Archaeological Service Associates.

Germick, Stephen. 1985. *An Archaeological Reconnaissance Along the San Juan and Lower Mancos Rivers, Northwestern New Mexico*. Archaeological Reports 748. Flagstaff: Northern Arizona University.

Gilpin, Dennis, Susan E. Perlman, Louise M. Senior, and Lynn A. Neal. 2002. Cultural Affiliation Study for Canyons of the Ancients National Monument, Southwest Colorado. Report prepared for the Bureau of Land Management,

Canyons of the Ancients National Monument, and Anasazi Heritage Center. Two Rivers Report TR-01. Dolores, CO.

Gladwin, Harold S. 1957. *A History of the Ancient Southwest*. Portland, ME: Bond Wheelright.

Gladwin, Winifred, and Harold S. Gladwin. 1934. *A Method for Designation of Cultures and Their Variations*. Medallion Papers 15. Globe, AZ: Gila Pueblo.

Glascock, Michael D. 1992. Neutron Activation Analysis. In *Chemical Characterization of Ceramic Pastes in Archaeology*, edited by Hector Neff, 11–26. Monographs in World Archaeology 7. Madison, WI: Prehistory Press.

Glassie, Henry. 2000. *Vernacular Architecture*. Bloomington: Indiana University Press.

Glowacka, Maria Danuta. 1998. Ritual Knowledge in Hopi Tradition. *American Indian Quarterly* 22 (3): 386–92.

Glowacki, Donna M. 1995. Patterns of Ceramic Production and Vessel Movement in the Mesa Verde Region. Master's thesis, Department of Anthropology, University of Missouri, Columbia.

———. 2001. Yucca House (5MT5006) Mapping Project Report. On file at Mesa Verde National Park and Crow Canyon Archaeological Center, Cortez, CO.

———. 2006a. The Social Landscape of Depopulation: The Northern San Juan, A.D. 1150–1300. PhD diss., Department of Anthropology, Arizona State University, Tempe.

———. 2006b. Architectural Change in Spruce Tree House (5MV640) During the Mid-to-Late 1200s: Main Street and Kiva G. Report Summarizing the 2005 Field Season. Manuscript on file with the Colorado Historical Society and Mesa Verde National Park, CO.

———. 2010. The Social and Cultural Contexts of the Central Mesa Verde Region During the Thirteenth-Century Migrations. In *Leaving Mesa Verde: Peril and Change in the Thirteenth-Century Southwest*, edited by Timothy A. Kohler, Mark D. Varien, and Aaron M. Wright, 200–221. Amerind Foundation Seminar Series. Tucson: University of Arizona Press.

———. 2011. The Role of Religion in the Depopulation of the Central Mesa Verde Region. In *Religious Transformation in the Late Pre-Hispanic Pueblo World*, edited by Donna M. Glowacki and Scott Van Keuren, 66–83. Tucson: University of Arizona Press.

———. 2012. The Mesa Verde Community Center Survey Documenting Large Pueblo Villages in Mesa Verde National Park, with Contributions by R. K. Bocinsky, E. Alonzi, and K. Reese. Manuscript submitted to the National Science Foundation and Mesa Verde National Park, on file with Crow Canyon Archaeological Center and Washington State University in compliance with NSF Grant DEB-0816400. Available at http://village.anth.wsu.edu/publications.

Glowacki, Donna M., Jeffrey Ferguson, Winston Hurst, and Catherine M. Cameron. n.d. Chacoan and Post-Chacoan Pottery Production and Circulation

Among Great House Communities in the Comb Ridge Locality, Southeast Utah. Manuscript in author's possession.

Glowacki, Donna M., and Hector Neff. 2002. Using INAA in the Greater Southwest. In *Ceramic Production and Circulation in the Greater Southwest: Source Determination by INAA and Complementary Mineralogical Investigations*, edited by Donna M. Glowacki and Hector Neff, 179–85. Monograph 44. Los Angeles: Cotsen Institute of Archaeology, UCLA.

Glowacki, Donna M., Hector Neff, and Michael D. Glascock. 1998. Initial Assessment of the Production and Movement of 13th Century Ceramic Vessels in the Northern San Juan Region. *Kiva* 63:217–40.

Glowacki, Donna M., Hector Neff, Michelle Hegmon, James W. Kendrick, and W. James Judge. 2002. Chemical Variation, Resource Use, and Vessel Movement in the Northern San Juan. In *Ceramic Production and Circulation in the Greater Southwest: Source Determination by INAA and Complementary Mineralogical Investigations*, edited by Donna M. Glowacki and Hector Neff, 67–73. Monograph 44. Los Angeles: Cotsen Institute of Archaeology, UCLA.

Glowacki, Donna M., and Scott G. Ortman. 2001. Distance Analysis of Mesa Verde Black-on-White Designs Among Mesa Verde Communities. Paper presented at the 66th Annual Society for American Archaeology Meeting, New Orleans.

———. 2012. Characterizing Community Center (Village) Formation in the VEP Study Area, AD 600–1280. In *Emergence and Collapse of Early Villages: Models of Central Mesa Verde Archaeology*, edited by Timothy A. Kohler and Mark D. Varien, 219–46. Berkeley: University of California Press.

Glowacki, Donna M., Charles Reed, R. Kyle Bocinsky, Shanna Diederichs, and Julie A. Bell. 2010. Making Sense of the Actual: Settlement Trends in the Southwestern Colorado VEP Study Areas. Paper presented in the Village Ecodynamics Project II at the 75th Annual Meeting of the Society for American Archaeology, St. Louis, MO.

Glowacki, Donna M., and Scott Van Keuren, eds. 2011. *Religious Transformation in the Late Pre-Hispanic Pueblo World*. Tucson: University of Arizona Press.

Glowacki, Donna M., Mark D. Varien, and C. David Johnson. 2003. Community Centers: Cycles of Aggregation in the Mesa Verde Region. Paper presented at the 68th Annual Meeting of the Society for American Archaeology, Milwaukee, WI.

Griffitts, Mary O. 1990. *Guide to the Geology of Mesa Verde National Park*. Mesa Verde Museum Association. Salt Lake City, UT: Lorraine Press.

Haas, Jonathan, and Winifred Creamer. 1993. Stress and Warfare Among the Prehistoric Kayenta Anasazi of the Thirteenth Century. *Fieldiana: Anthropology*, n.s. 21. Chicago: Field Museum of Natural History.

Habicht-Mauche, Judith, Deborah L. Huntley, and Suzanne L. Eckert, eds. 2006. *The Social Life of Pots: Glaze Wares and Cultural Dynamics in the Southwest, AD 1250–1680*. Tucson: University of Arizona Press.

Hannaford, Charles A. 1993. Prehistoric Communities in the La Plata Valley. Paper presented at the 5th Occasional Anasazi Symposium, San Juan College, Farmington, NM.

Harbottle, Garman. 1976. Activation Analysis in Archaeology. In *Radiochemistry*, vol. 3, edited by G. W. Newton, 33–72. London: Chemical Society.

Harkins, Michael E. 2004. Revitalization as History and Theory. In *Reassessing Revitalization Movements: Perspectives from North America and the Pacific Islands*, edited by Michael E. Harkins, xv–xxxvi. Lincoln: University of Nebraska Press.

Harry, Karen G., Timothy J. Ferguson, James R. Allison, Brett T. McLaurin, Jeff Ferguson, and Margaret Lyneis. 2013. Examining the Production and Distribution of Shivwits Ware Pottery in the American Southwest. *American Antiquity* 78:385–96.

Harry, Karen G., Paul R. Fish, and Suzanne K. Fish. 2002. Ceramic Production and Distribution in Two Classic Period Hohokam Communities. In *Ceramic Production and Circulation in the Greater Southwest: Source Determination by INAA and Complementary Mineralogical Investigations*, edited by Donna M. Glowacki and Hector Neff, 179–85. Monograph 44. Los Angeles: Cotsen Institute of Archaeology, UCLA.

Hassan, Fekri A. 2002. Paleoclimate, Food, and Culture Change in Africa: An Overview. In *Droughts, Food and Culture: Ecological Change and Food Security in Africa's Later Prehistory*, edited by Fekri A. Hassan, 11–26. New York: Kluwer Academic/Plenum.

Haug, Gerald H., Detlef Günther, Larry C. Peterson, Daniel M. Sigman, Konrad A. Hughen, and Beat Aeschlimann. 2003. Climate and the Collapse of Maya Civilization. *Science* 299 (5613): 1731–35.

Hayes, Alden C. 1964. *The Archaeological Survey of Wetherill Mesa, Mesa Verde National Park—Colorado*. Archaeological Research Series 7-A. Washington, DC: National Park Service, U.S. Department of the Interior.

———. 1981. A Survey of Chaco Canyon Archaeology. In *Archaeological Surveys of Chaco Canyon, New Mexico*, edited by Alden C. Hayes, David M. Brugge, and W. James Judge, 1–68. Washington, DC: U.S. Government Printing Office.

Hays-Gilpin, Kelley, and Eric Van Hartesveldt. 1998. *Prehistoric Ceramics of the Puerco Valley, Arizona*. Museum of Northern Arizona Ceramic Series 7. Flagstaff: Museum of Northern Arizona.

Healey, Christopher. 1990. *Maring Hunters and Traders*. Berkeley: University of California Press.

Hegmon, Michelle. 1991. Six Easy Steps to Dating Pueblo III Ceramic Assemblages: Working Draft. Manuscript on file, Crow Canyon Archaeological Center, Cortez, CO.

———, ed. 2000. *The Archaeology of Regional Interaction: Religion, Warfare, and Exchange Across the American Southwest and Beyond*. Proceedings of the 1996 Southwest Symposium. Boulder: University Press of Colorado.

Hegmon, Michelle, James R. Allison, Hector Neff, and Michael D. Glascock. 1997. Production of San Juan Red Ware in the Northern Southwest: Insights into Regional Interaction in Early Puebloan Prehistory. *American Antiquity* 62:449–63.

Hegmon, Michelle, Winston Hurst, and James R. Allison. 1995. Production for Local Consumption and Exchange: Comparisons of Early Red and White Ware Ceramics in the San Juan Region. In *Ceramic Production in the American Southwest*, edited by Barbara J. Mills and Patricia L. Crown, 30–62. Tucson: University of Arizona Press.

Hegmon, Michelle, Matthew A. Peeples, Ann P. Kinzig, Stephanie Kulow, Cathryn M. Meegan, and Margaret C. Nelson. 2008. Social Transformation and Its Human Costs in the Prehispanic U.S. Southwest. *American Anthropologist* 110:313–24.

Hegmon, Michelle, and Stephen Plog. 1996. Regional Social Interactions in the Northern Southwest: Evidence and Issues. In *Interpreting Southwestern Diversity: Underlying Principles and Overarching Patterns*, edited by Paul R. Fish and J. Jefferson Reid, 23–34. Anthropological Research Papers 48. Tempe: Arizona State University.

Heitman, Carolyn, and Stephen Plog. 2005. Kinship and the Dynamics of the House. In *A Catalyst for Ideas: Anthropological Archaeology and the Legacy of Douglas Schwartz*, edited by Vernon L. Scarborough, 69–100. Santa Fe, NM: SAR Press.

Herr, Sarah A. 2001. *Beyond Chaco: Great Kiva Communities on the Mogollon Rim Frontier*. Anthropological Paper 66. Tucson: University of Arizona Press.

Hewitt, Kenneth. 1983. *Interpretations of Calamity from the Viewpoint of Human Ecology*. Boston: Allen and Unwin.

Hill, J. Brett, Jeffery J. Clark, William H. Doelle, and Patrick D. Lyons. 2004. Prehistoric Demography in the Southwest: Migration, Coalescence, and Hohokam Population Decline. *American Antiquity* 69:689–716.

———. 2010. Depopulation of the Northern Southwest: A Macroregional Perspective. In *Leaving Mesa Verde: Peril and Change in the Thirteenth-Century Southwest*, edited by Timothy A. Kohler, Mark D. Varien, and Aaron M. Wright, 34–52. Tucson: University of Arizona Press.

Hilpert, Lowell S. 1969. *Uranium Resources of Northwestern New Mexico*. Geological Survey Professional Paper 603. Washington, DC: U.S. Government Printing Office.

Hoffman, Susanna M., and Anthony Oliver-Smith. 1999. Anthropology and the Angry Earth: An Overview. In *The Angry Earth: Disaster in Anthropological Perspective*, edited by Anthony Oliver-Smith and Susanna M. Hoffman, 1–16. New York: Routledge.

Holmes, William Henry. 1878. Report on the Ancient Ruins of Southwestern Colorado, Examined During the Summers of 1875 and 1876. In *United States*

Geological and Geographical Society of the Territories, Tenth Annual Report, 383–408. Washington, DC.

Huckleberry, Gary A., and Brian R. Billman. 1998. Floodwater Farming, Discontinuous Ephemeral Streams, and Puebloan Abandonment in Southwestern Colorado. *American Antiquity* 63:595–616.

Huntley, Deborah L. 2008. *Ancestral Zuni Glaze-Decorated Pottery: Pueblo IV Regional Organization Through Ceramic Production and Exchange*. Anthropological Papers of the University of Arizona 72. Tucson: University of Arizona Press.

Hurst, Winston. 1991. Analysis of Ceramics from Natural Bridges National Monument, Utah. In *Archeological Investigations in Natural Bridges National Monument, Utah*, by Karen Kramer, Alan Osborn, and Winston Hurst, 124–66. Midwest Archeological Center Technical Report 11. Lincoln, NE: U.S. Department of the Interior, National Park Service.

———. 1995. Ceramic Artifacts. In *Holocene Archeology near Squaw Butte, Canyonlands National Park, Utah*, edited by Betsy L. Tipps, 68–70. Selections from the Division of Cultural Resources 7. Denver, CO: U.S. Department of the Interior, National Park Service, Rocky Mountain Region.

———. 2006. Analysis of Ceramic Collections from the Canyonlands National Park SEUG River Corridor Survey (CANY-520), 2005–2006. Submitted to the U.S. Department of the Interior, National Park Service, Canyonlands National Park, Moab, UT.

Hurst, Winston, and Hugh L. Robinson. 2014. The Comb Wash Campground Survey: An Archaeological Surface Inventory of 2,200 Acres in San Juan County, Utah [draft]. Submitted to the Bureau of Land Management, Monticello Field Office, by Catherine M. Cameron, principal investigator, University of Colorado, Boulder.

Hurst, Winston, and Jonathan Till. 2009. A Brief Survey of Great Houses and Related Features in Southeastern Utah. In *Chaco and Post-Chaco in the Northern San Juan Region: Excavations at the Bluff Great House*, edited by Catherine M. Cameron, 44–80. Tucson: University of Arizona Press.

Ingold, Timothy. 2000. *The Perception of the Environment: Essays on Livelihood, Dwelling, and Skill*. London: Routledge.

Inomata, Takeshi. 2001. The Classic Royal Palace as Political Theater. In *Ciudades Mayas: Urbanización y organización especial*, edited by A. Ciudad Ruiz, 342–62. Madrid: Sociedad Española de Estudios Mayas.

———. 2006. Politics and Theatricality in Mayan Society. In *Archaeology of Performance: Theaters of Power, Community, and Politics*, edited by Takeshi Inomata and Lawrence S. Coben, 187–222. Lanham, MD: AltaMira.

Irwin-Williams, Cynthia. 2008. Chacoan Society: The View from Salmon Ruins. In *Chaco's Northern Prodigies: Salmon, Aztec, and the Ascendancy of the Middle San Juan Region After A.D. 1100*, edited by Paul F. Reed, 273–83. Salt Lake City: University of Utah Press.

Ives, John W. 2014. Resolving the Promontory Culture Enigma. In *Archaeology in the Great Basin and Southwest: Papers in Honor of Don D. Fowler*, edited by Nancy J. Parezo and Joel C. Janetski, 149–62. Salt Lake City: University of Utah Press.

Jennings, Jesse D. 1966. *Glen Canyon: A Summary*. University of Utah Anthropological Paper 81. Salt Lake City: University of Utah Press.

Jett, Stephen C. 1964. Pueblo Indian Migrations: An Evaluation of the Possible Physical and Cultural Determinants. *American Antiquity* 29:281–300.

Johnson, C. David. 2003. Mesa Verde Region Towers: A View from Above. *Kiva* 68:323–40.

Johnson, Gregory A. 1980. Rank-Size Convexity and System Integration: A View from Archaeology. *Economic Geography* 56 (3): 234–47.

Jolliffe, I. T. 1986. *Principal Component Analysis*. New York: Springer.

Judd, Neil M. 1959. *Pueblo del Arroyo, Chaco Canyon, New Mexico*. Smithsonian Miscellaneous Collections 138(1). Washington, DC: Smithsonian Institution.

Judge, W. James. 1979. The Development of a Complex Cultural Ecosystem in the Chaco Basin, New Mexico. In *Proceedings of the First Conference on Scientific Research in the National Parks* 3, edited by Robert M. Linn, 901–6. Washington, DC: Government Printing Office.

———. 1989. Chaco Canyon–San Juan Basin. In *Dynamics of Southwest Prehistory*, edited by Linda S. Cordell and George J. Gumerman, 209–62. Washington, DC: Smithsonian Institution Press.

———. 1991. Chaco: Current Views of Prehistory and the Regional System. In *Chaco and Hohokam: Prehistoric Regional Systems in the Southwest*, edited by Patricia Crown and W. James Judge, 11–30. Santa Fe, NM: SAR Press.

———. 2002. A Trial Timeline Model for Chaco Society and Polity. Paper presented at the Chaco Synthesis Capstone Conference, Santa Fe, NM.

Judge, W. James, and John D. Schelberg, eds. 1984. *Recent Research on Chaco Prehistory*. Reports of the Chaco Center 8. Albuquerque: National Park Service.

Kantner, John W. 2003a. Rethinking Chaco as a System. *Kiva* 69:207–27.

———. 2003b. Preface: The Chaco World. *Kiva* 69:83–92.

Kantner, John W., and Keith W. Kintigh. 2006. The Chaco World. In *The Archaeology of Chaco Canyon: An Eleventh-Century Pueblo Regional Center*, edited by Stephen H. Lekson, 153–88. Santa Fe, NM: School of American Research Press.

Kelley, J. Charles. 1952. Factors Involved in the Abandonment of Certain Peripheral Southwestern Settlements. *American Anthropologist* 54:356–87.

Kent, Kate Peck. 1983. Temporal Shifts in the Structure of Traditional Southwestern Textile Design. In *Structure and Cognition in Art*, edited by Dorothy K. Washburn, 113–37. Cambridge: Cambridge University Press.

Kenzle, Susan C. 1997. Enclosing Walls in the Northern San Juan: Sociophysical Boundaries and Defensive Fortifications in the American Southwest. *Journal of Field Archaeology* 24:195–210.

Kidder, Alfred V. 1924. *An Introduction to the Study of Southwestern Archaeology.* New Haven, CT: Yale University Press.

―――. 1958. *Pecos, New Mexico: Archaeological Notes,* vol. 5. Andover, MA: Phillips Academy, Robert S. Peabody Foundation for Archaeology.

Kidder, Alfred V., and Samuel James Guernsey. 1919. *Archaeological Explorations in Northeastern Arizona.* Bureau of American Ethnology Bulletin 65. Washington, DC: U.S. Government Printing Office.

Kinnear-Ferris, Sharyl, Winston Hurst, and Kelley Hays-Gilpin. n.d. Hopi Pottery and Prehistoric Salt Procurement in the Southern Utah Canyon Country. Draft manuscript.

Kintigh, Keith W. 1994. Chaco, Community Architecture, and Cibolan Aggregation. In *The Ancient Southwestern Community: Models and Methods for the Study of Prehistoric Social Organization,* edited by W. H. Wills and Robert D. Leonard, 131–40. Albuquerque: University of New Mexico Press.

Kintigh, Keith W., and A. Ammerman. 1982. Heuristic Approaches to Spatial Analysis in Archaeology. *American Antiquity* 47:31–63.

Kintigh, Keith W., Todd L. Howell, and Andrew I. Duff. 1996. Post-Chacoan Social Integration at the Hinkson Site, New Mexico. *Kiva* 61:257–74.

Kleidon, Jim, Shanna Diederichs, and Donna M. Glowacki. 2007. Long Mesa 2002 Fire Burned Area Archeological Inventory, Mesa Verde National Park, Colorado: Puebloan Settlement, Demographics, and Community Structure, A.D. 500–1300 on Chapin and Park Mesas. Division of Research and Natural Resources, Mesa Verde National Park, CO.

Kleidon, Jim, Michael Hendrix, Dani Long, Sarah Payne, Ed Rezac, Bryan Shanks, Shanna Diederichs, Jeremy Karchut, Vince Macmillan, and John Beezley. 2003. Bircher-Pony Post Fire Assessment Project. Division of Cultural and Natural Resources, Mesa Verde National Park, CO.

Kohler, Timothy A. 1992. Field Houses, Villages, and the Tragedy of the Commons in the Early Northern Anasazi Southwest. *American Antiquity* 57:617–35.

―――. 2010. A New Paleoproductivity Reconstruction for Southwestern Colorado, and Its Implications for Understanding Thirteenth-Century Depopulation. In *Leaving Mesa Verde: Peril and Change in the Thirteenth-Century Southwest,* edited by Timothy A. Kohler, Mark D. Varien, and Aaron M. Wright, 102–27. Tucson: University of Arizona Press.

Kohler, Timothy A., C. David Johnson, Mark D. Varien, Scott G. Ortman, Robert Reynolds, Ziad Kobti, Jason Cowan, Kenneth Kolm, Schaun Smith, and Lorene Yap. 2007. Settlement Ecodynamics in the Prehispanic Central Mesa Verde Region. In *The Model-Based Archaeology of Socionatural Systems,* edited by Timothy A. Kohler and Sander van der Leeuw, 61–104. Santa Fe, NM: School of American Research Press.

Kohler, Timothy A., Scott G. Ortman, Katie E. Grundtisch, Carly Fitzpatrick, and Sarah M. Cole. 2014. The Better Angels of Their Nature: Declining Conflict

Through Time Among Prehispanic Farmers of the Pueblo Southwest. *American Antiquity* 79:444–64.

Kohler, Timothy A., and Carla R. Van West. 1996. The Calculus of Self-Interest in the Development of Cooperation: Sociopolitical Development and Risk Among the Northern Anasazi. In *Evolving Complexity and Environmental Risk in the Prehistoric Southwest*, edited by Joseph Tainter and Bonnie Bagley Tainter, 169–96. Santa Fe Institute Studies in the Sciences of Complexity 24. Boston: Addison-Wesley.

Kohler, Timothy A., and Mark D. Varien. 2010. A Scale Model of Seven Hundred Years of Farming Settlements in Southwestern Colorado. In *Becoming Villagers: Comparing Early Village Societies*, edited by Matthew S. Bandy and Jake R. Fox, 37–61. Tucson: University of Arizona Press.

Kohler, Timothy A., Mark D. Varien, and Aaron M. Wright, eds. 2010. *Leaving Mesa Verde: Peril and Change in the Thirteenth-Century Southwest.* Tucson: University of Arizona Press.

Kohler, Timothy A., Mark D. Varien, Aaron M. Wright, and Kristin A. Kuckelman. 2008. Mesa Verde Migrations: New Archaeological Research and Computer Simulation Suggest Why Ancestral Puebloans Deserted the Northern Southwest United States. *American Scientist* 96:146–53.

Kolm, Kenneth E., and Schaun M. Smith. 2012. Modeling Paleohydrological System Structure and Function. In *Emergence and Collapse of Early Villages: Models of Central Mesa Verde Archaeology*, edited by Timothy A. Kohler and Mark D. Varien, 73–83. Berkeley: University of California Press.

Kowalewski, Stephen A. 2003. Scale and the Explanation of Demographic Change: 3,500 Years in the Valley of Oaxaca. *American Anthropologist* 105:313–25.

Kowalewski, Stephen A., Richard E. Blanton, Gary Feinman, and Laura Finstein. 1983. Boundaries, Scale, and Internal Organization. *Journal of Anthropological Archaeology* 2:32–56.

Kroeber, Alfred Louis. 1939. *Cultural and Natural Areas of Native North America.* Berkeley: University of California Press.

Kroskrity, Paul V. 1993. *Language, History, and Identity: Ethnolinguistic Studies of the Arizona Tewa.* Tucson: University of Arizona Press.

Kuckelman, Kristin A., ed. 2000. *The Archaeology of Castle Rock Pueblo: A Thirteenth-Century Village in Southwestern Colorado.* www.crowcanyon.org/castlerock (accessed February 2013).

———. 2002. Thirteenth-Century Warfare in the Central Mesa Verde Region. In *Seeking the Center Place: Archaeology and Ancient Communities in the Mesa Verde Region*, edited by Mark D. Varien and Richard H. Wilshusen, 233–53. Salt Lake City: University of Utah Press.

———, ed. 2003. *The Archaeology of Yellow Jacket Pueblo (Site 5MT5): Excavations at a Large Community Center in Southwestern Colorado.* www.crowcanyon.org/yellowjacket (accessed March 2013).

————. 2010. The Depopulation of Sand Canyon Pueblo, a Large Ancestral Pueblo Village in Southwestern Colorado. *American Antiquity* 75:497–526.

Kuckelman, Kristin A., Grant D. Coffey, and Steven R. Copeland. 2009. *Interim Descriptive Report of Research at Goodman Point Pueblo (Site 5MT604), Montezuma County, Colorado, 2005–2008*. www.crowcanyon.org/goodman point2005_2008 (accessed February 13, 2013).

Kuckelman, Kristin A., Ricky R. Lightfoot, and Debra L. Martin. 2000. Changing Patterns of Violence in the Northern San Juan Region. *Kiva* 66:147–66.

————. 2003. The Bioarchaeology and Taphonomy of Violence at Castle Rock and Sand Canyon Pueblos, Southwestern Colorado. *American Antiquity* 67:486–513.

Lancaster, James A., Jean M. Pinkley, Philip F. Van Cleave, and Don Watson. 1954. *Archeological Excavations in Mesa Verde National Park, Colorado, 1950*. Archeological Research Series 2. Washington, DC: National Park Service, U.S. Department of the Interior.

Larsen, Esper S., Jr., and Whitman Cross. 1956. *Geology and Petrology of the San Juan Region, Southwestern Colorado*. Geological Survey Professional Paper 258. Washington, DC: U.S. Printing Office.

LeBlanc, Stephen A. 1999. *Prehistoric Warfare in the American Southwest*. Salt Lake City: University of Utah Press.

Lee, E. S. 1966. A Theory of Migration. *Demography* 3:47–57.

Lekson, Stephen H. 1983. Dating the Hubbard Tri-wall and Other Tri-wall Structures. *Southwest Lore* 49 (4): 15–23.

————. 1986. *Great Pueblo Architecture of Chaco Canyon, New Mexico*. Albuquerque: University of New Mexico Press.

————. 1989. Kivas? In *The Architecture of Social Integration in Prehistoric Pueblos*, edited by William D. Lipe and Michelle Hegmon, 161–67. Occasional Papers 1. Cortez, CO: Crow Canyon Archaeological Center.

————. 1991. Settlement Patterns and the Chaco Region. In *Chaco and Hohokam: Prehistoric Regional Systems in the American Southwest*, edited by Patricia L. Crown and W. James Judge, 31–55. Santa Fe, NM: School of American Research Press.

————. 1999a. *The Chaco Meridian: Centers of Political Power in the Ancient Southwest*. Walnut Creek, CA: AltaMira.

————. 1999b. Great Towns in the Southwest. In *Great Towns and Regional Polities in the Prehistoric American Southwest and Southeast*, edited by Jill E. Neitzel, 3–21. Albuquerque: University of New Mexico Press.

————. 2006. Chaco Matters: An Introduction. In *The Archaeology of Chaco Canyon: An Eleventh-Century Pueblo Regional Center*, edited by Stephen H. Lekson, 3–44. Santa Fe, NM: School of American Research Press.

————. 2008. *A History of the Ancient Southwest*. Santa Fe, NM: School for Advanced Research Press.

Lekson, Stephen H., and Catherine M. Cameron. 1995. The Abandonment of Chaco Canyon, the Mesa Verde Migrations, and the Reorganization of the Pueblo World. *Journal of Anthropological Archaeology* 14:184–202.

Lekson, Stephen H., Curtis P. Nepstad-Thornberry, Brian E. Yunker, Toni S. Laumbach, David P. Cain, and Karl W. Laumbach. 2002. Migrations in the Southwest: Pinnacle Ruin, Southwestern New Mexico. *Kiva* 68 (2): 73–101.

Lekson, Stephen H., Thomas C. Windes, and Peter J. McKenna. 2006. Architecture. In *The Archaeology of Chaco Canyon: An Eleventh-Century Pueblo Regional Center*, edited by Stephen H. Lekson, 67–116. Santa Fe, NM: SAR Press.

Levy, Jerrold E. 1992. *Orayvi Revisited: Social Stratification in an "Egalitarian" Society*. Santa Fe, NM: School of American Research Press.

Lightfoot, Kent G., and Antoinette Martinez. 1995. Frontiers and Boundaries in Archaeological Perspective. *Annual Review of Anthropology* 24:471–92.

Lipe, William D. 1970. Anasazi Communities in the Red Rock Plateau, Southeastern Utah. In *Reconstructing Prehistoric Pueblo Societies*, edited by William A. Longacre, 84–139. Albuquerque: University of New Mexico Press.

———. 1989. Social Scale of Mesa Verde Anasazi Kivas. In *The Architecture of Social Integration in Prehistoric Pueblos*, edited by William D. Lipe and Michelle Hegmon, 53–71. Occasional Papers 1. Cortez, CO: Crow Canyon Archaeological Center.

———. 1995. The Depopulation of the Northern San Juan: Conditions in the Turbulent 1200s. *Journal of Anthropological Archaeology* 14:143–69.

———. 2002. Social Power in the Central Mesa Verde Region, A.D. 1150–1300. In *Seeking the Center Place: Archaeology and Ancient Communities in the Mesa Verde Region*, edited by Mark D. Varien and Richard H. Wilshusen, 203–32. Salt Lake City: University of Utah Press.

———. 2006. Chaco Notes from the North. In *The Archaeology of Chaco Canyon: An Eleventh-Century Pueblo Regional Center*, edited by Stephen Lekson, 261–313. Santa Fe, NM: School of American Research Press.

———. 2010. Lost in Transition: The Central Mesa Verde Archaeological Complex. In *Leaving Mesa Verde: Peril and Change in the Thirteenth-Century Southwest*, edited by Timothy A. Kohler, Mark D. Varien, and Aaron M. Wright, 262–84. Tucson: University of Arizona Press.

Lipe, William D., and Donna M. Glowacki. 2011. A Late Pueblo II Period "Surge" of Kayenta Ceramics into Southern Utah? Paper presented at the 76th Annual Meeting of the Society for American Archaeology, Sacramento, CA.

Lipe, William D., Donna M. Glowacki, and Thomas C. Windes. 2010. Dynamics of the Thirteenth Century Depopulation of the Northern San Juan: The View from Cedar Mesa. Paper presented at the 75th Annual Meeting of the Society for American Archaeology, St. Louis, MO.

Lipe, William D., R. G. Matson, and Jesse Morin. 2011. Report on Survey Conducted in 2009 in San Juan County, Utah, Under BLM Permit N0.085025.

Report submitted to the Bureau of Land Management, Monticello Field Office, Blanding, UT.

Lipe, William D., and Scott G. Ortman. 2000. Spatial Patterning in Northern San Juan Villages, A.D. 1050–1300. *Kiva* 66:91–122.

Lipe, William D., and Mark D. Varien. 1999a. Pueblo II (A.D. 900–1150). In *Colorado Prehistory: A Context for the Southern Colorado River Basin*, edited by William D. Lipe, Mark D. Varien, and Richard H. Wilshusen, 242–89. Denver: Colorado Council of Professional Archaeologists and State Historical Fund, Colorado Historical Society.

———. 1999b. Pueblo III (A.D. 1150–1300). In *Colorado Prehistory: A Context for the Southern Colorado River Basin*, edited by William D. Lipe, Mark D. Varien, and Richard H. Wilshusen, 290–352. Denver: Colorado Council of Professional Archaeologists and State Historical Fund, Colorado Historical Society.

Lister, Robert H., and Florence C. Lister. 1978. *Anasazi Pottery: Ten Centuries of Prehistoric Ceramic Art in the Four Corners Country of the Southwestern United States*. Albuquerque: University of New Mexico Press.

———. 1987. *Aztec Ruins on the Animas: Excavated, Preserved, and Interpreted*. Albuquerque: University of New Mexico Press.

Lucero, Lisa J. 2006. *Water and Ritual: The Rise and Fall of Classic Maya Rulers*. Austin: University of Texas Press.

Lucius, William A. 1982. Ceramic Analysis. In *Testing and Excavation Report, MAPCO's Rocky Mountain Liquid Hydrocarbons Pipeline, Southwest Colorado*, vol. 2, edited by Jerry E. Fetterman and Linda Honeycutt, 7.1–7.40. San Francisco, CA: Woodward Clyde Consultants.

Lyons, Patrick D. 2003. *Ancestral Hopi Migrations*. Anthropological Papers of the University of Arizona 68. Tucson: University of Arizona Press.

Lyons, Patrick D., and Jeffery J. Clark. 2008. Interaction, Enculturation, Social Distance, and Ancient Ethnic Identities. In *Archaeology Without Borders: Contact, Commerce, and Change in the U.S. Southwest and Northwestern Mexico*, edited by Laurie D. Webster and Maxine McBrinn, 185–207. Boulder: University Press of Colorado; Chihuahua: INAH.

Madsen, David B. 1994. Mesa Verde and Sleeping Ute Mountain: The Geographical and Chronological Dimensions of the Numic Expansion. In *Across the West: Human Population Movement and the Expansion of the Numa*, edited by David B. Madsen and David Rhode, 24–31. Salt Lake City: University of Utah Press.

Mahoney, Nancy M., Michael A. Adler, and James W. Kendrick. 2000. The Changing Scale and Configuration of Mesa Verde Communities. *Kiva* 66:67–90.

Malotki, Ekkehart, ed. 2002. *Hopi Tales of Destruction*. Lincoln: University of Nebraska Press.

Marshall, Michael, P., John R. Stein, Richard W. Loose, and Judith E. Novotny. 1979. *Anasazi Communities of the San Juan Basin*. Albuquerque: Public

Service Company of New Mexico; Santa Fe: New Mexico Historic Preservation Bureau.

Martin, Debra L., Ryan P. Harrod, and Misty Fields. 2010. Beaten Down and Worked to the Bone: Bioarchaeological Investigations of Women and Violence in the Ancient Southwest. *Landscapes of Violence*, vol. 1, no. 1, article 3:1–19. Available at http://scholarworks.umass.edu/lov/vol1/iss1/3.

Martin, Paul S. 1936. *Lowry Ruin in Southwestern Colorado*. Anthropological Series 21(1). Chicago: Field Museum of Natural History.

Mathien, Frances Joan. 1997. Ornaments of the Chaco Anasazi. In *Ceramics, Lithics, and Ornaments of Chaco Canyon: Analyses of Artifacts from the Chaco Project, 1971–1978*, vol. 3, edited by F. J. Mathien, 1119–1220. Reports of the Chaco Center 11. Santa Fe, NM: Division of Cultural Research, National Park Service.

Mathien, Frances Joan, and Randall H. McGuire, eds. 1986. *Ripples in the Chichimec Sea: New Considerations of Southwestern-Mesoamerican Interactions*. Carbondale: Southern Illinois University Press.

Matson, R. G. 1991. *The Origins of Southwestern Agriculture*. Tucson: University of Arizona Press.

Matson, R. G., William D. Lipe, and William R. Haase IV. 1988. Adaptational Continuities and Occupational Discontinuities: The Cedar Mesa Anasazi. *Journal of Field Archaeology* 15:245–64.

———. 1990. Human Adaptations on Cedar Mesa, Southeastern Utah. Department of Anthropology, University of British Columbia. Available at http://hdl.handle.net/2429/19586.

Maxfield, E. Blair. 1979. Geology of the Indian Creek, Beef Basin, Castle Valley, and Dolores Planning Units. In *A Stratified Random Sample of the Cultural Resources in the Canyonlands Section of the Moab District*, by Richard A. Thompson, 8–21. Cultural Resources Series 1. Report prepared for the Bureau of Land Management by International Learning and Research, Cedar City, UT.

McAnany, Patricia A., and Maxime Lamoureux St-Hilaire. 2013. Detaching from Place in Theory and Practice. Paper presented at the 78th Annual Meeting of the Society for American Archaeology, Honolulu, HI.

McAnany, Patricia A., and Norman Yoffee. 2010. Why We Question Collapse and Study Human Resilience, Ecological Vulnerability, and the Aftermath of Empire. In *Questioning Collapse: Human Resilience, Ecological Vulnerability, and the Aftermath of Empire*, edited by Patricia A. McAnany and Norman Yoffee, 1–17. Cambridge: Cambridge University Press.

McGimsey, Charles R., III. 1980. *Mariana Mesa: Seven Prehistoric Sites in West Central New Mexico*. Papers of the Peabody Museum of Archaeology and Ethnology 72. Cambridge, MA: Peabody Museum of Archaeology and Ethnology.

McGuire, Randall H. 2011. Rethinking Social Power and Inequality in the Aboriginal Southwest/Northwest. In *Movement, Connectivity and Landscape*

Change in the Ancient Southwest, edited by Margaret C. Nelson and Colleen A. Strawhacker, 57–73. Boulder: University Press of Colorado.

McGuire, Randall H., E. Charles Adams, Ben A. Nelson, and Katherine Spielmann. 1994. Drawing the Southwest to Scale: Perspectives on Macroregional Relations. In *Themes in Southwest Prehistory*, edited by George J. Gumerman, 239–66. Santa Fe, NM: School of American Research Press.

McGuire, Randall H., and Dean J. Saitta. 1996. Although They Have Petty Captains, They Obey Them Badly: The Dialectics of Prehispanic Western Pueblo Social Organization. *American Antiquity* 61:197–216.

McKenna, Peter J. 1998. The Cultural Landscape of the Aztec Ruins, New Mexico. Paper presented at the 63rd Annual Meeting of the Society for American Archaeology, Seattle, WA.

McKenna, Peter J., and H. Wolcott Toll. 1992. Regional Patterns of Great House Development Among the Totah Anasazi, New Mexico. In *Anasazi Regional Organization and the Chaco System*, edited by David E. Doyel, 133–43. Maxwell Museum of Anthropology, Anthropological Papers 5. Albuquerque: University of New Mexico.

McLellan, George E. 1969. The Origin, Development, and Typology of Anasazi Kivas and Great Kivas. PhD diss., University of Colorado, Boulder.

McPherson, Robert S. 1995. *A History of San Juan County: In the Palm of Time*. Salt Lake City: Utah State Historical Society, San Juan County Commission.

———. 2014. *Viewing the Ancestors: Perceptions of the Anaasází, Mokwič, and Hisatsinom*. Norman: University of Oklahoma Press.

McVickar, Janet L. 2001. *An Archaeological Survey of Natural Bridges National Monument, Southeastern Utah*. Intermountain Cultural Resources Management Anthropology Program, Professional Paper 64. Washington, DC: National Park Service, Department of the Interior.

Middleton, Guy D. 2012. Nothing Lasts Forever: Environmental Discourses on the Collapse of Past Societies. *Journal of Archaeological Research* 20:257–307.

Mills, Barbara J. 1999. Ceramics and the Social Contexts of Food Consumption in the Northern Southwest. In *Pots and People: A Dynamic Interaction*, edited by James Skibo and Gary Feinman, 99–114. Salt Lake City: University of Utah Press.

———, ed. 2000. *Alternative Leadership Strategies in the Prehispanic Southwest*. Tucson: University of Arizona Press.

———. 2002. Recent Research on Chaco: Changing Views on Economy, Ritual, and Society. *Journal of Archaeological Research* 10:65–117.

———. 2007. Performing the Feast: Visual Display and Suprahousehold Commensalism in the Puebloan Southwest. *American Antiquity* 72:210–39.

Mills, Barbara J., and William H. Walker. 2008. Introduction: Memory, Materiality, and Depositional Practice. In *Memory Work: Archaeologies of Material Practices*, edited by Barbara J. Mills and William H. Walker, 3–23. Santa Fe, NM: School for Advanced Research Press.

Minnis, Paul E. 1996. Notes on Economic Uncertainty and Human Behavior in the Prehistoric North American Southwest. In *Evolving Complexity and Environmental Risk in the Prehistoric Southwest*, edited by Joseph Tainter and Bonnie Bagley Tainter, 57–78. Santa Fe Institute Studies in the Sciences of Complexity 24. Boston: Addison-Wesley.

Morley, Sylvanus G., and Alfred V. Kidder. 1917. The Archaeology of McElmo Canyon, Colorado. *El Palacio* 4 (4): 41–70.

Morris, Earl H. 1928. *The Aztec Ruin*. Anthropological Papers of the American Museum of Natural History 26. New York: American Museum of Natural History.

———. 1939. *Archaeological Studies in the La Plata District, Southwestern Colorado and Northwestern New Mexico*. Publication 519. Washington, DC: Carnegie Institution of Washington.

Muir, Robert J., and Jonathan C. Driver. 2002. Scale of Analysis and Zooarchaeological Interpretation: Pueblo III Faunal Variation in the Northern San Juan. *Journal of Anthropological Archaeology* 21:165–99.

———. 2004. Identifying Ritual Use of Animals in the Northern American Southwest. In *Behavior Behind Bones: The Zooarchaeology of Ritual, Religion, Status, and Identity*, edited by Sharyn Jones O'Day, Wim Van Neer, and Anton Ervynck, 128–43. Proceedings of the 9th Conference of the International Council of Archaeozoology. Durham, NC: Oxbow Books.

Munson, Marit K. 2011. Gender, Art, and Ritual Hierarchy in the Ancient Pueblos of the Rio Grande Valley, New Mexico. In *Comparative Archaeologies: The American Southwest (AD 900–1600) and the Iberian Peninsula (3000–1500 BC)*, edited by Katina T. Lillios, 189–208. Oxford, UK: Oxbow Books.

Naranjo, Tessie. 1995. Thoughts on Migration by Santa Clara Pueblo. *Journal of Anthropological Archaeology* 14:247–50.

———. 2008. Life as Movement: A Tewa View of Community and Identity. In *The Social Construction of Communities: Agency, Structure, and Identity in the Prehispanic Southwest*, edited by Mark D. Varien and James M. Potter, 251–62. Lanham, MD: AltaMira.

Neff, Hector. 1994. RQ-Mode Principal Components Analysis of Ceramic Compositional Data. *Archaeometry* 36 (1): 115–30.

———. 2002. Quantitative Techniques for Analyzing Ceramic Compositional Data. In *Ceramic Production and Circulation in the Greater Southwest: Source Determination by INAA and Complementary Mineralogical Investigations*, edited by Donna M. Glowacki and Hector Neff, 15–36. Monograph 44. Los Angeles: Cotsen Institute of Archaeology, UCLA.

Neff, Hector, and Michael D. Glascock. 1996. Chemical Variation in Prehistoric Ceramics from Southwestern Colorado: An Update with New Data from the Lowry Ruin Excavations of W. James Judge. Report on file at Missouri University Research Reactor, Columbia.

Neff, Hector, and Donna M. Glowacki. 2002. Ceramic Source Determination by Instrumental Neutron Activation Analysis in the American Southwest. In *Ceramic Production and Circulation in the Greater Southwest: Source Determination by INAA and Complementary Mineralogical Investigations*, edited by Donna M. Glowacki and Hector Neff, 1–14. Monograph 44. Los Angeles: Cotsen Institute of Archaeology, UCLA.

Neily, Robert B. 1983. The Prehistoric Community on the Colorado Plateau: An Approach to the Study of Change and Survival in the Northern San Juan Area of the American Southwest. PhD diss., Southern Illinois University, Carbondale.

Neitzel, Jill E. 2000. What Is a Regional System? Issues of Scale and Interaction in the Prehistoric Southwest. In *The Archaeology of Regional Interaction: Religion, Warfare, and Exchange Across the American Southwest and Beyond*, edited by Michelle Hegmon, 25–40. Boulder: University Press of Colorado.

Nelson, Margaret C. 1999. *Mimbres During the Twelfth Century: Abandonment, Continuity, and Reorganization*. Tucson: University of Arizona Press.

Nelson, Nels C. 1919. The Archaeology of the Southwest: A Preliminary Report. *Proceedings of the National Academy of Sciences* 5 (4): 114–20.

Newsome, Elizabeth A., and Kelley Hays-Gilpin. 2011. Spectatorship and Performance in Mural Painting, AD 1250–1500: Visuality and Social Integration. In *Religious Transformation in the Late Pre-Hispanic Pueblo World*, edited by Donna M. Glowacki and Scott Van Keuren, 153–74. Tucson: University of Arizona Press.

Nickens, Paul R. 1981. *Pueblo III Communities in Transition: Environment and Adaptation in Johnson Canyon*. Memoirs of the Colorado Archaeological Society 2. Boulder: Colorado Archaeological Society.

Nordby, Larry V. 2001. *Prelude to Tapestries in Stone: Understanding Cliff Palace Architecture*. Mesa Verde National Park Archeological Research Series, Architectural Studies 4. Mesa Verde National Park, CO: Mesa Verde National Park Division of Research and Resource Management.

Nordenskiöld, Gustav. 1990. *The Cliff Dwellers of the Mesa Verde*. Reprint, Mesa Verde, CO: Mesa Verde Museum Association. Originally published 1893, Royal Printing Office, Stockholm.

O'Bryan, Deric. 1950. Excavations in Mesa Verde National Park, 1947–1948. Medallion Papers 39. Globe, AZ: Gila Pueblo.

Oliver-Smith, Anthony. 1996. Anthropological Research on Hazards and Disasters. *Annual Review of Anthropology* 25:303–28.

Orcutt, Janet D. 1991. Environmental Variability and Settlement Changes on the Pajarito Plateau. *American Antiquity* 56:315–32.

Ortiz, Alfonso. 1969. *The Tewa World: Space, Time, Being, and Becoming in a Pueblo Society*. Chicago: University of Chicago Press.

Ortman, Scott G. 2000a. Conceptual Metaphor in the Archaeological Record: Methods and an Example from the American Southwest. *American Antiquity* 65:613–45.

———. 2000b. Artifacts. In *The Archaeology of Castle Rock Pueblo: A Thirteenth-Century Village in Southwestern Colorado*, edited by Kristin A. Kuckelman. www.crowcanyon.org/castlerock (accessed May 3, 2002).

———. 2002. Artifacts. In *The Archaeology of Woods Canyon Pueblo: A Canyon-Rim Village in Southwestern Colorado*, edited by Melissa J. Churchill. www.crowcanyon.org/woodscanyon (accessed April 11, 2005).

———. 2003. Artifacts. In *The Archaeology of Yellow Jacket Pueblo (Site 5MT5): Excavations at a Large Community Center in Southwestern Colorado*, edited by Kristin A. Kuckelman. www.crowcanyon.org/yellowjacket (accessed May 21, 2012).

———. 2008. Architectural Metaphor and Chacoan Influence in the Northern San Juan. In *Archaeology Without Borders: Contact, Commerce, and Change in the U.S. Southwest and Northwestern Mexico*, edited by Maxine E. McBrinn and Laurie D. Webster, 227–55. Boulder: University Press of Colorado.

———. 2012. *Winds from the North: Tewa Origins and Historical Anthropology.* Salt Lake City: University of Utah Press.

Ortman, Scott G., and Bruce A. Bradley. 2002. Sand Canyon Pueblo: The Container in the Center. In *Seeking the Center Place: Archaeology and Ancient Communities in the Mesa Verde Region*, edited by Mark D. Varien and Richard H. Wilshusen, 41–78. Salt Lake City: University of Utah Press.

Ortman, Scott G., Donna M. Glowacki, Melissa J. Churchill, and Kristin A. Kuckelman. 2000. Pattern and Variation in Northern San Juan Village Histories. *Kiva* 66:123–46.

Ortman, Scott G., Donna M. Glowacki, Mark D. Varien, and C. David Johnson. 2012. The Study Area and the Ancestral Pueblo Occupation. In *Emergence and Collapse of Early Villages: Models of Central Mesa Verde Archaeology*, edited by Timothy A. Kohler and Mark D. Varien, 15–40. Berkeley: University of California Press.

Osborn, Alan P. 1971. *Archaeology of the Arizona Public Service Company 345KV Line.* Museum of Northern Arizona, Bulletin 46. Flagstaff: Northern Arizona Society of Science and Art.

Parks, James A., and Jeffery S. Dean. 1997. Interpretation of Tree-Ring Dates from Spring House and 20-1/2 House, Mesa Verde National Park, Colorado. Manuscript on file at the Laboratory of Tree-Ring Research, University of Arizona, Tucson.

———. 1998. Tree-Ring Dating of Balcony House: A Chronological, Architectural, and Social Interpretation. Manuscript on file at the Laboratory of Tree-Ring Research, University of Arizona, Tucson.

Parsons, Elsie Clews. 1939. *Pueblo Indian Religion.* Vols. 1 and 2. Chicago: University of Chicago Press.

Pauketat, Timothy R. 2001. Practice and History in Archaeology: An Emerging Paradigm. *Anthropological Theory* 1 (1): 73–98.

————. 2003. Resettled Farmers and the Making of a Mississippian Polity. *American Antiquity* 68:39–66.

————. 2011. Getting Religion: Lessons from Ancestral Pueblo History. In *Religious Transformation in the Late Pre-Hispanic Pueblo World*, edited by Donna M. Glowacki and Scott Van Keuren, 221–38. Tucson: University of Arizona Press.

Pauketat, Timothy R., and Susan M. Alt. 2005. Agency in a Postmold? Physicality and the Archaeology of Culture-Making. *Journal of Archaeological Method and Theory* 12:213–36.

Peckham, Stewart. 1963. *Highway Salvage Archaeology*, vol. 4. Santa Fe: New Mexico Highway Department and the Museum of New Mexico.

Peeples, Matthew A. 2011. Identity and Social Transformation in the Pre-Hispanic Cibola World, AD 1150–1325. PhD diss., Arizona State University, Tempe.

Petersen, Ken L. 1988. *Climate and the Dolores River Anasazi: A Paleoenvironmental Reconstruction from a 10,000-Year Pollen Record, La Plata Mountains, Southwestern Colorado.* Anthropological Papers of the University of Utah 113. Salt Lake City: University of Utah Press.

Pfaffenberger, Bryan. 1988. Fetishised Objects and Humanised Nature: Towards an Anthropology of Technology. *Man* 23:236–52.

Pierce, Christopher D. 1999. Explaining Corrugated Pottery in the American Southwest: An Evolutionary Approach. PhD diss., Department of Anthropology, University of Washington, Seattle.

Pierce, Christopher D., Donna M. Glowacki, and Margaret M. Thurs. 2002. Measuring Community Interaction: Pueblo III Pottery Production and Distribution in the Central Mesa Verde Region. In *Seeking the Center Place: Archaeology and Ancient Communities in the Mesa Verde Region*, edited by Mark D. Varien and Richard H. Wilshusen, 185–202. Salt Lake City: University of Utah Press.

Plog, Stephen. 1994. Introduction: Regions and Boundaries in the Prehistoric Southwest. In *The Ancient Southwestern Community: Models and Methods for the Study of Prehistoric Social Organization*, edited by W. H. Wills and Robert D. Leonard, 147–48. Albuquerque: University of New Mexico Press.

————. 1995. Equality and Hierarchy: Holistic Approaches to Understanding Social Dynamics in the Pueblo Southwest. In *The Foundations of Social Inequality*, edited by T. D. Price and Gary M. Feinman, 189–206. New York: Plenum.

————. 2003. Social Conflict, Social Structure, and Processes of Culture Change. Book Review Essay. *American Antiquity* 68:182–86.

————. 2011. Ritual and Cosmology in the Chaco Era. In *Religious Transformation in the Late Pre-Hispanic Pueblo World*, edited by Donna M. Glowacki and Scott Van Keuren, 50–65. Tucson: University of Arizona Press.

Plog, Stephen, and Carrie Heitman. 2010. Hierarchy and Social Inequality in the American Southwest, A.D. 800–1200. *Proceedings of the National Academy of Sciences of the United States of America* 107 (46): 19619–26.

Plog, Stephen, and Julie P. Solometo. 1997. The Never-Changing and the Ever-Changing: The Evolution of Western Pueblo Ritual. *Cambridge Archaeological Journal* 7 (2): 161–82.

Potter, James M. 1997. Communal Ritual and Faunal Remains: An Example from the Dolores Anasazi. *Journal of Field Archaeology* 24:353–64.

———. 2000. Pots, Parties, and Politics: Communal Feasting in the American Southwest. *American Antiquity* 65:471–92.

Potter, James M., and Jason P. Chuipka. 2007. Early Pueblo Communities and Cultural Diversity in the Durango Area. *Kiva* 72:407–29.

———. 2010. Perimortem Mutilation of Human Remains in an Early Village in the American Southwest: A Case for Ethnic Violence. *Journal of Anthropological Archaeology* 29:507–23.

Potter, James M., Jason P. Chuipka, and Jerry Fetterman. 2012. The Eastern Mesa Verde Region: Migrants, Cultural Diversity, and Violence in the East. In *Crucible of Pueblos: The Early Pueblo Period in the Northern Southwest*, edited by Richard H. Wilshusen, Gregson Schachner, and James R. Allison, 53–71. Monograph 71. Los Angeles: Cotsen Institute of Archaeology Press, UCLA.

Potter, James M., and Scott G. Ortman. 2004. Community and Cuisine in the Prehispanic American Southwest. In *Identity, Feasting, and the Archaeology of the Greater Southwest*, edited by Barbara J. Mills, 173–91. Boulder: University Press of Colorado.

Potter, James M., and Elizabeth M. Perry. 2000. Ritual as a Power Resource in the American Southwest. In *Alternative Leadership Strategies in the Prehispanic Southwest*, edited by Barbara J. Mills, 60–78. Tucson: University of Arizona Press.

———. 2011. Mortuary Features and Identity Construction in an Early Village Community in the American Southwest. *American Antiquity* 76:529–46.

Powers, Robert P., William B. Gillespie, and Stephen H. Lekson. 1983. *The Outlier Survey: A Regional View of Settlement in the San Juan Basin*. Albuquerque, NM: National Park Service.

Rands, Robert L., and Ronald L. Bishop. 1980. Resource Procurement Zones and Patterns of Ceramic Exchange in the Palenque Region, Mexico. In *Models and Methods in Regional Exchange*, edited by Robert E. Fry, 19–46. Society for American Archaeology Papers 1. Washington, DC: Society for American Archaeology.

Rautman, Alison E. 1993. Resource Variability, Risk, and the Structure of Social Networks: An Example from the Prehistoric Southwest. *American Antiquity* 58:403–24.

———. 1996. Risk, Reciprocity, and the Operation of Social Networks. In *Evolving Complexity and Environmental Risk in the Prehistoric Southwest*, edited by Joseph A. Tainter and Bonnie Bagley Tainter, 197–222. Proceedings, vol. 24, Santa Fe Institute Studies in the Sciences of Complexity. Reading, MA: Addison-Wesley.

Reed, Alan D. 1994. The Numic Occupation of Western Colorado and Eastern Utah during the Prehistoric and Protohistoric Periods. In *Across the West: Human Population Movement and the Expansion of the Numa*, edited by David B. Madsen and David Rhode, 188–99. Salt Lake City: University of Utah Press.

Reed, Erik K. 1958. *Excavations in Mancos Canyon, Colorado*. Anthropological Papers 35. Salt Lake City: University of Utah.

Reed, Lori. 2013. Notes on Aztec Pottery. Manuscript in the possession of the author. August 5, 2013.

Reed, Paul F. 2006a. *Thirty-Five Years of Archaeological Research at Salmon Ruins, New Mexico*. Vol. 1, *Introduction, Architecture, Chronology, and Conclusions*. Tucson, AZ: Center for Desert Archaeology; Bloomfield, NM: Salmon Ruins Museum.

———, ed. 2006b. *Thirty-Five Years of Archaeological Research at Salmon Ruins, New Mexico*. 3 vols. Tucson: Center for Desert Archaeology; Bloomfield, NM: Salmon Ruins Museum.

———. 2008a. Setting the Stage: A Reconsideration of Salmon, Aztec, and the Middle San Juan Region in Chacoan and Post-Chacoan Puebloan History. In *Chaco's Northern Prodigies: Salmon, Aztec, and the Ascendancy of the Middle San Juan Region After AD 1100*, edited by Paul F. Reed, 3–25. Salt Lake City: University of Utah Press.

———. 2008b. Salmon Pueblo as a Ritual and Residential Chacoan Great House. In *Chaco's Northern Prodigies: Salmon, Aztec, and the Ascendancy of the Middle San Juan Region After A.D. 1100*, edited by Paul F. Reed, 42–61. Salt Lake City: University of Utah Press.

———, ed. 2008c. *Chaco's Northern Prodigies: Salmon, Aztec, and the Ascendancy of the Middle San Juan Region After AD 1100*. Salt Lake City: University of Utah Press.

———. 2011. Middle San Juan Settlement Patterns: Searching for Chacoan Immigrants and Evidence of Local Emulation on the Landscape. *Kiva* 77:225–50.

Reed, Paul F., Gary M. Brown, Michael L. Brack, Lori S. Reed, Jeffrey Wharton, and Joel Gamache. 2010. *Aztec East Ruin Landscape Project*. Technical Report 2010-101. Tucson, AZ: Center for Desert Archaeology.

Reid, J. J. 1989. A Grasshopper Perspective on the Mogollon of the Arizona Mountains. In *Dynamics of Southwestern Prehistory*, edited by Linda S. Cordell and George J. Gumerman, 57–87. Washington, DC: Smithsonian Institution Press.

Renfrew, Colin. 2001. Production and Consumption in a Sacred Economy: The Material Correlates of High Devotional Expression at Chaco Canyon. *American Antiquity* 66:14–25.

Rice, Prudence M. 1987. *Pottery Analysis: A Sourcebook*. Chicago: University of Chicago Press.

Richert, Roland. 1964. *The Excavation of a Portion of the East Ruin, Aztec Ruins National Monument, New Mexico*. Southwestern Museum Association Technical Series 4. Globe, AZ: Southwestern Museum Association.

Robb, John, and Timothy R. Pauketat. 2013a. From Moments to Millennia: Theorizing Scale and Change in Human History. In *Big Histories, Human Lives: Tackling Problems of Scale in Archaeology*, edited by John Robb and Timothy R. Pauketat, 3–33. Santa Fe, NM: School of American Research Press.

———, eds. 2013b. *Big Histories, Human Lives: Tackling Problems of Scale in Archaeology*. Santa Fe, NM: School of American Research Press.

Roberts, Frank H. H. 1927. The Ceramic Sequence in Chaco Canyon, New Mexico and Its Relation to the Cultures of the San Juan Basin. PhD diss., Department of Anthropology, Harvard University, Cambridge, MA.

Robinson, Hugh L. 2005. Feasting, Exterior Bowl Design and Public Space in the Northern San Juan, A.D. 1240–1300. Master's thesis, Department of Anthropology, Washington State University, Pullman.

Rohn, Arthur H. 1963. Prehistoric Soil and Water Conservation on Chapin Mesa. *American Antiquity* 28:441–55.

———. 1971. *Mug House, Wetherill Mesa Excavations, Mesa Verde National Park, Colorado*. Archaeological Research Series 7-D. Washington, DC: National Park Service, U.S. Department of the Interior.

———. 1977. *Cultural Change and Continuity on Chapin Mesa*. Lawrence: Regents Press of Kansas.

———. 1989. Northern San Juan Prehistory. In *Dynamics of Southwest Prehistory*, edited by Linda S. Cordell and George J. Gumerman, 149–78. Washington, DC: Smithsonian Institution Press.

Roney, John R. 1992. Prehistoric Roads and Regional Integration in the Chacoan System. In *Anasazi Regional Organization and the Chaco System*, edited by David E. Doyel, 123–32. Maxwell Museum of Anthropology, Anthropological Papers 5. Albuquerque: University of New Mexico.

———. 1995. Mesa Verde Manifestations South of the San Juan River. *Journal of Anthropological Archaeology* 14:170–83.

Ryan, Susan C. 2008. Constructing Community and Transforming Identity at Albert Porter Pueblo. In *The Social Construction of Communities: Studies of Agency, Structure, and Identity in the Southwestern U.S.*, edited by Mark D. Varien and James M. Potter, 69–86. Walnut Creek, CA: AltaMira.

———. 2010. Environmental Change, Population Movement, and the Post-Chaco Transition at Albert Porter Pueblo. *Kiva* 75:303–25.

———. n.d. The Ritual Performance of Kiva Decommissioning. Manuscript in possession of the author.

Sahlins, Marshall. 1972. *Stone Age Economics*. Chicago: Aldine Atherton.

Salzer, Matthew W. 2000. Temperature Variability and the Northern Anasazi: Possible Implications for Regional Abandonment. *Kiva* 65:295–318.

Sanders, William T., Jeffrey R. Parsons, and Robert S. Santley. 1979. *The Basin of Mexico: Ecological Processes in the Evolution of Civilization*. New York: Academic Press.

Sayre, Edward V. 1975. *Brookhaven Procedures for Statistical Analyses of Multivariate Archaeometric Data*. Brookhaven National Laboratory Report BNL-23128. New York: Brookhaven National Laboratory.

Schaafsma, Polly. 2000. *Warrior, Shield, and Star: Imagery and Ideology of Pueblo Warfare*. Santa Fe, NM: Western Edge.

Schachner, Gregson. 2001. Ritual Control and Transformation in Middle-Range Societies: An Example from the American Southwest. *Journal of Anthropological Archaeology* 20:168–94.

———. 2007. Population Circulation and the Transformation of Ancient Cibola Communities. PhD diss., Department of Anthropology, Arizona State University, Tempe.

———. 2012. *Population Circulation and the Transformation of Ancient Zuni Communities*. Tucson: University of Arizona Press.

Schillaci, Michael A., Erik G. Ozolins, and Thomas C. Windes. 2001. Multivariate Assessment of Biological Relationships Among Prehistoric Southwest Amerindian Populations. In *Following Through: Papers in Honor of Phyllis S. Davis*, edited by Regge N. Wiseman, Thomas C. O'Laughlin, and Cordelia T. Snow, 133–49. Papers of the Archaeological Society of New Mexico 27. Albuquerque: Archaeological Society of New Mexico.

Schillaci, Michael A., and Christopher M. Stojanowski. 2002. Investigating Social Organization at Aztec Ruins Using Determinant Ratio Analysis. In *Forward into the Past: Papers in Honor of Teddy Lou and Francis Stickney*, edited by Regge N. Wiseman, Thomas C. O'Laughlin, and Cordelia T. Snow, 93–104. Papers of the Archaeological Society of New Mexico 28. Albuquerque: Archaeological Society of New Mexico.

Schlanger, Sarah H. 1988. Patterns in the Population Movement and Long-Term Population Growth in Southwestern Colorado. *American Antiquity* 53:773–93.

Schlanger, Sarah H., and Richard H. Wilshusen. 1993. Local Abandonments and Regional Conditions in the North American Southwest. In *Abandonment of Settlements and Regions: Ethnoarchaeological and Archaeological Approaches*, edited by Catherine M. Cameron and Steve A. Tomka, 85–98. Cambridge: Cambridge University Press.

Schwindt, Dylan, Scott G. Ortman, and Donna M. Glowacki. 2014. Comparing Demography and Population History Between the Northern San Juan and Northern Rio Grande. Paper presented at the the 79th Annual Society for American Archaeology Meetings, Austin, TX.

Sears, Julian D. 1956. *Geology of Comb Ridge and Vicinity North of San Juan River, San Juan County, Utah.* Geology Survey Bulletin 1021-E. Washington, DC: U.S. Government Printing Office.

Sebastian, Lynne. 1992. *The Chaco Anasazi: Sociopolitical Evolution in the Prehistoric Southwest.* Cambridge: Cambridge University Press.

Severance, Owen. 2003. Cultural Dynamics in Southeastern Utah: Basketmaker III Through Pueblo III. In *Climbing the Rocks: Papers in Honor of Helen and Jay Crotty,* edited by Regge N. Wiseman, Thomas C. O'Laughlin, and Cordelia T. Snow, 189–204. Papers of the Archaeological Society of New Mexico 29. Albuquerque: Archaeological Society of New Mexico.

———. 2005. A Controlled Surface Collection and Analysis of Ceramics at 42Sa5222 [Cottonwood Falls], Southeastern Utah. Report on file, Edge of the Cedars State Park, Blanding, UT.

Sewell, William H., Jr. 2005. *Logics of History: Social Theory and Social Transformation.* Chicago: University of Chicago Press.

Seymour, Deni J., ed. 2012. *From the Land of Ever Winter to the American Southwest: Athapaskan Migrations, Mobility, and Ethnogenesis.* Salt Lake City: University of Utah Press.

Shackley, M. Steve. 2009. Source Provenance of Obsidian Artifacts from Aztec Ruin National Monument, Northern New Mexico. Manuscript on file, Crow Canyon Archaeological Center, Cortez, CO.

———. 2010. An Energy-Dispersive X-Ray Fluorescence Analysis of Obsidian Artifacts from the East Ruin (LA 45) Aztec Ruin National Monument, Northern New Mexico. Manuscript on file, Crow Canyon Archaeological Center, Cortez, CO.

Sharrock, Floyd W., Keith M. Anderson, Don D. Fowler, and David S. Dibble. 1961. *1960 Excavations, Glen Canyon Area.* Glen Canyon Series 14, Anthropological Papers 2. Salt Lake City: Department of Anthropology, University of Utah.

Shepard, Anna O. 1939. Appendix A: Technology of La Plata Pottery. In *Archaeological Studies in the La Plata District: Southwestern Colorado and Northwestern New Mexico,* by Earl H. Morris, 249–87. Washington, DC: Carnegie Institution of Washington.

Shimada, Izumi, Crystal Barker Schaaf, Lonnie G. Thompson, and Ellen Mosley-Thompson. 1991. Cultural Impacts of Severe Droughts in the Prehistoric Andes: Application of a 1,500-Year Ice Core Precipitation Record. *World Archaeology* 22:247–70.

Silko, Leslie Marmon. 1996. Landscape, History, and the Pueblo Imagination. In *The Ecocriticism Reader: Landmarks in Literary Ecology,* edited by Cheryll Glotfelty and Harold Fromm, 264–75. Athens: University of Georgia Press.

Smith, Watson. 1952. *Kiva Mural Decorations at Awatovi and Kawaika-a with a Survey of Other Wall Paintings in the Pueblo Southwest.* Papers of the Peabody

Museum of American Archaeology and Ethnology 37. Cambridge, MA: Harvard University.

Sofaer, Anna. 1997. The Primary Architecture of the Chacoan Culture: A Cosmological Expression. In *Anasazi Architecture and American Design*, edited by Baker H. Morrow and V. B. Price, 88–132. Albuquerque: University of New Mexico Press.

Solometo, Julie. 2006. The Dimensions of War: Conflict and Culture Change in Central Arizona. In *The Archaeology of Warfare: Prehistories of Raiding and Conquest*, edited by Elizabeth N. Arkush and Mark W. Allen, 23–65. Gainesville: University Press of Florida.

Spielmann, Katherine A. 1991. *Interdependence in the Prehistoric Southwest: An Ecological Analysis of Plains-Pueblo Interaction.* New York: Garland.

———. 1998. Ritual Influences on the Development of Rio Grande Glaze A Ceramics. In *Migration and Reorganization: The Pueblo IV Period in the American Southwest*, edited by Katherine A. Spielmann, 253–61. Anthropological Research Papers 51. Tempe: Arizona State University.

———. 2004. Communal Feasting, Ceramics, and Exchange. In *Identity, Feasting, and the Archaeology of the Greater Southwest*, edited by Barbara J. Mills, 210–32. Boulder: University of Colorado Press.

Stein, John R., and Andrew P. Fowler. 1996. Looking Beyond Chaco in the San Juan Basin and Its Peripheries. In *The Prehistoric Pueblo World, A.D. 1150–1350*, edited by Michael A. Adler, 114–30. Tucson: University of Arizona Press.

Stein, John, and Stephen H. Lekson. 1992. Anasazi Ritual Landscapes. In *Anasazi Regional Organization and the Chaco System*, edited by David E. Doyel, 87–100. Albuquerque: University of New Mexico Press.

Stein, John R., and Peter J. McKenna. 1988. *An Archaeological Reconnaissance of a Late Bonito Phase Occupation near Aztec Ruins National Monument, New Mexico.* Santa Fe, NM: Southwest Cultural Resources Center, National Park Service.

Steward, Julian. 1937. Ecological Aspects of Southwestern Society. *Anthropos* 32 (1/2): 87–104.

Stone, Tammy. 1994. The Process of Aggregation in the Zuni Region: Reasons and Implications. In *Exploring Social, Political, and Economic Organization in the Zuni Region*, edited by Todd L. Howell and Tammy Stone, 9–23. Anthropological Research Papers 46. Tempe: Arizona State University.

Suina, Joseph H. 2002. The Persistence of the Corn Mothers. In *Archaeologies of the Pueblo Revolt: Identity, Meaning, and Renewal in the Pueblo World*, edited by Robert W. Preucel, 212–16. Albuquerque: University of New Mexico Press.

Sullivan, Allan P., and James Bayman, eds. 2007. *Hinterlands and Regional Dynamics in the Ancient Southwest.* Tucson: University of Arizona Press.

Swentzell, Rena. 1993. Mountain Form, Village Form: Unity in the Pueblo World. In *Ancient Land, Ancestral Places: Paul Logsdon in the Pueblo Southwest*, by Stephen Lekson, 139–47. Santa Fe: Museum of New Mexico Press.

Tainter, Joseph A. 1988. *The Collapse of Complex Societies*. Cambridge: Cambridge University Press.

Teague, Lynn S. 1998. *Textiles in Southwestern Prehistory*. Albuquerque: University of New Mexico Press.

Thompson, C., J. R. Allison, S. A. Baker, J. C. Janetski, B. Loosle, and J. D. Wilde. 1988. *The Nancy Patterson Village Archaeological Research Project: Field Year 1986—Preliminary Report No. 4*. Technical Series 87-24. Provo, UT: Brigham Young University Museum of Peoples and Cultures.

Till, Jonathan D. 2001. Chacoan Roads and Road-Associated Sites in the Lower San Juan Region: Assessing the Role of Chacoan Influences in the Northwestern Periphery. Master's thesis, Department of Anthropology, University of Colorado, Boulder.

Titiev, Mischa. 1944. *Old Oraibi: A Study of the Hopi Indians of Third Mesa*. Papers of the Peabody Museum of American Archaeology and Ethnology 22(1). Cambridge, MA: Harvard Museum.

Toll, H. Wolcott. 1991. Material Distributions and Exchange in the Chaco System. In *Chaco and Hohokam: Prehistoric Regional Systems in the American Southwest*, edited by Patricia L. Crown and W. James Judge, 77–107. Santa Fe, NM: School of American Research Press.

———. 1993. The Role of the Totah in Regions and Regional Definitions. Paper presented at the 5th Occasional Anasazi Symposium, San Juan College, Farmington, NM.

———. 2001. Making and Breaking Pots in the Chaco World. *American Antiquity* 66:56–78.

———. 2006. Organization of Production. In *The Archaeology of Chaco Canyon: An Eleventh-Century Pueblo Regional Center*, edited by Stephen H. Lekson, 117–51. Santa Fe, NM: SAR Press.

———. 2008. The La Plata, the Totah, and the Chaco: Variations on a Theme. In *Chaco's Northern Prodigies: Salmon, Aztec, and the Ascendancy of the Middle San Juan Region After A.D. 1100*, edited by Paul R. Reed, 309–33. Salt Lake City: University of Utah Press.

Triadan, Daniela, Barbara J. Mills, and Andrew I. Duff. 2002. From Compositional to Anthropological: Fourteenth-Century Red-Ware Circulation and Its Implications for Pueblo Reorganization. In *Ceramic Production and Circulation in the Greater Southwest: Source Determination by INAA and Complementary Mineralogical Investigations*, edited by Donna M. Glowacki and Hector Neff, 85–97. Monograph 44. Los Angeles: Cotsen Institute of Archaeology, UCLA.

Upham, Steadman, and Fred Plog. 1986. The Interpretation of Prehistoric Political Complexity in the Central and Northern Southwest: Towards a Mending of Models. *Journal of Field Archaeology* 13:223–31.

Van Buren, Mary. 2001. The Archaeology of El Niño Events and Other "Natural" Disasters. *Journal of Archaeological Method and Theory* 8:129–49.

Van Dyke, Ruth M. 2002. The Chacoan Great Kiva in Outlier Communities: Investigating Integrative Spaces Across the San Juan Basin. *Kiva* 67:231–47.

———. 2003. Bounding Chaco: Great House Architectural Variability Across Time and Space. *Kiva* 69:117–40.

———. 2004. Memory, Meaning, and Masonry: The Late Bonito Chacoan Landscape. *American Antiquity* 69:413–31.

———. 2007a. *The Chaco Experience: Landscape and Ideology at the Center Place*. Santa Fe, NM: School for Advanced Research Press.

———. 2007b. Reconceptualizing Regional Dynamics in the Ancient Southwest: Relational Approaches. In *Hinterlands and Regional Dynamics in the Ancient Southwest*, edited by Alan P. Sullivan and James M. Bayman, 201–10. Tucson: University of Arizona Press.

———. 2008. Sacred Landscapes: The Chaco-Totah Connection. In *Chaco's Northern Prodigies: Salmon, Aztec, and the Ascendancy of the Middle San Juan Region After A.D. 1100*, edited by Paul F. Reed, 334–48. Salt Lake City: University of Utah Press.

Van Dyke, Ruth M., and Anthony G. King. 2010. Connecting Worlds: PIII Towers in the Northern San Juan. *Kiva* 75:351–75.

Van Keuren, Scott. 2011. The Materiality of Religious Experience in East-Central Arizona. In *Religious Transformation in the Late Pre-Hispanic Pueblo World*, edited by Donna M. Glowacki and Scott Van Keuren, 175–95. Tucson: University of Arizona Press.

Van Keuren, Scott, Susan L. Stinson, and David R. Abbott. 1997. Specialized Production of Hohokam Plain Ware Ceramics in the Lower Salt River Valley. *Kiva* 63:155–75.

Van West, Carla R. 1994. *Modeling Prehistoric Agricultural Productivity in Southwestern Colorado: A GIS Approach*. Washington State University Department of Anthropology Reports of Investigation 67. Pullman: Washington State University.

———. 1996. Agricultural Potential and Carrying Capacity in Southwestern Colorado, A.D. 901 to 1300. In *The Prehistoric Pueblo World, A.D. 1150–1350*, edited by Michael A. Adler, 214–27. Tucson: University of Arizona Press.

Van West, Carla R., and Jeffrey S. Dean. 2000. Environmental Characteristics of the A.D. 900–1300 Period in the Central Mesa Verde Region. *Kiva* 66:19–44.

Van West, Carla R., and Timothy A. Kohler. 1996. A Time to Rend, a Time to Sew: New Perspectives on Northern Anasazi Sociopolitical Development in Later Prehistory. In *Anthropology, Space, and Geographic Information Systems*, edited by Mark Aldenderfer and Herbert D. G. Maschner, 107–31. New York: Oxford University Press.

Varien, Mark D. 1999. *Sedentism and Mobility in a Social Landscape: Mesa Verde and Beyond*. Tucson: University of Arizona Press.

———. 2000. Introduction. *Kiva* 66:5–18.

————. 2010. Depopulation of the Northern San Juan Region: Historical Review and Archaeological Context. In *Leaving Mesa Verde: Peril and Change in the Thirteenth-Century Southwest*, edited by Timothy A. Kohler, Mark D. Varien, and Aaron M. Wright, 1–33. Tucson: University of Arizona Press.

Varien, Mark D., William D. Lipe, Michael A. Adler, Ian M. Thompson, and Bruce A. Bradley. 1996. Southwestern Colorado and Southeastern Utah Settlement Patterns: A.D. 1100 to 1300. In *The Prehistoric Pueblo World, A.D. 1150*, edited by Michael A. Adler, 86–113. Tucson: University of Arizona Press.

Varien, Mark D., Scott G. Ortman, Timothy A. Kohler, Donna M. Glowacki, and C. David Johnson. 2007. Historical Ecology in the Mesa Verde Region: Results from the Village Ecodynamics Project. *American Antiquity* 72:273–99.

Varien, Mark D., Scott G. Ortman, Susan C. Ryan, and Kristin A. Kuckelman. 2008. Population Dynamics Among Salmon's Northern Neighbors in the Central Mesa Verde Region. In *Chaco's Northern Prodigies: Salmon, Aztec, and Ascendancy of the Middle San Juan Region After AD 1100*, edited by Paul F. Reed, 351–65. Salt Lake City: University of Utah Press.

Varien, Mark D., Carla R. Van West, G. Stuart Patterson. 2000. Competition, Cooperation, and Conflict: Agriculture and Community Catchments in the Central Northern San Juan Region. *Kiva* 66:45–66.

Vivian, R. Gordon. 1959. *The Hubbard Site and Other Tri-wall Structures in New Mexico and Colorado*. Archaeological Research Series 5. Washington, DC: National Park Service, U.S. Department of the Interior.

Vivian, R. Gordon, and Tom W. Mathews. 1965. *Kin Kletso: A Pueblo III Community in Chaco Canyon, New Mexico*. Southwest Monuments Association Technical Series 6, Part 1. Globe, AZ: Southwest Monuments Association.

Vivian, R. Gordon, and Paul Reiter. 1965. *The Great Kivas of Chaco Canyon and Their Relationships*. Monograph 22. Albuquerque: School of American Research and University of New Mexico Press.

Vivian, R. Gwinn. 1990. *The Chacoan Prehistory of the San Juan Basin*. New York: Academic Press.

Vokes, Richard. 2007. Rethinking the Anthropology of Religious Change: New Perspectives on Revitalization and Conversion Movements. *Reviews in Anthropology* 36:311–33.

Wallace, Anthony F. C. 1956. Revitalization Movements. *American Anthropologist* 58:264–81.

Wanek, Alexander A. 1959. *Geology and Fuel Resources of the Mesa Verde Area, Montezuma and La Plata Counties, Colorado*. Geology Survey Bulletin 1072-M. Washington, DC: U.S. Government Printing Office.

Ward, Christine G. 2004. Exploring Meanings of Chacoan Community Great Houses Through Chipped Stone: A Biographical Approach. PhD diss., University of Colorado, Boulder.

Ware, John A. 2001. Chaco Social Organization: A Peripheral View. In *Chaco Society and Polity: Papers from the 1999 Conference*, edited by Linda S.

Cordell, W. James Judge, and June-el Piper, 79–93. New Mexico Archaeological Council Special Publication 4. Albuquerque: New Mexico Archaeological Council.

———. 2014. *A Pueblo Social History: Kinship, Sodality, and Community in the Northern Southwest*. Santa Fe, NM: School for Advanced Research Press.

Ware, John A., and Eric Blinman. 2000. Cultural Collapse and Reorganization: The Origin and Spread of Pueblo Ritual Sodalities. In *The Archaeology of Regional Interaction: Religion, Warfare, and Exchange Across the American Southwest and Beyond*, edited by Michelle Hegmon, 381–409. Boulder: University Press of Colorado.

Weaver, Donald E., Jr. 1978. Prehistoric Population Dynamics and Environmental Exploitation of Manuelito Canyon District, Northwestern New Mexico. PhD diss., Arizona State University, Tempe.

Webster, David. 2002. *The Fall of the Ancient Maya: Solving the Mystery of Maya Collapse*. London: Thames and Hudson.

Webster, Laurie D. 2008. An Initial Assessment of Perishable Artifact Relationships Among Salmon, Aztec, and Chaco Canyon. In *Chaco's Northern Prodigies: Salmon, Aztec, and the Ascendancy of the Middle San Juan Region After A.D. 1100*, edited by Paul F. Reed, 167–89. Salt Lake City: University of Utah Press.

Whiteley, Peter M. 1998. *Rethinking Hopi Ethnography*. Washington, DC: Smithsonian Institution Press.

———. 2008. *The Orayvi Split: A Hopi Transformation*, pt. 1. Anthropological Papers of the American Museum of Natural History 87. New York: American Museum of Natural History.

Wilcox, David R. 1979. The Hohokam Regional System. In *An Archaeological Test of Sites in the Gila Butte–Santan Region*, edited by Glen E. Rice, David Wilcox, K. Rafferty, and James Schoenwetter, 76–116. Anthropological Research Paper 18. Tempe: Arizona State University.

———. 1999. A Peregrine View of Macroregional Systems in the North American Southwest, AD 750–1250. In *Great Towns and Regional Polities in the Prehistoric American Southwest and Southeast*, edited by Jill E. Neitzel, 115–42. Albuquerque: University of New Mexico Press.

Willey, Gordon R. 1953. *Prehistoric Settlement Patterns in the Viru Valley, Peru*. Bulletin 155. Washington, DC: Bureau of American Ethnology, Smithsonian Institution.

Willey, Gordon F., and Philip Phillips. 1958. *Method and Theory in American Archaeology*. Chicago: University of Chicago Press.

Wills, Wirt H. 2000. Political Leadership and the Construction of Chacoan Great Houses, AD 1020–1140. In *Alternative Leadership Strategies in the Prehispanic Southwest*, edited by Barbara J. Mills, 19–44. Tucson: University of Arizona Press.

Wilshusen, Richard H. 2002. Estimating Population in the Central Mesa Verde Region. In *Seeking the Center Place: Archaeology and Ancient Communities in the Mesa Verde Region*, edited by Mark D. Varien and Richard H. Wilshusen, 101–22. Salt Lake City: University of Utah Press.

———. 2009. East of the Animas–La Plata Divide: Is It Periphery of Mesa Verde or Chaco, Neither or Both? Paper presented at the Society for American Archaeology Annual Meeting, Atlanta, GA.

Wilshusen, Richard H., and Scott G. Ortman. 1999. Rethinking the Pueblo I Period in the Northern Southwest: Aggregation, Migration, and Cultural Diversity. *Kiva* 64:369–99.

Wilshusen, Richard H., Scott G. Ortman, Shanna Diederichs, Donna M. Glowacki, and Grant Coffey. 2012. Heartland of the Early Pueblos: The Central Mesa Verde. In *Crucible of Pueblos: The Early Pueblo Period in the Northern Southwest*, edited by Richard Wilshusen, Gregson Schachner, and James Allison, 14–34. Los Angeles: Cotsen Institute of Archaeology Press, UCLA.

Wilshusen, Richard H., Gregson Schachner, and James R. Allison, eds. 2012. *Crucible of Pueblos: The Early Pueblo Period in the Northern Southwest*. Los Angeles: Cotsen Institute of Archaeology Press, UCLA.

Wilshusen, Richard H., and Ruth M. Van Dyke. 2006. Chaco's Beginnings. In *The Archaeology of Chaco Canyon: An Eleventh-Century Pueblo Regional Center*, edited by Stephen H. Lekson, 211–59. Santa Fe, NM: School of American Research Press.

Wilson, C. Dean. 1991. Appendix A: Ceramic Analysis: Hovenweep Laterals Project. In *Archaeological Excavations on the Hovenweep Laterals*, by James N. Morris, 677–762. Four Corners Archaeological Project Report 16. Cortez, CO: Complete Archaeological Service Associates.

———. 2006. Ceramics. In *The La Plata Survey Report*. On file at the Museum of New Mexico, Santa Fe.

Wilson, C. Dean, and Eric Blinman. 1995. Changing Specialization of White Ware Manufacture in the Northern San Juan Region. In *Ceramic Production in the American Southwest*, edited by Barbara J. Mills and Patricia L. Crown, 63–87. Tucson: University of Arizona Press.

Windes, Thomas C. 1987. *Investigations at the Pueblo Alto Complex, Chaco Canyon, New Mexico, 1975–1979*, vols. 1 and 2. Publications in Archeology 18F, Chaco Canyon Studies. Santa Fe, NM: National Park Service.

———. 2004. The Rise of Early Chacoan Great Houses. In *In Search of Chaco: New Approaches to an Archaeological Enigma*, edited by David Grant Noble, 14–21. Santa Fe, NM: School of American Research Press.

———. 2010. Dendrochronology and Structural Wood Use at Pueblo del Arroyo, Chaco Canyon, New Mexico. *Journal of Field Archaeology* 35:75–95.

Windes, Thomas C., and Eileen Bacha. 2008. Sighting Along the Grain: Differential Structural Wood Use at the Salmon Ruin. In *Chaco's Northern Prodigies: Salmon, Aztec, and the Ascendancy of the Middle San Juan Region After A.D. 1100*, edited by Paul F. Reed, 113–39. Salt Lake City: University of Utah Press.

Windes, Thomas C., and Peter J. McKenna. 2001. Going Against the Grain: Wood Production in Chacoan Society. *American Antiquity* 66:119–40.

Winter, Joseph. 1977. *Hovenweep 1976.* Archaeological Report 3. San Jose, CA: Anthropology Department, San Jose State University.

———. 1981. Anasazi Agriculture at Hovenweep II: The Development and Use of Towers. *Contract Abstracts and CRM Archaeology* 2 (2): 28–36. Albuquerque: University of New Mexico Press.

Wobst, H. Martin. 1977. Stylistic Behavior and Information Exchange. In *Papers for the Director: Research Essays in Honor of James B. Griffin,* edited by Charles E. Cleland, 317–42. Anthropology Papers 61. Ann Arbor: Museum of Anthropology, University of Michigan.

Woodson, M. Kyle. 1999. Migrations in Late Anasazi Prehistory: The Evidence from the Goat Hill Site. *Kiva* 65:63–84.

Wright, Aaron M. 2010. The Climate of the Depopulation of the Northern Southwest. In *Leaving Mesa Verde: Peril and Change in the Thirteenth-Century Southwest,* edited by Timothy A. Kohler, Mark D. Varien, and Aaron M. Wright, 75–101. Tucson: University of Arizona Press.

———. 2012. Low-Frequency Climate in the Mesa Verde Region: Beef Basin Revisited. In *Emergence and Collapse of Early Villages: Models of Central Mesa Verde Archaeology,* edited by Timothy A. Kohler and Mark D. Varien, 41–57. Berkeley: University of California Press.

Yoffee, Norman. 1988. Orienting Collapse. In *The Collapse of Ancient States and Civilizations,* edited by Norman Yoffee and George L. Cowgill, 1–19. Tucson: University of Arizona Press.

Zedeño, M. Nieves. 1994. *Sourcing Prehistoric Ceramics at Chodistaas Pueblo, Arizona: The Circulation of People and Pots in the Grasshopper Region.* Anthropological Papers of the University of Arizona 58. Tucson: University of Arizona Press.

———. 1998. Defining Material Correlates for Ceramic Circulation in the Prehistoric Puebloan Southwest. *Journal of Anthropological Research* 54:461–76.

Zedeño, M. Nieves, and Daniela Triadan. 2000. Ceramic Evidence for Community Reorganization and Change in East-Central Arizona. *Kiva* 65:215–33.

INDEX

Page numbers in *italics* indicate illustrations.

Aztec-Chaco: and circular multiwalled
structures, 80–81, 206, 209; and civic-
ceremonial architecture, 84; collapse
of, 204–5; and decline of Chaco, 161,
162; and east vs. west differences,
153; and emigration in Eastern Mesa
Verde, 206; and extent of influence,
163; and historical landscapes, 145–53,
161–64; and power structures, 210–11;
and religious change, 163; and social
change, 209; and social stability, 198;
and use of the term, 145n; and West
Central Mesa Verde, 201, 202; and
Western Mesa Verde, 200–201
Aztec East: and construction style, 206;
dating of, 152, 162, 208; great house
at, 150; and multiwalled structures,
75, 76–77; and revitalization, 162; and
Salmon, 150
Aztec North, 146, 147, 149–50, 151
Aztec Ruins National Monument, 14, 34,
109
Aztec West: construction of, 151; and
construction style, 206; dating of, 208;
great house at, 150; plaza at, 173n; and
population growth, 146; and pottery,
125, 132, 136; and revitalization,
161–62; ritual landscape of, 154; and
multiwalled structures, 75, 76; and
Totah, 63

Balcony House, 205, 207
Barker Arroyo, 110, 183
Battleship Rock complex, 194
Bellorado, Benjamin A., 33
Billman, Brian R., 158
Bishop, Ronald L., 104
Bitsiel Biwall, 75
biwalled structures, 74, 75, 76; at Aztec,
76, 78, 88, 152; at Goodman Point-
Shields, 192; and population growth,
79, 84; at Yellow Jacket Pueblo, 75, 171,
187, 188; at Yucca House, 184
Blanton, Richard, 175
Blinman, Eric, 93
Bluff Great House, 136, 143, 144, 147,
179, 203
Bone Awl House, 22
Borck, Lewis, 214–15
bowls. *See* Mesa Verde Black-on-white
pottery
Bradley, Bruce A., 170–71
Breternitz, David, 74
Brown, Gary M., 152, 162

Burnt Mesa, 135
Butler Wash, 28, 138

Canyon de Chelly, 214
Canyons of the Ancients National
Monument, 14, 36
Carter, Sidney W., 128
Castle Rock Pueblo: abandonment of, 210;
and migration, 213; and pottery, 92,
95, 102, 113, 126, 127; and stone tool
procurement, 127
Cave Towers (42SA1725), 138
Cedar Mesa, 14, 38; and Chaco to Post-
Chaco transition, 197; and highly
valued commodities, 128; and Kayenta,
136; and long-distance interaction,
103–4; and pottery, 126; and settlement
patterns, 138; and site defensibility, 203;
and site density, 44; and textiles and
sandals, 142
Cedar Tree Tower, 81
Central Mesa Verde region, 22, 35–38;
and archaeology, 14; and Chaco, 148;
and community centers, 49, 57; and
intraregional variation, 26–27; and
megadrought, 154; and room-to-kiva
ratios, 64–65; and site density, 46; and
sociopolitical relationships, 85–86
ceremony: and Aztec, 146, 193; and Aztec
East, 152; and ceremonial networks,
132, 194, 199, 200–201, 202; and
Chaco Canyon, 145, 178, 179; and
Chaco to Post-Chaco transition, 155;
and community centers, 160; and
households, 167; and intensification,
130, 136–37, 172; and McElmo
Intensification, 164; and Pueblo society,
17, 18; and ritual knowledge, 175; and
West Central Mesa Verde, 201. *See also*
civic-ceremonial architecture
Chaco Canyon period: and agriculture,
147; and Aztec, 16, 150, 151; and
ceremonial system, 77; and Chaco
to Post-Chaco transition, 197; and
Chuskas, 160; and circular multiwalled
structures, 79, 80; and civic-ceremonial
architecture, 68, 85; decline of, 78,
91–92, 146, 154–55, 169, 186–87,
207; and depopulation, 7; and east vs.
west differences, 136; and exchange
networks, 92; expansion of, 146–47,
148, 178–80; and great houses, 73,
145, 146, 147, 186; and great kivas,
71–72; and hegemony, 148; and Mesa

35, 37; on the household, 167; on pueblo polities, 182n; on San Juan Pattern and Chaco, 167; on social power relationships, 85–86

Lister, Robert, 74

Long House: and aggregation, 205; and burned kivas, 207; plaza at, 69, 172, 184; and pottery, 95, 110, 126; and size, 62

Lower San Juan subregion, 38–39; and agriculture, 129; and Chaco, 199–200; and climate, 201, 202; and community centers, 49, 63; and great houses, 73, 74; and group-assembly architecture, 72; and intraregional interactions, 120–21, 128–30; and Kayenta, 136; and migration, 214; and occupation histories, 50, 54; and plazas, 69–70; and pottery, 95, 110, 111–12, 113, 114, 115, 116, 121, 126, 128; and room-to-kiva ratios, 65; and settlement organization, 44, 85, 138–39, 155–56

Lowry community, 87n, 111n, 112, 125

Lowry great house, 147

maize. *See* corn

Mancos River, 11, 35, 75

Manuelito Canyon, 75, 144

Martin, Debra L., 183

Maya, Classic period, 3, 4, 5, 7n, 12–13, 218

McAnany, Patricia A., 19–20

McElmo Creek, 35–36, 113, 132

McElmo Intensification, 164–65, 166; and community centers, 182; and religious change, 172; and sociopolitical landscapes, 185; and spatiotemporal variation, 85; and Western Mesa Verde, 200

McElmo-style great houses, 151, 152, 154

McElmo subregion, 35–37; and aggregation, 197; and agriculture, 90–91; and Aztec, 210; and Chaco to Post-Chaco transition, 197; and circular multiwalled structures, 79; and community centers, 57, 60–61, 63, 64, 160; and emigration, 166–67, 198, 207–10; and exchange networks, 93; and great houses, 73; and great kivas, 68–69; and group-assembly architecture, 71, 72; and immigration, 146–47, 147–48; and intraregional interactions, 117, 120, 121, 126, 128, 130–32; and multiwalled structures, 75, 163; and occupation histories, 50,

52–54; and plazas, 71; and population density, 160, 164–65; and population growth, 55, 56, 198; and pottery, 95, 110, 111–12, 114, 115, 122, 124–25, 131, 160; and production zones, 114; and settlement patterns, 44–45, 155–56; and sociopolitical influence, 77; and towers, 82; and triwalled structures, 76; and villages, 170; and violence, 157; and walls, 82–83

McGuire, Randall H., 178, 182

McKenna, Peter J., 23, 33, 150

McLoyd's Canyon, 38

McPhee Village, 135, 148, 176

Mesa Verde Black-on-white pottery: and Aztec, 78; and black paste, 112n, 130; and ceremony, 125; export of, 124–25; and interaction networks, 115; and intraregional exchange, *118*, 119, 121, 132; and Lower San Juan, 144; and Magdalena Black-on-white, 215; and NAA, 95, 114; and production, 100; and production zones, 114; uses of, 119, 125

Mesa Verde core, 35; and aggregation, 87; and Chuskans, 158; and civic-ceremonial architecture, 84; and intraregional interactions, 92, 119; and Kayenta pottery, 144; and lithic procurement, 93, 127; and Mesa Verde reformation, 202, 206, 210–11; and population growth, 166; and settlement patterns, 84–85; and social and political inequality, 169–70, 183; and villages, 169–70; and violence, 159

Mesa Verde cuesta, 24, 26, 27, 35, 205–6

Mesa Verde National Park (MVNP), 15, 35, 45–46, 73, 82–83, 156

Mesa Verde Proper subregion, 26, 35, 73; and Aztec, 160, 162, 194; and Aztec-Chaco, 194; and Chaco Canyon, 194; and Chaco to Post-Chaco transition, 197; and community centers, 49, 57, 61–62, 63; and emigration, 198, 205, 206; and great kivas, 68–69; and group-assembly architecture, 72; and intraregional interactions, 117, 119, 120, 121, 126, 130, 132; and McElmo, 93, 160, 206; and multiwalled structures, 75; and plazas, 71; and population, 55, 56, 160; and pottery, 95, 110–11, 112, 114, 115, 116, 124–25, 159, 160; and settlement patterns, 44–45, 50, 52–54, 155–57, 170; and social history, 194; and Totah, 206; and violence, 157

About the Author

DONNA M. GLOWACKI is currently the John Cardinal O'Hara CSC assistant professor of anthropology at the University of Notre Dame, a senior researcher on the Village Ecodynamics Project, and a long-time research associate with Crow Canyon Archaeological Center. She has conducted fieldwork at seventy-six of the largest sites in the Central Mesa Verde region and is interested in understanding long-term and large-scale social change, including the role of religious transformation and sociopolitical reorganization in the regional depopulation of the Northern San Juan region at the end of the 1200s. Her recent publications include the coedited volume *Religious Transformation in the Late Pre-Hispanic Pueblo World*, with Scott Van Keuren. She recently completed fieldwork at Mesa Verde National Park that focuses on village formation and aggregation at Spruce Tree House cliff dwelling and other large sites throughout the park.